GENEALOGY

OF THE

CULBERTSON AND CULBERSON FAMILIES

Revised Edition

Who came to America before the year 1800, and several
families that have come over since then; containing
biographical sketches of some of the more
prominent members of the various families.

BY

LEWIS R. CULBERTSON, M. D.

The Courier Co., Printers, and Binders, Zanesville, O.
1923

To my honored friend and co-worker, Rev.
John N. Culbertson, of Washington, D. C.
this work is respectfully dedicated.

INTRODUCTION

I have given in this work as accurate and complete a history of the Culbertson and Culberson Families as could be obtained from family records sent me by various families in this country, Scotland and Ireland; by searching the Will and Deed Records in many of the counties, and assess books in a few counties; also from records of French and Indian and Revolutionary War soldiers. I have obtained all marriages of Culbertsons given in Pennsylvania Colonial Archives. I have "not left a stone unturned" in obtaining full and accurate accounts of various families and my labor has been unceasing and difficult. I have classified the various families into Sections, Parts and Chapters. Have not attempted to give any of the purely Scottish families that came to America until after 1800. There were a great many Irish families came to America since 1800 but I do not include them—with two exceptions—as it would take too much time and labor to trace them out. I have used a key to simplify the work, which is as follows: Letter s means that party was Scotch and emigrated to Ireland. The capitals of alphabet indicate that party emigrated to America but do not mean that parties (capitals) are related. The children of each one that emigrated to America are numbered by Roman numerals I, II, &c., and the grandchildren are numbered 1, 2, 3, 4, etc. I am indebted to the following parties for valuable information: John N. Culbertson, Thomas G. Culbertson of Wheeling, Mrs. Rev. Bigham of Plain Grove, Pa.; Mr. Henry Culbertson, Medina, Wis.; Mrs. J. Witherspoon; Mrs. Sarah R. H. Culbertson; parties in Scotland and Ireland; W. W. Culbertson, Ashland, Ky.; Almon E. Culbertson, New York City; Mrs. Blanche C. French of New York City; Walter F. Beverly, Richmond, Va.; Frank Culbertson, Oil City, Pa.; James A. Culbertson, Cincinnati, O.; J. J. Culbertson, Paris, Texas; H. D. Culbertson, Albert Lea, Minn.; Mrs. R. H. Fink, Norton, Va.; J. W. Berryman, Ashland, Kan.; R. R. Culbertson, Central City, Ky.; Howard Cessna, Bedford, Pa.; John G. Orr, Chambersburg, Pa.; Mrs. Mary R. C. Hood, Joplin, Mo.; Mrs. Sevilla J. Kempton, Washington, D. C.; Major-

General E. M. Lewis, San Antonio, Texas; Mrs. George Spangler, Peoria, Ill., and many others too numerous to mention, to all of whom I return my sincere thanks. Likewise, I heartily thank all my subscribers and all who have aided me in any way.

The Revised Edition has been carefully compiled from family and Bible records, wills, deeds, settlements, sale-bills, inventories, tax records, U. S. Census records 1790, and in some instances 1800, pension records, land (pension) grants, Congressional Records, state land grants, State Archives, Colonial and Revolutionary and Historical works, and in some instances county histories.

LEWIS R. CULBERTSON, M. D.

Zanesville, Ohio, March 10, 1923.

CONTENTS

CHAPTER I

Origin of the name of Culbertson and meaning of same—Meaning of Cuthbert—King Malcolm's deed—The Norse in Scotland—Culuert—King Duncan—King Malcolm III —Duncan, father of Colbert—Our Celtic and Saxon origin—Invasion of Scotland by Irish and meaning of Mac. —Roxburgshire, the earliest home of Culbertsons—Description of Roxburgshire—Sketch of St. Cuthbert—The Cuthberts—Jean Baptiste Colbert, Minister of France under Louis XIV—What Mazarin said of him—Rev. Robert Culbertson of Morebattle, Scotland.

CHAPTER II.

Families in Ireland—Cuthberts and Culberts—Religion of Culbertsons—Wealth—Description of Scotch-Irish in America—Scotch-Irish—Historical sketch of Cumberland Valley—Rocky Spring Church.

SECTION FIRST

The three Scotch brothers who emigrated to Ireland between 1665-1685—King James II of England and Covenanters—Seige of Londonderry and triumph of William of Orange—Battle of Boyne—William or John (the Scotch brother) who settled in Londonderry Co. Ireland and issue—PART SECOND, John (A) and issue, chapter III and their descendants—PART THIRD of Section First (B)—PART FOURTH of Section First (C) Andrew from Ireland to Chester and Cumberland Cos. Pa. and descendants; Samuel of Washington Co., Tenn.; Andrew of Rockbridge Co., Va.; Col. Robert of Columbus, Ohio, including descendants in North and South Carolina, Ga., etc., Chapters V, XI, XVII, VI, VII, VIII, IX, X, XII, XIII, XIV, XV, XVI. (D) Section First PART Fifth, Samuel Culbertson from Ireland to Chester Co., Pa. and descendants Chapter XVIII in Silver Spring Tp., Cumberland Co., Pa. and Chapter XIX descendants in Mifflin Co., Pa., etc.—Section First PART SIXTH: (E)

Oliver Culbertson from Ireland to Chester Co., Pa. and
Franklin Co., Pa.—Armstrong Co., Pa., and Descendants
Chapter XX in Erie Co., Pa.

SECTION SECOND

PART FIRST—Culbertson of "Irish Row"—PART SEC-
OND Culbertson of "Irish Row" whose descendants went
to Lancaster Co., Pa· (present Franklin Co.) Pa. and established "Culbertson Row," Pa.—PART THIRD: The
first brother (E), Alexander of the "Row" and descendants. Chapter XXI, XXII, XXIII, XXIV, XXV.—PART
FOURTH: The second Irish brother (G) Samuel Culbertson and descendants, Chapters XXVI, XXVII,
XXVIII, XXIX, XXX, XXXI. PART FIFTH: The third
Irish brother Robert Culbertson (H) of Peters Tp., Cumberland Co., Pa. and descendants, Chapter XXXII. PART
SIXTH: Joseph Culbertson (J) of "Culbertson Row",
Pa., first cousin of the three Pa. "Row" brothers and
descendants, Chapters XXXIII, XXXIV, XXXV.

SECTION THIRD—PART FIRST

(K) Robert Culbertson (Irish) of Mill Creek Hundred,
New Castle, Pa., Del. and sons: Thomas, Robert and
Alexander of Delaware and Westmoreland Co., Pa., Chap-
ters XXXVI, XXXVII, XXXVIII, XXXIX·

SECTION THIRD—PART SECOND

(KK). John Culbertson (Irish) who emigrated from Ire-
land in 1746 to St. George's Hundred, New Castle Co.,
Del. and descendants, William, Chapter XLI; John XLII;
David, Chapter XLIII; Benjamin, Chapter XLIV.

SECTION FOURTH

Richard Culbertson (L) of Carlisle, Pa.—Cecil Co., Md.

SECTION FIFTH

Scotch-Irish Culbertson, name unknown, some of whose
descendants came to America before 1800. Lived in
Irish "Culbertson Row" at Ballygan, near Ballymoney,
·Co. Antrim, Ireland.

SECTION SIXTH

(L) John Culbertson of E. Hempfield Tp., Lancaster Co., Pa. (Irish) and descendants.

SECTION SEVENTH

(M) Elias Culbertson (Irish) of Washington Co., Pa., and descendants.

SECTION EIGHTH

Irish or Scotch (N) William of Mecklenberg Co., N. Car.; (O) John of Mecklenberg Co., N. Car.; (P) David of Burke Co., N. Car.

SECTION NINTH

(Q) James (Irish) of Mason Co., Ky. PART SECOND. (R) Robert of Harrison Co., Ohio. PART THIRD. (S) Irish William of America, residence unknown; (T) Irish Joseph of Huntington Co., Pa.-Belmont Co., Ohio, and descendants. PART FOURTH.

SECTION TENTH

The Newton-Stewart, Co. Tyrone, Ireland, family, eight of whom came to America after 1800—i. e. V. 1, James; V. 2, Allen; V. 3, Robert; V. 4, Wm. of Kenton Co., Ky.

SECTION ELEVENTH

(W) Patrick Culbertson (Irish) of Chester Co., Pa., Shermans Valley, Pa. and Venango Co., Pa. and descendants. PART FIRST. (Y) John Culbertson (probably a brother of Patrick) (W) of Shermans Valley, Pa. PART SECOND.

SECTION TWELVE—UNCLASSIFIED

James Culbertson of Pa. and Havre-de-Grace, Md. and descendants. (X) John Culbertson (fuller) Irish of Wayne Tp., Mifflin Co., Pa. (Z) Rev. John Culbertson of Lancaster Co., Pa. (Bart Tp.)—Miscellaneous data—Tax lists of Culbertsons of Chester Co., Pa. and Cumberland Co., Pa. 1750 to 1785. The "Flying Camp"; what it was. Also "Minute Men."

CHAPTER I

It has generally been supposed by the Culbertsons that their name was originally Cuthbertson and Cuthbert. William Arthur in his book on "Derivation of Family Names" says that Culbertson comes from the Gaelic word Culbheart, meaning crafty; and Culbertson, a son of Culbheart. In the same work he gives Cuthbert as a surname. He says that Cuthbert is from the Saxon and means "famous, bright, of clear skill or knowledge."

According to Camden, surnames began to be taken up in France about the year 1000 A. D. and in England at the time of the conquest (1066). Before this date in England all documents, etc., were signed thus, ✚Ego Edmundus (I, Edmund) do affirm, etc. The same author (Camden) says that in an old deed made by King Malcolm of Scotland and recorded in 1097, in which he deeds land for a church at Coldingham, one of the noblemen who witnessed the deed signed thus, S, ✚ Culuerti filii Doncani, etc., i. e. Culuert son of Duncan.

Culbert might have been derived from Culuert, as they are spelled almost alike. The Latin Culuertus would be pronounced Culwertus. The "w" may have been changed to "b" for sake of euphony. Or the "u" on the deed may have been intended for a "b", as it must have been difficult, in those days, for even a nobleman to write his own name. (The Latin for Cuthbert is Cudberctus). The coasts of Scotland were infested by Norse sea-pirates about this time and the Northmen added "son" to their surnames in the Tenth Century. The Scotch may have taken up the Norse custom of adding "son" to their surnames shortly after this. One might safely say, if a name terminates in "son," that it originated either in Scotland or Norway.

It is possible that Culbert, son of Duncan, was the first of the Culberts and from some of his descendants, perhaps his son, sprang the first Culbertson. This Culbert was one of the most prominent noblemen at that date.

The Duncan family (his father's) was then, and has always been a prominent family in Scotland. King Duncan Mac Crinan (1034-40) was slain in a battle with the forces of MacBeth, (Shakespeare says he was murdered by Macbeth), who reigned until 1057, when he was defeated and slain by Duncan McCrinan's eldest son Malcolm (Canmore) in 1057 who ascended the throne as Malcolm III and reigned until 1093. This Malcolm was a great and good king and greatly aided Scotland's welfare. It was he who made the deed to the church at Coldingham and he aided religion in every way possible. At his death he was succeeded by his brother Donald Bain, who was deposed in six months by Malcolm's son Edmund who had slain his half brother Duncan. Edmund was deposed three years later by Edgar Atheling, nephew of Donald. There is no doubt that Culbert, who witnessed the deed, was a nephew of Malcolm III (Canmore); and that Edmund who witnessed the same deed was the son of Malcolm III. It is probable that he was a younger son, hence did not inherit the title.

We are undoubtedly of Celtic origin, as the features indicate, i. e. the high cheek bones, blue eyes, broad chin, height, muscular development, and red hair that was found among some of those that came over in the 18th Century, but very rarely seen now. The "pug" nose—a Celtic feature—is very rarely seen among the Culbertsons; nearly all have good sized noses—another Scotch feature.

The early, and perhaps the majority of the Culbertsons of the present time, had light hair and blue eyes. This would indicate that centuries ago they either married Saxons or Norse or were descended from one or both of these races. The Saxons and Norse overran Northumbria—in which Co. the Co. of Roxburgh was situated—in the Seventh and Eighth Centuries.

The Celts crossed over from Ireland to Scotland about the Fifth Century and overran the Highlands defeating the Scots. It is from these that the Scotch got their red hair, likewise the Mac in their names which signifies "son." I have never heard of, nor have I been able to find in history, a McCuthbert or a McCulbert and do not believe such families ever existed. This fact would tend to show that the family has always lived in the Lowlands.

*If any of our name figured as chiefs of Highland Clans it must have been centuries past, as the name does not appear in Burke's Heraldry or in a work on The Scottish Clans.   *   *   *   *

I will mention a peculiar fact, that the Culbertson features are the same wherever you may meet them. This peculiarity occurs in many other families. I might mention the most marked of these features are the prominent nose, broad chin, heavy eye brows, as a rule blue eyes, high forehead and large frame.   *   *   *   *

The earliest home of the Culbertsons that I have been able to find is in the County Roxburg at a small village named Morebattle, eight miles south of Kelso, Scotland. Here the Culbertsons have lived continuously since the year 1400 A. D. This is in the Lowlands and is about five miles from the Cheviot Hills which form the boundary between Scotland and England, and is on a small stream which empties into the Tweed River. This was the most famous part of Scotland for battles. It was along this border that Earl Percy created such terror and likewise Claverhouse and Cromwell. Also where Wallace and Bruce defeated the English. The most dreadful cruelties were inflicted on these poor borderers by the English. **

This region abounds in beautiful scenery and historical relics. A few miles west of Kelso is Melrose Abbey where St. Cuthbert lived and preached in the Seventh Century. It was in this county that religion was first introduced to the Pagan Scots in the Dark Ages.

*From the fact that St. Cuthbert lived there 1500 years ago, some might believe we are descended from the Cuthberts, so we will make brief mention of St. Cuthbert. He was born in this Co., then a part of Northumberland Co., England. Lived at Melrose Abbey and Landisfarne. He was Scotland's Patron Saint. The Scottish battle cry was to St. Cuthbert. Pilgrimages were made yearly, by Christians, to his tomb and this custom was continued for several centuries. I will add in connection with the Cuthberts, that one family belonged to the nobility, and, until about seventy-five years ago, was quite a noted family and lived near Inverness. They are not among the nobility now.   *   *   *

Jean Baptiste Colbert of France claimed to be descended from a noble Scottish family. There is no doubt but what his statement was true. It is probable that his ancestor went to France with those Scottish soldiers of Lords

---

*There is no coat of arms of the Culbertsons. The Colberts of France have a serpent thereon, likewise the Cuthberts of Scotland have a serpent thereon. The serpent as an emblem is symbolical of wisdom or knowledge. (See previous reference to meaning of Culbert and Cuthbert.)

**There is a small stream in this region called Cuthbert's Hope, why so called we do not know.
*St. Cuthbert is buried in the Cathedral of Durham, England.

Buchan and Douglas who assisted King Charles VII of
France in opposing the English army of Henry V, about the
year 1400, some of whom were made nobles of France. Jean
Baptiste Colbert was born 1619 at Rheims, France. He began life as a woolen-draper, but soon after went to Paris
where his talents attracted the notice of the great Cardinal
Mazarin who was instrumental in making him Minister of
Finance. He did more for the financial welfare of France
than any Minister that country has ever had. It was under
his ministry that France first took rank as a naval power.
He founded Academies of Science, Architecture, etc., and
instituted stupendous and beautiful public works. France
never had but one man that did more for her welfare than
Colbert. *

Colberts ancestors may have come from Scotland; some
authors claim they did not.

It was Colbert who advised Cardinal Mazarin in everything and after the latter's death he was the "power be-
hind the throne" of Louis XIV, of France. Mazarin on his
death bed said to Louis, "Sire, I owe everything to you;
but I pay my debt to your majesty by giving you Colbert."

But to return to my subject, I have gotten the names of
all the Culbertsons in Scotland and find that they only live
in Roxburgh Co. and Kintyre, a peninsula on the West
Coast. Robert Culbertson of Kelso, Scotland, Co. Roxburgh, informs me that his great-great-grandfather left
Roxburghshire with his regiment, for Ireland about 1690,
to quell a rebellion and his regiment was stationed a long
time in Ireland. His time expiring he settled in Mayo Co.
and married. His great-grandson returned to Roxburghshire, Scotland, in 1845. (The Rebllion referred to was the
war between the Prince of Orange and James II.)

The following memoir of Rev. Robt. Culbertson was
written in 1826 by Alex. Duncan of Mid Calder, Scotland.
In it are named two Culbertsons; two Duncans one Simpson, which families have intermarried in the United
States: "James Culbertson, the father of the author, was
a farmer and a Fenar (or Renter) in Morebattle, a village
eight miles south of Kelso, Scotland. The mother of the
author was named Janet, a cousin of James C., her husband.
Robert, the author, was the eldest of seven children. He
was b. Sept. 1765—d. Dec. 1823. He entered the University

---

*Colbert's son was an Admiral in the French navy, and Minister of
Marine and built the Navy to wonderful efficiency.

of Edinburg in 1782. Licensed 1790, ordained 1791. He preached to the 'associate congregations' of St. Andrews and St. Leith. He married Elizabeth Richmond 1793. He is buried in the family vault at St. Leiths churchyard." He was the author of "Lectures on Book of Revelations", Ed. in 3 vols. Pub. London 1826, Dedicated to Marchioness of Huntley. Rev. Culbertson also pub. "Hints in the Ordinance in the Gospel Ministry."

Walter Culbertson of Morebattle writes me that in the old cemetery at Morebattle there are buried many generations of Culbertsons, but all the tombstones are too much worn to be legible except those named above, the first of whom (James) died in Jan. 1826, aged 98 years. The tombstone also says that Rev. Robert was minister of U. P. Church, St. Andrews street, Leith; and founder of the U. P. Church in the Islands of Orkney, Scotland in 1796." He also says that his (Walter) great-grandfather lived at Morebattle.

The Culbertsons of Kintyre date their ancestry thus: Lord Loudon of Ayrshire, Scotland, had a younger son James Campbell, who went from Ayrshire to Argyleshire (Kintyre) Scotland about 1660 A. D. This James Campbell had a daughter, Jean Campbell, who married James Culbertson who lived on a farm five miles north of Campbeltown, Kintyre. His farm was called then, as now, Laggan Farm and Culbertsons still live on this farm. This James Culbertson had a son Robert from whom many of the Scotch families in the United States are descended. Lord Loudon was one of the five signers of the first "Solemn League and Covenant" in 1638 and was foremost in the cause of the persecuted Covenanters.

I have not been able to trace any relation between this James Culbertson and the Scotch Covenanter brothers who went from Scotland to Ireland between 1665-1685. A grandson of James Culbertson (first) named James lived on Skerbolin Farm near Campbeltown, Kintyre, and his descendants still live on this farm.

*   *   *   *

I have had the following rare old works examined relative to obtaining the names or any information pertaining to the three Scotch brothers who went to Ireland 1665-1685: Bishop Wm. King's "State of the Protestants in Ireland;" "Bailles Letters and Journals" 1732-1737; Dodd's "Fifty Years Struggle"; Cotton's "Fasti Ecclesiae Hibernicae"; and others, which give no reference to the names Culbertson or Cuthbertson. In Hetherington's History of the Church of Scotland is a list of fines imposed by Middleton in Parliament, 1662, some 875 names, and among these was a "Robert Cuthbertson, Covenanter, fined 360 pounds." In the same work is a list of Fugitives proscribed by King Charles II, issued May 5, 1684 and containing names of 2000 Covenanters, in which the name Culbertson does not appear, but we find "Archibald Cuthbertson, a cooper, haunting about Caldermuir in Linlithgowshire." The Robert Cuthbertson, before mentioned also lived in Linlithgowshire.

The following books were also examined (these are all the books pertaining to the subject that can be found in Washington, D. C.) : Woodrow's "History of the Church of Scotland"; McCries "Sketches of Scottish Church History"; Burton's "History of Scotland" and other works but no reference to the name Culbertson or Cuthbertson was found. A careful examination of the entire list of Divines in the Westminster Assembly of 1638, fails to reveal the name Culbertson or Cuthbertson. Family tradition of all the families in America has it that they were Scotch Covenanters. The Secretary of War of Great Britain informs me that there are no rosters of the troops sent from Scotland to Ireland during the Revolution of 1688, hence we can glean no information from this source. You will all notice that the Duncan family was intimately associated with the Culbertsons both in Scotland and America and intermarried with them frequently.

Hannahs Scotch-Irish of America, Vol. 1, p. 356: "County of Cavan, precinct of Clanchy, 1000 acres Wm. Baillie. Two leases Stone Bawn Castle; building 4 leases. In 1629 there were eight leasees among whom were Guilbert Cuthbertson—cottagers. able to produce 28 men with arms."

Hannah, Ibid: "In list of banished out of parish of Kilmarnock (Ayrshire) in 1670, is John Cuthbertson (Culbertson)."

Rev. John N. Culbertson, Washington, D. C. writes me that he copied from a rare work in Cong. Library, Hills Plantations of Ulster as follows, "On p. 193, After the survey of 1609, Wm. Baillie of Scotland, was granted 1000 Acres in Co. of Cavan, Ulster, one of the lease-holders of said land was Guilbert Cuthbertson (or Culbertson). In

1629, said grant was made a manor, called Bailieborough, and is still on the map in the eastern part of Co. Cavan."

It will be seen, therefore, that the only Scotch Culbertsons or Cuthbertsons who resided in Ireland before 1700 were Guilbert before 1609; John 1670; Robert and Archibald 1662 and 1684. We do not know positively whether any of these were the ancestors of those that came to America, but no doubt they were.

Rev. John N. Culbertson says that, "In Sir Walter Scott's 'Tales of a Grandfather' he speaks of part of the Campbell Clan, who made a raid across the Scotch Border the night of Queen Elizabeth's death. They met a terrible defeat, and the upshot of the matter was they were transferred to the Northern part of Ireland. There is no doubt a list of these people, but the British Museum and Guild Hall Library in London possess no such list. I have no doubt some of the ancestors could be found on such a list."

It is probable that Guilbert Cuthbertson is descended from one of these. There is no Gilbert or Archibald among the Culbertsons who came to America before 1800.

CHAPTER II

Of the history of the families in Ireland, we know but little. There were living in Ireland (1892) families at the following places: Ballyscanlon and Gortnaskeagh, Co. Donegal; Dublin; Ballymoney, Co. Antrim; Bulaughmore, Co. Tyrone. The Robert Culbertson who owned the Ballysadare Woolen Mills came from Scotland and shortly after emigrating changed his name from Cuthbertson to Culbertson because his name had been written Culbertson in a deed. There are several families of Culberts in Ireland, and also Cuthberts.

A great many of the families that lived in Ireland have emigrated to America.

The Culbertsons of Ireland are, so far as I can learn Presbyterians.

Most of the families in America are Presbyterians. Most of the Culbersons in the Southern part of the United States are Methodists, while some are Baptists. Almost all the families in the North and West are Presbyterians.

As to riches, there are some very wealthy men of our name. One descendant very beautifully and truthfully described them when she said: "They were mostly farmers, industrious in their habits, and in quiet home life realized neither the pangs of poverty, nor the pride of riches." Many are moderately wealthy. Those who have attained wealth are honest and conscientious business men. Almost all who are wealthy are self-made men. Likewise they are warm-hearted, generous and progressive. The Culbertsons have adhered pretty closely to Horace Greely's advice, "Young man go West," and the majority have profited thereby.   *   *   *   *

No Culbertson came to America before 1700. *

A writer in The Cincinnati Enquirer of Feb. 20, 1893, says of the Scotch-Irish,—"Their beginning goes back to the invasion of Scotland by the missionary pupils of St. Patrick. He is a combination of the intellectual Irish who kept the light burning while all Europe was in dismal darkness; of the strong-bodied Scot; of the audacious Norman; the red-headed Dane and the conservative Saxon. The Scotch -Irish cared not for credit. Achievement was their aim. They led stormy lives in order to enjoy tranquility, that goal of human happiness that few attain.

All the great Indian fighters of Ohio were of this race.

Fifteen of the Presidents of the U. S. were of Scotch-Irish descent. Sixteen of our Premiers were of this race. Likewise nine secretaries of Treasury; nineteen out of forty-two War Secretaries; twenty-five out of forty-five Associate Justices of Supreme Court. In the Revolution forty generals were Scotch-Irish. Many generals of our other wars were of Scotch-Irish descent."

Let us go into the history of Pennsylvania as far as concerns Cumberland Valley and adjacent territory. McCauley says in his Hist. Sketch of Franklin Co.: "The first counties erected in the State were Philadelphia, Bucks and Chester, in 1682. The latter extended westward to the western boundary of Penn's territorial claim, and northward I know not exactly how far. It included however the territory embraced in this county. In May, 1729, the county of Lancaster was erected out of the western part of Chester Co., and this section of country was embraced within its limits, and there remained until the erection of Cumberland

*See Hotten's Work compiled from Her Majesty's Public Records.

Co. in 1750. There were no white settlers in this region, that I have been able to hear of, in 1729. There may have been occasional visits made by hunters and scouts but we have no records of them. Bands of Susquehanna and Shawanese Indians held a nominal possession of it but were under the Iroquois or Six Nations.

The lands of the Cumberland Valley were not purchased of the Indians until 1736, and were not therefore, before that time open for sale. History says that Benjamin Chambrs was the first white man who made a settlement in what is now known as Franklin Co., Pa. He was a native of Antrim, Ireland, of Scotch descent, and between the years of 1726 and 1730 emigrated with his brothers to Pa. He pushed bravely into the forest and was kindly received by the Indians and obtained permission to settle on the place of his choice and make it his own. This was about 1730 and in March 1734, Thomas Blounston, the agent of the proprietaries, gave him a license to "settle and improve 400 acres of land at Falling Springs mouth." The Scotch-Irish flowed into the valley in vast numbers and from 1730 to 1735 settled upon and improved large tracts of land from the Susquehanna to the southern line of the province. The precise date at which settlers began to locate at Greencastle, Rocky Spring, Middle Spring, Shippensburg, etc., are not known, as in many cases the earlier records of even the churches of the valley are lost; but they must have been commenced between the years 1730 and 1735, for within a few years afterwards Presbyterian congregations were organied at nearly all these places. By the year 1740 churches were found dotted over the broad bosom of this valley, almost invariably in a grove of shady trees, and near a spring of pure crystal water.

In 1735 "North Valley" was divided into two townships, "Pennsborough" and "Hopewell." In 1741 Hopewell was subdivided into Hopewell and Antrim Tps· Peters Tp. was settled as early as 1730. The "Upper West Conococheague Church" (Presbyterian) was organized in 1738. Lurgin Tp. adjoined Peters. Settlements were made in Letterkenny Tp. as early as 1730. Rocky Springs Church, organized about 1738, is in this Tp.

Green Tp. originally within Letterkenny Tp. In this Tp. lived the Culbertsons, McClays, Hendersons, Criswells, Johnsons, etc., who lived there many years and were buried there. "The church Records of Rocky Spring, as well as other churches, were destroyed during the Rebel raid on Chambersburg."

Rev. Nevin, in "Eminent Men of Cumberland Valley," says of the Rocky Spring Church: "It is on the Strasburg road about four miles from Chambersburg. The original edifice stood between the present building and the grave-yard. It was erected about 132 years ago (1740) and was a rough log building a story and a half high. It had one row of windows on the lower story, the lights of which were few and small in number. The present building was built in 1794. This has been enlarged from time to time by building additions. The first minister was Rev. John Craig-head—after whom Capt. John Culbertson of Cincinnati was named—next Rev. Francis Herron D. D. who preached here ten years, then became pastor of the First Presbyterian church of Pittsburgh; the pulpit was filled by Rev. John McKnight, who after preaching several years removed to Philadelphia. Rev. Nelson was preaching here in 1840." Rocky Spring Church is still standing and the name "Samuel Culbertson" carved one one of the pews. Old Fort Culbertson, built as a protection against the Indians, stood near the spring on Col. Joseph's farm. It has long since been pulled down.

General John Rea's pew, with his name carved thereon, is still in Rocky Spring church. "Gentleman James" Culbertson's farm lay north of Col. Sam's and separated by a lane. The farm of Joseph, son of Col. Robert, lay west of and adjoining that of "Gentleman James". Col. Robert's farm lay between Col. Sam's and Col. Joseph's farm.

Some fifteen years ago a large granite monument was erected in Rocky Spring Church yard with a bronze tablet containing the names of a number of Culbertsons who were in the Colonial and Revolutionary Wars. Rev. John N. Culbertson secured the money to do this by subscription. Another tablet has been put on (1922) containing names of all Culbertsons in America in Revolutionary, Colonial and early Indian wars. This was paid for by subscriptions of Culbertsons in 1921-22.

KEY

S. See Introduction.

A. B. C. D. etc. See Introduction.

I, II, III, etc. See Introduction.

1, 2, 3, 4, 5, 6, 7, etc., means that those designated by Arabic numerals are descendants of parties designated by Roman numerals; in some instances Roman numerals have not been used and the children and descendants have been designated by Arabic numerals only. In one or more instances I have used Arabic numerals thus, a. 1 or b. 1 to represent two different generations to prevent duplication of numbers and to simplify in several families where there was a longer descent and where information would come in after tables were made up.

ABBREVIATIONS

Co. means county.

b. means born.

d. means died.

Mar. means married.

Tp. or Twp. means township.

Arch. means Archives.

Prominent descendants of each Roman numeral will be found at the close of each chapter.

SECTION FIRST

The First Scotch-Irish Brother and Descendants

PART FIRST

William (?) Culbertson, who emigrated from Scotland to County of Derry near Londonderry, Ireland, about 1665-1687. One of his brothers settled in Omagh, Tyrone Co., Ireland; another at Ballygan, near Ballymoney, Co. Antrim, Ireland. The settlement of the last named brother was called "Culbertson Row", and it was from this the "Row" in Pennsylvania derived its name. These brothers were Scotch Covenanters and were driven from Scotland during the reign of James II of England.

King Charles II ascended the throne of England in the year 1660 and the persecutions of the Covenanters began about 1665 and continued throughout his reign. The poor Scotch Presbyterians being hunted down without mercy, sought refuge in northern Ireland. The emnity of the treacherous and false King Charles followed them to Ireland. Charles II on ascending the throne had promised the Scotch Presbyterians that he would protect them as his grandfather, James I, had done. (James I was a Presbyterian and was called "Good King Jamie" by the Scotch, he being a Scotchman.)

Charles II was a Catholic, as was also his father, Charles I. On the death of Charles II in 1685, his son, James II, ascended the throne. He immediately began to persecute the Covenanters in Scotland and Ireland. The Scotch-Irish rose in rebellion against King James II, and fled to several fortified cities in northern Ireland. One of these cities was Londonderry. Within its walls 7000 men were beseiged and at the end of the seige their numbers were reduced by famine and disease to 3000, all Protestants. King James was in command of the Catholic army. William, Prince of Orange, with a large fleet then sailed into Londonderry Bay and drove King James away in 1688. The Prince of Orange was a staunch Protestant and married Mary, the oldest daughter of James II of England, and by right the heir apparent. The great Battle of Boyne was fought in 1690, by the forces of King William and King James and the latter was completely routed and James became an exile, while William ascended the throne. After this the Scotch-Irish had comparative quiet.

William Culbertson (so say family records) was one of the defenders in the seige of that place in 1688. This was one of the most memorable seiges in history. The defenders were reduced to eating horse and dog flesh and even ministers fought on the walls. I am informed by parties in Londonderry, Ireland, that there are no Culbertsons living in the County Derry now, but there are Culbertsons living at Balyscanlon, Co. Donegal, which is not far from Londonderry. Wrote this family but received no reply. There was also a family lived at Newton Stewart, Co. Tyrone, Ireland, that may be descended from one of (s) Culbertsons. This town is very near Londonderry. The "Row" in Antrim Co., Ireland, is only a few miles from the boundary between Antrim and Derry Counties. (s) John(?) Culbertson who emigrated from Scotland to Ireland.

SECOND GENERATION

Issue:

A. **John,** b. 1680-90; d. Nov. 1756. (See Sec. First; Part Second.)

B. **Robert,** b. 1692 or before: d. 1762. (See Sec. First; Part Third.)

C. **Andrew,** d. 1746. (See Sec. First; Part Fourth.)

D. **Samuel,** d. 1749. (See Sec. First; Part Fifth.)

E. **Oliver,** d. 1792. (See Sec. First; Part Sixth.) Nephew of Robert, Andrew and Samuel.

The descendants of John (A) living in Erie Co., Pa., claim that (A) John's father was William Culbertson one of the defenders of Londonderry, Ireland—before mentioned—in 1788. (Colter Genealogy of Culbertsons of Erie Co., Pa., pub. 1889.) The above or part of them may be descended from Scotch—John Cuthbertson (Culbertson?) banished from Kilmarnock, Ayrshire, Scotland in 1670 (before mentioned).

The Culbertson-Colter Genealogy by J. P. Colter on page 83 says: "The earliest record we have of them in Ireland was at the seige of Londonderry. We learn from family records that Wm. Culbertson was one of the defenders of the Seige of Londonderry." Whether Colter actually had any Bible record of this I do not know. His statement would not tally with a statement of John Culbertson of Duluth,

Minn., in 1892. in which he said: "I have in my possession a cane brought from Ireland by John Culbertson, my ancestor, and which has been handed down through the family through seven generations of John Culbertsons." The man who made this statement was the seventh generation. The man who settled in Chester Co., Pa., in 1712 and on tax record there 1713 (A-John) was the second John, therefore the first John who had the cane was Scotch John and very likely the John Cuthbertson above mentioned as banished from Ayrshire in 1670.

PART SECOND

(A) IRISH JOHN OF CHESTER CO., PA., AND CUMBERLAND CO., PA.

THIRD GENERATION

(A) John Culbertson, emigrated to America in 1712 or before and settled in Londongrove Tp., Chester Co., Pa. He landed at New Castle, Del., and at once settled in Chester Co. with his brother Robert. Tradition says he had four sons but I here give facts taken from Will, Deed Records. First appears on tax records in 1713, in Chester Co. (Records of New Castle Co., Del. show that no Culbertson lived in Delaware at this early date.) His name does not appear on the tax books after 1726. Margaret Culbertson, who married in 1739, Robert Jackson at St. Paul's Episcopal Church at Chester (Pa. Col. Arch.) was either his daughter or niece. Whether or not he was the father of John Culbertson of Brandywine Tp., Chester Co., is a question, yet it is almost certain that he was. He left no will in Chester, Lancaster or Cumberland counties and no administration of his estate and no deeds to or from him. Many settlers located on lands in Pennsylvania before 1734 and paid taxes on same but could get no warrants until 1734. There is no warrant to this John Culbertson. John Esq. of Brandywine Tp., may have been his son, and probably was, and he left him in Chester Co. in 1727-8 (he would then have been 17 or 18 years of age); or John Esq. may have been a nephew and may have been raised in Chester Co. by his uncle Andrew or Robert, of Kennett Tp.

John moved to Lancaster Co., Pa. in 1727-8 to what was later Shippensburg, Cumberland Co., Pa., Wing's History of Cumberland Co., states, "Among the first twelve settlers at Shippensburg in 1730 were John Culbertson." Dr. Eagle in Queries on Culbertsons of Culbertson Row, states, "In the Indian foray, among the settlers killed in Nov. 1756 at

Shippensburg was John Culbertson." John Culbertson in a letter dated at Shippensburg May 7, 1756, writes Col. Burd, "that he had talked with an Indian at Big Cove, who had been captured at Ford Littleton and that this Indian was in the Battle of Sideling Hill, April 2, 1756, and that the Indians lost 17 killed and 21 wounded." John seems to have been a scout for Col, Burd. There is no deed or court record to show that Oliver Culbertson was a son of John Sr. or Shippensburg. It is my opinion that Oliver was John's son and a nephew of Irish Andrew of Shippensburg.

Issue of Irish John and wife:

(I) John (Esq. of East Coln. Tp., Chester Co., Pa.) b. 1710; d. Nov. 11, 1767. (Chapter III).

(E) Oliver (See Sec. First, Part Sixth).

There was a John Culbertson, Augusta Co., Va. in 1753-4. This was John Culbertson of Shippensburg, Pa., no doubt. No record of his appears prior to this in Orange Co., Va. or Augusta Co., Va. It is my opinion that he left Cumberland Co., Pa. in the spring of 1751 with Andrew Culbertson and went with him to Augusta Co., Va. The only record we have of him in Augusta Co., Va. is in Order Book No. 5, p. 20: "Nov. Court 1755, David Stuart vs. John Culbertson. Defendant being removed out of the county and not arrested, the suit dismissed." John of Rowan Co., N. Car. first appears on deed records of N. Car. in 1765. I do not believe he was of age before 1762-3. Rev. John N. Culbertson of Washington, D. C. has suggested that this might have been Irish John (First) of Shippensburg, sent to Va. on scout duty by Col. Burd. This John seemed to have no fixed abode, or at least had no property. John removed from Augusta Co. and returned to Shippensburg, Pa.

The Auditor of Taxes of Lancaster Co., Pa. informs me that they have none of the old tax books 1730-50 of the territory north and west of the Susquehanna. These have been lost or were taken to Harrisburg State Library years ago and any information therein transcribed to Colonial Archives. From these archives I have gleaned any information obtainable.

CHAPTER III

(I) **John Culbertson** came to America when a child. Was raised in Londongrove Tp., Chester Co., Pa. Was a prominent man of Chester Co., Pa. Was appointed Lieut. of Pa. Provincial Militia from Chester Co., Pa., in Col. Moore's Battalion in the year 1748. (See Pa. Colonial Arch.). Can find no further mention of him in Archives but presume he served in French and Indian War. 1st Battn. Capt. John McCall (Futhey's Hist.)

"By a Patent of the Penns he was, on Jan. 15, 1739, granted a tract of land in East Coln Tp., Chester Co., Pa." Here he died and was buried at Brandywine Manor. A deed at date of Oct. 1770 shows his children residing in the following Tps.: "Andrew in West Coln; James in East Coln; John in East Coln; Samuel in Carnarvon Tp.—Berks Co.; Benjamin in Chester Co. and son-in-law Benjamin Wallace." Sometime after the death of her husband (John I) his widow lived in Lancaster Co., Pa., and made her will in that Co. in 1809. Part of her farm was in Chester and part in Lancaster counties.

(1) John Culbertson was mar. to Eliza Rogers in 1731 at the First Presbyterian Church of Philadelphia, Pa. (Pa. Arch.). Part of his children were by this wife. She died. He married second, Mrs. Abigail Whitehill (from will) who had three children when he married her, namely Margaret, John and Jean Whitehill, who were named in John Culbertson's will, made in Chester Co., Pa., Aug. 26, 1767. His second wife, Abigail, made her will in Lancaster Co., Pa., in 1809, and in it she devises to her grandson, son of Jane Boyd; and to John Boyd, son of Margaret. I presume these two daughters must have been the Whitehill children, as Margaret and Jane Culbertson do not appear in John Culbertson's will. Numbers 1, 2, 3, 4, 5, 6 and 8 appear on his will. The other children were obtained from family records. .

FOURTH GENERATION

Issue, by both wives:
1. Andrew, b. 1731; d. 1797.
2. James, b. 1733; d. 1777.
3. Jane, b. 1735.
4. John, b. 1737; d. Sep. 12. 1794. Major.

5.   Samuel, b. 1744; d. Jan. 1782.   Capt. Flying Camp.
6.   Samuel, b. 1744; d. before 1770.
7.   Margaret, b. 1749.
8.   Benjamin, b. 1751; drowned.   Lieut.
9.   Ebenezer, b. 1757; d. young.
10. Esther, b. 1763; d. young.

FIFTH GENERATION

(1) Andrew Culbertson in 1775 moved from Chester Co., Pa., to Northumberland Co., Pa., and later to Wimsport, Lycoming Co., Pa. Mar. Jeannette Boyd at Philadelphia in 1763. Wife b.—; d. 1802.

Issue:

12. William, b. April 15, 1765; d. Nov. 11, 1843.
13. John Boyd, b. 1767; drowned.
14. Elizabeth, b. 1769; d. ——.   (Mrs. Matthew Wilson.)
15. John Boyd, (2nd.) b. 1770; d. called Boyd.
16. Andrew, b. 1772; d. ——. Erie Co., Pa.
17. James, b. 1774; d. ——.   Louisiana, Mo.
18. Samuel, b. 1776; do. ——.
19. Mary, b. 1780; d. ——.   (Mrs. Jas. Comings.)
20. Jeannette, b. 1783; d. ——.   (Mrs. Robt. McCaslin.)

(2) James Culbertson mar. Ann McNair, of Pa.   Killed by Indians in 1777. Widow and some of children moved to Livingstone Co., N. Y., in what is now Groveland Tp., where she is buried. At time of his death lived in Northumberland Co., Pa.   (Widow in Northampton Co., Pa. in 1790 Census.)

Issue:

21. John, b. 1762; d. 1777.   Killed by Indians.
22. Andrew, b. 1765; d. 1812.
23. James, b. 1767; d. 1848; bachelor.   Geneseo, N. Y.
24. William, b. 1770; d. 1808. Philadelphia.
25. Samuel, b. 1773; d. 1832.
26. Margaret, b. 1775; d. 1853.   (Mrs. J. McNair.)
27. Elizabeth, b. 1778; d. ——.

(4) Major John Culbertson mar. in 1761 to Sarah Denny. Lived, died and buried at Brandywine Manor, E. Coln Tp., Chester Co., Pa.
. Issue (from will and deeds) (2 over 16, 1 under 5; from Census 1790—Fuller) :

28. John, b. Jan. 27, 1762; d. ——.
29. William, b. Sep. 18, 1763; d. Mar. 1826.
30. Elizabeth, b. May 9, 1767; buried at Brandywine.
31. Margaret, b. Jan. 7, 1771; d. May 2, 1815.
32. James, b. Apr. 9, 1773; d. Sep. 1831.
33. Samuel, b. Mar. 8, 1780; d. Feb. 1858. Philadelphia.
     (5) Capt. Samuel Culbertson of Caernarvon Tp., Berks
Co., Pa., mar. *Margaret——. His farm was afterwards
(after 1770) included in Chester Co. and his widow made
her will in W. Nantmeal Tp.—which borders Berks Co. line
—on March 15, 1811. Samuel did not die in Berks Co. Died
Chester Co. Mar. before 1770.

Issue (from widow's will):

34. Elizabeth. (Mrs. Isaac Van Leer)
35. James.
     (6) Elizabeth Culbertson mar. Benjamin Wallace (from
old deed) of Dauphin Co., Pa., and moved to Erie Co., Pa.,
Mar.-Dec., 1767.
36. John Culbertson (Dr.) d. Erie Co., Pa.
     (8) Benjamin Culbertson of Chester Co., Pa. It appears
he did not marry. A deed in 1770 shows he was single.
Drowned in Delaware River, probably during Revolution.
Had no estate.

SIXTH GENERATION

(12) Wm. Culbertson mar. to second cousin, Mary Cul-
bertson, in 1794 and 1795 moved to Edinboro, Erie Co., Pa.
(Daughter of John and granddaughter of Samuel, son of
Robert of Kennett.)

Issue:

37. Andrew Columbus, b. June 20, 1795; d. Mar. 20, 1878.
38. Jeannette Cassander, b. 1797.
39. John Augustus, b. Mar. 26, 1800; d. Mar 16, 1872.
40. Wm. Washington, b. Feb. 22, 1802.

(12) Wm. Culbertson mar. second, Margaret Johnston of
Crawford Co., Pa., Jan. 1806.
41. Maria J., b. Nov. 17, 1806; d. ——.
42. James Johnston, b. Nov. 18, 1809.

*Family Bible of Samuel in possession of Mr. Stone of Dickson
Furnace, Tenn., says wife's name Margaret, wife of Samuel.

43. Josiah J., b. Feb. 26, 1812; d. May 19, 1868.
44. Cyrus A., b. May 23, 1814. d. ——.
45. Elizabeth. d. ——.
   (15) Boyd Culbertson moved West; am informed near Chillicothe, Ohio. None of descendants there now. Probably afterwards went to W. Va. Mar. Susan Douglas.

   Issue:

46. Joseph, d. ——. Was in War 1812. (Wellsburg, W. Va.)
46½. Benjamin, Erie Co., Pa.
   (16) Andrew Culbertson mar. first, Ann Culbertson, of Shippensburg, Pa., (a cousin several removed) moved to Washington Tp., Erie Co., Pa., where he died. Mar. June 17, 1797. (Wife b. 1773; d. 1808).

   Issue: (First wife died Jan. 1, 1808).

47. John Boyd, b. 1798; d. 1888.
48. Jane, b. 1800; d. Apr. 1888. Unmar.
49. Duncan, b. 1802; d. Dec. 1802.
50. Agnes, b. 1803; d. Nov. 20, 1803.
51. James, b. 1805; d. ——.
52. Eliza, b. 1807; d. ——. (Mrs. James Robinson)
   (16) Andrew Culbertson mar. second, Ann Morehead, of Lancaster Co., Pa., Feb. 9, 1809.

   Issue: (Wife d. Dec. 1847; wife b. Apr. 29, 1781.)

53. Thomas M., b. June 21, 1810; d. Oct. 15, 1881.
54. Andrew J., b. Apr. 21, 1812; d. 1883.
55. Wm. Patent, b. Dec. 3, 1819, Fulton, Illinois; d. ——.
   (17) James Culbertson moved to Washington Tp., Erie Co., Pa. Afterwards moved to Louisiana, Pike Co., Mo. Know nothing of descendants. Mar. Jane Maxwell.
   (18) Samuel Culbertson moved to Washington Tp., Erie Co., Pa. Know nothing of descendants. Mar. Jane Douglas.
   (22) Andrew Culbertson mar. Elizabeth Craig. Lived at Groveland, N. Y.

   Issue:

56. John, d. 1865. Bachelor. Tecumseh, Mich.
57. James, d. 1841. Bachelor. Tecumseh, Mich.
58. Samuel, d. 1857.
59. Thomas Craig, d. 1826. Bachelor. Groveland.
60. Ann, d. 1840. Geneseo, N. Y.

61. Robert, d. 1868. Bachelor. Tecumseh, Mich.
62. Eliza, d. 1875. Tecumseh, Mich.
63. Margaret. (Mrs. Buell) Grand Rapids, Mich.
64. Maria, d. 1864. Tecumseh, Mich.
      (24) Wm. Culbertson, mar. Miss Almon of Philadelphia,
Pa. Lived at Philadelphia.

Issue:

65. John. Know nothing of.
66. James, d. at Sparta, N. Y.
67. Wm., d. at Portland, Oregon. Bachelor.
68. Eliza, d. in Michigan. (Mrs. Mulhollen.)
      (25) Samuel C. mar. Anna S. Roup. Lived near Broken
Straw, Warren Co., Pa.

Issue:

69. Elizabeth, b. 1811. Geneseo, N. Y., d. ——.
70. Sarah, b. 1813; d. 1875.
71. Christiana, b. 1815; d. 1849.
72. Ann M., b. 1817; d. ——.
73. Charles W., b. 1819; d. 1890.
74. Fannie R., b. 1821; d. 1840.
75. Isaac V., b. 1823; d. 1856.
76. Mary K., b. 1826; d. ——.
      (26) Margaret Culbertson mar. first, Wm. Lattimore.

Issue:

77. Eliza. (Mrs. R. Wilcox.) Had issue.
      (26) Mar. Second, James McNair.
78. James Denny.
79. Richard, d. ——.
80. Ann, d. ——.
81   Andrew J. Honcut, California.
      (27) Elizabeth Culbertson mar. Issac Vandeventer. Died
at Logansport, Ind.

Issue:

82. Mary Ann, d. ——.
83. Christopher, d. ——.
84. James, d. ——.
85. Eliza, d. ——.
86. Rebecca, d. ——.
      (28) John Culbertson mar. Isabella——. Was a fuller of
cloth. Deed shows he moved to Crawford Co., Pa. after 1813.

Issue:

87. John H., Esq., b. 1823; d. Dec. 25, 1875. Crawford Co., Pa.
88. Samuel, d. ——.
89. Thomas, d. ——.
90. Denny, d. ——.
91. Lucretia, d. ——.
92. Letitia, d. ——.

(29) William Culbertson died at Barbersville, Jefferson Co., Ind. Know nothing of issue.

(30) Elizabeth Culbertson mar. Samuel Mackelduff.

Issue:

92 1-5. Rebecca. (Mrs. James McClure.) d. ——.
92 2-5. Mary Ann. (Mrs. David Krouser.) d. ——.
92 3-5. Elizabeth. (Mrs. John McClure, Sr.) d. ——.
92 4-5. Samuel.

(31) Margaret Culbertson mar. Capt. James Lockart, of Chester Co., Pa.

Issue:

92 6-5. Phoebe, d. Unmar.
92 7-5. Elizabeth, d. Unmar.
92 8-5. Isabel, d. Unmar.
92 9-5. Margaret. (Mrs. Samuel Pinkerton, who had issue: John P., Belle and S. Stanhope, of Pittsburgh, Pa. d.)

(32) James Culbertson mar. first, Hannah Murry. Moved from Chester Co., Pa., to Crawford Co., Pa., in 1797, where he mar. first wife. First wife d. 1799.

Issue:

93. Hannah. (Mrs. Samuel H. Wells, of Muskingum Co., O.) d.

(32) James C. mar. second, Miss Janet Dickson, daughter of (Scotch) James Dickson, Aug. 25, 1803. Afterwards moved to Logan Co., O., and was buried on McKee's Creek, four miles north of W. Liberty, Logan Co., O. Quit claimed in Chester, Pa., 1796.

Issue:

94. James Denny, b. Feb. 17, 1812.
95. Sarah, b. Sept. 4, 1814.
96. John H., b. Apr. 17, 1817.
97. Wm. G., b. Nov. 30, 1819.
98. Samuel D., b. Apr. 1, 1824.

Know nothing of Their Descendants.

(33) Samuel Culbertson mar. Susannah Myers Harrison. Lived at Philadelphia and buried at Brandywine Manor, Pa.

Issue:

98 1-5. Eliza Harrison, b. Dec. 9, 1813; d. Mar. 19, 1814.
98 2-5. Harrison, b. Dec. 3. 1818; d. Mar. 30, 1820.
98 3-5. John Harrison, b. Dec. 12, 1823; d. Sep. 30, 1892.
98 4-5. Walter Edwards, d. Aug. 21, 1872.
98 5-5. Louisa, b. Dec. 13, 1827; d. Aug. 30, 1828.
  (35) James Culbertson mar. ——. Issue:
99. Samuel. (From will.) d. Oct. 1826 in Chester Co., Pa. (unmar?)

SEVENTH GENERATION

(37) Andrew Columbus Culbertson mar. Margaret Alexander, Sep. 28, 1820. Farmer. Erie Co., Pa.

Issue:

100. Margaret J., b. Dec. 15, 1821. (Mrs. E. C. Rodgers.)
101. Mary Culbertson, b. Nov. 8, 1823; d.
102. William C., b. Nov. 27, 1825. (Congressman). d.
103. James A., b. Apr. 19, 1827; d.
104. Rebecca, b. Feb. 15, 1830. (Mrs. Geo. Wood.)
105. John, b. June 30, 1832; d. Dec. 2, 1895.
106. Alexander, b. June 11, 1835; d.
107. Charles, b. Apr. 12, 1839. Lumber. Argyle, Minn.; d.
  (38) Jeannette Cassander Culbertson mar. first, Loren West, July 14, 1825. Erie Co., Pa. Husband died.

Issue:

108. Loren West, b. Sep. 24, 1836; d.
  (38) Jeannette C. mar. second, Chauncey P. Roberts, Sep. 5, 1833.

Issue:

109. Chester C. Roberts, b. June 15, 1835; d.
110. Wm. b., Aug. 13, 1837; d.
111. Josiah B., b. Aug. 21, 1841.
  (39) John Augustus mar. Clarissa Harrison, Oct. 23, 1827. Was a cabinet maker; afterwards real estate agent, at Edinboro, Pa.

Issue:

112. Harrison, b. Sep. 25, 1829; d.
113. Louis C., b. Mar. 7, 1832. Covington, Ky.; d.

114. Johnston, b. Oct. 27, 1834; d.
115. Porter, b. Mar. 1, 1837; d.
116. Emily. (Intermar. John Proudfit.) ; d.
117. Edwin, b. May 11, 1843:d.
(41) Maria J. Culbertson mar. Thomas Colter, Jr. of Venango Tp., Crawford Co., Pa.

Issue:
118. Margaret. (Mrs. Jas. Mead) ; d.
119. Thomas W., d. young.
120. Elizabeth. (Mrs. H. Bunce) ; d.
121. Wm. Jackson; d.
122. Thomas Jackson; d.
123. Mary Cordelia.(Mrs. J. A. McKay); d.
124. Robert C; d.
125. Nancy Adeline. (Mrs. Niner) ; d.
126. Amos W.; d.
127. James P.; d.
128. I. S., d. Young.
129. Wilson H.; d.
(42) James Johnston C., mar. Jane Huntley, Jan. 17, 1830.
130. Cordelia, b. Aug. 22, 1833.
131. Julia, b. Oct. 4, 1835.
132. Louisa, b. 1840.
133. James J., b. Oct. 3, 1844.
(43) Josiah Jehosephat C., mar. Cordelia Stewart, Oct. 29, 1843.

Issue:
134. Celia, b. Jan. 28, 1846.
135. Celestia, b. Feb. 7, 1848.
136. Elliott, b. Nov. 4, 1849.
137. James, b. Oct. 2, 1856.
(44) Cyrus A. Culbertson mar. Catherine Willoughby. Wife d. 1882 .(Covington, Ky., and Edinboro, Pa.)

Issue:
138. Harriet, b. Jan. 28, 1839.
139. Dwight C., b. Mar. 25, 1840. Covington, Ky.
140. Xerxes W., b. Oct. 1, 1843. Covington, Ky.
141. Mattie, b. Nov. 6, 1845.
142. Sarah, b. June 15, 1849.
143. Deete, b. May 19, 1851.
144. Lansing B., b. May 13, 1855. Canton, Ohio.
145. Louie E., b. Mar. 11, 1857.

146. Lillie, b. Apr. 7, 1860.
(45) Elizabeth W. Culbertson mar. Wilson Colter, Apr. 8, 1835.

Issue:

147. Josiah J., b. Feb. 18, 1836.
148. Oscar C., b. Apr. 25, 1842.
(46) Joseph A. Culbertson, mar. Jane Martin, of Wellsburg, W. Va. Wife d. June 1852. He was a soldier in the war of 1812. (Lived at Wellsburg, W. Va.)

Issue:

149. Benjamin Martin, b. 1824. Soldier in Mexican and Civil Wars.
150. Wm. McC. Sea captain, not heard of for 30 years.
151. Joseph Alexander. Probably killed in Union army.
152. Lizzie. (Mrs. Watson.)
153. Eliza.
154. Priscilla.
155. Sarah.
156-161. Six others, d. young.
(47) John Boyd Culbertson mar. Miss Laughrey, of ——. Lived at Harbor Creek, Erie Co., Pa. until 1832, when he moved to Chandlersville, Muskingum Co., O., where he resided seven years. After this he moved to Licking Co., O., in 1840, and died in Paulding Co., O. (Was raised by his uncle Joseph C., of Salt Creek, Muskingum Co., O.)

Issue:

162. Andrew H. Bluffton, Ohio.
163. James W. Beloit, Kans.
164. William C.
165. John P.
166. Thomas L. Texas (soldier 7th Mo. Cav.)
167. Mary Ann. (Mrs. Sherman), Springfield, Mo.
168. Sarah Jane (Mrs. Hollinworth), Rockville, Mo.
169. Elizabeth C.
170. Charlotte P.
171. Rebecca M.
172. Martha E.
(51) James mar. Betsy Huntley. Know nothing about him.
(53) Thomas Culbertson mar. Nancy A. Norcross, Jan. 2, 1838. Lived in Erie Co., Pa.

Issue:

173. Maria L., b. Nov. 10, 1838. (Mrs. G. W. Moore.)
174. Catherine Ann, b. Sep. 13, 1841. Unmar.
175. John Norcross, b. Mar. 23, 1843.
176. Rachel McCord, b. July 19, 1847. (Mrs. Gay.)

(54) Andrew J. Culbertson, mar. Eliza J. Miller. Know nothing about him.

(55) Wm. Patent Culbertson mar. first, Mary McCord. Lives at Fulton, Whiteside Co., Ills. No issue; wife died. He mar. second, Helen Reed.

Issue:

177. Charles P., d. aet 35. Bachelor.
178. ——— dau. (Mrs. Prof. Lochmund.)

Issue: Franz C., Philadelphia.

(55) Mar. third, Mary Fay, who died without issue. He mar. fourth wife, Charlotte Hall. No issue.

(58) Samuel Culbertson mar. Nancy Johnson about 1828. Wife living 1893. She was born Mar. 7, 1805.

Issue:

179. John, b. Apr. 19, 1830 d. Oct. 1865.
180. Frank, b. July 3, 1832.
181. Margaret, b. 1834. San Francisco, Cal.
182. Samuel, b. Aug. 30, 1837.
183. Elizabeth, b. Dec. 25, 1839; d. Jan. 27, 1887.
184. Michael, b. Sep. 3, 1842.
185. Nancy, b. Nov. 14, 1845.
186. Matilda, b. July 7, 1848.
187. Edward J., b. Oct. 19, 1850. E. Groveland, N. Y.

(63.) Margaret Culbertson mar. Mr. Buell, of Grand Rapids, Mich. Know nothing of descendants.

(65) John. Know nothing about him.

(66) James, of Sparta, N. Y. Know nothing of descendants.

(68) Eliza Culbertson mar. Mr. Mulhollen. Know nothing of issue.

(71) Christina Culbertson mar. Abraham R. Cole, Sep. 2, 1840.

Issue:

188. ——— lived only two months.

(72) Ann M. Culbertson. Know nothing about issue.

(73) Charles W. Culbertson mar. Deborah H. Goheen, Nov. 20, 1845.

Issue:
189. Samuel Edward, b. Aug. 25, 1846.
190. John Edwin, b. Jan. 8, 1848; d. Nov. 20, 1867.
191. Chas. W., Jr., b. Mar. 3, 1854.
192. Fannie E., b. May 24, 1857. (Mrs. Weed.)
193. Lincoln, b. Aug. 3, 1860.
194. Anna S. May, b. May 16, 1863; d. Sep. 16, ——.
   (76) Mary K. Culbertson. Still living.
   (87) John H. Culbertson mar. Polly J. Merritt.
      Co. Recorder, Crawford Co., Pa., 1854.
Issue:
195. John T. Duluth, Minn.
196. Eugene M.
197. George D.
198. Ira W.
199. Herbert S.
200. Samuel H. Unmar.
201. Louise
202. Millie A.
203. Alonzo L. Unmar. Duluth, Minn.
   (98 2-3) John H. Culbertson mar. Theora Alethe Thomas.

Issue:
203 1-1. Samuel Harrison, b. Mar. 4, 1864; d. Aug. 10,
      1888.
203 1-2. Morgan Thomas, b. ——.
203 3-4. Elizabeth Denny b. June 6, 1865.
203 4-4. Walter Edwards, b. Aug. 21, 1872.

EIGHTH GENERATION

(102) Hon. Wm. C. Culbertson, of Girard, Erie Co., Pa.,
mar. Margaret Alexander.

Issue: (Girard, Erie Co., Pa.)
204. Cordelia A.
205. Kate.
206. James A.
207. Belle. (Mrs. Frank May.)
208. Wm. M. Miller, at Girard, Pa.
209. Margaret.
210. Charles B.
211. Archibald B., d. 1883.
   (103) James A. Culbertson. Manager Alleghany Springs,
Warren Co., Pa.

(105) John Culbertson. Lived in Sheffield, Pa.
.(106) Alexander Culbertson. Lived in California.
(107) Charles Culbertson mar. Mary Barker at Edinboro, Erie Co., Pa., in 1868. Moved to Augusta, Wis., in 1872, where he is engaged in farming and lumber business.

Issue:
212. Clarence B.
213. Andrew, d. young.
215. Bernice.
(——) Grandchildren of (39) Augustus Culbertson.
(113) Louis C. has a son, Halsey, living in Chicago.
Grandchildren of James Johnston Culbertson (42). Know nothing about.
Grandchildren of (43) J. J. Culbertson. Know nothing about.
Grandchildren of (44) Cyrus A. Culbertson. Know nothing about.
(149) Benjamin M. Culbertson mar. first, Catherine Snowden, of Wellsburg, W. Va. Wife died. Lives at Rolla, Mo.

Issue:
216. Samuel Snowden, b. Jan. 28, 1852. Washington, D. C.
217. Joseph Pearce, b. Jan. 9, 1855; d. ——.
218. Eliza Charlotte, b. July 21, 1857.
219. Alvin Dow, b. Feb. 20, 1860; d. Feb. 1861.
(149) Benjamin M. C., mar. second, Harriett Momen, of Rolla, Mo., Dec. 2, 1868.

Issue:
220. Stella Mae, b. Jan. 1, 1870; d. Jan. 1, 1870.
221. Benjamin Franklin, b. Mar. 16, 1871. Printer, Rolla, Mo.
222. Hattie Celestia Cyrene, b. Ap. 5, 1873. Unmar. Rolla, Mo.
223. Wm. Cliffton, b. Sep. 12, 1874. Printer. Rolla, Mo.
224. Clara Belle, b. Nov. 25, 1876; d. July 28, 1877.
225. Alice Daisy, b. June 7, 1878; d. Dec. 20, 1879.
(153) Eliza Culbertson mar. Mr. Crewson. Widow lives at Steubenville, O. Husband served in Union Army, all through war.

Issue:
226. Mary.
227. Alexander.

228. Edwin.
229. Emma. (Mrs. Young.)
230. Jennie, d.
231. Andrew.
232. Grant.

(155) Sarah Culbertson mar. Jas. A. Porter, of Fernwood, O., in 1865.

Issue:

233. George. Mar.
234. Sherman.
235. Albert Desmond. Mar.
236. Mary Florence. (Mrs. C. B. Parker.)
237. Charles Dayton.
238. James Garfield.

(163) James W. Culbertson mar. Miss Lucinda Reed, in 1847. Lived in Ohio 21 years; then went to Boonville, Mo.; in 1861, went to Iowa; in 1863, to Illinois; went to Kansas in 1873; to Barton Co., Mo., in 1891; now a Beloit, Kansas.

Issue:

238. Frances M. Mar. Miss Smith.
240. James B. Mar. Miss Coats.
241. John A. Unmar. Esrom, Mo.
242. Livinia E. (Mrs. D. F. Simpson), Beloit, Kans.
243. Mary.A.
244. Martha L. (Mrs. B. Pickering), Beloit.
245. Elvira P. (Mrs. B. King), Beloit, Kans.

(175) John N. Culbertson mar. first, Belle D. Blaine, Feb. 27, 1868. Wife d. Mar. second, Francis C. Chapman, April 17, 1878. Know nothing about issue.

(182) Capt. Samuel Culbertson mar. Sarah R. H. Johnston, dau. of J. M. Johnston, of Cincinnati, O. Lives at E. Groveland, N. Y. Was Capt. Co. B., 1st N. Y. Dragoons in Civil War.

Issue:

246. Margaret Bell.
247. Robert M.
248. Samuel Craig.
249. James J.

(184) Michael Culbertson mar. ——. Lives at E. Groveland, N. Y.

Issue:

250. Richard. J.

251. Anna S.
252. Nancy.
253. Augustus P.
    (189) Samuel E. Culbertson enlisted in the 6th Mich. Heavy Art'y, in Jan. 1864; discharged, Aug. '65. Mar. Mrs. Clara M. Buell, Dec. 18, '85.

Issue:

254. Fanny May, b. Jan. 18, 1887.
255. Bessie, b. Jan. 26, 1889; d. Aug. 1890.
256. Zoe Marie, b. Dec. 15, 1892.
    (190) John E. Culbertson enlisted in the 5th Mich. Inf., and was discharged in July, 1865. With Gen. Grant. Wounded at Appamattox. Died of wounds received in army. Was unmarried.
    (191) Charles W. Culbertson mar. Fannie E. Florence, Nov. 21, 1878. (P. M. at Ridgeway, Mich.)

Issue:

257. Carroll M., b. Jan. 11, 1880.
258. Florence May, b. Oct. 11, 1881.
    (192) Fannie E. Culbertson mar. Frank J. Weed, of Ceresco, Mich., Dec. 22, 1881.

Issue:

259. Charles J. Weed, b. Apr. 2, 1884.
260. Louise, b. Nov. 15, 1892.

NINTH GENERATION

    (195) John T. Culbertson mar. Orleana Kidner. Lives at Duluth, Minn.

Issue:

261. Lynn L.
262. John Byron.
263. Alvern.
    (196) Euguene M. C., mar. Ada Palmer.

Issue:

264. Grace.
265. Earle.
266. Rush.
267. Lilse.

268. Glennie.
  (197) George D. C., mar. Amy Harrington.

Issue:
269. Elva.
270. Earle.
  (198) Ira W. C. mar. Alice Coleridge.

Issue:
271. Lou.
  (199) Herbert S. C., mar. Jane Steele.

Issue:
272. Roy.
  (201) Louise Culbertson mar. Ira Hutton.

Issue:
273. Lena.
  (202) Millie A. Culbertson mar. W. Berrie. No issue.

PROMINENT DESCENDANTS OF JOHN (I)

(1) Andrew Culbertson was one of the early settlers of Williamsport, Pa. Cyrus Culbertson says he commenced a grist-mill, near Williamsport, in 1773. Deed Records of Chester Co., Pa., show that he deeded the last of his property in that Co., in July, 1775, to James Clemson, hatter. Owned a tract of land along the river below Deerstown, near Lewisburg, Pa. Was a private in Col. Hunter's Battalion of Associaters, from Northumberland Co., in July, 1776 and served until close of the war. Was in a battle with the Indians, on Bald Eagle Creek, Center Co., Pa., on Apr. 10, 1782, in which the whole force was killed excepting the commander, Major Moses Van Campen, Andrew Culbertson and one other. He was a wealthy man, and at his death left 907 acres in Lycoming Co., Pa. Appointed Chief Executive Officer of Northumberland Co. for carrying into effect the orders of Congress. (Pa. Arch.)

(2) James Culbertson was commissioned by Gov. Denny, of Pa., May 1, 1758, to be Ensign of a company, in Col. Hugh Mercer's Battalion (Regt.), the Third Bat. of Pa. Provincial Troops, in the French and Indian War. Ensign James marched to Ft. Duquesne in winter of 1758. He was in the Revolution, as well as his son, John, and while they were at home on a furlough and eating their dinners, the Indians took them by surprise and shot them down. The

son was only fifteen years old. His children (it is asserted) were granted a magnificent pension of almost a whole county in Va., or Maryland, but for some reason did not take up the claim, and their papers were foolishly destroyed. (I could find no evidence of this on any records.) The Pa. Archives, at Harrisburg, Pa., do not give his record, which was no doubt destroyed in Philadelphia in 1800. His descendants have his commission in the French and Indian War. There was no administration or will of his, nor deeds recorded in Lancaster or Chester Co., hence he lived in Northumberland Co. at his death. His brother Andrew probably bought his land, as deeds show that Andrew's Ex'rs., sold the "James Culbertson tract of 213 acres in 1797."

(4) Major John Culbertson was buried at Brandywine Manor, Chester Co., Pa. The following beautiful epitaph appears on his tombstone:

"My flesh shall slumber in the grave,
'Till the last trumphets joyful sound,
Then burst the chains with sweet surprise
And in my glorious image arise."

He was in the battle of Long Island in the fall of 1776, being a Major in Col. James Moore's Battalion (First) of Chester Co., Pa., Associaters of the "Flying Camp." (See Barrie's Army and Navy of the U. S., ed. de luxe, supplementary, p. 9.) He was commissioned Major, July 1, 1776. Stationed at Perth Amboy, N. J., under Gen. Mercer, Aug. 14, 1776; at Ft. Lee, Aug. 20, 1776 (Amer. Arch.) He was a "delegate to the Associated Battalion Convention, at Lancaster, Pa., July 4, 1776." (Pa. Arch.) His brother, "Andrew, a private from Northumberland Co., Pa., was also a delegate to this Convention." (Pa. Arch.) John was commissioned Major of Col. William Gibbons' Battalion (Seventh), of Chester Co., Pa., Associaters, May 17, 1777. In 1779, he was a Major of Lieut. Col. John Gardner's Battalion (Fifth), of Chester Co. Associaters. This made him virtually Lieut. Col. Was commissioned May 10, 1780, Major of Lieut. Col. John Gardner's (First) Battalion of Chester Co. Associaters." Futhey's Hist. Chester Co. says he was born 1739. Member Pa. Assembly 1777-80.

(5) Capt. Samuel Culbertson of Pikeland Tp., Chester Co., a member of the Com. of Public Safety, Oct. 23, 1775, at a meeting at which Anthony Wayne was chairman. (Pa. Arch.) Com. of Safety also published notice "for a meeting

to study the art of making a salt-petre, at the house of Mr. Culbertson at the Yellow Springs, on 4th and 5th of March, 1776." (Pa. Arch.). He was an inn-keeper on License Records up to and including 1782, but not in 1783, at which date his brother John's name appears.

I find in Deed Records of Chester Co., that on Mar. 1776, there was recorded a deed made by Samuel Culbertson to The Proprietaries of Pa., for land in Coventry Tp., Chester Co. This was for salt-petre beds. He was present at a meeting of the Com. of Safety at Downingtown, Chester Co., Pa., on July 1, 1776, where it was "agreed to raise a battalion of 652 men." (Pa. Arch.).

"Capt. Samuel was appointed, July 1776, Capt. in Col. Wm. Montgomery's Battalion of Chester Co. Associaters of the "Flying Camp." (Am. Arch. 4th ser., vol. VI, p. 1196.) The Flying Camp constituted the Brigade in New Jersey under command of Brig. Gen. Hugh Mercer. "Col. Wm. Montgomery's Regt. was at Perth Amboy in July, 1776, and remained there until August 14, 1776;; at Ft. Lee, N. J., Aug. 20, 1776. From Fort Lee, Gen. Mercer moved to Long Island." (Amer. Arch.) Saffell's Record of the Revolutionary War says of him: "Capt Samuel Culbertson, of Wm. Montgomery's Regt. was captured Nov. 16, 1776, at Ft. Washington. He was a prisoner, with certain bounds, on Long Island until Aug. 16, 1779, when he was ordered into the city prison of New York. Lewis Pintard and Col. Palfry supplied him in 1776 and '77 with money. He was exchanged Nov. 2, 1780, at Elizabethtown, N. J. and made his way to his place of abode at Yellow Springs, Pa. Capt. Culbertson was possessed of fine literary abilities and military talents." His administration shows that his wife died before he did.

Samuel Culbertson died in East Caln township, Chester Co., Pa. Letters of administration were granted for his estate January 8, 1783. Brother John, Admnr. Inventory of his estate shows "One silver stock buckle, one pair of silver sleeve buttons, two certificates for depreciation for pay as Capt. of the Flying Camp."

I neglected to state that the father of Isaac Vanleer, who married Elizabeth Culbertson, was Samuel Vanleer. Said Samuel was a captain in Chester Co., Pa. militia in the Revolution. He married Hannah Wayne, of Chester Co., Pa., a sister of Gen. "Mad Anthony" Wayne, of Revolutionary fame and a daughter of Isaac Wayne, an officer in the

French and Indian War. Samuel Vanleer had several sons: Anthony W. Vanleer, who went to Nashville, Tenn., and became one of the wealthiest iron-masters of Tennessee. One of his daughters, Mrs. Polk married a cousin of President Polk, and one of her daughters married one of the highest barons in Italy, and another a French count. Her son, Van Leer Polk, of Tennessee was Consul-General of the United States to Calcutta, India. Mrs. Polk moved to Rome, Italy, during the Civil War, and the family were intimate friends of King Humbert. Her daughter and her husband were warm friends of the Marquis and Marchioness of Lorne, and exchanged visits. The descendants of A. W. Van Leer's other daughter, Mrs. Kirkham, live in Nashville, being among the wealthiest people of that place. Her daughter married Capt Drouillard, U. S. Army, who became a Tenn. iron-master after the war and died over 55 years ago.

Another son of Isaac Van Leer was Bernard Van Leer, who was an iron-master at Nashville, another son of Isaac was William who died 1895 at Downington, Chester Co., Pa., aged over 90 years. His daughter married H. M. Richards, Sec'y of the German Society of Pa., and resides at Reading.

Issue Isaac Van Leer and Elizabeth Culbertson:

1. Hannah Vanleer, daughter of Isaac and Elizabeth Vanleer, b. Dec. 4, 1804.

2. Margaret Vanleer, daughter of Isaac and Elizabeth Vanleer, b. Dec. 14, 1805.

3. Linford L. Vanleer, b. Mar. 26, 1806 (son of Isaac and Elizabeth Vanleer).

4. Wayne Vanleer, son of Isaac and Elizabeth Vanleer, born June 24, 1810.

(1) Hannah Vanleer married first John Kennedy, of near Pittsburg, who moved to Tennessee in 1825, and had one child, who died young. Husband died in 1846, widow remarried to Hardman Stone, and had two sons, Samuel B. Stone and Robert B. Stone.

(2) Hannah Vanleer married a Mr. Nopper, and had children—Montgomery, Margaret and Mary Nopper.

(3) (Data not furnished).

The Census of 1790 for Tedriffen Tp., Chester Co., Pa., gives Isaac Van Leer, self and wife, 4 sons under 16 and 2 daughters. This makes it pretty certain that Bernard and William, sons of Isaac Van Leer, above were by the first wife. There were two other sons whose names I do not know, who may have died young. Elizabeth Culbertson (34) must have been his second wife. Her father was born 1744 and probably married 1763-5. If Elizabeth was born 1764-6 she would have been old enough to have married by 1783-5 and borne six children by 1790.

His brother-in-law Benjamin Wallace was a captain in Col. Wm. Montgomery's Bat. of the "Flying Camp," July 1, 1776, in Chester Co., Pa. Futhey's History of Chester Co., says that "In 1785 a change of election districts was made and the polling place of the Third Dist. was held at the sign of the Pennsylvania Arms, at the home of John Culbertson, of E. Coln Tp." Also, "among the first trustees of Brandywine Church, at the organization in 1786 were John Culbertson and (his cousin) Samuel." This church is in the northwestern part of the county. "Major John Culbertson was an active Whig during the Revolution." (Ibid). Was a fuller.

(9) Benjamin Culbertson was appointed Lieut. in Col. Wm. Montgomery's Battalion of Chester Co., Associaters of the "Flying Camp," July 1, 1776. (See Am. Arch., 4th ser. vol VI, p. 1196). Pa. Archives do not mention his service after Dec. 1776. Family records say he was "drowned in the Delaware River." (Probably during Revolution.)

(12) Wm. Culbertson was one of the early settlers of Edinboro, Erie Co., Pa., where he engaged in milling and farming. Was also Justice of the Peace.

(29) William served from 1778 to 1782 in Capt. Cornelius Atkinson's Co. Northumberland Co Mil." (Pa. Arch.). Not in Census alone or with his father, Chester Co., Pa., 1790. (See sons over 16).

(37) Andrew C. was in same business and his grandson, (102) Hon. Wm. C. Culbertson was a wealthy Congressman, capitalist and lumber merchant, of Girard, Pa. He had business interests in Erie Co., Pa., Michigan, Minnesota, Missouri, various places in Pennslvania, Kentucky, etc. For some time he was associated with his brother, J. A. Culbertson, in the lumber business with offices at Chicago,

Ill., and Covington, Ky., and they were rated by Bradstreet at over $1,000,000. They closed out their business at Chicago some years ago, and James A. now lives at Menominee, Mich. His brother Charles had extensive lumber and farming interests in Minnesota. William M. Culbertson, a son of the Congressman, is a wealthy miller at Girard, Pa. Hon. W. C. Culbertson of Girard, Pa., was Capt. in a Kentucky (Union) Regt. during the Civil War (1892).

(87) John H. Culbertson was recorder of Crawford Co., Pa. in 1854. His son John T. (195) is the owner of a cane which has been handed down through seven generations of John Culbertsons, having been brought from Ireland in 1713 and is, I presume, the oldest heirloom of any Culbertson family in this country. He is a prominent business man of Duluth, Minn. (1892).

(181) Miss Margaret Culbertson, Supt. of the Chinese Mission Home, San Francisco, went to California in 1878 and engaged in mission work among the Chinese. Her work has been one of the noblest and yet most difficult that man or woman has been called upon to perform. "When she first assumed charge of the home there were about ten girls. Since that time about four hundred women and children have found shelter there. She has defended these helpless ones even at risk of her life until the very police of Chinatown have come to say that she is braver than most men." (From Occidental Leaves).

PART THIRD

SECTION FIRST

Irish Robert (B) of Chester Co., Pa.

(B) PART THIRD (IRISH ROBERT OF KENNETT TP., CHESTER, PA.)

THIRD GENERATION

(B) **Robert Culbertson** (Irish) of Kennett Tp., Chester Co., Pa. made his will in Mar. 1762 and will was probated May 3, 1762. Devisees were wife Jean, son Samuel, and grandson John, son of his son (I) Samuel; daughters Mary, Martha, Isabella, Sarah. Recites that one-third of his estate shall go to his son Samuel, also a negro boy named Dirk, providing that Samuel takes his mother and sisters to Cumberland Co., Pa. and provides for them until his sisters' marriage, and in case he does not comply his one-third shall go to son-in-law Alex Porter. His widow Jane made her will in Sept 17, 1769 (probated Oct. 1769) and died shortly after. She devises to her daughters, and grandchild John, son of son Samuel. States that owing to the fact that son Samuel has not complied with his father's wishes she cuts him out in her will. In sale bill of Robert's est. Samuel refuses to act as ex'r. and the negro was sold at sale for £55, showing that Samuel received nothing. In the final account of widow's estate in 1773 shows Elizabeth, Martha and Isabella were dead. Exrs. paid £69 each to Jane (Hill), Mary (Gordon) and Sarah Barclay. The will states that Sarah Barclay is to receive £81, but £10 is to be deducted from this to pay grandson John Culbertson's bequest. This was done in settlement showing John was living. Samuel was given in the first edition of this Genealogy on Pages 21 and 45 as a son of Irish John of Londongrove Tp. (came over 1712), but Samuel was of too late a date to have been his son, also I could not find him on tax lists of 1740 or 1730, yet he must have been born by or befor 1741 as he is on tax duplicate in 1762 in Vincent Tp. His son Samuel was of age in 1771 (Jan 22) as Samuel and his son Samuel were deeded 200 acres by Jane Lockart, widow, and Robt. Lockart and wife in Vincent Tp., Chester

Co., Pa., Jan. 22, 1771. Samuel's son John did not participate in this transaction in 1771. This became the home farm of Samuel and son Samuel. John was not dead as he was mentioned in Samuel Sr.'s will in 1782. Not having participated in the purchase in 1771 he would not transfer in 1791.

Why Irish Robert of Kennett should have mentioned grandson John, and not grandson Samuel, I could not say, unless it be that grandson Samuel having ample means by inheritance through his wife Agnes Beatty did not need it. David Beatty had died before Irish Robert Culbertson. Neither Samuel nor his sons Samuel or John, are found on the tax list of Kennett in 1766. Widow Jane (or Robert) is on 1766. In the will of Samuel of E. Coln made 1782, the witnesses are Eliz. North, John Culbertson Esq. and wife Sarah. This was his second cousin, John of Brandywine, i. e. Major.

In his will probated May 9, 1788, he says: "And whereas I am now possessed of the one divided moiety or half part of the plantation on which I live, containing 200 acres together with half of the live stock and implements and half of all the household furniture now on farm. Item, I give to my nephew David, son of my son Samuel, all of my part of the above described plantation, &c." This real estate was subject to specific legacies of money to other heirs.

CHAPTER IV

FOURTH GENERATION

(1) Samuel Culbertson located in Vincent Tp., Mar. ——. First available tax list on which we find him is 1762 in above tp. He must have been born before 1725. Died in E. Coln Tp.

Issue: (from will) Trustee Brandywine Church 1786.
1. John. On tax, freeman, E. Nottingham Tp., Chester Co., 1776.
2. Samuel. Of age 1771 (deed).
3. Martha. (Mrs. Long).
4. Agnes (Mrs. McHenry).
5. Margaret (Mrs. Steel).

(II) Elizabeth Culbertson mar. Alex. Porter of Chester Co., (from will of her father).

Issue:

6. David
7. Samuel.
8. Nancy.

FIFTH GENERATION

(1) John Culbertson mar. first ———. Moved to Erie Co., Pa. as shown by Family Records of the Erie Co. Culbertsons (Colter and Culbertson Gen. by Robert Colter). On Census John Jr. 1790, Brandywine Tp., Chester Co., Pa., self and 1 son over 16; 1 son under 16, 2 fem.

Issue:

9. Son b. before 1774.
9½. Mary (Mrs. Wm. Culbertson) Edinboro, Pa.
9¾. Dan.
9 4-4. Dan.

(1) John Culbertson mar. second Mrs. Margaret Hamilton (Colter Gen.).

Issue:

10. Benjamin (Erie Co., Pa.).
11. Agnes (Mrs Robert Colter) Edinboro, Pa. b. Apr. 19, 1807.

(2) Samuel Culbertson mar. Agnes, daughter of David Beatty of Chester Co. moved to Crawford Co., Pa., after 1791, says Colter-Culbertson Gen., but Crawford Co. officials say no record of (if they told the truth). Census 1790 Chester Co., Pa., self and wife, four males over 16; 3 females. Brandywine Tp. No doubt part of these were nephews and nieces or nephews and sisters.

Issue:

12. David. Family records say moved to Blooming Valley, Crawford Co., Pa. Court officials claim no record of. Participates in a deed with his father and mother in Chester Co., Pa. in 1791. (Land from his grandfather Samuel Culbertson.)
13. Samuel, d. young.
14. Martha, d. young. She and brother Samuel named in grandfather's will.

SIXTH GENERATION

(9½) Mary Culbertson mar. Wm. Culbertson of Edinboro, Erie Co., Pa., a son of Andrew of Williamsport and grandson of John Esq., Sr., of Brandywine Tp., Chester Co., Pa. (Colter Gen. has it that she was a first cousin; that is a mistake as she was several cousins removed.) For descendants see descendants of Major John of Chester Co., Pa.

(11) Agnes Culbertson mar. Robert Colter of near Edinboro, Pa. Mar. July 15, 1824.

Issue:

15. John W., b. July 10, 1825.

16. Cyrus M., b. Aug. 4, 1827.

17. Darius J., b. Aug. 11, 1829.

18. Julia A., b. Oct. 19, 1831.

19. Thomas J., b. Dec. 1, 1833.

20. Levi A., b. Dec. 26, 1837.

21. Sarah J., b. Feb. 11, 1839.

22. Robert W., b. Feb. 13, 1841.

23. Francis M., b. Dec. 26, 1844.

24. Aaron B., b. Mar. 20, 1847.

25. Mary L., b. Apr. 30, 1851.

PART FOURTH

Irish Andrew (C) Lancaster County Pa. (Shippensburg)

(C) PART FOURTH

————————,

(C) **Andrew Culbertson** emigrated to America from Londonderry Co., Ireland, and settled in Kennett Tp., Chester Co., Pa., before 1726. He is on tax records of this county until 1728, but left Chester Co. in 1728-29 and settled in Hopewell Tp., Lancaster (now Cumberland Co., Pa.) Co., in 1729, being one of the very first permanent settlers of the present Cumberland Co., Pa. There is little doubt but that he was with the first party of Benjamin Chambers that went to Cumberland Co., Pa. He probably did not come to America with Chambers' party. He lived but a short distance from the Row and his descendants have always been regarded as belonging to the Row, but they did not, as that term was applied to the settlement of the three Irish brothers, Alex., Robert and Samuel and cousin Joseph. He was an uncle of the three "Pa. Row" brothers. Alex., Joseph and Samuel were named as his bondsmen in the administration of his estate, filed in 1746, and his (Andrew's) son, Samuel, was his administrator. An inventory of his estate was filed in 1747, of which I have a copy. On it his name is written Colbertson. It is quite interesting and shows that he was one of the wealthiest men of the Cumberland Valley. The total value of the inventory was about $4000, a very large sum for those days. Division of his estate was made in Cumberland Co., in 1750, from which I obtained names of his children, the last five being minors at that date. I should suppose from this that he must have been born before 1700. His land was assessed in inventory at £280. About this date the Proprietaries were receiving for land in Pa. £15, 10 shillings per 100 acres. The names of his children are derived from inventory and division of his estate.

In May 1748 his widow Janet took out a warrant for 50
acres in Hopewell Tp., Lancaster Co., Pa. Patent not returned on this until Jan. 18, 1775. This patent was returned
with 33 acres which evidently was allowed or purchased by
her from her first husband's estate. Order of resurvey was
given Mar. 5, 1767, and in this plat is 83 acres. Adjoining
land is Ed. Shippen, Isaac Miller, Sam Montgomery and Jas.
Silver. Pat recites "that Janet Culbertson intermarrying
with John Miller, by deed Jan. 13, 1775, granted said land
to Robert Culbertson." This was her son. Land was in Shippensburg.

The appraisers of his estate were John Miller, Allen Kil-
lough and Robert Dwining and they filed inventory at Lancaster, Pa., in March 1747. Janet Culbertson took out a warrant for land in what was then Lancaster Co., Pa. in 1748.
This was Andrews widow and she had not married John
Miller at that time.

Andrew (Irish) is first found on tax records of Chester
Co., Pa. in 1726. He is not on the records of 1713. The records for intervening years between 1713-1726 are missing
so we do not know just when he began paying taxes and
when he was of age, or when he came to America. Five of
his children were of age in 1750. He was probably married
about 1720 as several of his children were married in 1740.
He was an uncle, same say a cousin of the three brothers
of the "Culbertson Row." He received a Warrant from Gov.
Edward Shippen for 240 acres of land in Hopewell Tp., Lancaster Co., Pa. in 1740. This was partly outside and partly
inside Shippensburg. Tradition says he married a sister
of James Breckenridge; also that James Breckenridge
(First) was married to Andrew's sister. Also that he was a
brother-in-law to Robert (Irish) Culbertson of Peters Tp.
Andrew's widow, several years after his death, married
John Miller. He was one of the appraisers of Andrew's
estate in March, 1747. In 1751, James Culbertson of Hopewell Tp.; Wm. Carr and Elizabeth, his wife; Andrew Culbertson and wife, Esther, made a quit claim to their brother Samuel. Jane conveyed by her g'd'n N. Wilson, 1751.

In Nov., 1753, Samuel Culbertson, of Hopewell Tp., and
wife, Mary, deeded this property to Francis Campble
(275 A.), said Andrew having died intestate, 98 acres of
said tract fell to the share of the heirs Samuel, James,
Elizabeth and Andrew and Jane. The said Samuel having
purchased the shares of James, Elizabeth (now Mrs. Kerr),

Andrew and wife and Jane, by her Gd'n N. Wilson and Francis Campbell, Gd'n of Robert, Sarah and Rebecca, deed for them in 1753.

Andrew's son, James, moved to Chester Co., Pa., in 1751. In the old Genealogy, he was given by error as a son of Irish John of Chester Co., Pa., James willed to (Oct. 14, 1763) brothers: Samuel, Robert; sisters, Jane, Sarah (Breckenridge), Martha (Miller), Rebecca (Park).

It will be seen from this that three of his brothers and sisters are not mentioned, i. e. Andrew, Elizabeth and Margaret. It is my belief that in 1763 the two sisters were dead. There were no deeds to Margaret, showing she died in 1750-51. In his will he mentions Rebecca (Mrs. Park). This shows that she was married to Park in 1763, but later she became a widow and married Mr. Cravenstine, some records say from Va., but Census Records show they lived in Germantown, Philadelphia. Martha married Gideon Miller of Allegheny Co., Pa. (who served in Revolution with Cumb. Co. Ass'rs.) and afterwards moved to Allegheny Co., Pa. Elizabeth married Wm. Kerr of "Culbertson Row", Jane married Oliver Culbertson (Irish) of Lurgan Tp., Cumb. Co., Pa., and later moved to Armstrong Tp., Westmoreland Co., Pa.; Sarah married John Breckenridge before 1763 and lived in the "Row". Issue: Samuel, Janet (Mrs. Benj. Johnston), Sarah (unmarried), Elizabeth (Mrs. Jas. Herron), Polly (Mrs. Jas. Shoaff), Nancy (Mrs. Robert Culbertson of Ambersons Valley), Sarah (Mrs. Archibald Mahon).

The estate of James, son of Irish Andrew, was administered in Chester Co., Pa. Records there show he owned no real estate. James Reynolds and Robert Peoples, appraisers, were sworn in Cumb. Co. His brother Robert named executor—renounced.

THIRD GENERATION

Issue Andrew and Janet:

  I. **Samuel,** b.——; d. 1799, Washington Co., Tenn., (Chapter V).
 II. **James,** b.——; d. Nov., 1763, bachelor, Chester Co., Pa.
III. **Andrew,** b.——; d.——. (Chapter XI).
 IV. **Elizabeth,** b. ——; d.—— (Mrs. Wm. Kerr). Wm. Kerr killed Bloody Run, 1756. Wife died before 1763? Not on brother's will.

V. **Jane,** b.——; d.—— (Mrs. Oliver Culbertson),. West'm'd Co., Pa.

VI. **Robert,** b. 1741; d. 1821. (Col.) Columbus, Ohio. (Chapter XVII).

VII. **Martha,** b.——; d.——. (Mrs. Gideon Miller) Allegheny Co., Pa.

VIII. **Margaret,** b.——; d.young.

IX. **Sarah,** b.——; d.——. (Mrs. John Breckenridge) "Row."

X. **Rebecca;** married first Mr. Park; second Mr. Cravenstine, Germantown, Pa.

*　　　*　　　*　　　*　　　*

CHAPTER V

FOURTH GENERATION

(I) **Samuel** Culbertson married first to Mary ——. His will made in Washington Co., Tenn. shows that he had married a second time and that his second wife's name was Jane. I think it very probable that all his children were by the first wife. The youngest child named in his will was Mary, the same as his first wife's name. He left Cumb. Co. Dec., 1753 and moved to Va. (see Second Washington Va. Reports, page 54, James Burnside vs. A. Reid, Samuel Culbertson, etc.). This report shows that Andrew Culbertson made settlement on a piece of land known as "Culbertson's Bottom", and after living on it for a time, had to abandon it because of the Indians, and he sold it to his brother Samuel in 1754,. who lived on it for a while, but he, too, had to abandon it for fear of the Indians. Two other men settled on the land which led to a long law suit. It was finally settled in U. S. Supreme Court in favor of Samuel Culbertson, because he had first settled the land. This case was concluded in 1786. This land in 1779 was in Rockbridge Co., Va., between the Cow Pasture and Greenbrier River. Power of Atty. was given May 19, 1779 by Samuel Culbertson of Washington Co., N. Car. to A. Reid of Rockbridge Co., Va., relative to this land. This data shows he did not live in Va. during the Revolution and was not the Doctor of the 12th Va. line. He lived in Washington Co., N. Car. in 1787, as shown by a deed of Power of Atty. to S. Colwell on file in Cumb. Co., Pa., in which he authorizes him to sell land in Cumb. Co., Pa. Deed says he is a planter and is witnessed by his son, Joseph. Johnston's "Middle New River Settlements" says that "Culbertson Bottom" is near present Hinton, W. Va. (Crump's Bottom). The old Washington Co., N. Car.' occupied the eastern part of Tenn. in 1787. When the State of Tenn. was formed in 1796 that portion of N. Car. in which Samuel lived was included in Tenn. Old Washington Co., N. Car. was formed in 1777 from Orange Co., N. C. Samuel Culbertson, Sr., of Washington Co., Tenn., made his will in Dec., 1798, and will was probated in Feb. 1799. Lived on Indian Creek (now Unicoi Co., Tenn.). Devisees were wife, Jean; children: Andrew, Josiah, Samuel, Joseph, James and Mary (Weakfield). The witnesses to Samuel's will were James Deakens, John Young and Holland Higgins. Will proven at Feb. Session of Court (1799). Executors D. McCray and Robert Lowe. Wife Jane and Ex'rs. deeded some land of the est. Apr. 7, 1807, to Jos. Barnes; also 117 acres to Jos. Barnes, Jan. 10, 1807. Samuel received warrants of N. Car. land (Washington Co.) 900 acres in 1782. This included his original location in Wash. Co., N. C.; July 7, 1794, 400 acres on Indian Creek. Also grant July 12, 1794. His son Joseph rec'd a warrant for 120 acres on Indian Creek, Wash. Co., N. Car. July 12, 1794. Warrant states this land adjoins Samuel Culbertson's land. Joseph made entry of one 400 acre tract. Jos. also conveyed to Barnes. Samuel's home farm has passed through many hands and a part of it is now owned by the U. S. Fishery. I neglected to state that Thwaite's "Dunmores War" (1774) speaks of Ft. Culbertson "in Culbertson's Bottom." near Hinton, W. Va. and that troops marching to Point Pleasant, Va., stopped there.

The last name of Samuel's second wife is not known, nor is that of his first wife. Someone had a record which claimed that Mary Duncan was the wife of Irish Samuel the third Pa. Row brother. This was an error. It is possible that Samuel of Wash. Co., N. Car., married a Mary Duncan for his first wife.

The children are given as in will. Children are not always given in will as per order of birth and I am positive that Samuel did not give his children in order of their birth. A lady in Texas some twenty years ago sent me a typewritten mss. taken from a newspaper printed in Daviess Co., Ind. in 1839 giving the obituary of Josiah and it said he was born in 1742 in Lancaster Co., Pa. Therefore I am going to give

Samuel's children in different order from what they are given in his will.

FOURTH GENERATION

Issue:

a. 1. **James,** b. 1740?; d. ———. Chatham Co., N. Car. (Chapter VI).

a. 2. **Josiah,** b. 1742; d. Sept. 27, 1839. Daviess Co., Ind. Revolutionary hero. Left Spartansburg Co., S. Car. 1797. (Deed) (Chapter VII).

a. 3. **Joseph,** b. 1743?; d. 1814. Washington Co., Tenn. (Chapter VIII).

a. 4. **Andrew,** b. ———.; d. 1807. Chatham Co., N. Car. (Chapter IX).

a. 5. **Samuel,** b. ———; d. ———. Orange Co., N. Car., Spartansburg Co., S. Car.

a. 6. **Mary,** b. ———; d. ———. Mrs. Wakefield.

CHAPTER VI

FIFTH GENERATION

(a. 1) James took out a warrant, No. 17 in Jan., 1761, for 360 acres on North Hico and Limber Creek, in Orange Co., N. Car. In Oct., 1782, he took out a Warrant No. 340, for 300 acres of land on both sides of Hico Creek in Caswell Co., N. C. (Caswell formed from Orange Co. in 1777). In description of meets and bounds in latter warrant James, it says "Beginning at a large pine corner of his deeded line and running along said line." This refers to his warrant of 1761. Part of the lands he owned were in Chatham Co. and close to Pearson Co. line. It is possible that James swore he was of age in 1761 when he may have been only 17 or 18 years old. (As I have known of one instance in Pa.) James Culbertson of Orange Co., N. C. and Caswell and Chatham Co., N. C., besides Hico Creek farm owned 350 acres on Fall Creek, Chatham Co., N. C. This was deeded Nov. 19, 1824 by Josiah Culbertson acting by Power of Atty. then residing (Josiah) in Warren Co., Tenn. He deeded two-thirds interest of this 350 acres on Fall Creek, Chatham Co. to James Culbertson of Montgomery Co., N. Car. Josiah was attorney for William, Joseph, Lawrence, Andrew, Aaron and Jonathan Culbertson, all of Warren Co., Tenn., and heirs to James Culbertson of Chatham Co.,

deceased. He deeded land in Caswell Co. to a Joseph and
James Culbertson in 1787. This was his nephew Joseph
and son, James Jr.

James, Sr., Census 1790, self, two sons under 16 years,
wife and two daughters, Chatham Co. James apparently
did not die in Chatham or Orange Co., N. Car. Probably
died in Tenn.

Issue:

7. James, Montgomery Co., N. C. Sold farm Caswell Co.,
1795. Taxable 1790 Caswell Co.
8. William, Warren Co., Tenn.
9. Joseph, Warren Co., Tenn.
10. Lawrence, Warren Co., Tenn.   Deed Records of
11. Andrew, Warren Co., Tenn.   Warren Co., Tenn.
12. Aaron, Warren Co., Tenn.   Not searched.
13. Jonathan, Tenn.

Montgomery Co., N. C., Court Records destroyed by fire
1823.

(a. 1) James, Sr. The Clerk of Court of Warren Co.,
Tenn. finds no will or admin. of James or any other Cul-
bertson. Where did his sons move to from Warren Co.,
Tenn.?

*   *   *   *   *

CHAPTER VII

(a. 2) **Josiah Culbertson** born in Lancaster Co., Pa. The
mss. of newspaper article printed in 1839 in Daviess Co.,
Ind., I have lost, unfortunately. The history of Josiah reads
like a romance. Told of his wonderful feats of strength, his
fights with Indians and the British, also of the great
bravery of his wife in encounters with the Indians, and how
she carried powder to her husband when he was beseiged
by Indians, and how the Indians once cut off one of her
children's hands. He married a daughter of Col. John
Thomas in whose regiment he served. Pension Records at
Washington, D. C., give his service. "Served in John
Thomas' Reg't., S. Car. for two years. Was in engagements
Ramsours Mills, Cowpens and King Mt." Also "Private in
N. Car. troops, pensioned $80 a year. Pension commenced
Mar. 4, 1831." Commissioner U. S. Land Office says no
land military warrant to him. Residence Daviess Co., Ind."
Census 1790 S. Car. gives him in 96th Dist., Spartansburg

Co., self and wife, four sons under 16 years, four daughters. (Numbers 14 to 22).

Col. John Thomas and his sons, John and Wm. D. Thomas, are given in 1790 Census of S. Car. in Greenville Co. This county adjoins Spartansburg Co.

In Josiah Culbertson's biography (as given in Kings Mt. and Its Heroes, by Lyman Draper) he says: "His father settled at New River on the frontier of Va., thirty miles from any white settlement when Josiah was about 10 years old. Was living there in 1755-6 His father shortly after moved back to the Greenbrier River Settlements." He also says, "That he did not know Col. Isaac Shelby until he left N. Car. in the latter part of 1779.' I will digress here to quote from War. Dept. Reports, Vol. II, p. 11; Barrie's Army and Navy of the U. S.; Dunmore's War by Thwaites, etc.; "Isaac Shelby was a surveyor in the Western Virginia where he located in 1771 near Bristol, Tenn. In 1774 was a Lt. and in his father's company Va. troops in Dunmore's War. His bravery at Point Pleasant saved the day. Commissary-Gen. (Capt.) of Va. troops 1776; Col. in 1779. Was elected to Va. House of Delegates but after this date (1779) the line between Va. and N. Car. was extended and the survey threw Shelby into N. Car. He was then (1779) commissioned Col. of a Batt'n of Militia of Sullivan Co., N. Car. This was the time he first met Josiah Culbertson and they became fast friends. In 1776 east Tenn. belonged to N. Car. and was called Washington County. In 1784 this was called the Territory of Franklin and a governor was elected until Tenn. became a state. This data sustains Johnston's New River Settlements in statement that "Part of eastern Tenn. belonged to Va. before it belonged to N. Car."

After Samuel Culbertson left Greenbrier Settlement, Va., he moved to western N. Car. Josiah served with N. Car. troops. Have not been able to get the regiment in which Josiah served in N. Car.

Gen. John Sevier, of Tenn., lived only five to ten miles from Josiah Culbertson and his father Samuel. He lived at Wataugua Settlement and it is highly probable that they were personal friends of the Immortal John Sevier.

Barrie's Army and Navy of the U. S., Vol. VII, p. 26, says: "Forces from Sullivan Co., N. Car., at Battle of Kings Mountain under Col. Isaac Shelby of Tenn."

Josiah says in his biography: "Removed to N. Car. before 1770, with my father, Samuel. That I (Josiah) was in

Gov. Geo. Tryon's Army in 1770, when he defeated the 'insurgents'; afterwards (after 1779) removed to S. Car. Was married in 1774."

Josiah's eldest son was Andrew. He witnessed a deed for his father in Spartansburg Co., S. C., Jan. 7, 1797.

Josiah's wife does not participate with him in deed in S. Car. in Jan. 7, 1797 (other Culbertsons in same state at that date in making deeds the wife participates). She, no doubt was dead at that time; likewise family tradition says she was buried on Fair Forest Creek in S. Car.; also Josiah left the state in 1797.

In his pension application he says: "I was born in 'Culbertson Row', Pa., near Shippensburg, Pa., in 1742. My father moved to New River, Va. in 1753."

"Enlisted in N. Car. Flying Camp, 1776. At Siege of Savannah, Kings Mt., Ninety-Six, Musgrove's, Cedar Springs, Cowpens, etc." (See Dr. Lyman Draper's Kings Mt. and Its Heroes. Also Summer's S. West Va.)

Dr. Lyman Draper's "Kings Mt. and Its Heroes," gives some interesting reminiscenes of Josiah Culbertson, a member of Col. Shelby's Regt. (from N. Car.). In 1892 a gentleman by the name of Scott said that his father served in the same company with Josiah Culbertson and that he often related to him the bravery and heroic deeds of Culbertson during the Revolution. Col. Shelby led the charge at Kings Mt. Court records of Daviess Co., Ind., show a son of Josiah died in that county in 1862. Court records Daviess Co., Ind., show no will or settlement Josiah, Sr. No other issue given. There was one other son who ran away and whereabouts unknown, until the author received a letter from a descendant in Tennessee. He was William Davies Thomas Culbertson, named after his uncle, who moved with his father from N. Car. to S. Carolina, then in 1797 to Warren County, Tennessee, and after 1824 moved to Daviess County, Indiana. 1815 took out warrants for 1130 acres in Greenville Co., S. Car. This son went from Indianapolis, Ind., to N. Car. where he married Narcissa Wood about 1829, and later to Jonesboro, Ala., later to Winston Co., Miss., where he died 1863. His descendants have an old powder gourd used by Josiah in the Revolution and which had belonged to Irish Andrew and said to be 250 years old having been brought from Ireland. They also have a Bible printed in the Welsh language which belonged to Josiah's wife's father, Col. John Thomas, printed 1561. Wm. D.

Thomas Culbertson was an educated man, a doctor and also a preacher in Miss. His daughter married a Mr. Suttles and their son is J. H. Suttles, a professor in a Memphis Business College.

Homes' ·"History of the Presbyterian Church" and Johnson's "Traditions of the Revolution" speak highly of Col. John Thomas and his son John, afterwards Col., and son-in-law Josiah Culbertson, Sr.

Sullivan and Washington Counties, N. Car. adjoin and went into Tenn. when that state was formed (Sullivan formed from Washington). Josiah Culbertson, Sr·, was probably in Col. Isaac Shelby's Regt. before he went to S. Car. Went to S. Car. 1779. Left S. Car. 1797.

CHAPTER VIII

(a. 3) **Joseph Culbertson** remained with his father until 1802. He witnessed a deed for his father in 1779 and in 1787, residence Washington Co., N. Car. He took out a warrant in Tenn. for 120 acres on Indian Creek, Washington Co., land adjoining his father's in 1794. Also 100 acres (1797) on north side of Flat Creek on Bald Mt. Road, Buncombe Co., N. Car., near Tenn. land. I have not been able to ascertain whether he was married or single. The census 1790, 1800, 1810, for Tenn. was destroyed 1812 when the British sacked Washington. Joseph sold all of his land in Washington Co., N. Car. in 1802 and then moved into Buncombe Co., N. Car. This is no doubt one reason why Samuel Culbertson, Sr., did not name him exr. of his will.

Joseph made a deed Apr. 22, 1806, and another Dec. 19, 1806, for land in Buncombe Co., N. Car. His wife did not sign—if married—he signed "Joseph Culbertson of Buncombe Co., N. Car."

These deeds were made by him a year after administrator was appointed for Joseph Culbertson of Russell and Scott Co., Va·, proving that Joseph of Washington Co., Tenn., and Buncombe Co., N. Car., was a son of Samuel. County Clerk of Buncombe Co., N. Car., says that he made a number of deeds in his county and there is no will or administration of him in his county showing he moved out of that county—I know not where—could not ascertain if he was married.

There was an Andrew Culbertson took out a warrant for 50 acres in Buncombe Co., N. Car., in 1817. He may have been a son of above Joseph.

Many of the Buncombe Co., N. Car., records were destroyed during the Civil War.

There was a grant to one Wm. H. Culbertson, Dec. 19, 1853, for 15 acres on French Broad River and on Pole Creek. Wm. H. Culbertson was grantee of 100 acres on west side of French Broad River, near Haywood Co., July, 1854. An attorney living in Asheville says he knew this Wm. H. Culbertson many years ago and he had a son named Hill Culbertson. Does not know what became of him.

I am inclined to think that Wm. H. was a son of Andrew. The Marriage Bond Records of Washington Co., Tenn. were examined thoroughly and the names of Joseph and Andrew Culbertson do not appear, nor do the names of any other Culbertsons appear. This proves that Joseph did not marry in Washington Co., N. Car. and must have married (if he did marry) in Buncombe Co., N. C.. It also proves that Samuel, Sr., did not marry in N. Carolina.

There is no will of Joseph in Buncombe Co., and no administration. Examination of Henrico records from 1750 to 1850 do not show Joseph nor Andrew.

Census of Henrico Co., Va. and Richmond does not show Joseph or any other Culbertson for 1830. This proves that Joseph Culbertson was not living in Henrico Co. when pension was allowed. Joseph of Buncombe Co., N. Car., was not on Census 1820 or 1830 in that county, showing he had either moved away or died before 1820·

Joseph's brother, Josiah, said in his autobiography (as given in Dr. Lyman Draper's "Kings Mt. and Its Heroes), "That his father, Samuel, moved to N. Car. before 1770." Joseph's brother, Samuel, who fought against the Regulators (Sons of Liberty) in 1771, resided in Orange Co., N. Car. Orange Co. was a very large county and in 1770 extended into eastern Tenn. Josiah's statement shows that his father had left the State of Va. before 1770 and therefore Samuel, Sr. and his sons were not in Virginia during the Revolution. The state line between Va· and N. Car did not extend far enough south to take in Samuel and Joseph of N. Car. When the Va. State Line was changed in 1779 a portion of Va. was thrown into N. Car· (Vide Chapter VII) This included all or a part of what is now Sullivan Co., Tenn. I have not been able to secure a map of Va. State Line prior to 1779 but the Holston river was the dividing line. Samuel, Sr. and Joseph lived probably fifteen miles south of the Holston.

Summers, in his "History of Southwestern Virginia," pages 695 and following discusses the Tennessee-Virginia boundary line in 1777. (I find no map giving this line at that date, and it seems to have been very vaguely determined before 1779.) In the spring of 1777 the election of Anthony Bledsoe and William Cocke, delegates-elect from Washington County, Virginia, was contested on the ground that they were elected by votes of citizens living in (then) North Carolina. But they won the contest and "citizens living as far down as the Long Island of Holston were accepted as legal voters in said election." (Bristol is in Washington County.)

Previous to 1776 commissioners had extended the dividing line as far west as Steep Rock Creek (now Beaver Dam Creek). The line was supposed to be 36 degrees and 30 minutes north latitude, in conformity with the old Charles II charter. This makes it positive that Joseph, son of Samuel Culbertson of Washington Co., N. Car., was not living in Va. during or after the Revolution.

CHAPTER IX

(a. 4)   **Andrew Culbertson** married Ann Elizabeth Quackenbush of Caswell Co., N. Car. Wife died 1816. Andrew lived in Chatham Co., N. Car. Chatham Co. was taken off of Caswell after 1777. First warrant we find to him was No. 568, Oct. 23, 1782, for 400 acres on south side of Rocky River, another No. 1108 for 180 acres on Rocky River, adjoining his other farm, also got a warrant 1782 for land on Deep River, Chatham Co. His will was executed in 1802, and probated in 1807. Devisees were, wife Anne Elizabeth and children (name spelled with "t"). (Wife died in 1816 in Chatham Co., N. Car.) Census 1790, self and wife; 2 sons over 16; 6 daughters. Chatham Co., One son under 16.

FIFTH GENERATION
Issue:

1. John Culbertson.
2. Samuel.
3. Elizabeth.
4. Mary.
5. Rebecca Susanna (Mrs. Russel Dorset).
6. Sarah.

7. Rhoda (Mrs. Alex. McCracken) mar. Oct. 15, 1813.
8. Anna.
9. Rachel.
10. Keziah (Mrs. David Forrester).
10½. Son, d. young.

NOTE:—In Andrews (a. 4) will he says, single daughters Elizabeth, Mary, Rachel, Rebecca, Sarah, Rhoda and Anna. Married daughters Susanna (Mrs. Russell Dorset), Keziah (Mrs. David Forrester). With all those unmarried daughters he could not have been a very old man. His widow Anna, in her will made 1816, devised to her daughters, Ann Elizabeth and Rhoda (Mrs. Alex McCracken). She must have been a second wife of Andrew.

SIXTH GENERATION

(1) John Culbertson mar. ——. Resided on his father's place on Rocky River, Chatham Co., N. Car. His will was executed in 1849 and probated Aug. 7, 1849, in Chatham Co. Issue (from will; owned 1000 acres):

11. James W. Culbertson (Chatham Co., N. Car.).
12. Samuel T. Culbertson (Chatham Co., N. Car.).
13. John J. Culbertson.
14. Minerva Culbertson.
15. Matilda Culbertson (Mrs. Turner).
16. Maria Culbertson (Mrs. Marley).

(2) Samuel Culbertson made his will in 1817 in Chatham Co., N. C. Wife Sarah.

Issue:

17. William Culbertson, lived in Chatham Co., N. Car. in 1839 (deed).
18. John C., Issue: 25. Samuel, and 26. Nancy.
19. Andrew, lived Chatham Co., awhile but moved away.
20. Polly.
21. Elizabeth.
22. Sarah.
23. Amy
24. Bethiana.

(12) Above Samuel had issue: 27, Sarah; 28, Wm. T. (living in 1892 at Swans Sta., N. C.) ; 29, Geo. H.; 30, Daniel S.; 31, Melie R.; 32, Eddie Lee.

CHAPTER X

(a. 5) **Samuel Culbertson** mar. Sue ———. Samuel was in the "Regulators" (akin to the Sons of Liberty) in 1771 and was arrested and imprisoned and declared a traitor by the Colonial Legislature in 1771. Several of these Regulators were hung by Gov. Tryon of N. Car. in 1771 (See N. Car. Colonial Archives). We are not informed how Samuel Culbertson was released or escaped. He got in the game early against the British. He was declared a Traitor to King George, Mar. 11, 1771; residence Orange Co., N. Car. He was a ring-leader in the Regulators. Caswell Co., N. Car. was formed from Orange Co. in 1777. Washington Co. was formed off Orange Co. in 1777.

Census of 1790 for So. Car., Dist. 96, Spartansburg Co., gives him and wife and three sons under 16 years (Numbers 1-3). The famous Mecklenburg Declaration (the first Declaration of Independence), was made in Mecklenburg Co., N. Car. in 1775. This county adjoined Orange County and probably was taken off of Orange before 1766. Have not been able to ascertain whether Samuel or any of the Culbertsons signed this Declaration.

Court records of Spartansburg Co., S. Car., show no wills or administration of Culbertsons. The deed records reveal the fact that Samuel Culbertson, Sr. of Spartansburg Co., S. Car., had a son, Samuel Culbertson, Jr. who was just of age and deeded 26 acres in April 1795 to Henry O'Neil. Wife's name Celia. Made another deed to O'Neil May 14, 1796, wife Celia. It appears from a deed made by him Sept. 12, 1798, that his first wife had died, as on this deed of Samuel, Jr. to Samuel Culbertson, Sr. the name of Samuel. Jr.'s wife is Jane. This deed was for 290 acres. I do not know what became of him after this. Samuel, Sr., was deeded by his brother, Josiah Culbertson, Jan. 7, 1797, 179 acres. This deed shows Josiah Culbertson's wife (Thomas) did not sign (no doubt dead). Witnesses: E. Smith, W. D. Thomas (bro.-in-law) and Andrew Culbertson (Josiah's son?). In 1811 Samuel Culbertson (Sr.) conveyed 340 acres to O. Wingo. Wife Sudie. Do not know what became of him after this, nor do I know names of his other children.

As Samuel, Jr., was of age in 1795 he must have been born late in 1774 as Census 1790 shows he was under 16 years old at that date (1790). Therefore his father was married by or before 1773. Hence he was undoubtedly the

Samuel of Orange Co., N. Car. who in 1771 was declared a traitor to King George. As he is not on the deed records or Census of N. Car., I surmise that when he was declared a traitor to King George that he fled to S. Car. Name on deeds spelled with "t".

A warrant was issued to David Culbertson Feb. 5, 1798 for 445 acres in Spartansburg Co., S. Car; also a warrant for 500 acres, Feb. 5, 1798, to John Culbertson in Spartansburg Co.. S. Car. I am strongly of the opinion these were sons of Samuel of Spartansburg, and that these were taken out when they had just attained their majority. This would tally with the Census report of 1790 as to their ages.

Marriage records of Orange Co., N. Car., searched at State Library at Raleigh, N. Car. and no Culbertson found.

CHAPTER XI

(III) ANDREW CULBERTSON, SON OF IRISH ANDREW OF SHIPPENSBURG, PA. AND DESCENDANTS.

(III) **Andrew Culbertson**, son of Irish Andrew of Shippensburg, Pa.. quit claimed with his wife Esther, Apr., 1751, in his father's estate to his brother Samuel. In 1751, he moved to Augusta Co., Va., and in 1753 to the New River, between the Greenbrier and Cowpasture Rivers and his place of settlement was called "Culbertson's Bottom" or later Crump's Bottom. In 1754 he sold this place to his brother Samuel. It is in what is now Summers Co., W. Va. Johnston's "Middle New River Settlements" says: "At one time—when the first settlements were made—Augusta Co., Va., embraced all that vast domain" beyond the Alleghenies westward to the Mississippi river. This embraced what is now Washington Co., Tenn., also called Territory of Franklin or Tenn. This was at one time supposed to be in N. Car. But Washington Co., Tenn., was not formed until after Washington Co., Va. Botetourt Co. was formed from Augusta, Fincastle was formed 1769 from Botetourt, Rockbridge formed 1778 from Botetcourt and Augusta, Washington formed 1776 from Fincastle and Montgomery split off the latter at the same time; Wythe formed 1790 from Montgomery and Tazewell. Tazewell 1790 from Russell and Wythe. Russel formed 1786 from Washington, Lee from Russel 1792 and Scott from Russel 1814. I have had all these county court records searched and nothing found except Russel, Lee and Scott, Augusta and Rockbridge. I have had records searched in Rockbridge, Clarke, Shenandoah, Loudon, Highland, Bath, Allegheny, Frederick, Greenbrier, Pocahontas Counties, Va.; and Washington and Sullivan Co., Tenn.; and Orange, Caswell, Pearson, Guilford (formed 1770), Alamance, Durham, Chatham, McDowell, Burke, Washington, Chowan, Bertie, Martin, Beaufort, Hyde and Tyrrell, Mecklenberg in N. Car., but can get no trace of Andrew or where he died. Am sure he died in Va., but where? The census of 1790 for Va. was destroyed by fire when the British sacked Washington in 1812. The Gov't has published taxpayers lists 1781-85 of about 40 counties of Va. (not on these) but the county in which he located—if he was then living—is missing. He is not on Census 1790 in North or South Car. The Territory of Tenn. Census was destroyed (1790) in 1812. If living he would have been too old to have served in the Revolution. We know that Robert of Laurens Dist., S. Car. was his son. James of Laurens Dist., S. Car. lived adjoining Robert and was undoubtedly his brother. Age of his children (1790 Census) shows he was not Robert's son. This is undoubtedly James the 2nd Lieut. with Col. Daniel Morgans Regt. at Valley Forge (Va. Line). John Culbertson of Rowan Co., N. Car. (first on deed 1765) was no doubt his son. His descendants in 1895 stated they had an old letter which they read in youth which was written in Va. during the Revolution by relatives telling of the surrender of Cornwallis at Yorktown. Robert in his pension application says he "was born in Lancaster Co., Pa., near Shippensburg 1750." His father must have married about 1730 or before. Johnston's Settlements says, "Andrew came from near where Chambersburg, Pa., is situated to Culbertson's Bottom 1753."

The Line Regiments were generally made up of soldiers from different parts of a state. I believe the Dr. Samuel Culbertson of the 12 Va. Line (Col. James Woods) 1776-78 was Andrew's son. Col. James Woods was from Winchester but records there and adjoining counties show nothing of Dr. Samuel. A Martinsburg court record was found in 1807 where some Samuel Culbertson sued a man for $12

FOURTH GENERATION

Andrew Culbertson (III) of Shippensburg and Va. mar. Esther ———.

Issue (Marriage Bond Records of Orange Co., N. Car. thoroughly searched but no Culbertson found):

a. 1. **John**, Rowan Co., N. Car. and Tenn (Chapter XII).
a. 2. **James** (Lieut.), Rockbridge Co., Va. and Laurens Co., S. Car. (Chapter XIII.)
a. 3. **Robert**, Rockbridge Co., Va. and Laurens Co., S. Car. (Chapter XIV).
a. 4. **Joseph**, Rockbridge Co., Va. and Russell Co., Va. (Chapter XV).
a. 5. **Samuel** (Dr.) Rockbridge Co., Va. (Chapter XVI).
a. 6. **Sarah?** (Mrs. Thos. Fallin of Ky.?)

Records of Guilford Co. N. Car. before 1799 destroyed. County formed 1770 from Rowan and Orange Counties.

A most thorough search of Va. Court Records seventy counties fails to reveal any will or administration or deeds (save Culbertson Bottom Deed of 1754) as does N. Car. records—of Andrew Culbertson. Part of his children remained in Rockbridge County until near the close of the Eighteenth Century. It is my opinion that Andrew died in Augusta or Rockbridge Co., Va. I have not been able to get any trace of him in North or South Carolina.

From the fact that James, brother of Andrew of Shippensburg, who died in Chester Co., Pa., in Oct. 1763, and mentioned all his living brothers and sisters, save Andrew, I am now convinced that Andrew was dead was the reason he was not mentioned in aforesaid will; also that he had no property is the reason we have not been able to find him on the court records. Not on marriage or court records of N. Car. I sent a professional genealogist to Augusta, Rockbridge and Orange Counties, Va., to personally examine the court records, including marriage records, of those counties for Andrew Culbertson. The portion of Augusta Co., Va. where the Culbertsons lived was thrown into Rockbridge Co. when the latter county was formed in 1778. Postmaster of Staunton, Va., says no Culbertsons residing in Augusta Co., Va., now.

Summer's Hist. of Southwest Va. says "Culbertson's Bottom was settled in 1753 by Andrew Culbertson and was the first settlement in all the section of the New River country."

CHAPTER XII

a. 1. **John Culbertson** of Rowan Co. N. Car., son of Andrew Culbertson (III) of Va. and grandson of Irish Andrew of Shippensburg, Pa., was deeded land in 1765 in Rowan Co., N. Car. by John Gillespie, also deeded land by Wm. England in 1773. Rec'd a warrant for 250 acres from the state in 1782 in Rowan Co. Deeded land to his son Samuel in 1802 and 1804. Family records say he came from Va. His great grandson stated in 1895 that he remembered of reading a letter when a boy which was sent to his great-grandfather John, by relatives in Va. announcing the surrender of Cornwallis. Lived on So. Yadkin River in Rowan Co. Family records state that most of his sons moved to Tenn. and that he followed them and died in Tenn.

He did not leave any will or administration in Rowan Co., N. Car. John Culbertson mar. ——.

FIFTH GENERATION
Issue:

2. Samuel, b. 1768; d. 1843. Rowan Co., N. Car.
3. Agnes (Mrs. Knox), Rowan Co. Issue: Absolom Knox (of Saulsbury, N. C.).
4. Jane (Mrs. John Marlin). Issue:Samuel, Jesse, John, Margaret.
5. Son, d. 1773.
6. Peggy (Mrs. James Elliott). Williamson Co., Tenn.
7-8. Two other daughters—names not given; d· young.
9. Benjamin, Williamson Co., Tenn., in 1827. Do not know about issue.
10. Daniel, of Elkton, Todd Co., Ky. Issue: Peggy Elliott, Dolly, Ann, Martha, Jane, Fanny.
11. James, mar. Mary ——. Issue: 12, Elizabeth; 13,. Thomas; 14, John; 15, James; 16, Daniel; 17, Nancy. All lived in 1821 in Robertson Co., Tenn. These men were great athletes and it is said some of them could leap over a covered wagon.

The Census of 1790 gives John, Sr· and wife, one son over 16 years and four sons under 16 and five daughters (Rowan Co., N· C.).

SIXTH GENERATION

(2) Samuel Culbertson mar. Lydia Gillespie, Jan. 28, 1797. Remained in Rowan Co., N. Car.

Issue:

18. Gillespie, b. 1800. Woodleaf, Rowan Co., N. C.
19. John, bachelor.
20. Knox. (Issue: Hiram who went to Tenn.). Rowan Co., N. C.
21. Daniel. Rowan Co., N. C.
22. Elizabeth (Mrs. Turner). No issue.
23. Jane (Mrs. E. Rice). Issue: Wm., Nancy, Lydia.
24. Nancy (Mrs. Robinson). No issue.

(4) Jane Culbertson mar. John Marlin. A grandson of this union is John Marlin, President of Lafayette College, Ala., in 1895.

SEVENTH GENERATION

(18) Gillespie Culbertson mar. Susan S. Grey, Nov. 20, 1822. Lived at Rowan Co., N. C.

Issue:

25. Richard. Mebane, N. C.
26. Samuel Steele.
27. William, d. young.
28. Margaret, d. young.

(21) Daniel Culbertson mar. Miss Lydia S. Repult, Feb. 4, 1851.

Issue:

29. John, of Chicago, Ills., dead.
30. Lizzie (Mrs. J. H. Rice). Living.

EIGHTH GENERATION

(25) Richard Culbertson mar. Miss Fanny Knox, March 6, 1854. Lived at Mebane, N. C.

Issue:

31. James.
32. Richard W. (minister). Charlotte, N. Car.

(26) Samuel Steele Culbertson mar. Barbara C. Fraley, Feb. 22, 1853.

Issue:

33. John Knox, lives at Woodleaf, N. Car.

NINTH GENERATION

(32) Rev. R. W. Culbertson mar. Miss Johnstone.

Issue:

34. Mary.
35. Jetson.
36. Frances.
37. Ruth.
38. Lucy.
39. Knox.
40. Clara.
41. Kingsley. This fine young man joined (volunteered) in the Aviation Corps in the World War and was crushed to death by his plane at an aviation field.

(33) John Knox Culbertson mar. Miss Harte.

Issue:

42. Wm., in World War. Army. In camp, volunteer.
43. Leo, in World War. Aviation. Vol.
44. Richard, in World War. U. S. Navy. Still in Navy (Ensign). Stationed at St. Paul Island, Alaska.
45. Glenn. In World War. Vol. Camp.
46. John Steele.
47. Fay.
48. Jean.

John Knox Culbertson (33) has the old grandfather's clock brought by his ancestor John, from Pennsylvania to Va. and N. Car., being 175 years or more old and still in use. The home built by John in N. Car., Rowan Co., is still standing, but not occupied by Culbertsons.

(33) J. Knox Culbertson's daughter, Lottie Fay (47), mar. Hugh S. Bailey. Issue: 49 Wm. Douglas Bailey, aged 3 years; 50 Hilda Hart Bailey, aged 2 years.

Ensign Richard Culbertson, son of John K. Culbertson, volunteered during the World War for four years in the U. S. Navy, and the government sent him to Harvard College from which he came out and was made an Ensign in one year's training. He served his time and was honorably discharged. He was offered a position in Alaska with the Bureau of Fisheries and Commerce which position he now holds at St. George's, Alaska. Jean, the second daughter of J. K. Culbertson, is a student in the W. C. College for Women at Greensboro, N. Car.

(20) Samuel Knox (called Knox), married Feb. 20, 1833 to Ruhamah Briggs.

CHAPTER XIII

(2. a.) **James Culbertson,** son of Andrew (III) and grandson of Irish Andrew of Shippensburg, Pa. Born in Pa. Revolutionary Service: (Waldron), Barrie's Army and Navy Reports "Lt. James Colbertson or Culbertson of Col. Daniel Morgan's Regt. took the Oath of Allegiance at Valley Forge, in the Fall of 1777. Daniel Morgan, Col. 11th Va. Line, designation changed to 7th Va. Line, Sept. 14, 1778." He moved from Va. to S. Carolina. Census 1790 gives him Dist. 96, Laurens Co., S. Car. (same district his brother Robert was in), self and one male over 16 yrs., one male under 16, wife and 2 females.

There is no will or administration of his estate in Laurens Co. He first purchased land in this county July 26, 1792, and later sold this place and evidently moved out of the county. Wife's name Nancy. Col. Daniel Morgan's Regt. of Riflemen took part in the battle of Saratoga (one of the Fifteen Decisive Battles of the World as given by Creasy), in Oct., 1777. This regiment was then taken to Valley Forge, Pa. Vol. 1, page 167, Augusta Co., Va. Records (Chalkley Abstracts) "May 22, 1772, James Culbertson to be paid as patroller."

"Col. Daniel Morgan's invincible Riflemen was composed in greater part of Pa. men. Morgan was from Va. (Hist. Perry Co., Pa.).

"Morgan's Pa.-Va. Riflemen were not at Brandywine, having been sent to Gen. Gates at Stillwater (Battle of Saratoga)." (From Bruce's Battle of Brandywine).

CHAPTER XIV

(3. a.) **Robert Culbertson** son of Andrew of Va. and grandson of Irish Andrew of Shippensburg, Pa., says in his application for pension. "Was born in Lancaster Co., Pa. In early life removed to Caswell Co., N. Car. Enlisted in Capt. John Grove's Co. of N. Car. Was in the battle of Camden; the defeat of Gen. Gates. Then re-enlisted in Col. Williams' Regt. Was in battle of Cowpens and Kings Mt. Then re-enlisted in Col. Campbell's Regt. Was in skirmish at Wetzels Mills and two skirmishes near Wilmington. Claim for pension made 1832. Annual allowance $40. Age 83 years. Private in N. Car. militia. He removed to Laurens Dist., S. Car. in 1785." Received a grant for land on the Reedy

River in 1785. (S. Car.). Can find no Col. Campbell with N. Car. troops. There was Col. Campbell of Va. line.

The Census 1790, S. Car. Dist. 96, Laurens Co., gives him 4 sons under 16 years, wife and 3 daughters. This tallies with the family records. Had 5 sons but one remained in Va. (Wm. P.) with his mother (first wife). Family history says:

Robert has a most interesting family history. "He entered the army at the beginning of the Revolution and served until the close. His wife heard nothing of him during this time and supposed he was dead, remarried. At close of the war he returned home—and his wife left her second husband and would not live with either one. Her first husband then took his oldest son and left his second son with his wife. The father and son then went to N. Car. where he remarried. He was wounded at the Battle of Kings Mountain, S. Car., for which he was pensioned."

He moved to Charlotte, N. Car. before his death. His widow filed a newspaper clipping with the Pension Dept, in which it stated that he had died at his home near Charlotte in 1848. Widow filed claim for pension.

If Robert left his first wife in Virginia, then it must have been 1776 to 1777 as he served with the N. Car. troops. Putting the family version together with facts from court records he must either have left her about 1776-7; or must have married his second wife about 1780-82 (note number of children he had on Census 1790). Marriage bonds had to be filed in court in N. Car. at this date and there is no bond of Robert Culbertson and Dolly Pleasant. Census 1790 of N. Car. shows three Pleasants living in Gloucester Dist. of Caswell Co. There are no Pleasants living in S. Car. 1790 Census. I did not have divorce records of Caswell Co., N. Car., nor Va., examined for Robert and Elizabeth Culbertson. On Census of 1790 Robert is given in Laurens Co., S. Car., self and wife, 4 males under 16 years, and three females. Family history says he only had two sons by first wife. I have given children from family history. I am inclined to believe one or two daughters were by the first wife. There were no marriage (court) records kept in S. Car. until 1914.

John Grove was on Census 1790 in Rowan Co. N. Car. J. M. Barrie's Army and Navy of U. S. Vol. VII, p. 26, says "There were two Col. Williams from N. Car., Col. James Williams commanded a regiment of Rangers and Partisan

Corps; and Col. John Williams the 9th N. Car. Line. Battle of Camden the attack was led by Col. Williams' Volunteers."

The only two James Williams on 1790 Census (N. Car.) in territory where Culbertsons were located were in Rowan Co. (none in Caswell). Robert states in his pension papers he "was in N. Car. Militia", so this shows he must have been in James Williams Regt. Vol. II, p. 422, Abstracts of Augusta Co., Va., by L. D. Chalkley, says, "Delinquents Augusta Co., Va. Levy 1779, Robert Culbertson gone from county." This is Robert of Laurens Co., S. Car.

FIFTH GENERATION

(3. a) **Robert Culbertson** mar. first, Miss Elizabeth Porter, before the Revolution in Va. (Augusta Co. ?). Left Va., 1776.

Issue:

1. b. James, b. before Revolution. Went to S. Car.
2. b. Wm. Porter, b. before Revolution. Remained in Va.

(3. a.) **Robert Culbertson** after the close of the Revolution went to Laurens Co., S. Car., where he had taken up a large tract of land on the Reedy River. Mar. Miss Dolly Pleasant of Glouster Dist. Caswell Co., N. Car.

Issue:

3. b. John.
4. b. Alexander.
5. b. Josiah.
6. b. Robert.
7. b. Sarah   .
8. b. Martha.

SIXTH GENERATION

(1. b.) **James Culbertson** went from Va. to Caswell Co., N. Car. when a small boy with his father and afterwards went with him to Laurens Co., S. Car.

Issue:

9. Hiram.
10. Young J.
11. John (Capt.).
12. Porter.

13. Isaac Newton, d. 1853.
14. Olive.
15. Edney (Mar. Wilson Cooper).

(2. b.) Wm. Porter Culbertson raised in Va. by his mother and after his marriage in Va., moved to Madison Co., Ga. His family afterwards moved to Texas. Do not know where, nor names of any of them.

(3) John Culbertson. I think this is the John Culbertson who many years ago moved to Missouri and whose son, A. J. Culbertson, is president of a bank in Stewartsville, Mo., but I am not sure as to this.

(b. 4.) Alexander Culbertson mar. Miss Johnson. Lived in Laurens Co., S. C., then before 1861, moved to Ga., and later to Gadsden, Ala.

Issue:

16. Nancy (Mrs. James Grimes).
17. Haley (Mrs. Geo. Weldon).
18. Mary. Mar. Lived in Georgia (Mrs. Sprewel).
19. Martha. Mar. Lived in Georgia.
20. Robert.
21. Butler.
22. George Washington.
23. Henry.

SEVENTH GENERATION

(9) Hiram Culbertson mar. ——.

Issue:

24. John M. Had a son, Joel Andrew.
25. William.
26. Andrew.
27. James.
28. Nancy.
29. Martha.

(10) Young J. Culbertson mar. ——.

Issue:

30. Andrew Porter.
31. Andrew.
32. James.
33. Lettie.
34. Francis.
35. Elizabeth.
36. Margaret.
37. Olive.

(11) John Culbertson mar. first Martha Babb.
Issue:
38. Mary Porter, b. 1823. (Mrs. Elledge).
(11) John Culbertson mar. second Luranah Pitts.

Issue:
39. Young J. (Capt.), Ekom, S. Car.
40. Martha J. (Mrs. Cooper).
41. Hannah E. (Mrs. Watkins).
42. Sarah C. (Mrs. Fuller).
43. Mary O. (Mrs. Baldwin).
44. Nancy H. Unmar.
45. Edney S., b. Dec. 6, 1841; d. Aug. 11, 1917.
46. James H., Enoree, S. Car.
47. Henry L. (Dr.), Washington, Ga.
48. John R. (Dr.), Greycourt, S. C.; b. 1847; d. 1910.
(12) Porter Culbertson, Texas.
(13) Dr. Isaac Newton Culbertson mar. Jane Cunningham. Moved to Ga.

Issue:
49. Wade Anderson (Dr.), Cave Springs, Ga.
50. Amanda Evaleila, d. 1882 (Mrs. Rev. J. C. Browne).
(20) Robert Culbertson mar. Miss Nancy Henderson. Lived and died in Laurens Co., S. Car.

Issue:
51. Wiley, d.
52. Carter, d.
53. Hugh, d.
54. Young.
55. Warren, d.
56. Candace, d.
57. Mary.
(21) Butler Culbertson mar. Miss Polly Lander. He died in Civil War.

Issue:
58. Mateson, d. Greenwood, S. Car.
59. William.
60. Eliza.
61. Mellie.
(22) George Washington Culbertson mar. Parmelia Ann Godfrey of Laurens Co., S. Car. in 1848. Served in Confed. Army 61-65, Capt. 14th S. C. Regt. He died 1907. Was a magistrate of Co. a number of years.

Issue:

62. Juretie, b. 1849; d. 1859.
63. Mary E., b. 1851.
64. J. Lawrence, b. 1853.
65. John, b. 1855; d. 1859.
66. William P., b. 1857.
67. W. Wister, b.1859.
68. Lula J., b. 1861.
69. Washington L., b. 1864.
70. Andrew B., b. 1868.
71. Burley Y., b. 1871.

(23) Henry Culbertson lived in Alabama. Married twice and had issue. Could not obtain names of his wives or children. He was a prominent Baptist minister.

EIGHTH GENERATION

(38) Mary P. Culbertson mar. James M. Elledge. Living at Landrum, S. Car. (Husband dead.)

Issue:

72. John Porter. Served in S. Car. Confed. Regt.
73. Martha Emma, d. 1856.
74. Jacob Harrison, d. 1856.
75. Newton A., d. 1889. Laurens Co., S. Car.
76. Sarah J., d. 1856.

(39) Young J. Culbertson mar. first Nancy F. Culbertson. Ekom, S. Car.

Issue:

77. Ellen.
78. Evaleila.
79. Jane.
80. James Wade.

(39) Young J. mar. second Marget J. Watkins. Laurens Co., S. Car.

Issue:

81. Myrtle.
82. James Dennis.
83. W. Black.
84. . Robert.
85. Homer. Laurens Co., S. Car.
86. B.
87. Francis.
88. Virginia.

(40) Martha J. Culbertson mar. Thomas J. Cooper, who died during the war.

Issue:

89. John Young.
90. James L. Laurens Co., S. Car.
91. Henry D.
92. Ellen.

(41) Hannah Elizabeth Culbertson mar. H. H. Watkins. Anderson S. Car.

Issue:

93. John B. (Prof.). Belton, S. Car.
94. James N. Greenville, S. Car.
95. Henry Hitt (Judge). Anderson, S. Car., b. June 24, 1866.
96. Margaret L.
97. Henrietta.
98. Fannie B.
99. Sarah Stepp.

(43) Mary Olive Culbertson mar. James E. Baldwin.

Issue:

100. James.
101. Wm. Y.
102. Austin.
103. Powell.
104. Robert. Laurens Co., S. Car.
105. Lawrence.
106. Lodie.
107. Emma.
108. Othello.
109. Sarah.

(42) Sarah C. Culbertson mar. Henry Y. Fuller. Live at Honea Path, S. Car.

Issue:

110. Wm. Benton.
111. Lettie Francis.

(45) Edna S. Culbertson mar. Joel Andrew Culbertson, April 22, 1869, of Crosshill, S. Car. Her husband was a son of (24) John M.

Issue:

112. John M. (Rev.) Honea Path, S. Car., b. July 4, 1873.
113. Shelton. Trough, S. Car., b. May 8, 1877.

114.   Nancy Arcanie, b. Feb. 18, 1870.
115.   Bessie Susanna, b. Oct. 27, 1871.
116.   Cora Lee, b. July 19. 1881.
117.   Olive Porter, b. July 21, 1875.
    (46) James Newton Culbertson. Mar. first Olive Culbertson. Wife d.

    Issue:
118.   Sarah Olive.
    (46) James N., mar. second Millisant Redden.

    Issue:
119·   John.
120.   James.
121.   Clarence. Enoree, S. Car.
122.   Lida.
123.   Claude.
124.   Clyde·
    (47) Dr. Henry L. Culbertson mar. Cora Shadric.

    Issue:
125.   Hattie.
126.   Preloe.
    (48) Dr· J. R. Culbertson mar. Mrs. Hattie White, Greenville, S. Car. No issue.
    (49) Dr. Wade Anderson Culbertson mar. ——.

    Issue: 127-134·

    (50) Amanda Evaleila Culbertson mar. Rev. J. Courtney Browne, of Aiken, S. Car.
    Issue: 135-140.
    One daughter Adrienne (Mrs. Gantt).
    (58) Matison Culbertson mar. Mrs. Gaines of Laurens Co., S. Car. Lives Greenwood, S· Car. In Confed. Army.

    Issue:
141.   James.
142.   Arthur·
143.   Daughter.
144.   Daughter.
145.   Daughter.
146.   Daughter.
147.   Daughter.
148.   Daughter.
    (59) William Culbertson mar. Miss Susan Mathers of Laurens Co·, S. Car. Wife living. No issue.

(63) Mary Etta Culbertson mar. Samuel M. Cooper. Both living at Donald, S. Car.

Issue:

149. Othello Cooper, d.
150. William Irvin, Greenwood, S. Car. (Mar.)
151. Samuel, Mullins, S. Car. (Mar.)

(64) J. Lawrence Culbertson mar. Miss Lou Cooper in 1873. Wife d. 1879.

Issue:

152. Lawrence (dau.), Laurens, S. Car.

(66) William P. Culbertson mar. Miss Ellen Culbertson in 1881. Has been a prominent teacher of Laurens Co., S. C., for 43 years. Cross Hill, S. C.

Issue:

153. Eugenia Blanche, b. 1882. Mar. S. J. Rasor in 1904. Issue: Lewis, b. 1907; Samuel b. 1909; Ellen, b. 1913. Mountville, S. Car.
154. Lillie Francis, b. 1887. Mar. E. A. Adams of Mountville, S. Car. in 1918. Issue: Mary Ellen, b. 1918; Lyle, b. 1920.
155. Henry Grady, b. 1890. Served in World War. 2nd Lt. Quartermaster Dept. Mar. Miss Hester Richey, 1919. Lives at Cross Hill, S. Car. Issue: Grady, b. 1920; Wm. b. 1922.

(67) Warren Wister Culbertson mar. Miss Mary Cooper, 1877. Living Laurens Co., S. Car.

Issue:

156. Lydie (Unmar.).
157. Margie mar. Clarence Culbertson, lives Newberry, S. Car., has several children.
158. Hosey, d. 1918.
159. Maggie mar. Eugene Elmore of Laurens Co., S. Car. Issue, several children.
160. Etta, mar. Otis Martin. Issue, Jones.

(68) Lulu J. Culbertson mar. Calvin Cheek in 1885. Lives at Laurens, Co., S. Car.

Issue:

161. Melvin, mar., has several children, Greenville, S. Car.
162. Annie mar. Posey Bobo; Issue, 5 children.
163. Ewel.
164. Jerul, mar. Miss Cook, 1921. Issue, one son 1922.

(69) Washington Lee Culbertson moved to Gadsden, Ala. in 1886. Mar. Annie Sikes 1888; moved to Georgia and now preaches at Commerce, Ga.

Issue:

165. Broadus.
166. Aubrey.
167. Otto.

(69) Washington L. Culbertson mar. second Miss Jessie Sanders, of Cuthbert, Ga. No issue.

(70) Andrew B. Culbertson mar. Miss Barbara Godfrey in 1890. Laurens Co., S. C.

Issue:

168. Lonnie, b. 1891. Mar. Miss Alta Martin, 1916.
169. Jessie.
170. Washington.
171. Rylan.

(71) Burley Y. Culbertson mar. Miss Alma Langston in 1898. Editor of the Laurensville Herald, Laurens, S. Car.

Issue:

172. Thomas b. 1899, mar. Miss Proffet, 1919.
173. Harold, b. 1902.
174. Annette, b. 1907.

(95) Judge Henry Hitt Watkins mar. Maude Wakefield, Dec. 27, 1892. Issue, none.

NINTH GENERATION

(112) Rev. John M. Culbertson mar. Kate Clement, Dec. 22, 1898.

Issue:

175. Lowell Earl.

(113) Shelton Y. Culbertson mar. Mamie Lee McPherson June 12, 1917.

Issue:

176. Shelton Young, Jr., b. July 16, 1919.
177. James Lee, b. Jan. 27, 1921.

(114) Nancy Arcanie Culbertson mar. James Clement Wells, of Mountville, S. Car. (a widower with several children when he married her), b. Jan. 27, 1873. No issue.

(115) Bessie Susannah Culbertson mar. John Smith, Feb. 14, 1889. She died Feb. 11, 1914. Husband died June 29, 1914.

Issue:

178. John Quincy.
179. Henry Hitt.
180. Willie Stepp.
181. Jos. Blanton.
182. Ola Susan.
183. Sallie Pearl..
184. Lydie Arcanie.
185. Myrtle Edna.
186. Mattie Sophia.
    (116) Cora Lee Culbertson mar. Samuel Cleland,. Mar. 25, 1914.

Issue:

187. Joel Samuel Cleland.
    (117) Olive Porter Culbertson mar. M. W. Hill, June 7, 1911.

Issue:

188. Edna Lucy Hill.
189. Francis Lee.
190. Wilma Hill.

PROMINENT DESCENDANTS OF (3A) ROBERT

(15) Edney Culbertson daughter of James Culbertson (1. b.) married Wilson Cooper and had issue, Rev. John A. Cooper who had a son, Henry Cooper. This Henry Cooper is the father of Gov. Cooper of S. Car. 1920-23.

(95) H. H. Watkins is U. S. District Judge. Is honorably mentioned in Who's Who in America, as follows:

"Henry Hitt Watkins son of Henry Hitt and Elizabeth Culbertson. M. A. Furman Univ., Greenville, S. C., 1883. Univ. Va. Law 1890. Teacher eight years. Admitted to bar, S. C., 1892, practiced Anderson, S. C. Member of firm Bongane, Watkins & Allen; Vice Pres. Brogan Cotton Mills. Peoples Bank, Belton Savings & Trust Co,, Q. M. on Staff Gov. Hayward; Capt. Co. C. 1st S. C. Regt. U. S. V. 1898. Chairman Co. and State Dem. Com.; Dem. Pres. Elector 1904; Dem. delegate at large Dem. Natl. convention 1908. Pres. of trust of Anderson Col. 1911; Trust Anderson Hosp. Asso.; Library Ass'n; Baptist; Mem. Am. Bar Ass.; S. C. Bar. Ass.; Sigma Alpha Epsilon; Mason (K. T.). Clubs, Rose Hill, Poinsett. U. S. District Judge.

CHAPTER XV

(4. a.) **Joseph Culbertson**, son of Andrew and grandson of Irish Andrew of Shippensburg, Pa. Family records say that "he moved south by way of Va. long before the Revolutionary War; raised his family in Caswell Co., N. Car. and about 1793 moved with part of his family to Russel Co., Va. (taken from family records). Was fifty or sixty years old when he moved to Va. Was buried two miles north of Ft. Blackmore, on the Clinch River in Scott Co.,. Va. Joseph Sr. must have married about 1760-2. The following is a verification of part of the above: Administration Records of Russel Co., Va. show that Agnes Culbertson (wife) was appointed administratrix of his estate in 1805 and filed her accounts but did not mention names of children. His son Joseph's est. was administered in Scott Co. and settled in 1820.

The Census for Russel, Rockbridge and Washington Counties 1790, 1800, 1810, Va., was destroyed in 1812 when the British sacked Washington. Census for Caswell Co., N. Car. for 1790 (destroyed but tax list substituted for Caswell) does not show Joseph, Sr., there. It shows Joseph, Jr., James (this James was a son of James, Sr., who sold land to Jos. and James, Jr., 1787); William (this was Joseph, Sr.'s son who remained in Caswell Co., N. Car.), Joseph, Jr. went to Russell Co., Va.

James went to Russell Co., Va. in 1786, probably. I did not get date of warrant but patent was issued to him for 100 acres on north side of Moccasin Ridge, June 7, 1789. In those days it generally took several years after warrant was issued before survey was made and patent issued. He sold his farm in Caswell Co., N. Car. in 1785 and married in Dec. 1785 (Marriage Bond). His land in Va. was close to Gate City. Owned 400 acres 1799. There is no deed to either Joseph until 1800 in Russel Co., Va.

Joseph, son of Samuel and grandson of Irish Andrew of Shippensburg, took out a warrant for 120 acres July 12, 1794 in Washington Co., Tenn. on Indian Creek along side of his father's land. This locates him living in Tenn., while his cousin Joseph was living in Virginia. It had been a long hard fight to get these two Josephs properly placed. David had moved out of Caswell Co. in 1789, not to Virginia. Joseph, Jr., deeded his farm of 200 acres for £200 July 15, 1791, near Leasburg in Hightowers Tp., Caswell Co., N. Car. on N. Hico Creek to Benj. Douglas. He then moved to Russell Co., Va. His land in N. Car. adjoined land of James Culbertson, Jr. and John Currie. His wife did not sign deed as it was not necessary for wife to do so in N. Car. Only deed in Caswell Co., N. Car. in which Joseph was grantor. Census 1790 Henrico Co., Va., does not give Joseph Culbertson or Daniel Gildier.

Joseph, Sr., is not found on any warrant or deed nor Census 1790 of N. Car. His descendants had a tradition that he lived in N. Car. but there is absolutely no record of it. I found a deed and a release given by A. Reid of Rockbridge Co., Va., to Samuel Culbertson of Washington Co., Tenn. for land in Washington Co., Tenn. These documents were signed and witnessed in Rockbridge Co., Va. by Andrew Alexander, Joseph Culbertson, Wm. Carothers, Alex. Shields, David Shields, James Carothers, on Dec. 7, 1795. The Joseph Culbertson witnessing the above was Joseph son of Andrew from Shippensburg and locates him living in Rockbridge Co., Va. in 1795, while Samuel's son Joseph, resided in Washington Co., Tenn. It also shows that he did not move to Russel Co., Va. until after 1795. His children had left him when very young and moved to Caswell Co., N. Car., but he remained in Rockbridge Co., Va. The latter county was formed in 1778 off of Botetourt and Augusta and Botetourt was formed off of Augusta in 1770. Therefore the territory in which he resided was before 1776 in Botetourt Co. Court Records Henrico Co., Va., do not mention Joseph.

The War Dept. Reports (Pensions) is given: "Joseph Culbertson, pr., March 3, 1830, Henrico Co., Va. Amount of pension $48 per year. Paid total $192.13. In 4th Va. Line Capt. Daniel Gilder." (War Dept. Records 1835, Vol. II, p. 11). Also Eckerode, Va. Arch. 1911. "Col. Geo. Walls, Capt. Daniel Gilder, 4th Va. Line 1776." (Barries Army and Navy of U. S.). I have not been able to ascertain what part of Va. this regiment was from or where its officers were from.

Joseph of Buncombe Co., N. Car. was in Washington Co., N. Car. in 1779.

Joseph of Va., son of Andrew died 1805, his son Joseph 1820.

A most thorough search of the court records of Henrico Co., Va., from its formation to date of 1840, fails to reveal Joseph, or any other Culbertson. These records at the court house and State Library have been searched twice and nothing found. I have found no positive evidence that Joseph of Buncombe Co., N. Car. was married. Census 1830 shows no Joseph Culbertson in Henrico Co., Va.

This shows that the War Dept. Report on Pension of above Joseph Culbertson refers no doubt to where Joseph enlisted in 1776. All court records searched show only one Joseph Culbertson in Virginia from 1776 to 1790 and that was Joseph of Rockbridge Co. It is my belief that either Joseph had made application for pension before he died in 1805, or that his widow filed claim. We do not know date of her death. The paper does not say when he died only when pension was granted.

His descendants say he was wounded by a musket ball in Revolution and drew pension for same. There is no deed to or from him in Washington Co. (formed in 1776 from Botetourt) nor Russel Co.—formed from Montgomery and Washington (1787); nor in Montgomery; nor in Scott or Lee Counties, Va. He lived in Russel Co., Va. and died on his farm on Clinch river as shown by family and court records. There are no deeds to or from him in Washington, Scott and Lee or Henrico Counties. His wife Agnes was made his administratrix in Russel Co., Va. in 1805. She made no deeds in Russel or Scott Counties. His widow filed her account but did not mention names of children in same. He was buried two miles north of Ft. Blackmore on the Clinch River in what is now Scott Co. Joseph and Agnes (Family Bible). Bible owned by Mrs. R. H. Lyons of Mt. Sterling, Ky., in 1892. Gives children as below.

FIFTH GENERATION

2. b.   David Culberson.   Greene Co., Ga.
3. b.   James Culberson, b. Jan. 19, 1764; d. Jan. 14, 1823. Scott Co., Va.
4. b.   Joseph Culberson, d. 1815-20.   Scott Co., Va.
5. b.   William Culberson, Caswell Co., N. Car.
6. b.   Robert Culberson, unmar. killed by Indians in Va.

SIXTH GENERATION

(2. b.) **David Culberson** lived in Caswell Co., N. Car. Mar. Miss Clara Browning of Caswell Co., N. Car. Feb. 24, 1782 (from license) Farmer.

David Culbertson (2b.) left Caswell Co., N. Car. before 1790, as he does not appear on tax lists 1785. Nor does he appear Census S. Car.; Georgia Census 1790 destroyed. He

moved to Georgia 1789. The Clerk of Court of Greene Co.,
Ga. writes me that he can find no will of David Culbertson
from 1786 to 1850, but says the records in Probate office
are not complete, and that some years ago some of these
records between 1800 and 1817 were loaned to some one in
Atlanta, who was writing a history of Ga. and were never
returned. If these could be found a will might be found
among them. He also says "I find on deed records No. 1,
p. 544, Jan. 18, 1790, a deed from John Cassna to David
Culbertson for 400 acres, but cannot find any will or deed
whereby he disposed of this, so there must be a will some-
where disposing of this land between 1790 and 1817." The
deed above to David Culbertson in Jan., 1790, shows he was
in Greene Co., Ga., when Census 1790 was taken (Census of
Ga. destroyed by British in 1812). The family records show
positively that his widow lived in Greene Co., Ga., at time
of her second marriage to Jonathan Harrolson. David's
son lived in Greene Co., Ga., for a time. State Land Grant
was made to David Culbertson in 1789 for 400 acres on
Stephens Creek, Franklin Co., Ga. Clerk of Court of Franklin Co., Ga. informs me that he looked for a will or administration of David Culbertson but could find none, showing
he died in some other county. This was, no doubt, David
Culbertson of Greene Co., Ga. After his death his widow
lived in Greene Co., Ga. He moved to Greene Co., Ga., in
1789-90.

Issue:

7. Isaac Culbertson, b. Oct. 30, 1784; d.
8. Jeremiah. Know nothing of him.
9. John. Lived in Harmonton, Miss. Know nothing of
    his family.
10. James, d. 1863.
11. David B. Culberson (Rev.).
12. Elizabeth (Mrs. Eliza Harrolson). Alabama.

Widow of David Culbertson (2) mar. Jonathan Harrolson
of Greene Co., Ga.

Issue:

Jonathan Harrolson. Moved to Alabama.

Kinchen L. Brownsville, Tex.

Hugh A. Mar. (La Grange, Ga.). Was congressman
    many years from Fourth Cong. Dist. of Ga.: one
    of his daughters mar. Chief Justice of Ga., Logan
    A. Blakely; another dau. mar. Ex-Gov. Gen. J. B.
    Gordon, of Atlanta, Ga.; another dau. mar. Capt.
    Pace of Covington, Ga.

(b. 3.) James Culberson, mar. in Caswell Co., N. Car. (Marriage Bond) Miss Mary Kilgore, Dec. 15, 1785. Moved to Scott Co., Va., 1787. Wife b. Feb. 13, 1766; d. Mar. 1845. Estate settled Scott Co., Va., 1823.

Issue: (From old Family Bible). On tax 400 acres Russel Co., Va., 1799.

13. Sidney, b. Sept. 17, 1786; d.
14. Tyree, b. Oct. 17, 1788; d.
15. Elizabeth, b. Aug. 29, 1791; d. (Mrs. Walker) Tenn.
16. Sibella, b. Aug. 10, 1793; d.
17. Mary, b. Sept. 21, 179—; d. Missouri.
18. John, b. Jan. 1, 1798; d. July 23, 1843. Mo.
19. Charles, b. Jan. 27, 1800; d. ("Big Charles")
20. James, b. May 21, 1802; d.
21. William, b. Jan. 31, 1805; d. 1843 (Bachelor). Mo.
22. Joseph, b. May 22, 1807; d.
23. Martha, b. Aug. 22, 1809; d.
24. Jephthah, b. May 30, 1813; d.

Part of the children of James (3. b.) dropped the "t" from their name, but on the death of their father they all resumed the "t" and their descendants retained it. Mar. license issued in Caswell Co., to Jas. Culberson.

(4. b.) Joseph Culbertson probably mar. after 1790. Moved to Scott Co., Va. Joseph was deeded 150 acres on north side of Clinch River in 1800 by R. Price for £200. No marriage bond to him in Caswell Co., N. Car. Lt. Militia Scott Co., Va., in 1814.

Issue:

25. Jerry.
26. David.
27. James.
27½.—Dau. (Mrs. Zach Wills). Issue Thos. Zach, Wm., Jerry, Robt., Jacob, Stephen, Jemima, Betsy, Abigail and Sally.

Settlement Records Scott Co. show that on Dec. 13, 1820, Geo. Stacy, admr. of Jos. Culberson made settlement with Jeremiah, James anud David Culberson and Zachiriah Wills in sum of $1124. Joseph deeded his farm in Caswell Co., N. Car. in 1791 and he probably was married that year.

(5. b.) William Culberson of Caswell Co., N. Car., did not follow his father to Va. Census 1790 gives him as taxable Caswell Co., N. Car. The legislature in 1784 ordered that the county in which he lived (Hillsboro Dist.) issue him a new money warrant for county warrant (not Revo-

lutionary) destroyed by water. He deeded a negro in Caswell Co. in 1804. Farm was on county line on Haw Creek adjoining his brothers. He was married to Miss Mary Browning in Caswell Co., N. Car., May 29, 1800 (from license.) Children from family record verified by will in Caswell Co., N. Car. Can find no Revolutionary Record of him. The money warrant destroyed was not for Revolutionary service, the state Librarian informs me. Died 1824. Do not know which children by first wife.

Issue: (second wife Mary), from will.

28. William Culberson. Know nothing of.
29. Sibella (Mrs. Parks).
30. Hiram Culberson, Lincoln Co., Tenn. Married Nancy Hightower of Caswell Co., N. Car. (formerly of Halifax Co., Va.) Dec., 1806. Moved to Lincoln Co., Tenn. Issue: (of Hiram and Nancy) a. James S.; b. David Thomas; c. Hiram; d. Pamela; e. Mary; f. Sarah; g. Wm. C. (bachelor in 1892). Stock raiser living at El Campo, Tex.; h. Iverson Green.
31. Edney (Mrs. Wm. Price). E. Tenn.
32. Susannah (Mrs. Joshua Rudd).
33. Tibitha (Mrs. Rudd).
34. Mary (Mrs. Joshua Price).
35. James, d. young (not in will).
36. David, died young (not in will).

SEVENTH GENERATION

(7) Isaac Culbertson mar. Dec. 2, 1807 to Miss Mary Houston, of Morgan Co., Ga. Both died in Troup Co., Ga.

Issue:

37. Elizabeth Ann Culber(t)son b. Dec. 10, 1808; d. Apr. 26, 1844.
38. David H. Culber(t)son, b. June 8, 1810; d. Mar. 12, 1866.
39. James H. Culber(t)son, b. Oct. 21, 1813; d. Apr. 6, 1884.
40. Isaac L. Culber(t)son, b. July 7, 1815; d. May 28, 1835.
41. Nancy E. Culberson (no "t"), b. July 22, 1817. Gilman, Tex.
42. William P. Culberson, b. Mar. 29, 1819. Gilman Tex.
43. Mary Eunice, b. Dec. 5, 1820. Living Newman, Ga.
44. Augustus B. Culberson, b. Dec. 5, 1822; d. Feb. 24, 1889.

45. Marcus L. Culberson, b. July 29, 1824; d. July 24, 1883.
46. Alonzo Browning Culberson, b. Feb. 28, 1827; d. Mar. 26, 1852.
47. Columbus Y. Culberson, b. July 6, 1829; d. 1879. Tex.

(8) Jeremiah Culbertson mar. in Ga. The records furnished me by Culbersons in 1892 stated that "they did not know what became of him." I am convinced from the data furnished by Dr. James Culbertson of Maud, Okla., that Jeremiah was the ancestor of Dr. James Culbertson and will place Jeremiah (8) as the grandfather of Dr. James. He states that his father had but two children 48 Augustus and 49 Allen Turner Culbertson. Augustus is an unusual name among the Culbertsons and this name (Augustus Browning) occurs among the descendants of Isaac, a brother of Jeremiah (8). Dr. James states his father went to Calif. and was never heard from. Does not know whether his father married again in Calif. His letter as follows: "I have been trying to gather some data of my ancestors from an old uncle of mine still living, but find that he can't give me any information prior to my father's marriage to his sister. My father, Allen Turner Culbertson was born either in Ga. or N. Car. and grandfather started to California in or about 1832 to the great gold rush, and was never heard of any more. I don't know his name. My father was born in Ga. about 1821, died 1905, and while a young man settled in Ala. and married a Miss Adline Houston, a relative of the Gov. Samuel Houston family. My father was in Montgomery, Ala. for many years. About 1869 he moved to north Ark. and entered the live stock business and lived there for many years, and moved to Okla. and died Apr. 16th, 1905, aged 84 years. He was a very peculiar man, never mentioning any history of himself to his family, or any one else. I have heard him say that he was a distant relative of Senator Culberson of Texas. I have also heard him say that he had relatives in New Orleans who were in the banking business. My sister says she heard father say several times that his father's name was Jerry. I can only give you a little history of myself which will probably be of no benefit. However I am sure I belong to the family that settled in the east many years ago.

"I was born at Montgomery, Ala., Oct. 27, 1867. Moved to Arkansas in 1869. Attended the common schools of that state and the Ark. University, taking my first two years in the Medical Department. I finished my medical education in the College of Physicians, St. Louis, Mo., in 1898. Attended Post work in New York, Baltimore and New Orleans. "Jan. 15th, 1890, I married Miss Fannie Burton, daughter of S. Burton, a Methodist clergyman. We have four sons and one daughter. My oldest son, Dr. R. R. Culbertson, born in Greenwood, Ark., Jan. 16, 1891. He is now practising with me. My daughter, Mrs. Edith Duke, was born at Chismville, Ark., Dec. 18th, 1893. Leonard Culbertson, born at Ft. Smith, Ark., May 11th, 1895. Gus Culbertson, born Ft. Smith, Ark., May 22nd, 1900, now a traveling salesman in San Francisco, Calif. The above Leonard Culbertson is a druggist, here with me. My father only had two sons, myself and my older brother, Augustus Culbertson, born Sept., 1861. About 1885, he married Miss Mary Beasley, in Newton Co., Ark., and lives there now. He had three sons, Claud, who was born Feb., 1888; d. Feb., 1914; Albert, B., b. Apr. 2, 1890, now teaching in Okla. City public schools; Olin, b. Sept., 1900, now a druggist in Okla. City, Okla. You might note my brother's name Augustus and my name also. I feel that Jeremiah was my grandfather, as I am sure from your letter that John, was not. I heard my father say, if I am not mistaken, that his grandfather in Ga. lived to be 109 years of age. He raised my father after my grandfather went west, and was never heard from. I feel that the Culbersons of San Francisco are probably my near relatives.

"This additional information might not be out of place. Dr. R. R. Culbertson, my oldest son, educated in Ark. U. and his Med. Education, at National U. Med. Dept., St. Louis, Mo. Leonard the druggist, University of Okla. and Colorado. (Married Miss Cora Ogee, Jan. 14, 1922); Gus, University of Colorado; Otto, University of New York; Edith, my daughter, Central Baptist College, Conway, Ark. My oldest son, Dr. R. R. Culbertson, served as Capt. in Medical Corps, and was Equitation Instructor at Camp Greenleaf, Ga. all during the war, and now Capt. in Medical Reserve Corps U. S. A."

(10) James Culbertson mar. first Miss Sarah M. Wilkinson, dau. of Revolutionary soldier of Greene Co., Ga. Moved from Greene Co., Ga., to Troup Co., Ga., where he died. Wife d. 1860.

Issue:

50. Eliza B., d. La Grange, Ga.
50½. Martha A. Living at La Grange, Ga.
50¾. Mary L. Living at Clayton, Ala.

51.   S. F. (Dr.) Snyder, Scurry Co., Tex.
52.   John Pope (Col.) Atlanta, Ga.
53.   Sarah A. Living at Atlanta, Ga.
54.   Margaret P. Atlanta, Ga.

(10) James C. mar. second Mrs. Libby Ashford. No issue. Widow lives Greenville, Ala.

(11) Rev. David B. Culbertson mar. Miss Lucy Wilkinson and moved to Texas in 1853. Formerly lived in Alabama. Was a prominent Baptist minister.

Issue:

55.   David Browning Culbertson. Jefferson, Tex. (Congressman and Senator).

(14) Tyree Culbertson mar. Miss Mattie Vickers. Moved to Russell Co., Va.

Issue:

56.   William, d. Killed in Civil War.
56¼.   James. Lived in Russell Co., Va. Killed in Civil War.
56½.   Henry, d.
56¾.   Sarah, d.
56 4-4. Agnes, d.
57.   Lydia (Mrs. Salyer), d.
57¼.   Martha, d.
57½.   Nancy d.
58.   Betty, d. unmar.
59.   Thomas, living 1923.

(18) John Culbertson mar. Miss Comfort Osborne, Aug. 16, 1827. After living a few years in Scott Co., Va., moved to Hickory Co., Mo. Wife b. Oct. 18, 1806; d. June 26, 1873.

Issue:

60.   Nancy, b. May 28, 1828; d. June 26, 1875.
61.   Jane, b. Jan. 16, 1830; d. Sept. 21, 1888.
62.   William, b. July 24, 1832. Gravel Ford, Ore.
63.   John A., b. Feb. 6, 1833. Bachelor. Phoenix, Ariz. (1892).
64.   Stephen, b. Oct. 8, 1834. Lived at Nelson, Mo.
65.   Jephthah, b. July 20, 1836.
66.   Erena, b. May 21, 1838.
67.   Pauline, b. Jan. 2, 1840; d. Feb. 22, 1864.
68.   Rebecca, b. Dec. 9, 1841; d. Sept. 16, 1864.

(19) Charles Culbertson mar. Miss Nancy Osborne. Lived in Scott Co., Va.

Issue:

69. Charles W. Morgan Co., Ky.
70. William. Mar.
71. Stephen.
72. David.
73. John W.
73½. Sarah (mar. David C. Powers, Wise Co., Va·)
(20) James Culbertson mar. Miss Elizabeth Harris. Lived in Scott Co., Va.

Issue:

74. James E. Texas.
75. Edward J., d. in Civil War.
(22) Joseph Culbertson mar. Miss Dorton. Lived in Scott Co·, Va·

Issue:

76. Edward D.
77. Joseph. Lived in Scott Co., Va. in 1861.
78. David.
(24) Jephthah Culbertson mar. Miss Elmina Pullum of Mo. Lived in Mo. for a short time and then moved back to Va. in Scott Co. in 1845.

Issue:

79. Wm. J. Dead. Merchant, Nicklesville, Va· No issue·
80. Robert C., d. young.
81. George W., dead.
82. Cassandra.
83. Elizabeth (Mrs. D. C. Powers), dead.
84. Mary, dead·
85. Lucinda, living.
86. Louisa, living. No issue.
87. James M., dead. Lived Wise Co. Va. Farmer.
88. Cordelia.
(24) Jephthah Culbertson mar. second Miss Eliza Moore.

Issue:

88½. Margaret, dead. (Mrs. ——) Issue: Mabel, Paul, Muriel.
89. Benjamin T. Prominent banker and merchant at Dungannon, Va.
89½. Geneva (Mrs. Whiteside). Living at Erlanger, Ky. No issue.

(25) Jerry Culbertson mar. ———. Moved to Indiana.

Issue: Know nothing of.

(26) David Culbertson mar. Miss Livingstone. Lived in Scott Co., Va.

Issue:

90. Livingstone. Scott Co., Va.
91. Jerry. Scott Co., Va.

EIGHTH GENERATION

(37) Betsey Ann Culberson mar. John Conyers. Know nothing of.
(38) David Culberson. Know nothing of.
(39) James E. Culberson mar. first Miss Park.

Issue:

92. Augustus L.
93. Alonzo B. Bachelor.
94. Wm. Columbus.
95. Achsah O.
96. Charles Y.
(39) James H. mar. second Miss Johnston.

Issue:

97. Gracie. Alameda, Cal.
98. Clifford. San Francisco.
99. James H. mar. Alameda, Cal.
(41) Nancy E. Culberson mar. Fred Palmer. Living, Gilman, Texas. Know nothing of them.
(42) Wm. P. Gilman, Tex. Know nothing about him.
(43) Mary Eunice Culberson mar. Benj. Leigh, of Newman, Ga. Know nothing of.
(44) Augustus B. Culberson mar. Margaret H. Caldwell, Feb. 23, 1847.

Issue:

100. Ovid Isaac, b. Dec. 21, 1847. Atlanta, Ga.
101. Gerald Harrington, b. Oct. 26, 1849. Atlanta, Ga.
102. Alevilda Mary, b. Mar. 13, 1852.
103. John Caldwell, b. Apr. 3, 1854.
104. Leila Hinton, b. Aug. 11, 1857.
105. Hubert Leon, b. Feb. 7, 1860.
106. Corinne Eloise, b. Dec. 23, 1861.

107. Augustus B., Jr., b. Dec. 12, 1863; d. Aug. 30, 1889.
108. Maggie, b. Nov. 13, 1867; d. Dec. 1867.
    (45) Marcus L. Know nothing about.
    (46) Alonzo B. Know nothing about.
    (47) Columbus Y. Know nothing about.
    (48) Eliza B. Culberson mar. A. G. Hightower of La
Grange, Ga.

Issue: two sons and three daughters. 109-114.

(49) Martha A. Culbertson mar. first, Thos. Cox, who
died. No issue. Widow mar. second, Thos. J. Thornton of
Harris Co., Ga.

Issue:

115. J. P. Thornton. La Grange, Ga.
116. A. E. Thornton. Atlanta, Ga.
117. Tommie (Mrs. Banks). La Grange.
    (50) Mary L. Culberson mar. A. H. Borders a Baptist
minister. In 1861 moved to Clayton, Ala.

Issue:

118. Mary Moore. (Mar. Judge J. A. Foster, Chancellor
       of 3rd Jud. Dist. of Alabama.)
119. Sarah, d. (Mar. Rev. Paidine (Baptist) Clayton, Ala.)
120. James C. Killed in Civil War.
121. Augustus. Mar. Clayton, Ala.
    (51) Dr. F. S. Culberson mar. first Miss Cornelia Lewis,
of La Grange, Ga. Wife died.

Issue:

122. Sherwood F. Killed in war at Marietta, Ga.
123. James, b. 1853. Living in Texas.
124. John P., d. in Tex.
125. Hattie, d. (Mrs. Johnson of Louisiana.)
    (51) Dr. F. S. Culberson mar. second Miss Doney Nichol-
son of Shreveport, Tex. Wife died. (Moved to Texas
about 1855.)

Issue:

126. Hazel   } Twins
127. Sherwood
128. Victor Stanley. Stock farm, Silver City, N. M.
129. Maud.
130. Anna.
131. Walter.

(51) Dr. F. S. Culberson mar. third, Mrs. Morgan. Live at Snyder, Scurry Co., Tex. Issue: None living.

(52) Col. John P. Culberson mar. Miss Romelia Bird at La Grange in 1853. Live at Atlanta, Ga.

Issue:

132. Sarah L. (Mrs. J. K. McCall). Atlanta, Ga.
133. J. Pope, Jr., b. 1859. Mar. (Southern Ex. Co.)
134. Joseph B. Conductor in S. America. Mar.
135. Lila Romelia. (Mrs. Dr. G. W. Bishop, Atlanta.)
136. Fannie.
137. Mary Lee. (Mrs. S. L. Ivy, Atlanta, Go.)
138. Charles H. R. R. conductor, Marshall, Tex. Unmar.
139. Annie P. (Mrs. Marion S. Perry). Atlanta, Ga.

(53) Sarah A. Culberson mar. Dr. Dudley Sneed, of La Grange, Ga., who d. 1847.

Issue:

140. Dau. (Mrs. T. N. Hall, Atlanta, Ga.)

(54) Margaret P. Culberson mar. Gen. J. W. B. Eadwards of Atlanta, Ga.

Issue:

141. Sallie (Mrs. Chas. Handy). Atlanta.
142. Willie F. (Mrs. Frank Reid).
143. Dovie. (Mrs. Jas. H. Carter).
144. S. J. B. (Dr.), mar. lived in Gadsden, Ala.

(55) Hon. David Browning Culberson mar. Eugenia Kimbal, daughter of Dr. Allen Kimbal. Congressman from Jefferson, Tex. many years. Formerly lived at Dadeville, Ala.

Issue:

145. Charles A., b. June 10, 1855. U. S. Senator from Tex.

(56½) Henry Culbertson lived in Russel Co., Va. in 1861. (I will state here that Miss Winifred Culbertson, of Cincinnati, O., writes me—1923—that her grandmother now living says that her husband, Henry Culbertson, was from the western part of Old Virginia and that he moved from Va. to Grayson Co., Ky. in 1862, and that she thinks he was a son of Tyre Culbertson and Mattie Vickers. I have written to an old lady in Va. and told her to forward my letter to Thomas Culbertson, the only surviving brother of Henry Culbertson of Russel Co., Va. and asked him to confirm this. He is over ninety years old. At time of going to press I have not received reply to this letter. I will insert this

Henry Culbertson in here with this reservation. Editor.)
Henry Culbertson mar. Mary Elizabeth Drake and moved
in 1862 to Grayson Co., Ky.

Issue: ——.

(——) Frank C. Culbertson, born May 14, 1851. Mar.
Mary Elizabeth Diedrich, Feb. 14, 1877, and had issue: Fred
M., b. 1879, d. 1917 Louise W., b. Dec. 29, 1880, mar. Bose
Watson, lives in Ashland, Ky, issue six children; May
Jeanette, b. March 29, 1885, mar. Walter Matthews, d. 1907;
Vida, b. July 29, 1887, mar. Fred Mannon, lives Holden, W.
Va., issue three children; Winifred, b. Feb. 24, 1891, trained
nurse, lives in Cincinnati, O., was in U. S. Military Service
as trained nurse in World War; Ernest, b. Feb. 12, 1895, d.
1895; Josephine, b. June 29, 1886, who mar. Roy Reynolds,
lives in Ashland, Ky. and has four children; Beatrice, b.
June 23, 1898 mar. Orie McKenzie, lives Russell, Ky., 6
children.

(57) Lydia Culbertson, mar. first —— Dorton, issue not
known.

(57) Lydia Culbertson mar. second in 1834 to Samuel Sal-
yr, Jr., of Scott Co., Va. He died 1911 in Wise Co., Va.,
aged 114 years. Born 1797.

Issue:

146.   Logan H. N. Salyer (Col.) of Letcher Co., Ky., b.
1835, d. May 3, 1916. Married four times (wives
not given). Issue: Helen C., Drewery W., Dicey
Elizabeth, Annie, Hattie Maud (Mrs. H. N. Taylor
of Norton, Va.), Lelia, Samuel T., John, Effie,
Clarence, Slemp.

146¼.   Lydia Drusilla (Mrs. Henry Frazier of Norton,
Va.) who had issue: (a) H. T. Frazier of Lee Co.,
Va. A son is Prof. Clark Frazier of Jonesville, Va.
(b) Martha Frazier mar. David F. Beverly and
had issue: Lillian Mae Beverly, born Dec. 1, 1893,
married Nuttar Cart, 1920, and now living in
Louisville, Ky.; was with the American Army as
a graduate nurse; Bessie Belle Beverly born Feb.
22, 1895, married Dr. Ralph C. Bray, 1916. Her
husband was in the army. They live at Appalachia, Va. She has two children, Beverly (1918)
and Doris (1920); Charles F. Beverly, born April
17, 1897, married Carrie West of Jackson, Ky.,
1916. He has four children, Robert (1917), Elmer
and Margaret (1918), and Mildred (1921). He

lives at Norton, Va.; Walter F. Beverly, born Sept. 29, 1889, married Belle Pearce of Richmond, Va., 1915 and have three children, William Morgan, born (1917), Walter Frazier, Jr. (1919), and Martha Bell (1921). (c) Mary Frazier married John Jenkins and had issue: Elmer Jenkins, Lt. U. S. Army. A graduate of West Point and served in the World War in Siberia. Now in the Philippines. His brother, Wm. Jenkins, is a prominent business man of Norton, Va. (d) —— Frazier (Mrs. C. G. Connar of Norton, Va.).

146½.   Tyre T. Salyer.
146¾.   Martha M.
146 4-4.   Frank, mar. issue: Ida (Mrs. Geo. Jenkins) of Appalachia, Va.

(61) Jane Culbertson mar. R. H. Lyons of Mt. Sterling, Ky. The given data from the Family Bible of James (3. b.) in 1892.

Issue:

147.   James J. Lyons, b. Jan. 6, 1858; d. Mar. 20, 1859.
147½.   Trinvilla, b. Dec. 28, 1859; d. July 31, 1861.
148.   Caleb F., b. Dec. 31, 1861; d. July 4, 1864.
149.   Orman E., b. Feb. 28, 1864.
150.   Melinda, b. Apr. 14, 1866.
150½.   Herbert K., b. Dec. 2, 1868.

(62) William Culbertson mar. Miss Jane Dingus. Know nothing about.

(64) Stephen Culbertson mar. Martha Ann Dennis, Aug. 3, 1859. (Lived at Nelson, Saline Co., Mo.)

Issue:

151.   Nancy, b. May 30, 1860.
152.   Jefferson B., b. 1861.
153.   James, b. Dec. 10, 1862.
·154.   Martha M., b. Jan. 19, 1864.
155.   Wm. W., b. May 3, 1865.
146.   Mary A., b. June 4, 1866.
157.   Benjamin F., b. Apr. 29, 1867.
158.   John A., b. Apr. 24, 1869.
159.   Comfort, b. Aug. 4, 1880.

(65) Jephthah Culbertson mar. Miss Mary Bird. Lived in Bath Co., Ky.

Issue:

160.   John.
161.   Stephen A.

(73) John W. Culbertson mar. Lucinda Gose. Know nothing about him.

(74) James E. Culbertson mar. Miss Winnie Kilgore. Lived in Texas.

(75) Edward J. Culbertson mar. Miss Gibson. Lived in Scott Co., Va. Killed in Civil War.

(76) Edward D. Culbertson mar. Miss Wolfe. Lived in Scott Co. before the war.

(81) George Culbertson mar. ———. Lived Wise Co., Va.

Issue:

162. Myrtle.
163. May.
164. Robert.
164. Elsie.
166. Sarah.

(82) Cassandra Culbertson mar. J. R. Hartsock.

Issue:

167. Geneva.
168. Wm. J.
169. Julia.

(83) Elizabeth Culbertson mar. David Crocket Powers of Wise Co., Va. Wife died.

Issue:

170. Mary (Mrs. R. H. Fink). Issue: Robert Powers Fink, b. 1901, d. 1914. Living at Norton, Va. Teacher for 25 years.
171. Nancy Louisa (Mrs. D. B. Crawford of Norton, Va.) Issue: Bruce, Jr., Wm. H., Elizabeth,. Virginia.
172. Stella (Mrs. L. H. Dooley of Roanoke, Va. Live at Norman, Okla.). Issue: Mary Nancy, Lillian, Paul, Elizabeth.

David Crocket Powers mar. second (73½) Sarah Culbertson daughter of Chas. Culbertson (19).

Issue:

173. Robert E. Powers, Hobart, Okla. (Mrs. Eliza Kilgore of Va.) Issue: Ruby, Elbert, Clyde, Myrtle, Raymond, Hazel.
174. Geneva (Mrs. C. Parsons) Davenport, Ia. Issue: David, Bruce, Olin.

(85) Lucinda Culbertson mar. Mr. Johnston.

Issue:

174½.   Wm. J. Johnston.
175.   Andrew.
176.   Ellen.
177.   City.
    (87) James Culbertson mar. ——. Lived in Wise Co., Va.

Issue:

178.   James N.   Lives at Dooley, Va.
179. to 189.
    (88) Cordelia Culbertson mar. P. C. Hartsock.

Issue:

190.   Jephtha Hartsock.
191.   Ida.
192.   Roy.
193.   Pleasant.
    (89) Benjamin T. Culbertson, merchant and banker at
Dungannon, Va. Mar. first Laura Compton, Jan. 20, 1897.
She died Feb. 7, 1904.

Issue:

194.   Cecelie Fay, b. July 14, 1898.
195.   Mark Somers, b. Jan. 4, 1900.
    (89) Benjamin T. Culbertson mar. second Margaret
Wolfe, Nov. 30, 1905.

Issue:

196.   Benjamin Cline, b. Aug. 10, 1907.
196½.   Margaret Ruth, b. July 27, 1909.
196¾.   Chas. Leonard, b. June 17, 1911.
197.   Eliza, b. Nov. 22, 1915.
    (90) Livingstone Culbertson mar. Mary E. Douglas, July
26, 1868. Lived at Scott Co., Va. Moved to Rich Hill, Mo.,
1866.

Issue:

198.   Jeremiah, b. Sept. 12, 1869.   Kansas City, Mo.
199.   Finley, b. May 15, 1872; d. May 1, 1888.

NINTH GENERATION
    (92) Augustus L. Culberson mar. Philia Fricks.

Issue:

200.   Mattie, d.

201.   James Wm.
202.   Edward.
203.   Sallie.
204.   Beatrice.
    (94) Wm. Columbus Culberson mar. Mollie Jones of De
Kalb Co., Ala.

Issue:

205.   Lilla.
    (97) Achsah O. Culbertson mar. J. S. Green of Zebulon,
Pike Co·, Ga.

Issue:

206.   Oscar·
207.   Alonzo.
208.   Emma.
209.   Harvey.
210.   Lizzie.
211.   Frank,
212.   Claude.
    (96) Charles Y. mar. Annie Jones of De Kalb Co., Ala,

Issue:

213.   Hattie.
214.   Truman·
215.   Gerald.
    (99) James H., Jr., mar. ——.

Issue:

216.   Grace.
    (100) Ovid I. Culberson mar. Annie E. Stewart, Aug. 22,
1869.

Issue:

217.   Maggie Wright, b. July 16, 1870.
218.   Lillian, b. Sept. 23, 1872.
219·   Rhea, b. July 12, 1875; d. Mar. 19, 1879.
    (101) Gerald H. mar. Sallie Reid Battle, June 18, 1874.
Manufacturer of agricultural implements, Atlanta, Ga.

Issue:

220.   Gerald H., Jr., b. Dec. 1, 1879 (Rev.) Portsmouth, O.
221.   Emeline Howell, b· Jan. 1881.
    (103) John C. mar. Sallie May Williams, Jan. 15, 1880.

Issue:

222. Mary Lou, b. Nov. 30, 1880.
  (105) Hubert L. mar. Katherine Bleckley, June 1, 1880.
Lawyer, Atlanta, Ga.

Issue:

223. Caroline Lewis, b. Apr. 3, 1888; d. July 19, 1898.
  (145) Senator Charles A. Culberson of Dallas, Tex., mar.
——, daughter of Col. W. W. Harrison, of Ft. Worth, Tex.

Issue:

224. Mary.
  (198) Jeremiah Culbertson mar. Feb. 20, 1901, to Miss
Josephine Parsons, daughter of Mr. and Mrs. J. C. Parsons
of Harrisonville, Mo. Lives Kansas City, Mo.

Issue:

225. Judith Douglass, b. July 7, 1902.
226. Kathryn Nevin, b. Apr. 21, 1904.
227. Eleanor Wade, b. July 3, 1907.
228. Joseph Livingstone, b. Jan. 5, 1922.
TENTH GENERATION
  (220) Rev. Gerald H. Culberson, Jr. married Mary
Syme of Winchester, Va., Sept. 17, 1902. Minister in Chris
tian Church, Portsmouth, O.

Issue:

229. Gerald Culberson, b. June 13, 1903, at Winchester,
  Va.
230. Ruth Culberson, b. Sept. 30, 1904, at Chester, W. Va.
231. Grey Culberson, b. Apr. 14, 1906, at Winchester, Va.
  (221) Emeline Culberson mar. B. H. Alexander. Live at
Lake Wales, Fla.

Issue:

Prominent Descendants of Joseph (a. 4.), son of Andrew (III) of Shippensburg, Pa. and Rockbridge Co·, Va.

David (2. b.) Culberson had a son (11) Rev. David B.
Culberson, a prominent minister of Alabama, who had a
son, David Browning Culberson, Jr., of Dallas, Tex., Con
gressman from Texas for many years. In 1892 it was said
he had made the greatest mark of any Culbertson who had
been in Congress· Congressman Joe Cannon, said of him.
"He was the best posted man in Congress on legal techni-

calities." He showed a true Culbertson characteristic. viz.. simplicity in dress. It is said that he was never known to wear a dress coat even at state receptions. In 1892 he was at the head of the free silverites in Congress.

(145) Culberson, Chas. A. (senator) b. Dadeville, Ala.. June 10, 1855; son of D. B. (congressman Tex. 22 years) and Eugenia (Kimball) Culbertson;, grad. Vir'g. Mil. Ins't, 1874; law student Univ. Va. 1876-7; settled in Tex. 1856. Practiced Dallas, Tex. since 1887. Co. Att'y Marion Co.; Att'y Gen. Tex. 1890-4; Gov. Tex. two terms; U. S. Senator 1899-05, 05-11, 1911-17, 1917-23. Delegate Nat. Dem. Convention 1896-1904. Dallas, Tex. Married daughter of Col. W. W. Harrison of Ft. Worth, Tex.—(From Who's Who in America.)

(198) Jerry Culbertson, Specialist in Industrial Development, is descended from a prominent family of the Old Dominion. He was born in Bates County, Missouri, September 12th, 1869, the son of Livingston and Mary E. (Douglas) Culbertson. His father was born in Scott County, Virginia and removed to Missouri in 1866, becoming a pioneer farmer and merchant of Bates County, and the founder of the town of Rich Hill, which he named, and in which he established the first store. The elder Culbertson was a son of David Culbertson a native of Virginia and a member of the legislature of that state in 1838. The latter, a native of Virginia and a descendant of Scotch ancestry, was a member of the family from which the famous Culbertson family of Texas is descended. Mary E. Douglas, our subject's mother, was a daughter of Colonel Geo. Douglas. (From the Encyclopedia of the History of Missouri, Page 204.)

Jerry Culbertson received his elementary education in the common schools of Bates County and at the age of eighteen years St. Francis Institute (Catholic) at Osage Mission, Kansas. A year later he took a course in Bryant College at Sprague, Bates County, Missouri, after which he was, for a year principal of the graded school at College Hill in the same county. After a year's course in the state university he taught one year at Old Rich Hill, then took another year in special studies in the state university, devoting his time chiefly to literature, economics and metaphysics. He then entered the law department of the university, and after two year's course, was graduated therefrom, June 3, 1896. Four days later he was admitted to the bar before Judge Lay at Butler, Mo., and at once opened an office at Rich Hill, Missouri. Nov., 1900, he was elected prosecuting attorney of Cass County on the Democratic ticket.

In 1905 Mr. Culbertson became aware of the greater op-portunities that Kansas City had to offer to the young business man, and has made it his home since then, devot-ing his time to the study of permanent investments. He is the founder and president of both the International Ex-ploration Company and the Culbertson Realty-Stock-Bond Corporation. Fraternally, he is a Mason, an Elk and a Modern Woodman.

Reverend Gerald Culberson (220), son of Gerald H. Cul-berson (101). Born Waynesville, N. C., reared in Atlanta, Ga., entered an East Tennessee Bible College in 1899. After three years of preparation there entered Bethany College, W. Va., receiving degree in 1905. Has held pastorates in churches of the Disciples of Christ in West Virginia, Vir-ginia, Indiana and Texas. Now pastor of the First Chris-tion Church, Portsmouth, Ohio, one of the largest and most influential congregations in the Communion.

(61) Mrs. R. H. Lyons (nee Jane Culbertson), of Mt. Sterling, Ky. a daughter of (15) John Culbertson and granddaughter of b. 3. James Culbertson of Scott Co., Va., stated in 1892 that the old Family Bible of James Culbert-son (b. 3.) giving his wife's name (marriage record of same obtained in Caswell Co., N. C.) and dates of birth, etc., also names of James' father and mother, i. e. Joseph and Agnes of Russel Co., Va., was in possession of her brother Stephen of Nelson, Mo. Mrs. Lyons' brother, J. A., living in Ari-zona in 1892, gave me a great deal of information on the Culbertsons of So. West Va. The aforementioned Bible al-so gave the names of the children of Joseph and Agnes of Russel Co., Va. J. A. also said Joseph was wounded in Rev-olution and that his sons lived in Caswell Co., N. Car., for a time; latter statement confirmed by records. Mrs. Lyons copied dates from her Bible and these dates she had copied from the original Bible in possession of Stephen Culbert-son, of Nelson, Saline Co., Mo. In 1892 Wm. J. Culbertson (92), of Scott Co., Va., wrote me a conference he had had with an aunt ninety years old and she told about the ances-tors coming from Pa. to Va., then going to Caswell Co., N. Car. and when Joseph was 50 or 60 years old moved back to Va. in Russell Co., with part of his sons and died in Rus-sel Co., Va.

CHAPTER XVI

(5. a.) Samuel Culbertson (Dr.) of the 12th Va. Continental Line, 1776-78, Col. Woods (Va. Arch.). All trace of him is lost to record after 1778. It is my belief that he owned no property but remained in Rockbridge Co., Va. There was an Alexander Culbertson married to Polly Barclay, March 5, 1799 (bond) in Rockbridge Co., Va., whom I think was Dr. Samuel's son. This Alexander Culbertson and wife, Polly, conveyed 80 acres to John Barger, lying on the James River at the Great Road. One of the witnesses H. Barclay. Date May 1, 1802. Know nothing more of him. There was a Mr. Culbertson of Rockbridge Co., Va., married Martha Allen Bridgeland-Smith of that county many years ago and moved to Fairland, Ind., and had issue. No Culbertsons at Fairland, now. (The regiment in which Dr. Samuel Culbertson served was commanded by Col. James Wood. Col. Woods was from Winchester, Va.)

CHAPTER XVII

FOURTH GENERATION

(VI.) **Col. Robert Culbertson** of Hopewell Twp., Cumberland Co., Pa., moved to Columbus, O., in 1801. Mar. first ——, mar. second Mrs. Elizabeth (Davis) Irwin. (Irwin was her second husband; her first husband was David Jamison, son of Col. David Jamison, M. D., an officer of French and Indian War and the Revolution.)

Issue: (Most of these by first wife.)

1. Andrew, d. Apr., 1826. Lived at Columbus, O.
2. James, d. Lived at Columbus, O.
3. Rebecca d. (Mrs. Moore).
4. Jane, d. (Mrs. Park).
5. Agnes, d. (Mrs. Park).
6. Keziah,d. (Mrs. Brotherton).
7. Martha, d. (Mrs. Brotherton).
8. Margaret, d. (Mrs. Keller).
9. ——, d. (Mrs. Breckenridge).
10. Sarah, d. (Mrs. David Jamison).
    —From Jameson Genealogy and Will of Robert Culbertson.

FIFTH GENERATION

(1) Andrew Culbertson is given Hopewell Tp., Cumb. Co.,
Pa. Census 1790, self and wife, one son under 16, and one
daughter. Andrew first appears as a taxable in Hopewell
Tp., Cumb. Co., in 1788. He was of age before that. He
moved with his father to Columbus, Ohio, in 1801. Died
intestate at Columbus, O., in 1826 and Mr. Deshler (D. W.)
of the wealthy Deshler family, was appointed administrator. His children are not given in settlement of his estate
but widow Esther is given. In the old Genealogy (Culbertson) the names of his children were taken from the Jameson Genealogy, but the writer of this work failed to mention the son Robert. It was through the Pension office
records and correspondence with descendants in Ills. that I
was able to connect Robert their ancestor, with the War of
1812 soldier. In pension application he says "Born 1790,
drafted into Ohio Militia, Capt. Geo. Gibson's Co., at Columbus, Ohio, Oct., 1814."

Residence at time of application Washington, Tazewell
Co., Ills. Descendants say "Robert was born at Columbus,
O. Owned land on Scioto at Columbus, Ohio. Had a brother
Andrew, who died young. Had a sister who married a
Shannon. Grandmother died young and gradfather did not
remarry. He was in the War of 1812. He moved to Washington, Tazewell Co., Ills. He and his sons owned land
there. He afterwards moved to Gilman, Ills. and lived with
his son Joseph and died there about 1870." Records show
that Andrew (1) married his cousin Esther Culbertson,
daughter of Robert Culbertson, son of Irish Samuel of Pa.
"Row." (priv. 1776-7 in Revolution, i. e. Robert.) In his
est. inventory filed 1826, only $150 of pers. property and
no realty, hence names of heirs not given save in surety of
Esther as admn'x.

Issue:

11. Alexander, d. Columbus, O.
12. Elizabeth, d. (Mrs. Andrew Dill), Columbus, O.
13. Isabella, d. (Mrs. John Emmick), Columbus, O.
14. Rebecca, d. (Mrs. Nathaniel W. Smith), Columbus, O.
15. Mary, d. (Mrs. Wm. W. Shannon), Columbus, O.
16. Robert, d. about 1870. Gilman, Ills.

　　—These four sons-in-law on bond for widow as ad-
　　ministratrix in 1826. She was removed two years
　　after.

(2) James Culbertson mar. Emily Jamison, graddaughter of Col. D. Jamison.

Issue:

17. John, d.
18. Robert, b. 1805; d. 1826. Bachelor.
19. David, b. 1808; d. Feb. 17, ——. Tanner, Columbus (Bachelor).
20. James, b. Jan. 30, 1810; d. ? Lawyer. Columbus (Bachelor)
21. Elizabeth, b. 1815; d. Unmarried.
22. Emily, b. Mar. 14, 1819; d. Unmarried.
23. Jane, d. Unmarried.
24. Andrew, b. 1817. Columbus, Ohio.
25. Samuel, b. Feb. 21, 1821; d. 1850. Columbus.

(6) Keziah Culbertson mar. Mr. Brotherton, of Columbus, Ohio.

Issue:

26. Elizabeth Brotherton.
27. Margaret.

(7) Martha Culbertson mar. Mr. Brotherton.

Issue:

28. Robert Brotherton.
29. Margaret.

(8) Margaret Culbertson mar. Mr. Kellar.

Issue:

30. Robert Keller.
31. Jane.
32. Eliza.

SIXTH GENERATION

(16) Robert Culbertson mar. Moved first to Washington, Tazewell Co., Ills. and later to Gilman, Ills.

Issue:

33. Henry, Chatsworth, Ills.
34. Joseph, Gilman, Ills.

(17) John Culbertson mar. ——.

Issue:

35. Samuel.
36. John H.
37. B. Seip.
38. Catherine.

39. George. Unmarried.
40. James. Columbus, Ohio.
    (24) Andrew Culbertson mar. ——.

Issue:

41. Wm. H.
42. David James.
43. Mary Ellen. (Mrs. Turbett).
44. Martha Ann. (Mrs. Hoover).
45. Robert W.
46. Melissa Turbett.
47. Emily Spafford.
48. Alfred, d.
49. Silas, d.
50. Josephine Huff, Mar.
51. James Monroe. Unmarried.
52. Alice Reiselt. Mar.
    (25) Samuel Culbertson mar. Miss Flennieken of Washington Co. Pa. Widow lived in N. Y. City.

Issue:

53. James, b. 1845. Lawyer. Abilene, Kans.
54. Libbie Mary, b. 1847. Lives N. Y. City. (Mrs. McCune).

SEVENTH GENERATION

(33) Henry Culbertson mar. ——. Lived at Washington, Ills., until about 1868 when he moved to Chatsworth, Ills.

Issue:

55. Hettie (Mrs. Woods) St. Louis, Mo.
56. Dessie (Mrs. Douglas) St. Louis, Mo.
57. Charles. St. Louis, Mo.
58. Ida. (Mrs. Smith). Trenton, Mo.; died Feb., 1915.
59. Robert McClane, d. Sept. 6, 1916.
    (34) Joseph Culbertson lived at Gilman, Ills. Mar. and had issue.
    (35) Samuel Culbertson mar.

Issue:

60. Son, d. 61-62.
    (36) John H. Culbertson mar.

Issue:

63. Joseph. Columbus, Ohio. 64-69.
    (40) James Culbertson mar. ——.
    Issue: Three daughters, 70-73.
    (41) Wm H. Culbertson mar.

Issue:

74. Ida Bell, d.
75. Charles. Unmar.
76. Andrew. Unmar.
77. Abe. Unmar.
(42) David Culbertson mar.

Issue:

78. Ralph George.
(43) Mary Ellen Culbertson mar. Mr. Turbett.   Issue:
Three sons and four daughters, viz; 79-86.
(44) Martha Ann Culbertson mar. Mr. Hoover.   Issue:
Four sons and three daughters, viz: 87-94.
(45) Robert W. Culbertson mar.

Issue:

95. Frank.
96. Lillie.
97. Emry.
98. Cory.
99. Clay.
100. Harry.
(46) Melissa Culbertson mar. Mr. Turbett.   Issue: Son
and daughter. 101-102.
(48) Alfred Culbertson mar.

Issue:

103. Rose.
104. Ola May.
105. Iva Bell.
106. Clarence.
(50) Josephine mar. Mr. Huff.
Issue : Three daughters: 107-110.
(52) Alice (Reiselt). Issue: Two daughters 111-112.
(53) James Culbertson mar. Caroline Junkin, of Abilene,
Kans. in 1873.   No issue.
EIGHTH GENERATION
(59) Robert Culbertson mar. Isabel Murdock. Lived Ills.

Issue:

113. Estella (Mrs. Kelley) Brimfield, Ills.
114. Raymond, Akron, Col. who mar. and had issue: Clyde,
     Edith, Harry. Verne. (Harry and wife Mabel both
     met death on wedding trip by R. R. accident.)
115. Helen (Mrs. Tucker) issue: Wilbur and Ruth.   Live
     at Brimfield, Ills.

(VI) COL. ROBERT CULBERTSON AND PROMINENT DESCENDANTS

Col. Robert Culbertson of Hopewell Tp., Cumb. Co., Pa. (later of Columbus, Ohio). *"Was commissioned Lt. Col. of First Batt. Class One of Assr's, called out July 31, 1777; Col. James Dunlap, Major James Carnahan, Lt. Col. same Batt'n and officers called out May 14, 1778. Major Sixth Batt'n, Cumb. Co. Assr's May 10, 1780, Lt. Col. James Dunlap." Census 1790, Hopewell Tp., Cumb. Co., Pa., Self; 2 sons under 16; wife; 5 daughters.

A deed made in Cumb. Co., Pa., Dec. 4, 1779 by Capt. Robert and Capt. Joseph Culbertson of Letterkenny Tp. and James Breckenridge (which they bought of John Montgomery's exrs. in Aug., 1779) deed land in Lurgan Tp. to Col. Robert Culbertson of Hopewell Tp. Cumb. Co., 300 acres for £3000 lbs. land adjoining Daniel Duncan. His brother-in-law or father-in-law, Col. John Davis, bought a portion of this land in 1782 and they participated in a deed of this to Samuel Blythe in 1782. (Robert's wife was Elizabeth (Davis) Irwin). Robert did not live on this farm. He owned a tract of 617 acres in Hopewell Tp. which he sold in 1801 for $36,000. He called this Culbertsonia (See Culbertson's Row in the Eighteenth Century, by John G. Orr), lying between Middle Spring Road and the Cumb. Val. R. R. In 1775 he erected a large stone mansion yet standing on the farm. (This land embraced the Himes and Nevins farms.) James Moore, who bought it, stocked its cellars with wine, built a race course and soon came to grief. Col. Robt. on tax 1762. First deed to him Oct., 1763. Col. Robert was a member of Middle Spring church. He never lived in the "Row." He owned land for a time in Westmoreland and Huntingdon Counties which he sold. Paid pew rent 17s, 6d at Middle Spring. Not old enough to serve in French and Indian War. "He was one of the first settlers of Franklinton (now Columbus), Ohio, in 1801, and purchased extensively on both sides of the Scioto river, above and below, as well as in Columbus and Franklinton. Also took up some military land on Scioto. He was an elder and prominent member of the Presbyterian church of Columbus and signed the call for the first pastor, Rev. Dr. Hoge, of Richmond, Va. Near Col. Culbertson lived many families that

* Wings Hist. of the Three Counties says: "Robert Culbertson, Elder in Mid. Spring Church. Lt. Col. in Jos. Dunlap's 1st Regt.

had been prominent in Franklin Co., Pa., viz.: Stewarts, Johnsons, Jamisons and Lindseys, and a number of Culbertsons had married into these families. For years he was proprietor of a hotel in Columbus. His second wife was the widow of a son of Col. David Jamison, a noted officer in the Revolution, and father of Dr. Horatio Gates Jamison, one of the greatest surgeons of his day ,who was a professor in a medical college at Baltimore, and who was sent by the government as a minister to one of the smaller European countries (From History of Jamison Family). Took out military warrant, 30 acres on Scioto in 1812, nine acres surveyed but no patent returned (5 miles south of Columbus west side).

(50) James Culbertson, great-grandson of Col. Robert, in 1892 was an attorney. He served one term as County Atty. of Dickinson Co., Kans.; three terms as Probate Judge of same county, and twelve years as City Attorney of Abilene, Kans. Was in the Civil War at age of fifteen years as a drummer boy, Co. I, 26th O. V. I. and served until discharged for disability in 1862.

PART FIFTH
Irish Samuel (D) of Chester Co., Pa.
SECTION FIRST

PART FIFTH

SECTION FIRST

SAMUEL CULBERTSON (D) as shown by tax records of Chester county, Pa., first paid taxes in that county in 1730, in Londongrove Township. I found a release made by Wm. Finley, of the same county to a mortgage on property of the heirs of said Samuel Culbertson. The lease recites "that said Wm. Finley and Michael Finley, yeomen, of York County, Pa., were issue of William Finley and Catherine (Culbertson) Finley, his late wife. Also Samuel Daniel, of West Marlboro township, Chester county, Pa., yeomen, and Catherine, his wife, the said Samuel being the only surviving issue of John Daniel, late of Londongrove township, Chester County, aforesaid, deceased, who married Jane Culbertson. Said Jane and Catherine being the only daughters of Samuel Culbertson, deceased.

(D) **Samuel Culbertson,** son of (s) —— Culbertson, of Co. Derry, Ireland, emigrated to America and settled in Londongrove Twp., Chester Co., Pa., in 1729. He does not appear on Tax Records before 1730. Deed Record show that "Geo. Hodgson conveyed to Samuel Culbertson, Apr. 6, 1736, land" in this Twp. He made his will May 15, 1741. Names of his children are obtained from will and deeds. His wife Francis ——, died shortly after. His oldest son was his executor. Died Apr. 1749. In his will he bequeathes to his grandson "Samuel." This is Samuel Daniel. Jane (Daniel) was dead at time of making of Samuel's will, i. e. May 15, 1741. All or part of Samuel Culbertson's children evidently were born in Ireland and as the daughters were mentioned last I would infer that they were younger than the sons. Jane I would infer must have been born about 1720-22. Kittren was first married before 1741. William was executor of his father's estate and conveyed his interest to his brother John, June 18, 1753. In 1755 John placed a mortgage on this to Samuel Fisher for £729. This was released in Dec., 1764. In 1771 (Oct.) this was sold to Geo. Passmore.

It is my belief that William was born 1714-16 and John 1716-18. Samuel Culbertson also gave a mortgage on this property to son-in-law John Daniel, before 1749. In Oct., 1771, John Daniel gave release to this for 20 shillings to John Culbertson.

THIRD GENERATION

Issue:
I.   **William,** b. 1718 or before; d. Apr., 1785. See Chapter XVIII.
II.   **John,** b. 1720 or before; d. May, 1785. See Chapter XIX.
III. **Kittrena** (Mrs. Dongrey in father's will made 1741 and evidently no children by Dongrey; later mar. Wm. Finley. Issue: Michael and William).
IV.   **Jane** (Mrs. John Daniel). Issue: Samuel.

CHAPTER XVIII
FOURTH GENERATION

(I) ·WILLIAM CULBERTSON, son of Samuel (D), of Londongrove Tp., Chester Co., Pa. Was granted land in East Pennsborough Tp., (now Silver Spring Tp.) Cumberland Co., Pa. Made his will in this Co. Mar. Margaret ——. Lived seven miles east of Carlisle, Pa. Warrant issued 1750 for land.

Issue: (Taken from will, corroborated by records.)
1.   Samuel b. 1742; d. Apr. 1, 1807.
2.   William, b. 1760; d. May 18, 1798.
3.   Frances.

FIFTH GENERATION

(1) Samuel Culbertson mar. Elizabeth Loudon, of Pa. Wife b. 1765; d. July 24, 1803. Lived on old farm in Cumberland Co., Pa. (Tanner).

Samuel Culbertson served in Revolution "July 1778, pr. in Third Batt'n Cumb. Co., Pa., Ass'rs., Col. James Bell. Also 3rd Bat. 1781-2, Col. James Bell." (Pa. Arch.) Census 1790, self and wife; 1 son over 16; 1 son under 16. Cumb. Co., Pa.
4.   William, b. 1801; d. 1878.
5.   James, b. Mar. 12, 1803; d. Mar. 30, 1854. Dr.
6.   Sarah, d. young.
7.   Margaret, d. young.

(2) William Culbertson mar. Miss Nancy ("Agnes" in will) Bell of Cumb. Co., Pa. (wife b. 1767; d. Aug., 1805). Lived on farm in Silver Spring Tp., Cumb. Co., Pa.

"William served in Revolution July. 1778, in Third Batt'n Cumb. Co., Pa. Associaters, Col. James Bell. Also pr. in 3rd. Batt'n 1781-82. Col. James Bell" (Pa. Arch.) Col. Bell was his father-in-law. Also probably the Wm. in Frontier Rangers for a time. Census 1790, self and wife; one son over 16 years; 2 sons under 16; 4 females.

Issue:

8.   Sarah, b. 1778-90 (Mrs. Jas. Dunlap).
9.   Margaret, b. 1792-3 (Mrs. Johnston).
10. John, b. 1795; d. Apr. 15, 1850. (Farmer.)
11. Samuel, b. 1796; d. Dec., 1826.
12. Wm. (bachelor).
     (3) Francis Culbertson mar. Mr. Johnston of Va.

Issue:

13. Wm. Johnston.
14. James.
15. John.
16. Jean.

SIXTH GENERATION
     (4) Wm. Culbertson mar. ——. Was a dry goods merchant at Lewistown, Pa., from 1825 to 1837, after which he retired to his farm in Silver Spring Tp., Cumberland Co., Pa.

Issue:

17. Ellen.
18. Thomas H., (Capt.) Killed in railroad accident at Dennison, Tex., in 1889.
     (5) Dr. James Culbertson mar. Miss Mary Steel, of Lewistown, Pa., July 3, 1839. (Lived at Lewistown,. Pa.) Wife b ——; d. Apr. 19, 1885.

Issue:

19. Wm. A., b. May 29, 1840; d. Oct. 3, 1843.
20. Horace J., b. May 25, 1842. Lawyer. Living, Lewiston, Pa..
     (10) John Culbertson mar. Hannah Reed. Wife b. 1809; d. Apr. 15, 1850. (Lived on farm, Silver Spring Tp., Cumberland Co., Pa.)

Issue:

21. C. R., b. 1834; d. July 3, 1884.
22. Wm. F., b. Dec. 13, 1835.
23. Samuel D., b. Sept. 5, 1839. (Dr.) Died.
24. A. F., (dau.), b. June 25, 1841; d. Dec. 29, 1877. Unmar.
25. Joseph W., b. Apr. 28, 1843; d. May 16, 1845.
26. Sarah M., b. Apr. 28, 1843; d. Feb. 25, 1867. Unmar.

27.   James, b. June 12, 1848.   Unmar.

27½   Nancy Bell, b. 1837; d. Apr. 23, 1907.

(11) Samuel Culbertson mar. Polly Urie of Sandy Hill, Perry Co., Pa.

Issue:

28.   Wm. H. (Sandy Hill, Pa.)

28.   Benjamin.

29.   Eleanor.

30.   Rose Anna.

(8) Sarah Culbertson mar. James Dunlap, in 1807, at First Presbyterian church, Carlisle, Pa.

Issue:

31.   John C. Dunlap, b. Feb. 5,. 1809; d. 1869. Bachelor.

32.   Armstrong, mar.; d. Oct., 1850 aet. 36.

(9) Margaret Culbertson mar. John Johnston, in 1809, at First Presbyterian church, Carlisle, Pa.

Issue:

33.   John Johnston.

34.   Culbertson Johnston.

SEVENTH GENERATION

(17) Ellen Culbertson intermar. with John Irvine of Carlisle, Pa.

Issue:

35.   Wm. C., Denver Col.

36.   Kate. Carlisle, Pa.

37.   John. Pittsburg, Pa.

(18) Capt. Thos. H. Culbertson.   Know nothing of descendants.

(20) Horace J. Culbertson mar. Miss Julia M. Watts, dau. or Hon. Frederick Watts, of Carlisle, Pa., Feb. 6, 1867. Wife d. Nov. 6, 1886. Lawyer at Lewistown, Pa.   Graduate of Lafayette College.   Was District Attorney one term.

Issue:

38.   Frederick Watts, b. Mar. 21, 1868. Lawyer. Lewistown.
       State Senator.

39.   Mary Steel, b. Jan. 20,. 1870.

40.   Julia, b. Aug., 1876.

41.   Anna M. R., b. Apr. 2, 1880.

(21) C. R. Culbertson mar. Nancy ———.

Issue:

42.   Charles.

43. Wm.
44. Nelie Bell, d. infancy.
   (22) Wm. F. Culbertson mar. Luella Carmichael, Jan. 13, 1869. Live at Blanchard, Ia. (Served in Union Army three years.)

Issue:

45. Rosa Belle, b. 1873. (Mrs. C. Maginnis).
46. Samuel, b. 1875.
47. Bessie Pearl, b. 1878.
48. Daughter d. infancy.
   (23) Dr. Samuel D. Culbertson mar. Clara K. Culver, of Carlisle, Pa. Moved to Piper City, Ills., in 1867. Physician and druggist.

Issue:

49. John C., b. Feb. 6, 1869. Pharmacist, d. Nov. 22, 1922. Piper City.
50. Samuel Carey (Dr.) b. Oct. 5., 1872. Chicago, Ills.
51. Helen M.,. b. May 15, 1876.
52. Josephine, b. Oct. 24, 1870; d. Apr. 5, 1916. Married.
53 Ira D., b. Feb. 15, 1877; d. July 14, 1877.
   (28) William Culbertson mar. first ——. Mar. second ——.

Issue:

54. Samuel B.
55. Margaret (Mrs. Mohler).
56. Victoria L. (Mrs. Jones)
57. Jane Mary (Mrs. McMillen).
58. Nancy Bell (Mrs. Kinch).
59. John Urie.
60. Sarah Ann (Mrs. Benner).
61. Wm. Frank.
62. James R.
63. Emma.
64. Elmer V.

EIGHTH GENERATION

   (49) John C. Culbertson of Piper City, Ills., married Grace Kirkley. Issue: none.

   (50) Dr. Samuel Carey Culbertson of Chicago, Ills. married Katherine Graham. He is an eminent surgeon of Chicago.

Issue:

65. John Carey.
66. Virginia Graham.

(52) Josephine Culbertson mar. Dr. R. S. McCaughey of Hoopestown, Ills.

Issue:

67. Thomas Culbertson McCaughey.

68. Robert Culver McCaughey.

PROMINENT DESCENDANTS OF WM. CULBERTSON, OF E. PENNSBOROUGH TWP., CUMBERLAND COUNTY PENNSYLVANIA

(1) Samuel was a member of the Supreme Executive Council of the State of Pa. and resided part of time on farm, and part of time in Harrisburg. His son, (5) Dr. James, graduated at Dickinson college, in 1824, and studied medicine and graduated at University of Penna., Apr. 1827. Located at Lewistown, Pa., and practiced there until his death. Another son, (4) Wm., was a dry goods and grain merchant at Lewistown, and later retired to his farm.

(18) Capt. Thomas H., entered the 9th Pa. Cav., as Serg't and mustered out as Capt.; was on staff of Brig. Gen. Thomas Jordon.

(20) Is a prominent lawyer at Lewistown, Pa.; a graduate of Lafayette college. Admitted to bar, 1866. His son, Fred W., is State Senator.

(23) Dr. Samuel D. Culbertson born and raised on the farm. Enlisted in Co. F, 130 Pa. Vol. Inf. under Col. Zinn. Was in battles of Bull Run (second), South Mt., Antietam, Marey's Hill, Chancellorsville, etc. After the expiration of his term of service he took up the study of medicine and graduated from Jefferson Med. College in 1866, and located at Piper City, Ills., in spring of 1867. He was prominent in the care of the wounded in the great Chatsworth railroad wreck in 1877. Was commander of Piper Post, G. A. R., and member of Ill. State Med. Society and member of other societies. His son (50) Dr. Samuel Cary Culbertson is an eminent surgeon of Chicago (1923).

CHAPTER XIX

FOURTH GENERATION

(II) **John Culbertson,** of Armagh Twp., Cumberland Co., Pa. (now Mifflin Co.), who settled there in 1774, moved from Londongrove Tp., Chester Co., Pa. (Deed Records) Mar. Agnes ——. Wife b. 1726; d. 1808. Probably mar. about 1747. Made will in Armagh Tp., Cumberland Co., Pa., in 1785, from which the names of his children are obtained.

Issue:

1. Samuel.
2. William Hannah
3. John, b. 1753; d. Feb. 15, 1808. (Col.)
4. ——, d. (Mrs. John Campbel.)
5. Jean, d. (Mrs. McFarlin); mar. 2nd McCartney.
6. Frances, d. (Mrs. Orr).
7. Agnes, d. (Mrs. Thompson).
8. Elizabeth, d. Unmar. at date of will.

FIFTH GENERATION

(1) Samuel Culbertson moved from Chester Co., Pa., about the time of the Revolution, and settled in the Kishocoquillas Valley, Mifflin Co., (then Cumberland Co.) Pa. Cannot find him on Deed Records of Cumberland Co. Mifflin Co. was organized in 1789. Mar. ——.

Issue:

9. James, living in 1794, Mifflin Co. (Warrant), d. soon after moving to Miffiln Co., Pa.
10. Joseph, d. Went west, do not know where.
11. David, d. Remained in Lancaster Co.(?)
12. Wm., d. 1873, aet. about 93 years.
13. Martha, d. (Mrs. Major, Lewistown, Pa.)
14. John, d. remained in Lancaster Co., Pa.

(2) Wm. Hannah Culbertson no doubt died before 1790. Know nothing about him. Not mentioned in his mother's will; am inclined to think he died a bachelor.

(3) Col. John Culbertson mar. Mary ——*. Lived at Lewistown, Mifflin Co., Pa. Census 1790 Mifflin Co., self

* A John Culbertson and Mary Augeer mar. 1787 at Paxtang, near Harrisburg, Pa.

and one male over 16 (brother?) ; one son under 16; wife and four females.

Issue:

15. Jeremiah, b. 1788; d. 1832.
16. Nancy, b. 1790; d. June, 1825.
17. John, b. 1792; d. Oct., 1866.
18. Lydia Maria, b. 1797; d. Apr.. 1822. Unmar.
19. Wm. H., b. 1800; d. 1821.
20. Samuel, b. 1802; d. Apr., 1865.
21. Ezra Doty, b. 1805; d. July, 1872.

(7) Agnes Culbertson mar. Mr. George Thompson of Huntingdon Co., Pa.

Issue:

22. Nancy.
Do not know others.

SIXTH GENERATION

(11) David. Know nothing of.

(12) ·Wm. Culbertson mar. Barbara Cohill. Was one of the first settlers of Allenville, Mifflin Co., Pa.

Issue:

23. Samuel, d. act. 83.
24. Wm.
25. James, d. June 4, 1891, aet. 75.
25½. David.
25¾. Joel.
26. Ezra.
27. John (Newton, Hamilton, Mifflin Co., Pa.).
28. Nancy.
29. Mary.
30. Martha.

(14) John. Know nothing of.

(15) Jeremiah Culbertson mar. Susan ——. Lived at Boalsburg, Center Co., Pa.

Issue:

31. John, d. Sep., 1889.
32. Susan.
33. Maria.

(16) Nancy Culbertson, mar. Mr. James Watson.

Issue:

34. John Watson.

35.   Wm. H., Ferguson Tp., Huntington Co., Pa.
36.   Ann.
37.   Eliza. (Mrs. Wharton Morris), Milesburg, Pa.
37½. Nancy (Mrs. Orr).
    (17) John Culbertson mar. Miss Maybury. Moved to Lawrence Co., Ohio. Iron merchant.

Issue:

38.   Cambridge, b. 1816. Living 1893.
39.   John, d.
41.   Harriet, d.
42.   Lawrence, d. young.
43.   Mary Anne, d.
    (18) Lydia Maria mar. Wm. Murray of Center Co., Pa.

Issue:

John.
Margaret.
    (20) Samuel mar. Mary A. Kennedy, Sept. 15, 1834, of Philadelphia, Pa. Lived in Adams Co., O.

Issue:

44.   Wm. Wirt, b. Sep. 23, 1835. (Capt.) d. (Congressman.)
45.   Kennedy R., b. May 12, 1840. (Hon.) d.
46.   Mary, d.
47.   Samuel B.
48.   John Janeway, d.
49.   Maxwell.
    (21) Ezra Culbertson mar. ——, iron manufacturer. (Lived in Vinton Co., Ohio.)

Issue:

50.   Arthur.
51.   John J. Oreton, Vinton Co., O.
52.   Marion.

SEVENTH GENERATION

    (23) Samuel Culbertson mar. Mary Gibbons. Lived in the Kishocoquillas Valley, Pa.

Issue:

53.   John. Siglerville, Mifflin Co., Pa.
54.   Wm.
55.   Elizabeth.
56.   Louisa. (Mrs. King), Huntingdon, Pa.
57.   Mary. (Mrs. Dinges), Walla Walla, Wash.

58. Catherine.
59. Libbie.
60. Susan.
61. Ellen.
   (24) Wm. Culbertson mar. Margaret Polliard in 1847. Lived at Rimersburg, Clarion Co., Pa.

Issue:

62. Samuel, d. Feb. 25, 1855.
63. Wm. (Butler, Pa.) Private in Civil War, from Pa.
64. Thurza E. (Mrs. Pollock), Eldred, Pa.
65. Calista J., unmar. Rimersburg, Pa.
66. John C., Knapp Creek, N. Y.
67. Rachael A., d. Nov. 30, 1872.
68. Catherine E. (Mrs. J. T. McIlvaine), Oakdale, Pa.
69. Margaret A. (Mrs. R. C. Crick), Breneman, Pa.
70. Edward A. Coraopolis, Pa.
72. George B. (farmer), Rimersburg, Pa.
   (25) James Culbertson mar. Rachael Jenkins. Lives at Allensville, Mifflin Co., Pa.

Issue:

73. Wilson W., Huntingdon, Pa.
74. James O., near Allensville, Pa.
75. Ira M., near Allensville, Pa.
   (25½) David Culbertson mar. Miss McGowen.

Issue:

76. Lewis.
77. David.
   (25¾) Joel Culbertson mar. Harriet Jenkins.

Issue:

78. Mary (Mrs. Witman), West Liberty, Logan Co., O.
79. Sarah (Mrs. Witman), West Liberty, Logan Co., O.
80. Thos. H., near Bellefontaine, O.
81. Wm., near Bellefontaine, O.
82. John W., Lawrence Co., Pa.
83. Sardis W., near Bellefontaine, O.
84. Elmer E., Bellefontaine, O.
85. Harry F., Altoona, Pa.
86. Frances S., Allensville, Pa.
87. James Bruce, Allensville, Pa.
   (26) Ezra Culbertson mar. Belle Bortle. Lives at Rimersburg, Pa.

Issue:
88.   Cain.
89.   Ezra.
90.   James.
   (27) John mar. Mary J. Morrison. (Saddler.)

Issue:
91.   Anna E. (Mrs. T. Davis) Hagerstown Md.
92.   M. Ella. (Mrs. Sunderland), Hagerstown, Md.
93.   Esther M. Unmar.
Four sons d. infancy. 94-97.
   (28) Nancy Culbertson mar. David Johnson, of Mifflin
Co., Pa.

Issue:
 98.   Wm. Johnson, Pleasant Gap, Pa.
 99.   Mary. (Mrs. Knepp) Allensville, Pa.
100.   Elia. (Mrs. Axe), Menno, Pa.
101.   Sarah. (Mrs. Miller), Reedsville, Pa.
102.   Matilda. (Mrs. McColm), Allensville, Pa.
   (29) Mary Culbertson mar. Edward Wheaton. No issue.
   (30) Martha Culbertson mar. Charles Crownover.

Issue:
103.   Edward Crownover. Mill Creek, Pa.
   (31) John Culbertson mar. Margaret Jones. of Hollidaysburg, Pa. Moved from Boalsburg, Pa., to Tipton, Iowa.

Issue:
104.   John Tipton.
105.   Susan, d.
106.   Ellen, d.
107.   Margaret, d.
   (32) Susan Culbertson mar. Col. Thos. H. Benton, nephew
of Senator Benton, of Ills.

Issue:
108.   Maria. (Mrs. Hon. Ben. Cable, Rock Island, Ills.)
109.   ——, d. infancy.
   (33) Maria Culbertson mar. James Boreland. Issue not
known.
   (38) Cambridge Culbertson, mar. ——.

Issue:
111.   Frank R., Supt. "Tiger Mine", Burke, Idaho.
112.   Harriet, d.
113.   Ella. Ironton, O.

114.   Jennie.   Ironton, O.
115.   Edmund S. Ironton, O.
   (40) Priscilla Culbertson mar. Mr. Shakelford, of Kentucky.   Wife died.

Issue:

116.   George T.   Denver, Colo.
117.   Edmund J.   Mt. Sterling, Ky.   Husband remarried
          to Melissa Walker of Ky.   Son, John W.
   (41) Harriet Culbertson mar. Mr. Clarke, of Lawrence
Co., O.

Issue:

118.   John Clarke, Toledo, O.
119.   Jennie.
120.   Cambridge. Ironton, O.
   (43) Mary A. Culbertson mar. Mr. Garrett.

Issue:

121.   John, d. 1882. Several children.
122.   Samuel, d. 1863.
123.   Mary (Mrs. Henderson). One dau., Mrs. K. H. Perrin, Pikeville, Tenn.
124.   Susan. (Mrs. Glidden), Spokane, Wash. Several children.
   (44) Hon. Wm. Wirt Culbertson mar. first, Miss Jennie
Means, daughter of the millionaire, Thos. W. Means of
Hanging Rock, O., Feb., 1865. Wife d. Sept. 19, 1874.

Issue:

125.   Thomas Means. Ashland, Ky.
126.   ——, d. young.
127.   ——, d. young.
   (44) Hon. W. W. Culbertson mar. second, Miss Lucy Hardy of Frankfort, Ky., in 1880. Widow lives at Miami, Fla.

Issue:

128.   Wm. Wirt, Jr. Miami, Fla.
129.   Henry Hardy.
130.   Lucia Robertson.
131.   Samuel Kennedy.
132.   Jupiter Ammon.
   (45) Kennedy Culbertson mar. ——.

Issue:

133.   Kennedy.

EIGHTH GENERATION

(53) John Culbertson mar. ——. Served in Civil War.
Issue:
134. Wm. H., lumber dealer. Milheim, Center Co., Pa.
135. Nancy Catherine (Mrs. Peacht), Siglersville, Pa.
136. James, d. young.
137. George, d. young.
138. John, d. young.
(104) John Culbertson mar. Martha Black, of Pittsburg, Pa. Lived in Pittsburg.
Issue:
139. Susan J. Unmar. Pittsburgh, Pa.
140. John Benton, Pittsburgh, Pa.
141. Herman Brandt.
125) Thos. M. Culbertson mar. Jan. 27, 1897 to Mary Pollard of Boyd Co., Ky. Issue: Mary, Margaret, Sarah, Viriginia.

PROMINENT DESCENDANTS OF JOHN (II)

(II) John Culbertson was a miller in Londongrove Twp., Chester Co., Pa. His brother, William, conveyed to him property in this Twp., in 1753. I presume that Wm. moved away at this date, to Cumberland Co., Pa., as he does not appear on tax lists for 1757, in Chester Co. John last appears on the Tax Records of Chester Co., in 1773. In "March 6, 1755, John Culbertson and wife, Agnes, gave a mortgage to John Richardson on a grist-mill and one hundred acres of land in Londongrove Twp." He is found on Tax Records of 1769 and '73, when he paid taxes amounting to 7s. 6d., more than any other Culbertson in the county. He sold his farm and mill Nov. 30, 1771. He disappears from tax lists of Chester Co. after 1773. Then moved to Armagh Twp., Cumberland Co., Pa.

His name does not appear on tax records of Chester Co. in 1774. The deed records of Mifflin county, Pa. recite that "John Culbertson and wife Mary, of Armagh Township, Mifflin county, in 1793 deeded land to J. Holly; that said land was sold to John Culbertson, father of aforesaid John Culbertson, by Joseph Armstrong of Carlisle in 1775. John Culbertson, Sr. left one-half of said tract to his son John. Land situated on west branch of Kishocoquillas. The division of said tract was made by mutual consent of heirs." First on tax list Armagh Twp. 1774. I find in the Pennsylvania Colonial Arch. on page 506 in a "list of offi-

cers of Two Associate Regiments of Chester Co., Pa., 1747-
48, John Culbertson, Lieut., Col. Andrew McDowell (Futhey's Hist.)" (There were two Lieutenant John Culbertsons in Chester Co. at the same date. One of these was (II)
John of Londongrove (this chapter) and the other John
Esq. of E. Coln Tp. (died 1767). His wife died in March,
1808. In her will (made in Center Co., Pa.) her devisees
are: Nancy Orr (granddaughter), Jean (McCartney), Elizabeth (daughters); John (son), Jeremiah, grandson John;
son John Culbertson's seven children. No account filed.

In will of Agnes Culbertson, the mother of Col. John Culbertson of Lewistown, which was made Nov. 9, 1807, and
probated March 30, 1808, her residence is given as Alexandria Borough, Huntingdon county, Pa. She bequeathes
the lot in Alexandria to her grandson Jeremiah. The only
other court proceedings were appraisement and inventory
including wearing apparel, furniture, cash, notes, bonds,
etc. and the lot before mentioned. No account filed. A
deed was made by John Taylor and wife, Derry Tp., Cumb.
Co., Pa., to John Culbertson, Jr., of Armagh Tp., Cumb. Co.,
for 120 acres and 118 p. of land in Barree Tp., Bedford Co.,
Pa., adjoining John McNitt and John Dickey's places, made
Feb. 29, 1780. Consideration £2750. This same land or a
portion of it was sold by John Culbertson and wife Mary,
Dec. 3, 1796, said John Culbertson, living in Lewistown,
Mifflin Co., Pa. Sold to James Irwin for £300 lbs. Land in
Barree Tp., Huntingdon Co. formerly in Bedford Co. Futhey's History of Chester Co., Pa., says of John Sr. "Among
those who were leading men at Fogg's Manor at this period
(1767) was John Culbertson." Fogg's Manor is in the
southwestern part of the county, and is one of the oldest
churches in the county, and is only a short distance from
the home of John, of Londongrove Twp. He made his will in
Armagh Twp., Cumb. Co., Pa. Armagh Twp. is at present
in Center Co. Mifflin Co., Pa. was organized in 1787. It
appears he owned land both in Center and Mifflin counties. His grandson, John Culbertson, inherited a part of the
land on which Lewistown is built; sold his share for a horse,
on which he rode to Ohio, in search of work as a clerk. This
was when Lewistown was a small village.

(3) Col. John Culbertson of Lewistown, Pa., Revolutionary Record, Pa. Arch. Vol. VI, p. 574, 5th. Ser. "John Culbertson enlisted in the 8th Battn., Cumb. Co., Pa. Militia,
Capt. Robert Samuels, in 1782 and served in the Kishocoquillas Valley. Also served two other enlistments as his

name appears on a list of those who were paid for services in the War of the Revolution."

(2) William Hannah Culbertson. Revolutionary Services the same Batt'n and Co. as his brother, i. e. 1782.

Pa. Archives, new series by Bruce, says, "Col. John Culbertson was appointed Brigade-Inspector of Center, Mifflin and Juniata Counties, Pa." and in the same vol. his letter of acceptance dated from Lewistown. This was a state office. "He was killed in the performance of his duty, when he was thrown from his horse, his foot hung in the stirrup and he was dragged to death." He was appointed to this office just after the Revolution. He lived at Lewistown and owned the greater part of the land on which that town was built, also a large tract in the Kishocoquillas Valley.

There was a story written by a minister, Rev. Cyrus Jeffries of Perry Co., Pa., called "Jack Culbertson, The Indian Hunter of the Juniata." Could never ascertain who the hero of this story was (or whether he was a real character) if such a real character existed; it may have been Col. John as he lived on the Juniata. Story said to be founded on facts.

Huntingdon County, Pa., records show that Mary Culbertson, wife of John Culbertson, Jr., died 1832-3. Orphans Court records show names of James Watson and wife Nancy's children were: Ann, John, Nancy, Eliza, William, living in Ferguson Tp., Huntingdon County, Pa.; children of Wm. Murray and wife, John and Margaret, of Center County, Pa. Have found no deed or will whereby to connect the Culbertsons and Augeers. The church records of Paxtang Church show that "John Culbertson and Mary Augeer were married Nov. 20 ,1787, by Rev. John Elder." (Pa. Arch.) Omitted in Census 1790, Mifflin County, Pa.

(17) John Culbertson moved from Pa. to Lawrence Co., O.; then removed to Greenup Co., Ky.; was there a few years; after that removed to Lowrence Co., O. He was first engaged in the iron business in Adams Co., O. Engaged in same business in Lawrence Co., O., without much success, but after that was engaged in the Lawrence Furnace, Lawrence Co., O., in which business he remained until his death. After being engaged in this business for some years he succeeded in accumulating a fortune of not less than $160,000. He was one of the most respected and prominent citiens of Southern Ohio.

(20) Samuel Culbertson born in Mifflin Co., Pa., and moved to Greenup Co., Ky., and engaged in merchandising,

but soon after became an iron manufacturer in Ohio and Ky., and moved to West Union, Adams Co., O., and held an interest in the Vinton Furnace. He was a thorough business man and eminently characterized by his religious and moral worth. He died in Adams Co., O.

His son (44) Hon. W. W. Culbertson, received a common school education at Ironton, O. He early became a clerk in his father's store at Greenup Furnace Greenup Co., Ky., and later in same position, Adams Co., O. After this he became storekeeper at Clinton Furnace, and later assistant manager at Vinton Furnace, and subsequently clerk and manager at Ohio Furnace, Scioto Co., O. In 1861 he raised a company of men, and was made a Captain in 27th O. V. I. Was at battle of Lexington, Mo., Blackwater, Springfield and Island No. 10; seige of Corinth, Iuka, second Corinth, and participated in Sherman's march. Was mustered out in spring of '64. After this he took charge of the Pine Grove Furnace. He also took charge of the Buena Vista Furnace, Ky. This furnace was afterwards owned by Culbertson, Means & Culbertson, with W. W. C. as treasurer and supt. He was still later engaged with his brother, Kennedy, in building the new furnace, "The Princess", ten miles from Ashland, and also owned by Culbertson, Means & Culbertson. The large and superior quality of output of all the furnaces, with which he was connected, was due to his energy, sound judgment and progressive spirit. In 1871 he removed to Ashland. Was mayor of the place ,and later was a member of State Senate. Was a member of Republican Nat. Conventions in '76, '80, '84. Chairman Rep. Dist. Com. Was elected to the U. S. House of Representatives, in 1882, from a strong Dem. district. In 1886 was tendered the nomination for Congress by acclamattion, but declined the distinguished honor. His first wife was the daughter of Thos. W. Means, the distinguished millionaire iron manufacturer of Hanging Rock, O. After being a widower six years, he married Miss Hardie, who belonged to one of Kentucky's oldest families. He built the Ashland Ferry, and is a stockholder in Big Sandy Packet Co. Was in the wholesale and retail drug business; also president and secretary of Ashland Foundry and Machine Co.; and president Spring Mont. Distil. Co.

(45) Hon. K. R. Culbertson, a brother of W. W. C. born at Knightstown, Ind., lived several years with his parents in Iowa and Ky., and moved to Ohio at age of twelve. His education was same as his brothers. In 1862, he received a

Captain's commission and recruited Co. F., 91st O. V. I., and served with Gen. Cox, in the Kanawha campaign, with Gen. Crook, at Cloyd Mt.; Gen. Hunter at Lynchburg; and the Shenandoah campaign; Battles of Strasburg and Winchester. On his return from the army, in the fall of '64, he assumed charge of the Buena Vista Furnace, in Boyd Co., Ky. He was a stockholder in several furnaces belonging to Culbertsan, Means & Culbertson, being a member of the firm.

He was olso one of the owners of the Cherokee Iron Works, in. Alabama. Was elected to Ky. State Legislature in 1875, on Republican ticket. He was a man of imposing appearance, as is also his brother.

(21) Ezra Culbertson moved to Vinton Co., O., where his son, John (28), is engaged in ore mining and merchandising.

(40) Priscilla (Culbertson) Shakelford had a son, George (116) who was Col. of the 18th Ky. Regt. of the Union Army. The husband of Priscilla, remarried and had a son, John W. Shakelford, who was a strong Union officer, and was offered a Brig. Generalship by President Lincoln but refused. He was a warm friend of Abraham Lincoln when he (Lincoln) was a school teacher.

(108) Maria Benton mar. Hon. Benjamin Cable, Congressman from Rock Island, Ills.

(125) Thomas Means Culbertson was born Nov. 13, 1870, at Hanging Rock, Lawrence Co., Ohio but was reared in Ashland, Kentucky, where he obtained his elementary education. Completing his early studies at the Georgetown University, in Washington, D. C., he was subsequently storekeeper at Pine Grove Furnace for two years, after which, he was for two years secretary of the Ashland Fire Brick Company. Public spirited and progressive he has been actively identified with the upbuilding of Ashland and a promoter of any of its more important industrial and business enterprises, serving as director and stockholder in each. Always taking an intelligent interest in the affairs of the city, he has been very active in real estate deveolpment and improvement, and in addition to having built many modern residences erected "The Elms", the finest modern apartment building in this section of the Blue Grass state.

Following in the footsteps of his father, he is a staunch Republican, actively interested in municipal and party affairs, and stands for honesty and stability in politics and public matters. On January 1st, 1910, he was appointed by the council as city treasurer for a period of two years, and serving with characteristic fidelity and ability in that capacity. He was appointed by Gov. Willson as a delegate to represent Kentucky at all meetings of the Lincoln Centenary Committee, held at the Lincoln Farm in Larue Co., Feb. 9, 1909, when the corner stone of the Lincoln Memorial was laid and the old log cabin and farm were dedicated. President Roosevelt being the chief of ceremonies and the principal speaker of the day.

SECTION FIRST
Irish Oliver (E) of Chester and Cumberland Co., Pa.
PART SIXTH

Oliver was, in my opinion, a son of (A) John, of Chester Co., Pa. and Shippensburg, Pa., although there is no will, settlement or deed to prove this.

PART SIXTH

(E) **OLIVER CULBERTSON** (Irish) of Chester County, Pennsylvania and Lurgan Tp., Cumb. Co., Pa., a nephew of Andrew, Robert and Samuel of Chester Co., Pa. John Culbertson, Jr., of Lurgan Tp., Cumberland Co., Pa., was his son as the following will prove.

A deed made June 24, 1768, by John Culbertson (no wife given) of Lurgan Tp., Cumb. Co., Pa., to John Herron of Lurgan Township, assignment for order of survey for 100 acres, dated January 20, 1767, No. 2503. Oliver on tax list 1750 acres in Cumb. Co., Pa. Deed made April 21, 1798. "John Culbertson of Southampton Township, Franklin County Pennsylvania, to M. Mauk, Sr. of Southampton Township, same county, one-half interest in 6 acres-17 p. of land in Southampton township same county, part of 314 acres-24 p. granted Oliver Culbertson, January 20, 1767, and one-half interest conveyed John Culbertson by deed from Oliver Culbertson, September 8, 1774." This was in Culbertson Row. A History of Erie County says, "he settled there in 1799. Came from Lancaster Co., Pa."

"John Culbertson and Jean his wife, Erie Township, Allegheney County, Pennsylvania, to John Herron of Southhampton Township, Franklin County, Pennsylvania, May 25, 1799, for 150 acres and 135 p. etc. of land in Southhampton Township obtained by grant from Oliver." John G. Orr says this was the "Row Mill" site owned by the Herrons on Herrons Branch.

Oliver conveyed 157 acres in Lurgan to J. Miller in 1775 (Jean not on deed in 1774 so must have married between 1774-75), for £525. These deeds show John moved to Erie Township, Allegheny County, Pa. (after 1799 this was Erie County). Oliver moved to Armstrong Tp., Westmoreland County, Pennsylvania.

Oliver married Jean, daughter of Irish Andrew Culbertson of Shippensburg. Issue: from will recorded August 2,. 1792. Oliver on Census 1790 in Armstrong Tp., Westmoreland co., Pa., self and wife, one male under 16, grandson, and one female (dau. Mrs. Griff).

Issue:

I. John.
II. Jean (Mrs. Wm. Griff who had a son Wm. Griff).

John to whom Oliver granted a half interest in his land in Lurgan was his son by a former wife. Oliver Culbertson paid taxes in Londonderry Township, Chester County, Pa., in 1735, therefore he must have been born by 1713 anyway. Cannot say whether in America or Ireland. John (2nd) was no doubt a son by first marriage and Jean (Mrs. Griff) by second marriage. Oliver's wife Jean named as executor of his will. Do not know date of Oliver's marriage, possibly in 1768-9 as Jean did not sign assignment of order of survey in 1768 Oliver to John. This would have given 21 years for Oliver to have become a grandfather to his daughter Jean's son, Wm. Griff (will made in 1790). Oliver in his will bequeaths $3.00 to son John (showing he had already received his share of his father's property by deed), daughter Jean £5, Wm. Griff grandson £5, and wife Jean (Executrix) household goods, cattle, etc. Estate not settled in Orphans Court and no deeds in Westmoreland Co. Olivers wife Jean is mentioned simply as Jean in her brother James' will in 1762. She might have been married then as her married name was still Culbertson, her brother did not put her married name in brackets, yet I do not believe she married until after 1768.

John served as private in Capt. Noah Abraham Co., Col. James Dunlap (First) of Cumb. Co. Ass'rs. Enlisted October 2, 1777 (Pa. Arch. Vol. 23, 3rd Ser. p. 623).

"Aug. 30, 1780, Pr. John Culbertson, 4th class, 3rd Co., 4th Batt'n, Col. Samuel Culbertson, Cumb. Co., Pa., Ass'rs." (Pa. Arch. 5th Ser. page 280.)

CHAPTER XX

(1) John Culbertson son of Oliver (made his will in Erie Co., Pa., in 1816), is found on the Census of 1790 in Southhampton Tp., Franklin Co., Pa., given males over 16 yrs. one (self), males under 16, five, females, including wife 4.

Some family records give wife's name Mary. This is wrong unless he married twice. He died in Erie Co., Pa.

FOURTH GENERATION

Issue:

1. John, b. Mar. 5, 1782; d. 1851.

2.   Andrew J., b.
3.   Joseph, d. 1884.
4.   William.
4½.   Son, d. young.
5.   Margaret (Mrs. Geo. Parker) Rising Sun, Ind.
6.   Rebecca (Mrs. Sam'l Davis), Leesburg, Ohio.
7.   Mary Ann (Mrs. Andrew Culbertson) of Erie Co.,
      Pa. (See Sec. First) Son of Andrew of Chester Co.
      and Williamsport, Pa. b. 1773; died Erie Co., Pa.
      1808.

FIFTH GENERATION

*(1) John Culbertson mar. Mary McClemthan, of Edinboro, Erie Co., Pa. Lived at McLallen's Corners, Erie Co., Pa. Wife in will, Susan. (Susan b. Sept. 14, 1781).

Issue:

8.   Robert A., d. Feb. 3, 1873; b. Mar. 12, 1806.
9.   Wm. D.
10.   Stephen.
11.   Sarah.
12.   Jane.
13.   John, d. Feb., 1854.
14.   Mary A.
15.   Susannah.
16.   Andrew.
17.   James.
18.   Sylvester.

(2) Andrew J. Culbertson, born in Erie Co. Went to Pittsburg and learned saddler's trade, and in 1815 left Pittsburg. He probably went from there to Zanesville. He does not appear on tax books of Muskingum Co., O. He soon left Zanesville, and moved to Princeton, Gibson Co., Ind., where he soon after married Hannah Humphreys. Later about 1839—moved to Livingstone Co., Mo., and after 1846, moved to California, where he died.

Issue:

19.   Jane, b. 1820. Sturges, Mo.
20.   John, b. 1822; d. young.
21.   Elijah Humphreys, b. 1824.
22.   Mariah, b. 1827. (Mrs. Geo. Shriver) Montana.
23.   Mary, b. 1831; d. (Mrs .Brigmon.)
24.   Letitia, b. 1833; d. (Mrs. Billings.)

* History of Erie Co. Pa., (1890) says, "John Culbertson Sr., came from Lancaster Co., Pa." This is an error. Came from Franklin Co., Pa.

25. Andrew J., b. 1836.
26. Alexander b. 1838; d. young.
27. Marion, b. 1840. Mar. Pleasant Home, Ore.
28. Theophilus, b. 1843.
29. Frances, b. 1846; d. young.

(3) Joseph Culbertson moved to Salt Creek, P. O., (Chandlersville), Muskingum Co., in 1825. Will Records show that he died in 1884, and that he "bequeaths his property to his wife, Mattie, and to Harriett Reynolds." He had no living children and probably no grandchildren. He raised his nephew (son of his sister), John Boyd Culbertson.

(4) William Culbertson. Know nothing about.

(8) Robert A. Culbertson mar. ——. Lived in Washington Tp., Erie Co., Pa.

Issue:

30. Lucina.
31. Stephen Decatur. Bachelor.
32. Henrietta. Unmar.
33. Marietta.
34. James. Unmar.
35. Melvina. Unmar.

(9) Wm. D. Culbertson mar. ——. Lived at Edinboro, Erie Co., Pa.

Issue:

36. Joseph.
37. Jane. Unmar.
38. Charles.
39. Susannah.
40. Annie.
41. Marietta.
42. Melvern.

(10) Stephen Culbertson mar. ——. Washington Twp., Erie Co., Pa.

Issue:

43. Adaline.
44. Nancy.
45. George. In Civil War.
46. Wesley.
47. Sylvester.
48. Fred. Unmar.
49. Robert.
50. Austin.

(11) Sarah Culbertson mar. Mr. Clemons. Lives at Venango, Crawford Co., Pa.

Issue:

51. Alvius Clemens.
52. Susan.
53. Sophia.
54. Josephine.
55. Oscar D.
56. Sabra.

(12) Jane Culbertson mar. Mr. Allen, of Fairview, Erie Co., Pa. First son was in Civil War.

Issue:
57-63.   Joshua, Leander, Obediah, Martha, Mary, Andrew, Ebenezer.

(13) John Culbertson mar. ——. Lived in Lebuff Twp., Erie Co., Pa.

Issue:

64. Mifflin.   In Civil War.
65. Charles.
66. Celia.
67. Ferris, d. young.
68. Ettie.

(14) Mary A. Culbertson mar. Mr. Skinner. Lived in Waterford Twp., Erie Co., Pa. Now in West.

Issue:

69.   Charles.
69¼.   James.
69½.   Maria.
69¾.   Carolina.
70.   Ranseler.
70½.   Ritner.

(15) Susannah Culbertson mar. Mr. McLallen, of McLallen's Corners, Erie Co., Pa. First son in Civil War.

Issue:

61. Halsey.
72. Fernandc.
73. William.
74. Andrew.

(16) Andrew Culbertson mar. ——. Lived in Washington Twp., Erie Co., Pa.

Issue:

75. Annette. (Mrs. Adams.)

(17) James Culbertson mar. ——. Lives at Union City, Pa.
Issue:
76. Halsey. Unmar.
77. Zilpha. Unmar.
78. . Mary, d. young.

(18) Sylvester Culbertson mar. ——. Died at Geneva, Ashtabula Co., Ohio.
Issue:
79. Frank E. A sailor. Whereabouts unknown.
80. Lee. Unmar.
81. Fred. Unmar.

(19) Jane Culbertson mar. Robert M. Steen. Widow lives at Sturges, Mo.
Issue:
82. John A. Concho Co., Tex.
83. James K. (Rev.) Served in Union Army two years; also, in Regular Army after the War. (Sturges, Mo.).
84. Mary A.
85. Robert T.
86. Letitia F.
87. Sarah J.
88. Wm. A.
89. George W.
90. Francis M.

(21) Elijah H. Culbertson mar. first in 1845, to Eliza Crim. Then lived in Livingstone Co., Mo. Wife died.
Issue:
91. Andrew J., Oct. 29, 1846. Unmar.
92. Caroline, b. Jan. 24, 1849; d.
93. Catherine, b. Sept. 25, 1851.

(21) Elijah H. Culbertson mar. second, in 1854, Helen H. Curtner. Moved to Tarront Co., Texas, about 1860; about 1870 moved to Choctaw Nation, Indian Ter. Now lives at Savannah, Indian Ter. Mechanic and farmer
Issue:
94. Frances, b. Apr. 18, 1855. (Mrs. E. A. Robinson.)
95. Wm. T., b. June 22, 1857.
96. Mary B., b. June 16, 1860. d. unmar.
97. Charles E., b. Feb. 15, 1863.

98. Medora J., b. Aug. 14, 1865. (Mrs. L. Smith.)
99. George D., b. Mar. 1, 1868. Unmar. Accountant.
100. Josephine Ann, b. Aug. 1, 1870. (Mrs. J. W. Collard.)
101. Jesse W., b. Feb. 13, 1873. Mar.
102. Alice M., b. Feb. 15, 1876. (Mrs. Wm. Branson.)
103. John M., b. June 24, 1879. Unmar.

SIXTH GENERATION

(30) Lucina Culbertson mar. Benjamin F. Trow, of Chautauqua, N. Y., Nov. 24, 1850. Now live at McLallen's Corners, Erie Co., Pa.

Issue:
104. B. F. Trow, Jr., b. Mar. 11, 1855.
105. Arminta, b. Apr. 15, 1857.
106. Effie A., b. July 4, 1864.
107. Lester, b. Oct. 7, 1859.
108. Alfred, b. Jan. 14, 1871.

(33) Marietta Culbertson mar. Mr. McLallen.
Issue:
109. Myra.
110. Louvern.
111. Luella.
112. Nellie.
113. Ida.
114. Robert.
115. Harriett.
116. Arthur.

(36) Joseph Culbertson mar. ——.
Issue: ·
117. Elmer.

(38) Charles Culbertson mar. ——.
Issue:
118. Lizie.
119. Flora.
120. Lola.

(39) Susannah Culbertson mar. ——.
Issue:
121. Jennie.

(40) Annie Culbertson mar. Mr. Melspaw.
Issue:
122. Lillie.

123. Wm.

(41) Marietta Culbertson mar. ——, and has three children. 124-127.

(42) Melvern mar. ——, and has one child.   128.

(43) Adaline mar. Mr. Mitchell.
Issue:
129. Ella.
130. Florence.

(44) Nancy Culbertson mar. Mr. Hodge.
Issue:
131. Lodema.

(45) George Culbertson mar. ——.
Issue:
132. Carrie.

(46) Wesley Culbertson mar. ——.

Issue:
133. Emma.

(47) Sylvester mar. ——.

Issue:
134. Myrtie.
135. Maud.
136. De Etta.
137. Grace.
138. Willow

(49) Robert Culbertson mar. ——.

Issue:
139. Blanche.

(64) Mifflin Culbertson mar. ——.

Issue:
140. Minnie.
141. Elvira.
142. Grant.
143. ´ Clyde.

(65) Charles Culbertson mar. ——.

Issue:
145. ——.
145. ——.

(66) Celia Culbertson mar. Mr. Tew.
Issue:
146.   Lottie.
147.   John.
148.   Millie.

(68) Ettie Culbertson mar. ——.
Issue:
149.   ——.

(75) Annette Culbertson mar. Mr. Adams.
Issue:
150.   Fannie.
151.   Forest.

(92) Caroline Culbertson mar. L. H. Priddy. Husband
lives at So. Canadian, Ind. Ter.
Issue:
151.   Melvin, b. Oct. 11, 1878.

(93) Catherine Culbertson mar. Wm. Coil. Both dead.
Issue:

152.   Lemma, b. Aug. 17, 1877. Savannah, Ind. Ter.
(94) Frances Culbertson mar. E. A. Robinson of Kiowa,
Ind. Ter.
Issue:
153.   Odus B., b. May 10, 1872. Salesman, Kiowa, I. T.
154.   Oliver L., b. Mar. 6, 1875; d.
155.   Ora L., b. Mar. 31, 1877.
156.   Ouray L., b. May 12, 1880.
158.   Oscar L., b. July 29, 1886.
157.   Orva L. b. Apr. 17, 1883.
159.   Edward A., b. Aug. 11, 1889.

(95) Wm. T. Culbertson mar. ——.   (Lives at Savannah,
Ind. Ter.)
Issue:
160.   Edwin E., b. Sep. 30, 1888.

(97) Charles E. Culbertson mar. ——.   (Lives at Savannah, Ind. Ter.)
Issue:
161.   Charles E., Jr., b. Apr. 19, 1893.

(101) Jesse W. Culbertson mar. ——. Lives at Savannah, Ind. Ter.
Issue:
162.   Theo. P., b. May 15, 1893.

(102) Alice M. Culbertson mar. Wm. Bronson, of Kiowa, Ind. Ter.

Issue:

163.   James E., b. Apr. 17, 1891.
164.   Jessie May, b. Nov. 2, 1892.

SECTION SECOND
The Second Scotch-Irish Brother and Descendants.

PART FIRST

(Scotch) —— Culbertson settled at Ballygan, near Bally-money, County Antrim, Ireland, and called his settlement "Culbertson Row." He died in Ireland. Tradition says he left Scotland between 1665 and 1690.

SECOND GENERATION

Issue:

I. ——, b. ——; d. ——. "Irish Row." (See Part II, Section II.)

(I) PART SECOND

(I) —— Culbertson, son of Scotch —— Culbertson who emigrated from Scotland to Ireland between 1660-1685? Lived and died in "Culbertson Row", at Ballygan, near Ballymoney, Co. Antrim, Ireland.

Issue:

THIRD GENERATION

(F) **Alexander,** b. May 17, 1714(?); d. Apr. 2, 1756. Capt. (Part Third.)

(G) **Samuel,** b. 1719(?); d. Sept. 9, 1789. (Part Four).

(H) **Robert,** b. before 1722; d. 1762. (Part V) Peters Tp.

* * * * *

(J) **Joseph,** b. ——; d. Dec. 1794. (Part VI). First Cousin of the above three Row brothers.

All four emigrated to America and settled in Lancaster Co., Pa., in what was afterwards Cumberland Co., and still later Franklin Co. Pa. Called their settlement "Culbertson Row". The "Row" proper was seven miles north of Chambersburg; four miles from Rocky Spring and six miles from Middle Spring.

(E) PART THIRD
OF SECTION SECOND

Captain Alexander Culbertson of Culbertson Row, Pa.

(E) PART THIRD

(E) **Capt. Alexander Culbertson,** of Lurgan Tp., Cumberland Co., Pa., emigrated to America between 1730-35, from Ballymoney, Co. Antrim, Ireland ("Irish Row") He settled about six miles from the town of Chambersburg, Pa. —his cousin, Joseph, came over in 1743—and his farm and that of his two brothers and cousin together with the farms of their children, were called "Culbertson Row". In 1755 Alexander Culbertson was commissioned Captain in Col. Burd's Regt. of Pa. Provincial Troops in the French and Indian War. (See Pa. Arch. N. Ser. Vol. 11, p. 519). In April, 1756, he was a Captain in Lieut. Col. John Armstrong's Regt. (Second) of Pa. Prov. Troops and was killed near McCord's Fort, April 2, 1756." (Pa. Arch. New Ser. Bruce.) The following is an account of the engagement, taken from a letter written by Hanse Hamilton, at Fort Littleton, Apr. 9, 1756. (See Pa. Arch. 2nd Ser., p. 540). "These come to inform you of the melancholy news of what occurred between the Indians that had taken many captives from McCords Fort, and a party of men under Capt. Alex. Culbertson, and nineteen of our men, the whole amounting to about fifty, who came upon the Indians with the captives and had a sore engagement, many of both parties being killed, and many wounded, the number unknown." In another letter he says that "The Indians had taken and burnt up McCord's Fort, and taken many captives, upon the news of which Dr. David Jameson, with nineteen men went over to Rays, near Sideling Hill, and came up with the Indians and captives and a sore engagement happened. Only five of our men returned, mostly wounded, Capt. Culbertson and Dr. Jameson were thought to be killed, having received many wounds. Our men engaged two hours, being about thirty-six in number, and would have had the better had not thirty Indians come to their assistance. Some of our men fired twenty-four rounds apiece, and when their ammunition failed, were obliged to fly." McCord's Fort was near Parnels Knob, Franklin Co., Pa., in Egles Hist. of Pa., quoting Col. Tate: "The battle of Bloody Run (the run derived its name from this battle) was fought on the Culbertson tract, a short distance east of the steam mill. Traces of the old road can yet be seen near Culbertson's Hill." (The Culbertson tract belonged to Robert, son of Capt. Alex.) This was also called the Battle of Sideling Hill, and is in the present county of Bedford, at the county line of Bedford and Fulton Counties.

Capt. Culbertson was stationed at Ft. Augusta, near Shamokin, under Col. Burd, in 1755.

Cumberland Co. Records show that inventory of his estate was filed June 11, 1757, about one year after his death. Received warrant for land Oct. 19, 1749. A deed in Cumb. Co. shows he deeded land to one of the McConnells in 1743.

Irish Alexander appears on the tax lists of Fannett Tp. in 1762 (land); in 1767, this was thrown into Colerain and Cumberland Valley Tp., Cumb. Co., Pa. and in 1771 this was thrown into Cumberland Tp., Bedford Co., Pa.

Alexander (Irish) had three tracts of land; one patented 307 acres-30 p. to himself Nov. 18, 1752 (home farm), and two under warrant. One of these was patented to Samuel and in the Orphans Court proceedings one was patented to heirs: Elizabeth, Robert, James, Alexander, John and Joseph (but Joseph having died 1776 did not appear on tax records), Robert, James and Alexander appear on tax records in Cumb. Tp., Cumb. Co., 1771, also together with sister Elizabeth in Cumb. Tp., Bedford Co. in 1771 and in 1776 they are found in Cumb. Tp., Bedford Co., as is also John (land only, not personal) and also 1779 (John 60 acres but disappears after 1779). Tanner Alex was taxed 1770 in Cumb. Tp., Cumb. Co. 200 acres warranted and in 1771, 150 acres located, 2 horses and 2 cows, showing he lived there a short time, but was back in Letterkenny 1772.

A portion of Irish Alex's land lay in Lurgan Tp. Col. Samuel bought this in 1770 from the heirs, while the other heirs took the Bedford Co. land. John is not found on Bedford or Cumberland Co. records after 1779 and not on Census 1790 any place in Penna. He went to Ky. 1779-80.

(E) Capt. Alexander (Irish) married Margaret (there is a record which gives her name Mary Duncan, b. Mar. 15, 1725, in Lancaster Co., Pa., d. Aug. 3, 1794, married Nov. 4, 1740 in Lancaster Co., Pa.) this is an error as his wife's first name was Margaret—whether Margaret Duncan I could not state. Alexander's administrator's—Joseph Culbertson and Margaret Stuart were appointed in March, 1757. Joseph was appointed Gd'n for Samuel and Alex. minors and James Breckenridge gd'n for Robert in 1758. In May, 1763, James, son of Alex. dec'd, being 14 years of age, chose N. Wilson as guardian. Chas. Stuart was appointed guardian of John and Joseph being under 14 years af age. Margaret, widow, had remarried by or before March, 1757. Capt. Alexander's widow remarried before 1758 to John Stuart as shown by the following Release of Dower, "John Stuart and Margaret his wife, being the relict of Alexander Culbertson, dec'd, late of Letterkenny Tp., Cumb. Co., Pa., whom said John Stuart has intermarried, in consideration of £60 paid by Alex's eldest son, Samuel, do hereby release all claim on the estate of Alexander Culbertson. Made 1765, Recorded 1795." Capt. Alex. had two other warrants one of which was in Cumb. Valley Tp., Bedford Co., Pa.

FOURTH GENERATION

Issue:
I. **Samuel** (Col.) b. Dec. 21, 1741; d. Feb. 4, 1817 (Chapter XXI).
II. **Robert** (Col.) b. ——, 174—; d. —— (Chapter XXII)
III. **Elizabeth** (Mrs. Col. Chas. Cessna), b. Jan. 31, 1747; d. ——.
IV. **James,** b. 1748-9; d. 1805. Capt. ("Baron James") Chapter XXIII.
V. **Alexander,** b. 1750; d. Dec. 13, 1822. Tanner Alex. Chapter XXIV.
VI. **John,** b. 1753; d. Nov. 1844. Lieut. (Chapter XXV).
VII. **Joseph,** b. 1755-6; d. 1776 (Killed, Three Rivers, Can., March 1776) Ensign.

A quit claim made Mar. 4, 1770 and recorded in Dec. 26, 1774, by Charles Cessna and Elizabeth, his wife; Robert Culbertson, both of Lurgan Tp., Cumb. Co., Pa. (no wife given of Robert) quit claim to brother, Samuel Culbertson. A quit claim made Dec. 26, 1774, by James Culbertson of Cumb. Tp., Bedford Co. (no wife), Alexander Culbertson (no wife) and John Culbertson (no wife) both of Letterkenny Tp. to brother Samuel Culbertson, 307 acres for £440 in Lurgan and Letterkenny Tps. This is when John attained his majority. Joseph's name does not appear. He would not then have been of age and would have had to have signed by Gd'n or waited until he became of age in 1775-76. Joseph was killed at Three Rivers, Canada, 1776, the above deed states that this land was patented to Alexander Culbertson, father of the above heirs in 1752. Elizabeth Culbertson married Chas. Cessna, March 4, 1770. Col. Chas. Cessna was one of the first Commissioners of Bedford Co.,

Pa., was Major of Second Batt. Bedford Co. Militia, Col. George Wood commanding July, 1776; Lt. Col. First Bat. Bedford Co., Col. Wm. Parker, Dec., 1777; Lt. Col. commanding First Bedford Batt., 1781 (Pa. Arch.). Col. Chas. Cessna was a prominent man in Bedford Co. His father, John Cessna lived near Shippensburg.

Col. Charles Cessna was on Bedford Co., Pa. tax lists 1783. Was a member of the Pa. Assembly 1781. In 1782 the Pa. Gen. Assembly voted that the Controller-General call on all officers of State to give accounting of public monies in their hands. Among those called on was Col. Chas. Cessna. He did not respond and Sept. 11, 1783, the assembly directed that action be brought against him for forgery and perjury. Action was brought. Old Pa. Supreme Court papers show that his case continued from time to time and kept alive on records as late as 1807. This confirms the conclusion that he left the state to escape prosecution. These crimes, I have been informed, at that time were punishable by death. He was not on 1790 or 1800 Census of Pa. and not on tax or other court records. My belief is that he went to Kentucky under an assumed name (either William Cessna or some other name). It is my belief he was the father of Robert Cessna of Muhlenburg County, Ky. There was a record collected by one claiming to be his descendant (Mr. Martin, Supt. of Pullman Car Company on Pa. R. R.) but his record undoubtedly is wrong as he gives Col. Charles Cessna and wife Elizabeth's first born 1788 and other children up to 1802 born in Bedford County. He undoubtedly is giving the children of Charles Cessna of Bedford Co. Pa., a son of Major John Cessna, Jr., of Bedford Co., Pa. (a brother of Col. Charles) and mentioned in Major John Cessna's will 1794. This Charles would have come of age about 1788.

While it is possible that Wm. Cessna of Muhlensberg Co., Ky., was Col. Chas Cessna in disguise, yet he may have been Wm. Cessna of Franklin Co., Pa., son of John Cessna, Sr., of Shippensburg. Can find no court record of either one in Ky.

Alexander Culbertson's family furnished more officers to the Revolutionary Army than any other Culbertson family. Col. Chas. Cessna and wife not on 1790 Census of Penna. Probably went to Ky. The Census of 1830 for Muhlenburg Co., Ky., gives Elizabeth Cessna (widow of Robert). This is the only Cessna found. She was a daughter of Capt. John Culbertson of Muhlenburg Co., Ky.

A Wm. Cessna died at Cessna, Ills., many years ago who may have been Wm. Cessna, early settler of Muhlenburg Co., Ky.

CHAPTER XXI

FIFTH GENERATION

(I) **Col. Samuel Culbertson,** eldest son of Irish Alex. Culbertson of "Culbertson Row," Pa. Samuel was like a father to his brothers and sisters. His will was made June 9, 1813, and probated Feb. 27, 1817, in Greene Tp. Left his widow $2000; left $1000 to each of his children, but sums given them during life were to be charged off against this. His property was sold and amounted to $10,000, paid out—exclusive of sums he gave children during his lifetime. Executors Gen. John Rea, Adam Harbison and John Thompson. Final acc't filed 1824 and showed all bequests were paid. He only left "Devil Alex" $27, but Alex's children got $400. In regard to Col. Samuel's mother, Margaret Stewart, we do not know just where she resided or if she had children by John Stuart, or when she died. Col. Samuel married first Margaret Henderson of Lurgan p., Cumb. Co., Pa., Mar. 20, 1761. Wife b. 1743, d. April 30, 1775. Census 1790 self and wife, 3 males over 16 years 6 under 16; 3 females.

Issue:
1. Gustavus, b. Dec. 28, 1761; d. young.
2. Elizabeth, b. 1764; d. young.
3. Alexander ("Devil Alex"), b. 1765; d. in fifties.
4. Margaret, b. 1767, d. (Mrs. Cunningham.)
5. Robert, b. 1770; d.
6. Joseph, b. 1772; d.
7. Samuel, b. Apr. 8, 1775; d. Feb. 20, 1811.

(I) Col. Samuel Culbertson mar. second, Miss Elizabeth McClay of Lurgan Twp., daughter of Hon. John McClay, Feb. 4, 1777, at Rocky Spring Church. (Wife b. 1755; d. June 4, 1817).

Issue:
8. John, b. Oct. 1777, or 8 d. July, 1830.
9. Elizabeth, b. Mar. 3, 178—; d. June, 1836.
10. James, b. Oct. 14, 1785; d. Feb. 22, 1847. (Minister.)
11. Charles McClay, b. Oct. 19, 1787; d. Apr. 20. 1848.
12. David, b. Jan. 16, 1789; d. Jan. 1839 Unmar. Franklin Co., Pa.

13.   Eleanor, b. Aug. 9, 179—; d. Jan. 19, 1852.
14.   Amelia, b. Oct. 19, 179—; d.
15.   Cynthia, b. May 12, 179—; d. young, after 1813.

SIXTH GENERATION

(3) Alexander Culbertson ("Devil Alex") mar. his cousin Margaret daughter of James Culbertson (IV). Lived in South Mountain, Franklin Co., Pa. (Distiller). Census 1800 self and wife age under 45; one son under 10 years; 3 daughters under 10 years.

Issue:
16.   Margaret, b. ——; d. March 20, 1862.
17.   Polly. d.
18.   Alexander Samuel, d.
19.   Jane, d. Unmar.
19½. Elizabeth.

(4) Margaret Culbertson intermar. Wm. Cunningham, of Franklin Co., Pa. Lived near Brownsville, Pa. Had issue; do not know names.

(5) Robert Culbertson mar. first ——. Lived in "Row" until after his second marriage, when he moved to Bedford Co., Pa. Living with father 1800. Census 1810-20. Inn-keeper. Bedford, Pa. Went to Md., 1821. Do not know which children are by each marriage.

Issue:
20.   Samuel, b. 1807; d. Nov. 21, 1887.
21.   Joseph, b. ——; d.
22.   Mary, b. 1805; d. 1891. (Mrs. Lindsay).
23.   Emily, b. ——; d. ——. (Mrs. Betts.)
24.   Son, d. young.
25.   Son, d. young.

(6) Joseph, son of Col. Samuel. A nephew living in 1892 stated Joseph moved to Meadville. Court Records of Craw-ford Co, Pa. show no Culbertsons. I find in final acct. of John Thompson ex'r Col. Samuel that all of the bequests of Col. Samuel were paid.

(7) Samuel Culbertson moved from "Row" to Maysville, Ky., in 1796. Mar. Miss Martha Mitchell, from near Brad-docks Field, Pa., at Maysville, Ky., Dec. 12, 1798. Merchant; wife b. Sept. 2, 1777; d. Sept. 2, 1836.

Issue:
26.   Samuel Henderson, b. Sept. 25, 1800; d. after 1855.
27.   Julius (Dr.) b. Nov. 12, 1804; d.

28. Cicero, b. Feb. 5, 1807. d. young.
29. Milton, b. Aug. 27, 1808; d. (bachelor).
30. Margaret, b. Dec. 25, 1810; d.

(8) John Culbertson of "Row" and Chambersburg, Pa., mar. by Rev. Francis Herron to Miss Margaret Greer, of Franklin Co., Pa., May 8, 1804. Farmer and merchant.

Issue:
31. Samuel, b. April, 1805; d. young.
32. Thomas Greer, b. April 11, 1807. Living 1893.
33. James, b. June, 1809; d. Aug., 1846.
34. John McClay, b. July, 1811; d. 1848 in California.
35. Elizabeth G., b. 1813; d. in infancy.
36. Sarah Milnor, b. Aug., 1815; d. Aug., 1880.
37. Cynthia McClay, b. Aug., 1813; d. July, 1845.
38. Elizabeth Greer, b. Mar., 1823; living, 1893.
39. Mary Jane, b. July 1826. Living 1893.

(9) Elizabeth Culbertson mar. Major-Gen. John Rea, of Chambersburg. Pa.

Issue:
40. John Rea (Dr.), d. 1885. Mar. Hannah B. Laughlin, of Pittsburgh. Had issue: Dr. Samuel C. Rea; Mary A., d. 1885; Elizabeth Laughlin (Mrs. E. L. Simonds).
41. William Rea, b. ——; d. 1892. Mar. Matilda Robinson, of Pittsburgh. Had issue: Wm. H., lives at Pittsburg.
42. Samuel Culbertson, d. Pittsburg. Mar. Elizabeth J. McKee. Had issue: Mrs. Ayres.
43. James D. Rea, d. 1858. Hollidaysburg, Pa. Mar. Ruth Blair Moore of Hollidaysburg, Pa. Issue: Thomas (bachelor); Samuel, mar. Miss Black; Jane Rea.
44. David, d. young.
45. Elizabeth McClay (Mrs. Wm. Scott, of St. Louis). Living 1893, aet. 75. Issue: Helen Rea Scott (Mrs. McDonald), St. Louis, Mo.
46. Andrew Jackson, mar. Jane Maloney (d. July 4, 1841, at Hollidaysburg, Pa.) Issue: Jas. N., Johnstown, Pa.
47. William, d. young.
48. Charles, b. 1823. Lived at Pittsburg. Mar. Elizabeth Cochran. Served three years in Civil War. Priv. Co. F., 46 Pa. V. I. Issue: Chas. Stanley, b. 1859; Louisa Harbaugh, b. 1875.
49. Hannah, d. young.

(10) Rev. James Culbertson moved to Zanesville, O., in 1811. Mar. first Miss Sarah Milnor of Pa. Wife d.
Issue:
50. ——, d. infancy at birth. Both buried Pioneer Park Hill, Zanesville, O.

(10) James Culbertson mar. second Miss Eleanor Colhoun, daughter of John Colhoun, of Chambersburg, Pa., Oct. 17, 1817. Wife b. Mar. 28, 1792; d. Feb., 1853.
Issue:
51. Milnor, b. Aug. 15, 1820; d. Jan. 3, 1828.
52. John Colhoun, (Maj.) b. Oct. 27, 1822; d. July 18, 1872.
53. Dr. Howard (Capt.), b. Feb. 17 1828; d. June 18, 1890.
54. Elizabeth Ann, b. Aug. 4, 1830; d. 1914.

(11) Charles McClay Culbertson, Sr., raised in Row and moved to Madison, Iowa, where he died. Mar. Sep. 8, 1809, to Elizabeth McKemey, of Pa., a descendant of the first Presbyterian minister in the United States. Wife b. Aug. 15, 1872; d. Dec. 4, 1823.
Issue:
55.   Elizabeth McC., b. Dec. 13, 1810; d. 1885.
55½.   Mary Jane, b. Jan. 5, 1812; d. Mar. 15, 1815.
56.   Josephine, b. Sep. 9, 1813; d. 1836.
57.   Samuel, b. Jan. 8, 1815; d. Sep. 12, 1815.
58.   James McKemey, b. Feb. 23 , 1817; d. 1864. (Bachelor.)
59.   Charles McClay (No. 2), b. Aug. 5, 1819. Living, 1893.
60.   Milton, b. Jan. 24, 1821. Whereabouts unknown. Went west, probably to Australia.

(11) Charles McClay Culbertson mar. second Mariah Logan of Virginia, July 25, 1825. (Wife b. Sept. 9, 1799, Peru, Neb., d. Oct. 1900.)
Issue:
61   Margaret Manison, b. Aug. 17, 1826; d. 1854.
62. Samuel, b. Jan. 22, 1828.
63. Mariah Jane, b. Feb. 13, 1830; d. Feb. 5, 1920.
64. Emily Edith, b. Feb. 11, 1833.
65. Julius Theodore, b. Oct. 15, 1838. (Bachelor.) Was Union soldier in Rebellion.

(12) David Culbertson in the first edition of this Genealogy was credited with having gone to Kentucky; this is an error. Rev. Thos. G. Culbertson of Wheeling, W. Va., who left the row about 1828 stated in 1892 that David was

a bachelor. There was a David Culbertson for whom an administrator was appointed Jan. 19, 1839 (Ad'm'r. Wm. S. Davis). Davis was a surveyor and court official of that county. There was no account or appraisement filed. I take this evidence as pretty conclusive that this was Col. Sam's son and that he was a bachelor and had no property as there were no deeds to or from him or his admin'r. All of Col. Sam's descendants had left Franklin Co. by this time.

(13) Eleanor Culbertson mar. Wm. McEwen or McCune of Franklin Co., Pa. before 1813 in Franklin Co., Pa. In 1833 they moved to near Columbus, Ohio, and in 1836, moved to Lacon, Marshall Co., Ills. He was injured the following year in a stage coach accident and died soon after. Eleanor (Culbertson) McCune was a devisee in her father's will written 1813 and she was left $800, exclusive of what she had already received. Executors accounts show she was paid her share. After her husband's death she continued to reside in Lacon, Ills. and was an active member of the First Pres. Church of that place. She is buried there. Her husband died July 14, 1837.

Issue:

(a) Samuel Culbertson McCune (Presbyterian minister) mar. Lettie Clark of Penna. Issue: Alex., d. in Civil War; Dr. Harold of Kirkville, Ia., who had a daughter who was a nurse in the World War; Mary Ellen (Mrs. Lake of Gallipolis, Ohio.); Jennie (Mrs. John Watt); Elizabeth (Mrs. Jos. DeVault); Chas. Culbertson.

(b) Emily Culbertson McCune mar. Wm. Spangler of Franklinton, Ohio (b. July 18, 1811) Mar. 1835, wife born July 16, 1818; d. June 29, 1883.

Issue:

1. Samuel McC. Spangler b. 1836, d. June 24, 1877, mar. Minerva Stevenson; 2, Wm. Findlay Spangler, b. June 26, 1838, d. Feb. 8, 1908, and mar Mary Dougal Porter, daughter of Rev. Geo. Porter and Sarah Jane McCoy, a granddaughter of Jane Culbertson, the latter was a daughter of "Gentleman James" Culbertson of Culbertson Row, Pa. in Millerstown, Pa., Feb. 20, 1841, d. Jan. 12, 1912; 3, David Spangler, b. 1840, d. age 21; 4, John Breece Spangler, b. Dec. 31, 1842, d. Feb. 21, 1903, mar. Eliz. DeVault, b. April 17, 1849; 5, Margaret E. Spangler, b. Jan. 2, 1844, d. Jan. 11, 1868, mar. J. R. Iliff

Nov. 3, 1833, d. Apr. 2 1906; 6, James Culbertson
Spangler (twin) b. Nov. 3, 1847, mar. Armanda J.
Carrithers, b. Feb. 3, 1851. Live at La Rose, Ills.,
mar. Jan. 18, 1872; 7,Chas. Culbertson Spangler
(twin to James) b. Nov. 5, 1847, mar. Margaret
Kelly; 8, Mary Spangler, b. Feb. 13, 1851, mar.
James Ramp, lives Lacon, Ills.; 9, infant Emma J,,
d. young; 10, Carrie A. Spangler, b. Apr. 8, 1860,
lives Peoria, mar. H. G. Foster; 11, Ida Belle
Spangler, b. May 21, 1863, mar. Wm. T. Iliff,
Peoria

(c) Mary Jane McCune, b. May 1816, d. 1863. Mar. W. T.
Clemens, Feb. 9, 1841. Issue: Chalmers and Thompson.
(d) Eleanor McCune, b. Penna. Aug. 24, 1824, d. La Rose,
Ills. Mar. Harvey Scott. Issue: Wm. and Margaret.
(e) Elizabeth M. McCune, b. Jan. 3, 1826, d. June 3, 1865.
Mar. Abija Smith Sherwood. Issue: Eliz. and Ed Lomax.
(f) Wm. McCune, d. June 19, 1854, age 26 years.
(g) Margaret McCune, b. Aug. 31, 1830. Mar. Jacob Hol-
lenbach of Rehobeth, Perry Co., Ohio. Issue: Margaret E,
Josiah K., Jacob H., Clara Belle, Chas. C.
(h) John, d. infancy.
(14) Amelia Culbertson mar. John Thompson of Franklin
Co., Pa., in 1811, and moved to Blue Rock Tp., Muskingum
Co., Ohio, in 1825. Made will 1842.
Issue:
79. Elizabeth.
80. Samuel Culbertson.
81. Joseph.
82. James.
83. John Rea.
84. Amelia.

SEVENTH GENERATION

(16) Margaret Culbertson mar. Joseph McAnulty. (Children dropped "A" from name.) Joseph McNulty died Apr.
16, 1854.
Issue:
85. Samuel McNulty. Bachelor.
86. Charles. Bachelor.
87. William, d. 1890. Lived Ashland, O. Hotel proprietor.
88. Isaac. N. Y. City b. Apr. 27, 1827; d. Nov. 16, 1897.
      N. Y.
89. John. Bachelor.

90. Augustus.
91. Margaret. (Mrs. Bittenger.)
92. Eliza. (Mrs. Wm. Baughman.)
93. Elizabeth, b. ——; d. June 3, 1852.

(17) Pollie Culbertson mar. Wm. C. Greer. No issue.
(18) Alexander Samuel. Know nothing of.
(20) Samuel Culbertson mar. Miss Matilda De Hart in 1831. Moved to Williamsport, Md.
Issue:
94. Samuel, b. 1841. Hagerstown, Md.
95. Mary.
96. Matilda.
97. Kate, b. 1842.
98. Ida.
99. Cora.

(21) Joseph Culbertson mar. ——. Manufacturer woolen goods. Emmettsburg, Md.
Issue:
100. Elizabeth (Mrs. Prof. Gilson.)
101. Samuel. York, Pa.
102. John. York, Pa.
103. James. Hanover, Pa.
104. Robert, d. young ⎫ Twins
105. ——, d. young. ⎬
106. Louis Oscar, b. July 11, 1852. Gnadenhutten, Ohio.
107. William. Carlisle, Pa.
108. Son.
109. Sarah. d. aet. 13.

(26) Samuel H. Culbertson mar. Catherine ——. Lived in Montgomery Co., Ohio, in 1856.
(27) Dr. Julius Culbertson mar. Mary Charlotte Purnell at Natchez, Miss., Feb. 11, 1834. Lived at Madison Parish, La.
Issue:
110. Levi Purnell, b. 1835; d. 1865 at Alto, Tex. (Bachelor.)
111. Julius. Ft. Worth, Tex.

(29) Milton Culbertson mar. Miss Margaret Byrne, of Philadelphia, Pa. No issue. Was a stock raiser at Maysville, Ky.
(30) Margaret Culbertson mar. first, Thos. D. Purnell, May 12, 1836, at Madison Parish, La.
Issue:
112. Mattie Purnell (Mrs. Irvine.)

113. ——, dau., d.

(30) Mrs. Margaret C. Purnell mar. second Rufus Case, a man of wealth.

Issue:

114. Laura Case, d. young.
115. Margaret Extina, Mar. (Cleveland, Ohio.)

(32) Thomas Greer Culbertson mar. first by Rev. Francis Herron, to Miss Sarah Ann Steel Greer, Sep. 21, 1828. (Wife d. 1837.)

Issue:

116. Margaret Greer, b. June 30, 1830; d. May, 1870.
117. Mary Adaline, b. Jan., 1833. (Mrs. H. C. Greer.)
118. David Thompson, b. Feb., 1835; d. Mar. 1839.

(32) Thomas Greer Culbertson mar. second Martha Dickey, of Wheeling, W. Va., Feb. 1840. Wife d. Feb., 1883.

Issue:

119. Sarah Jane, b. May, 1842.
120. John Dickey, b. Sept., 1844. Wheeling, died.

(33) James Culbertson mar. Louisa S. Willey, of Baltimore, Md., Sep. 21, 1835.

Issue: (Baltimore, Md.)

121. Isaac Greer.
122. Annie, d. young.
123. James. Killed in railroad accident, 1861.
124. Thomas, d. infancy.
125. Margaret, d. young.
126. Louisa.

(36) Sarah Milnor Culbertson mar. Robert McClean, of Fayetteville, Pa. Both dead.

Issue:

127. William, d. in Union Army.
128. Margaret Culbertson (Mrs. Falconer) N. Y.
129. Agnes (Mrs. A. Campbell). Kansas City.

(37) Cynthia McClay Culbertson mar. Thos. Owings, Owings Mills, W. Va., Oct. 10, 1839. Both dead.

Issue:

130. Wm. Owings, d.
131. Alfred. Wheeling.

(38) Elizabeth Culbertson mar. Rev. F. S. DeHass, Apr. 14, 1845. Lived in Wheeling. Widow lived in N. Y. City.

Issue: None.

(39) Mary Jane Culbertson mar. Alfred Caywood, of Somerset, O., May 3, 1848. Live at Clarksburg, W. Va.

Issue:

132. Charles Caywood, d.
133. John.

(52) Major John Colhoun Culbertson mar. Mrs. Mary Thomson Crawford, of Chambersbug, Pa., dau. of Hon. Wm. Thomson, in 1850. Moved to Iowa City; later to Springfield, Mo. Banker.

Issue:

134. Ellen.
135. Mary, d. young.
136. Clementina, born ——; d. Nov., 1910.
137. Wm., d. young.
138. Lucy, d. Oct. 9, 1918.
139. Frank. Civil Engineer, Pa. R. R. b.——; d——.

(53) Capt. Howard Culbertson, M. D., mar. Miss Louisa Maria Safford, dau. of Dr. Elial Safford, of Parkersburg, W. Va., Nov. 16, 1854. Wife b. June 24, 1836; d. Feb. 28, 1885.

Issue:

140. Herbert John, b. Aug. 23, 1855; d. June 3, 1897.
141. Anne Virginia, b. Nov. 16, 1857; d. Dec. 6, 1918.
142. Ernest (mar. Miss Gilmore), b. June 30, 1860; d. Aug. 1895.
143. Sydney Mathiot, b. Nov., 1864.
144. Lewis Rogers (Dr.), b. Jan. 16, 1867.
145. Cornelia Swift, b. June 25, 1869.
146. Claude Lanier, b. Jan. 19, 1877; d. Dec. 13, 1918.

(54) Elizabeth Ann Culbertson mar. Rev. W. E. Ijams, a prominent Presbyterian minister, formerly of San Francisco, Cal.; Germantown, Philadelphia, and Iowa City. No issue. Both dead.

(55) Elizabeth McClay Culbertson mar. first Col. Joshua Wilkinson, U. S. A., of Newport, Ind.

Issue:

147. John. Mar. Had a dau. Alice (Mrs. Dr. R. Gillette, Danville, Ind.). Both dead.

Issue:

148. Mary Belle. (Countess Uda). Naples, Italy.
149. Kate Scott, Danville, Ills.
150. W. H. Scott, Jr., d. aet. 20, from Army service during Civil War.

(56) Josephine Louisa Culbertson mar. first, Rev. John Black, Presbyterian minister. Moved to Ky. and Miss., where they resided eleven years; then moved to Allegheny, Pa. Husband died.

Issue:

151.   John Charles (Brig. Gen.), dead. Ex. Com. Pensions, Chicago. Issue: Helen, Grace, John D.
152.   Wm. P. (Capt.) Lawyer, Chicago. No living issue.
153.   Rose, d. Unmar.
154.   Mary. (Mrs. Geo. Hart.) Chicago. No issue.

(56) Josephine L. Black mar. second, Dr. Wm. Fithian, a man of means, of Danville, Ills. Mar. in 1850. No issue. Both dead.

(59) Charles McClay Culbertson (No. 2), mar. Miss Rhoda A. Williams, at Newport, Ind., Dec. 1, 1842. Wife b. Apr. 11, 1825.

Issue:

155.   Willis Godfrey, b. Sep. 1843. Chicago.
156.   James McKemey, b. Sep. 10, 1845; d. May 6, 1876. (Bachelor.)
157.   Florence.
158.   Candace Josephine, b. Nov. 4, 1849. Unmar.
159.   Charles McClay, b. Sep. 4, 1852. (Bachelor.)
160.   Lucy, b. Apr. 10, 1855.
161.   Mary, b. Mar. 16, 1858.
162.   Rhoda Anna, b. Mar. 20, 1860.

(61) Margaret Manison Culbertson mar. Dr. Draper of Danville, Ills.

Issue:

163.   Charles Draper, d. 1850.

(62) Samuel Culbertson mar. Eliza Jane Brazelton, of Lancaster, Ind., Nov. 19, 1850.

Issue: (Peru, Neb.)

164.   Charles Wm., Shelbyville, Ind.
165.   Alice.
166.   Lucius. (Bachelor.) Lancaster, Ind.
167.   Nettie.
168.   Harry Wilbur.
169.   Nelia Bell, b. Nov. 28, 1867.
170.   Leafie Emma, b. June 13, 1870.
171.   Grace Daily. Unmar. Peru, Neb.

(63) Maria Jane Culbertson mar. June 8, 1850 to William Daily (born July 24, 1828. Still living), Auburn, Neb.

Issue:
172.   Harry Clay Daily, d. infancy.
173.   William, d. infancy.
174.   Charles, d. infancy.
175.   Alice Estella.
176.   Anna Maria.
177.   Joe.
178.   Katherine, d. 1918.
179.   Sarah Emily (also called "Fay" Daily Hoadly), b.
       Oct. 14, 1864.

EIGHTH GENERATION

(94) Samuel Culbertson mar. ———. U. S. Int. Revenue Collector, Hagerstown, Md.

Issue:

180.   Mary C.
181.   Alice M.

(95) Mary Culbertson mar. Louis F. McComas, of Hagerstown, Md.

Issue:

182.   Boy.
183.   Boy.
184.   Boy.
185.   Girl.
186.   Girl.
187.   Girl.

(96) Matilda Culbertson mar. D. Darby, of a prominent manufacturing firm, of Baltimore, Md.

Issue:

188.   Boy.
189.   Boy.
190.   Boy.
191.   Girl.
192.   Girl.
193.   Girl.

(97) Kate Culbertson mar. first Rev. Dr. Joseph Moody, of Shippensburg, a prominent minister, in 1858. Husband died.

Issue:

194.   Florence Culbertson.

(97) Kate C., mar. second, Burns Downey, a lawyer, of

Leesburg, Va. No issue. Husband d. Widow lived at Baltimore.

(98) Ida Culbertson mar. J. W. Trammelle of Martinsburg, Va. Lived at Oxford, Neb.
Issue:
195.   Albert C. Trammelle.

(99) Cora Culbertson mar. B. Frank Darby, a prominent manufacturer cf Baltimore, Md.
Issue:
196. Albert W. Darby.
197.   Ethel M.
198.   Walter C.

(100) Elizabeth Culbertson mar. Prof. Gilson.
Issue: Not known.

(102) John Culbertson mar. ——.
Issue: Lived at York, Pa.
199.   Daughter, d.
200.   Daughter, d.

(106) Louis Oscar Culbertson mar. ——. Manufacturer carpets, d'lr's windmills, etc. Gnadenhutten, Ohio.
Issue:
201.   L. May, b. Dec. 12, 1880.
202.   Elmer Ellsworth, b. Apr. 19, 1884.
203.   Harry Winfield, b. Nov. 28, 1887.
204.   Louis Oscar, Jr., b. Aug. 15, 1891.

(107) Wm. Culbertson mar. ——. Lived at Carlisle, Pa. Know nothing of issue.

(111) Julius Culbertson mar. Emma Searles, of Vicksburg, Miss., Ncv. 15, 1860. Lived formerly at Madison Parish, La.; later at Maysville, Ky., and recently at Ft. Worth, Tex. Wholesale wagon manufacturer.
Issue:
205.   Julius, d. infancy.
206.   Carrie Purnell.
207.   Levi.
208.   Mary Markham. Unmar.
209.   Milton, St. Louis, Mo.
210.   Charles Searles.

(116) Margaret Greer Culbertson mar. Wm. Clark, of Martins Ferry, W. Va.
Issue:

211. Clara Greer Clark. Unmar. Brooklyn, N. Y.
212. ——. (Mrs. Burritt.)
213. Thomas Greer (Rev.), Grand Rapids, Neb.

(117) Mary Adaline Culbertson mar. Henry C. Greer.
Issue:
214. Daughter.
215. Son.

(119) Sarah Jane Culbertson mar. S. B. McColloch, of
Wheeling, W. Va., Sept. 1, 1863. Owatonna, Minn.
Issue:
216. Martha. (Mrs. C. F. Williams.) Minneapolis.
217. Maria Reed. Unmar. Owatonna, Minn.

(120) John Dickey Culbertson mar. Sallie McF. Tingle, of
Wheeling, W. Va., Aug. 25, 1870. Lived at Wheeling. Iron
manufacturer. Widow lives at Pittsburg, Pa.
Issue:
218. John D., Jr., Pittsburg, Pa.
219. Tingle Woods. Wheeling, d.

(121) Isaac Greer Culbertson mar. first, Sarah E. Baur-
ber, Baltimore, Md. Wife died Sept. 15, 1868.
Issue:
220. Anna Greer Culbertson (Mrs. Capt. Jos. Cole.)
221. Mary (Mrs. Frank Bantz.)
222. Warren Robuck.
223. Wm. Greer.

(121) Isaac Greer Culbertson mar. second in Mar., 1869,
to Mrs. George Hilbert.
Issue: 224, Harry Stone; 225, James Cloud, single; 226,
  Mattie, single, d.; 227, Edith, single, d.; 228, Amy,
  single; 229, Bessie, single; 2 latter Cecilton, Md.

(126). Louisa Culbertson mar. first H. C. Moores. No
issue. Husband died. Mar. second, D. H. Seebold, of Baltimore, Md. Second husband dead.
Issue:
229½. Mary Louise, d.

(134) Ellen Culbertson mar. Frank Hill of Carthage, Mo.,
a wealthy miller and bank president. Husband dead.
Issue:
229¾. James Fiske.
230. Henry.
231. Elizabeth.

232.   Frank Culbertson.
233.   Eleanor Norwood.

(135) Clementine Culbertson mar. J. H. Culbertson, her cousin.

Issue:
234.   Daughter, d. infancy.

(138) Lucy Culbertson mar. Henry C. Whitlock, a wealthy lawyer, of Philadelphia. Wife dead. No issue.

(139) Frank Culbertson mar Miss Letitia B. Toohill, of Pa. Civil Engineer, Pa. R. R. Issue: Five or six children. 235-241.

(140) Herbert John Culbertson mar. (135) Clementina Culbertson of Springfield, Mo.
Issue:dau. d. young.

(142) Ernest Howard Culbertson mar. Miss Gilmore of Macomb, Ills.

Issue:
243.   Ernest Howard. Lives at N. Y. City.
244.   Harold, d. young.

(143) Sydney Mathiot Culbertson mar. July 12, 1893, Miss Edith McDaniels of Columbus, Ohio. Wife d. June 13, 1911.   Lives at Denver, Colo.   Prominent business man.
Issue:
245.   Emily, Denver, Col., mar. Bruce Kistler, Dec. 9, 1922.
246.   Katherine, mar. 1923 to H. Frank; chemist.

(144) Dr. Lewis Rogers Culbertson .mar. first Miss Blanche M. Adams of Dresden, Ohio. Wife born 1876; d. Sept. 5, 1900. No issue.

(144) Dr. Lewis R. Culbertson mar. second Miss Edith Sophia Popp, of Zanesville, Ohio., Oct. 3, 1910. Lives at Zanesville, Ohio. Wife b. June 21, 1888.
247.   Constance Maxine, b. July 26, 1911.
248.   Howard Louis, b. Apr. 14, 1914.
249.   Edith Janet, b. Oct. 11, 1915.

(145) Cornelia Swift Culbertson mar. Abraham Gordon-Winstanley.

No issue. Lives at Pittsburg, Pa.

(146) Claude L. Culbertson mar. Mabel Virginia Cosgrave, Sep. 25, 1901. Wife b. Nov. 12, 1879. Lived at

Zanesville, Ohio. Graduate of O. S. U. Druggist and prominent citizen. Family resides Zanesville, Ohio.

Issue:
250. William Howard, b. Mar. 2, 1903.
251. Virginia, b. Feb. 11, 1908.
252. Mary Louise, b. July 24, 1910.
253. Eleanor Frances, b. June 29, 1917.

(155) Willis Godfrey Culbertson mar. Lottie E. Ball. Lived at Fayetteville, Ind.

Issue:
254. James Ball, b. 1877.

(157) Florence Culbertson mar. Frank C. Remick, of Chicago, Ills.

Issue:
255. Edward Culbertson, b. Apr. 4, 1881.

(160) Lucy Culbertson mar. W. McCarty, of Chicago, Ills.

Issue:
256. Florence Culbertson, b. Aug., 1882.

(161) Mary Culbertson mar. Richard Nash, of Chicago, Ills.

Issue:

257. Margaret Culbertson ⎫ b. 1886.
258. Madeline Arthur ⎬

(162) Rhoda Anna Culbertson mar. Arthur E. Havens, of Chicago, Ills.

Issue:
259. Katherine, b. 1890.
260. Charles Culbertson, b. 1892.

(164) Charles William Culbertson mar. first Lydia Harris, of Lancaster, Ind., Nov. 9, 1871. Wife d. Shelbyville, Ind.

Issue:
261.Charles Draper b. Sep. 28, 1873. Shelbyville.
262. Laura Louise, b. July 28, 1877.

(164) C. W. Culbertson mar. second, Eugenia L. Bone, Oct. 10, 1883.

Issue:
263. Alice Charles, b. July 26, 1884.
264. Edith Patience, b. Apr. 20, 1885.

(165) Alice Culbertson mar L. H. Fort, of Red Cloud, Neb. Husband Clerk of Court.

Issue:
265. Grace.
266. Charles.
267. Nettie.
268. Nellie.

(167) Nettie Culbertson mar. C. M. Wherry, of Council Bluffs, Ia.

Issue:
269. Lee Bye Wherry.

(169) Nelia Bell Culbertson mar. Horton Wallace Bedell, of Peru, Neb., Dec. 17, 1885. Husband b. Apr. 12, 1865.
Issue:
270. Bessie Culbertson Bedell, b. Oct. 6, 1886.
271. Ralph Benjamin, b. Feb. 28, 1888.

(170) Leafie Emma Culbertson mar. Geo. Rogers of Omaha, Neb.

Issue:
272. Floyd B., b. 1891.

(179) Sarah Emily "Fay" Daily mar. Jan. 8, 1885 to Benj. Bates Hoadley. Auburn, Neb.

Issue:
273. Wm. Daily Hoadley, Jr., B. Oct. 9, 1895.
274. Donald Eldridge, d. infancy.
275. Ben. Bates, Jr., d. infancy.
276. Mary Abby, b. June 22, 1889. (Mrs. Fitts). Scottsbluff, Neb.
277. Dexter B. Farnsworth, b. Sep. 14, ——; married.
278. Alice, Apr. 7 —— (Mrs. Young). Peru, Ind.
279. Dorothy Margaret, May 24, ——.
280. Martha Daily, July 22. (Mrs. Kinsey).
281. Ben Bates, Jr., Dec. 8, ——. Served in World War. 134 Inf. Neb. Trained at Camp Cody N. M. Corp. promoted to Segt. Served in France from Oct. '18 to Feb., '19. Married.

NINTH GENERATION

(206) Carrie Purnell Culbertson mar. N. S. Wood, of Maysville, Ky.

(207) Levi Culbertson mar. Miss Lucy Pitty, of Liberty, Mo. Live at Ft. Worth, Tex.
Issue:
282. Julius.

(220) Anna Greer Culbertson mar. Capt. Jos. Cole.
Issue:

(221) Mary Culbertson mar. Frank Bantz.
Issue: Not given.

(222) Warren Robuck Culbertson mar. Olivia Burton.
Issue:
283. Rachel.
284. Corben, single.
285. George (Unmarried).
286. Nathan Corben.
287. Mary Woorks.
288. Elizabeth.

(223) Wm. Greer Culbertson mar. Anna Blondell.
Issue:
289. Warren.
290. Anna.
291. Elsie.

(224) Harry Stone Culbertson mar. Francis M. Kelly. Lives at Baltimore, Md. Conductor B. & O. R. R.
Issue:
291½. Amy Marie (mar. to Capt. Chas. Meekins).
292. Edith May.
292½. Harry Vincent (mar. Jessie Stricker).
293. Harry Stone.
294. Jessie Parmelia.
295. Virginia May.
296. Helen Marie.
297. Louis Vincent.
298. Thelma Parmelia (Mrs. Geo. Kelner).

(270) Bess Culbertson Bedell is Principal of the Rose Hill School, Omaha, Neb. Graduate from Peru Normal. Has taught in Omaha for 14 years.

(271) Ralph Benjamin Bedell mar. Mabel Adair Brown, of Smith Center, Kans., Aug. 20, 1911. Wife b. Nov. 13, 1884.
Issue:
299. Margaret Bess Bedell, b. June 26, 1915.
300. Alice Ann Bedell, b. Oct. 28, 1918.

(271) Ralph B. Bedell received his B. A. degree from State Teachers' College, at Peru, Neb. and his M. A. from Neb. Univ. Now Supt. of Ashland, Neb. schools.

(276) Mary Abby Fitts. Husband Alden C. Fitts. Their children:
301.   Emily Jane Fitts.
302.   Wm. Alden Fitts.
303.   Mildred Fay Fitts.

(277) Dexter B. (Hoadley) Farnsworth and wife Zelma Young Farnsworth. Children:
304.   Dexter B. Farnsworth, Jr.
305.   Russell Daily Farnsworth.

(278) Alice Hoadley Young; husband Fred R. Young. Children:
306.   Marjorie Alice Young.
307.   Kenneth Daily Young.

(279) Dorothy Margaret Hoadley; unmarried.

(280) Martha Daily Kinsey; husband C. W. Kinsey. Issue:
308.   Robert Daily Kinsey.

(281) Ben. B. Hoadley, Jr.; Helen Jones Hoadley (wife). Issue:
309.   Betty Lou Hoadley.

(I) COL. SAMUEL CULBERTSON AND PROMINENT DESCENDANTS

Col. Samuel Culbertson, born and raised in Row. Of his early history we know but little. No record of him can be found in the French and Indian War. Rev. A. Nevin, in his work "Men of Mark of Cumberland Valley," says of him: "Col. Samuel Culbertson was the most noted of the family. He raised a company of Provincial Troops and marched them to the spring running through Robert's (Culbertson) farm where he formed them in confronting lines on the opposite banks. Then clasping hands across the stream swore fidelity to the cause of their country. This was a form of Scotch swearing, solemn and irrevocable. After the vows were uttered the oaths were confirmed by draughts from a tinful of whiskey, which Col. Robert supplied from his still house which stood at the head of the famous spring. He was a Ruling Elder of the Rocky Spring

Church, and was a member of the Assembly for a number of sessions." Col. Sam's grandson (87 years old 1892) Thomas G., of Wheeling, says of him: "He was a dignified military looking old gentleman, over six feet in height and straight as an arrow, and the father of a goodly number of descendants who all thought it a great glory to have a son to call 'Sam'." Dr. McClay of Greenville, Pa., said of him: "He was the most prominent man of Franklin Co.; the pillar of Rocky Spring Church, and was truly a noble type of a 'fine old Irish gentleman,' as well as an officer of standing in the Revolution. His fine old stone mansion built 1786 is still standing. Its massive walls, great substantial chimneys (a style of that day) with the name 'Sam Culbertson, 1786,' cut on them. This fine old house stands on a high eminence overlooking the beautiful valley below for miles. His farm of 400 acres of limestone land was all cultivated."

Daniel Foust, aged 90 years, who knew Col. Sam., says: "He was a powerful man, and could throw a shoulder stone farther than any man in his regiment."

His second wife belonged to one of the most prominent families of Franklin Co. Her brother, Capt. Chas. McClay, was killed with his whole company (all over six feet in height) in the surprise by the Indians at Crooked Billet, Pa. in 1778. Several of her uncles were Congressmen. One of them was Hon. Wm. McClay of the first U. S. Senate, who wrote an interesting journal on the proceedings of the First Senate. The father of Col. Sam's second wife was Hon. John McClay, a member of the first conference at Carpenters Hall, Philadelphia, in June, 1776. His brother, Hon. Samuel McClay, was U. S. Senator from Pa., from 1802-1809. Col. Sam Culbertson's first wife was also of a prominent family of Franklin Co., Pa.

In the Rocky Spring Church there still remains the pew of Col. Sam Culbertson, with his name painted thereon. He was buried in this churchyard, but his grave is unknown.

The first call ever issued to the Rev. Francis Herron—who preached so many years in the First Presbyterian Church of Pittsburgh, was written and signed by "Sam. Culbertson, Elder," of Rocky Spring Church.

The following is his Revolutionary Record from Pa. Archives: "Lt. Col. Fred Watts, Capt. Samuel Culbertson of First Cumb. Co. Batt'n of the 'Flying Camp,' in Camp at Lancaster July 4, 1776." (Minutes of Council of Safety, Pa.) "Capt. Samuel Culbertson Sept. 26, 1776, paid £23, .7s, Captain's pay..' (p. 258 Pa. Assembly Minutes) "Dec. 8,

1776, Col. Fred Watts, Lt. Col. Samuel Culbertson, Cumb. Co., Pa., 'Flying Camp' " (Pa. Arch.). Stryker's Battles of Trenton and Princeton says "In 1777, Samuel Culbertson was commissioned Col. of the Sixth Batt'n of Cumb. Co., Pa. having been Lt. Col. in a former organization. Dr. Wing in History of the Three Counties says: "Two regiments of Pa. Militia were sent to Washington at Long Island, the First Cumb. commanded by Col. Fred Watts. Watts with part of his reg't was captured at Ft. Washington but he was soon after exchanged and re-entered to service again." This shows Col. Samuel was in the defeat at Ft. Washington but we do not know if he was captured. July 31, 1777, commissioned Col. of Sixth Batt'n of Cumb. Co., Pa. Ass'rs; May 14, 1778, Col. of Sixth Batt'n Cumb. Co.; May 10, 1780, Lieut. Col. Fourth Batt'n Cumb. Co. (Pa. Archives).

This data shows he was a Captain in Sept., 1776, and on Dec. 8, 1776, was a Lieut. Col. while there was a Capt. Samuel Culbertson app. Capt., Dec. 8, 1776, in Armstrong's 5th Batt'n. (The latter was Samuel "of the Creek," son of Irish Joseph.)

(3) Alexander Culbertson ("Devil Alex," "Old Nick") was a giant, some say seven feet in height, others seven feet six inches. Daniel Foust, who knew him, says: "He was a powerful, red-haired man and followed the business of making whiskey. Had a distillery at the foot of South Mountain, Franklin Co. Everybody was afraid of him, and he had the reputation of throwing a live cat in a kettle of boiling apple butter." Another gentleman who knew him says of him: "He was as though of iron, and I am told he would rise from his bed any time of the night and go twenty miles to have the pleasure of a fistic encounter. Had he taken care of himself, his constitution would have carried him to a great age. I think he was near one hundred years old at his death." His grandson, Wm. McNulty, had one son, Wm. I. McNulty, Civil Engineer, Public Works, St. Louis, Mo.; another a Dr. in Duluth, Minn. Another grandson, Wm. McNulty, of New York, had a son, George W., who is Chief Engineer of the Broadway Cable Construction Co. "He (G. W.) was educated at University of Va., and N. Y. Polytechnic. Left college at the early age of eighteen and engaged in surveying. He applied for the position of assistant engineer of the great Brooklyn Bridge, but was refused. He then offered to work for nothing, and his services were accepted. He supervised the laying of the corner stone of the Brooklyn tower, and superintended the mason-

ry work on both sides, caissons, and the dock at the base of the Brooklyn tower. The magnificent and architecturally beautiful Brooklyn approach was constructed under his supervision. He is one of the most accomplished engineers in the land."—N. Y. Paper (1892).

His brother, Joseph McNulty, is a graduate of Columbia College; Royal School of Mining Engineers, Freiburg, Germany, and is now a mining engineer in S. Carolina (1892).

(7) Samuel H. Culbertson moved to Maysville, Ky., where he built the first brick house in that place which is still standing and belongs to the Library Association of that place. A portrait of him hangs in the Library. He is buried just back of the Library. He was one of Maysville's earliest and most respected citizens. His son, Dr. Julius (27), studied medicine and graduated at the Jefferson Medical College, Philadelphia, practiced a few years in Maysville, Ky., and then removed to a plantation in Miss., just opposite Vicksburg, where he resided until his death. He was a self-made man, having earned the money that paid for his education. At his death, before the war, he owned one hundred and fifty slaves and left an estate valued at $150,000. His sons Julius and Levi resided on the plantation until breaking out of the war, when they entered the army. Levi died in the army. The loss of the slaves and deterioration in land ruined Julius, who moved to Maysville, in 1869, and engaged in various pursuits, and in 1890, sold out and moved to Texas and engaged in wagon manufacturing.

(29) Milton lived at Maysville. Was a stock-raiser and was also considered the best judge of stock in that part of the state (the "Blue Grass Region"). He was also an amateur artist. Also at one time was proprietor of a hotel, Lee House, at Maysville.

(30) Margaret Culbertson mar. Rufus Case, a very wealthy man, son of Reuben Case.

(20) Samuel Culbertson, son of Robt. (5), was one of Williamsport's (Md.) most respected citizens, and a Ruling Elder in the First Presbyterian church of that place.

(8) John Culbertson was appointed Lieut. of Sixth Co., State Militia, 73d Regt., Aug. 1800; Capt. of Sixth Co., Pa. Militia (73rd) Regt., Aug. 3, 1803; Lieut. Col. of 73d Regt. Pa. Militia Aug. 3, 1807; Brigade Major, Aug. 3, 1811. His regiment was preparing to march to Baltimore when they were notified their services would not be needed. He was appointed Justice of Peace, of Green Tp., in 1813. He also held other offices of trust.

(32) His son, Thomas G. Culbertson, moved to Wheeling in 1830, and engaged in the stove and tin business. During the last thirty years of his life he has been engaged in the foundry business; the original firm being Ott, Culbertson & Greer; then Thos. G. Culbertson; then Culbertson & Fisher. He was also engaged in the same business for a few years in Martins Ferry (opposite Wheeling), the firm there being Culbertson, Wiley & Co. He retired from business about 1880. He had the Culbertson build, being six feet in height, weighed 210 pounds and was a hale, hearty old gentleman of 87 in 1892. His son (120) John D. Culbertson began business as clerk in a bank, and soon went into the iron business, and has continued in that business up to date. Was secretary and treasurer of the Riverside Iron Works since its organization, now one of the largest concerns south of Pittsburgh. It includes bar mills, nail factories, etc., at Wheeling; steel plant, etc., at Benwood and furnaces, etc., at Steubenville. The Riverside Iron Works was rated by Bradstreets 1892 at over $1,000,000. A newspaper article states that the Riverside Iron Works has in its employ 4000 men (1892). Shortly after entered the U. S. Steel Corporation and moved to Pittsburg, Pa. In a testimonial to John D. Culbertson's widow the U. S. Steel Corporation said, "He exemplified in the highest degree in his social and business life, every quality of the courteous, conscientious, Christian gentleman."

(36) Sarah (Culbertson) McClean's daughter, Margaret, married W. H. Falconer, a prominent real estate agent of New York City.

(38) Elizabeth married Rev. F. S. De Hass, who was pastor of the Methodist church, of Washington, of which Gen. Grant was a member. He was afterwards appointed Minister to Jerusalem by President Grant.

(9) Elizabeth Culbertson marrried Maj. Gen. John Rea. "John Rea was a captain in Col. Joseph Armstrong's Battalion of Cumberland Co., Pa. Associaters (Fifth Battalion), in December, 1776." which battalion at that date marched to the defense of Philadelphia. "July 31, 1777 was commissioned Captain of the Eighth Co., of Col. Abraham Smith's Regt. (Eighth) of Cumberland Co., Pa. Associaters. May 14, 1778, was commissioned Captain of the Eighth Co., in the Eighth Regt. (Smith's), of Associaters. May 10, 1780, was commissioned Captain of the Second Co., of the Second Battalion (Col. James Johnston's), of Cumberland Co., Pa., Associaters." (See Pa. Archives)   "He was commissioned

Brig.-Gen. in 1812." (Pa. Arch.) Was commissioned Major-General, in 1814." (From commission). He represented the Franklin and Bedford district in Congress, from 1803 to 1811; also from 1813 to 1815. He served in the Pa. Legislature (House) from 1785-86-89-90-92-93-96-97-93-1800-01, and in the State Senate from 1823-24, when he resigned. he was the first coroner of Franklin Co., Pa.

The following romantic story is told of him: "When a young man of perhaps twenty-five or twenty-seven, during the Revolution or at its close, he went to call on his friend, Col. Samuel Culbertson. While there he was shown the new baby, Elizabeth. After admiring her, he said, 'Sam, you must save her for me.' When he was fifty years old he married her." He was one of Franklin county's most prominent citizens. He died at Chambersburg, Pa., and was buried at Rocky Spring Church. His wife was buried at Maria Forge, Blair Co., Pa.

His son, John Rea, was a physician of great ability and means, and married a daughter of the wealthy iron manufacturer, Alexander Laughlin, of Pittsburg. Charles Rea lives in Pittsburgh and is connected with the Robinson Rea Manufacturing Co., manufacturers of machinery of all kinds, and a very large concern.

(41) William Rea resided in Pittsburg, being one of the most prominent citizens of that place. Was president of two banks in Pittsburg, and a large stock-holder in the Robinson Rea Mf'g. Co.

(42) Samuel C. Rea was a wealthy and prominent citizen of Pittsburg.

(43) James D. Rea was a judge and prominent citizen of Hollidaysburg, Pa. His widow resided in Pittsburg (1892).

(46) Andrew J. Rea was a prominent citizen of Hollidaysburg, Pa. All the children of Gen. Rea were very handsome and people of great influence and culture.

Samuel Rea, son of James D. (43) was born in Hollidaysburg, Blair County, Pa., Sept. 21st, 1855. His mother, who died in 1908, was a daughter of Thomas Blair Moore, of that county, and his father, James D. Rea, who died in 1868, was a well-known resident of Hollidaysburg. Mr. Rea's first connection with The Pennsylvania Railroad Company was in the Engineering Dept. where he began on July 17th, 1871, as a chainman and rodman on the Morrison's Cove Branch and was located at Roaring Spring. On February 10th, 1897, Mr. Rea was appointed First Assistant to the President of the Pennsylvania Railroad Company, ef-

fective Jan. 1st, 1913, to succeed Mr. James McCrea, resigned.   Later he was elected a Director and President of the
other principal railroad corporations constituting the Pennsylvania System.

For many years Mr. Rea was interested in the project to
bridge the Hudson river from Hoboken to New York City,
and thus establish in the metropolis a terminus for the railroads using ferries from the New Jersey side.   He was one
of the incorporators of the North River Bridge Co, char-
tered by an Act of Congress in 1890 to build that bridge.

When other railroad companies failed to join the Pennsylvania Railroad Company in the project to bridge the Hudson, and after a very careful examination and report on the
entire project by engineering experts, The Pennsylvania
Railroad Company determined to build two single track
tunnels under the Hudson river and four single-track tunnels under the East River, with a large station in the heart
of New York City.   After this plan had been approved by
President Cassat and the Board of Directors of The Pennsylvania Railroad Company, Mr. Rea was given direct
charge of what was regarded as the most important and difficult piece of engineering work in this country, and carried
it to a successful conclusion.   As a part of this project may
be considered under his direction, of the "Hell Gate Bridge
Route" by the New York Connecting Railroad Company,
jointly owned by The Pennsylvania Railroad Company and
the New York, New Haven & Hartford Railroad Company,
which, with the tunnel extension of the Pennsylvania Railroad Company, forms a through route for railroad trans-
portation between the Southern, Western and New England
States.   On April 11th, 1917, he was appointed a member
of the Executive Committee of the Special Committee on
National Defense (Railroads' War Board), of the American
Railway Association, which Committee supervised the oper-
ation of the railroads of the United States from that time
until they were taken over by the Government on Dec. 28th,
1917.   He is a member of the Philadelphia and Rittenhouse
Clubs (Philadelphia) ; Union Club and Century Association
(New York) ; Metropolitan Club (Washington) ; an Honor-
ary Member of the American Society of Civil Engineers and
a member of the Institution of Civil Engineering (London) ;
Pennsylvania Society Sons of the Revolution; Society of
War of 1812, etc. (From Penna R. R. Biographies).—Extracts.

(10) Rev. James Culbertson received his academical edu-

cation at Jefferson College, Washington, Pa., which he entered quite young. He prosecuted his theological studies under the direction of Drs. King and Herron, and was licensed to preach the gospel in 1811, by the Presbytery of Carlisle. In the summer of 1812, he went to Zanesville, Ohio, then a small village of log cabins chiefly. In 1816, a brick church was built, corner Fourth and South streets, and in 1839 a much larger church (the First Presbyterian) was built, corner Sixth and Market Streets. He preached fully 4000 sermons during his lifetime, and preached altogether thirty-four years. He was said to have been the best and most brilliant minister that ever filled a pulpit in Zanesville. He was perhaps as fine a scholar as ever lived in Zanesville, being well versed in Latin, Hebrew, Greek, French and German. He was a man of tall and commanding figure, very magnetic and eloquent in address. He thought nothing of riding a hundred miles on horseback to fill a brother minister's pulpit. He once received a call to fill the pulpit of one of the largest Presbyterian churches in Philadelphia, which paid a very large salary, but he declined, saying that "his duty lay in Zanesville. The salary had no consideration for him. His nephew, T. G. Culbertson, of Wheeling, says of him: "Another trait of his character was his quiet, unassuming modesty. When a certain institution wished to add D. D. to his name, he refused positively to permit it, and informed his friends never to address him that way.". His first wife was of a prominent family of Pa. His second wife was a daughter of one of Franklin County's most prominent citiens, John Colhoun, who was a Revolutionary soldier, merchant, banker. He was one of the founders of the first bank in Chambersburg. Also was a member of the first Conference, at Carpenter's Hall, June, 1776.

(52) John Colhoun Culbertson, son of Rev. James was educated at the Ohio University, at Athens, standing at the head of the noted class of '43. Was a man of brilliant intellect. Went from Zanesville to Iowa City, before the war and engaged in banking. His bank failed in '57, because of "wild-cat" currency in Illinois. On leaving college he studied law with Hon. Judge Thomson of Chambersburg, whose daughter he married. She was a sister of First Vice-President Thomson, of Penna. R. R. and Dr. Thomson, the noted Philadelphia oculist. At breaking out of war, he served State of Iowa as paymaster of Troops, and Nov. 26, 1862, was appointed by the President, Major and Paymas-

ter, U. S. Army. Resigned Aug. 8, 1863, because of disability incurred in line of duty. Organized the First National Bank, of Springfield, Mo., in 1867, and became its cashier, and retained this position until his death, which occurred in 1872, as a result of disease contracted during his army service.

(53) Howard Culbertson, M. D., was born and raised in Zanesville. Received a common school education at Howe's Academy Zanesville,. At the age of seventeen he went to Cincinnati and became a machinist—for which work he possessed great adaptability—having shown great mechanical genius as a boy, and when a youth built a steam engine, making all the parts himself. The work in the machine shop was too heavy for his slight frame, hence he soon gave up his trade and began the study of medicine under Dr. Little, of Zanesville, and took his first course of lectures at the Ohio Medical College, Cincinnati; his second course at Jefferson Medical College, Philadelphia, graduating in 1850. Practiced in Zanesville until fall of 1862. Was Acting Asst. Surgeon of 62d O. V. I. from Aug. 11 to Sept. 13, 1862, in. camp at Zanesville; appointed Surgeon U. S. Vols., Nov. 7, '62; appointed Asst. Surg. U. S. Regular Army, Feb. 28, 1866; appointed Capt. and Asst. Surg., July 8, '66. Brevet Rank Lieut.-Col., U. S. Vol. Oct. 6, '65, "for faithful and meritorious services." Actual rank in Vols. was Major. Honorably mentioned a number of times in the Medical and Surgical History of the Rebellion.

Services:—Served as Acting Asst. Surg. at camp near Zanesville in '62; in charge of hospitals at Rolla, Mo., Nov. '63; in charge of Harvey U. S. Gen. Hospital at Madison, Wis., to Oct. 1, '65; Act. Asst. Surg. Camp Butler, Ills., from Nov. 14, '65 to Dec. 25, '65; and at Louisville, Ky., to May 27, '66; post hospital, Louisville, Ky., to July '66; with 2d U. S. Infantry at Taylor Barracks, Louisville, Ky., to Oct. 66; ordered to Memphis, then to Louisville, to attend cholera patients; on sick leave May to Aug. '68, with congestive fever and retired because of disability caused by the fever.

He then removed to Zanesville, where he devoted himself to general practice, and soon after took up specialties of diseases of the eye and ear to which he devoted himself until his death. His skill as a surgeon is shown in the Surgical History of the Rebellion. He wrote a work entitled, "Excision of the Larger Joints of the Extremities," which is considered the authority on the subject today. It was the prize essay of the American Medical Association, in 1876. The great Prof. Louis Sayre, M. D. of New York, in presenting him to the Society, said: "Gentlemen, I have the honor, to present to you, a man who has accomplished a task which no other man in the United States would have had the courage to undertake and patience to finish." The work was tabular, chiefly, and require.d in its preparation an immense correspondence with surgeons of every nation. He was looked up to by oculists all over the United States, and was regarded by them as one of the best. To show how highly they esteemed him:—A gentleman who had procured glasses of him afterward consulted the great oculist, Dr. D. B. Roosa, of New York, regarding his eyes. Roosa asked him who had given him glasses. The gentleman told him and in reply Dr. Roosa said: "If you got them of Dr. Culbertson, it will be unnecessary for me to examine your eyes." Similar illustrations might be given of praise to him by other great eastern oculists. He numbered among his personal friends such oculists as Roosa, Chisholm, Stevens, Agnew, Thomson, Wordsworth, Alt, Green, Hotz, etc., etc. and among surgeons, such men as Sayre, Gross, Ashurst, Bartholow, Hamilton, etc.

He was a contributor to a number of medical journals, and one of the Asst. Editors of the American Journal of Ophthalmology. Was the inventor of a number of delicate eye operating instruments; also of the Prisoptometer, an instrument for examining the eyes for glasses; also, a meerschaum probe for bullets. Was examining surgeon on the Pension Board, at Zanesville, for twenty-two years. One of the Medical Referees of the Pension Dept. said "With but one exception, he was the best pension surgeon in the United States." He was the best posted physician in Forensic Medicine that Zanesville has ever had. Was a member of the American Med. Association; American Ophthalmological Society; Ohio State Med. Association, etc., etc. Was a Deacon in the Second Presbyterian church at Zanesville, for many years.

His son (144) Dr. Lewis R. (the author), is a graduate of Jefferson Medical College, class of 1890, and a specialist

on the eye and ear.　Holds position of Expert Eye and Ear
Examiner to the U. S. Pension Bureau, and other positions.
Studied his specialties under his father and in Philadelphia.
Post graduate course at Royal Ophthalmic Hospital, and
Golden Square Nose and Throat and Prof. Lewis Anatomi-
cal school, London 1906. Also Royal Vienna Univ. 1906.
Contributor to Eye and Ear Journals.　Mem. Amer. Med.
Ass'n., Ohio State and Musk. Co. Acad. Med., American
Academy of Oph. and Otol., etc., etc.　Eye and Ear Surg.
Penna R. R.

(141) Culbertson, Anne V.　Educated common schools
and Putnam Seminary, Zanesville, Ohio. Unmarried.　Since
1893 engaged as a writer and author-reader, giving enter-
tainments in which she read her own writings and poems
and dialect songs.　Contributed to magazines and papers in
verse and dialect stories chiefly in negro dialect and dialect
of mountain whites of the South and French patois.

Author of Lays of a Wandering Minstrel, 1896; At the
Big House, 1904 (A Book of Negro and Indian Folk Lore) ;
When the Banjo Talks, 1905.　Published by Bobbs, Merrill
Co., Indianapolis, Ind. (Extracts from Who's Who in America.)　Some of her best poems are unpublished and were
written during the World War.　She belonged to the Vigi-
lantes, a national society of poets and writers, formed during the World War to write patriotic articles and poems to
stimulate patriotism.　A number of these beautiful patriotic poems were published in newspapers and magazines
and reprints sent to the sick and wounded soldiers in this
country and Europe.　She numbered among her friends
such great writers as Joel Chandler Harris, Ella Wheeler
Wilcox, James Whitcomb Riley, etc., etc.　She at one time
spent a summer in the Great Smoky Mountains of N. Car.
in order to study the folk-lore of the Indians there.　She
stated that many of these Indian stories were given by the
Indians to the Negroes and thus quite a number of folk-lore
stories of the latter originated.　She studied the Negroes
in Virginia.　Died Dec. 1918.

Lack of space prevents publishing herein any of Anne
Virginia Culbertson's poems but we will give one verse of
one of her most beautiful poems published in 1895.　The

title of the poem is "The Blue Muskingum", an ode to the
beautiful river in Ohio, which flows through her native vale.

"Though I wander far and wide,
Though I see and stand beside
All the classic streams of earth
They shall seem as nothing worth
While I miss the sudden thrill
When my eager eyes alight
Where the sun is glancing bright
On the waxes that wind and trail
Through my lovely native vale.
Like a silver serpent flung
Green-clad hills and dailes among
Ah, thy praises, sweet to sing them
Well beloved, blue Muskingum!

*   *   *   *   *

We will also copy one of her most beautiful war poems
in full.

AT PARTING

I will not say "goodbye," dear heart,
It is a word
So often heard
It means too little when we part—
I will not say "goodbye," dear heart.

May "God-be-wi'-ye," so it reads
In ancient Anglo-Saxon screeds—
"Goodbye" we speak it in our day:
The time-worn phrase I will not say
As trembling hands together cling,
Because it asks a needless thing;
I will not ask that He may go
With you, dear one, because I know
That God is with you, that with Him
You cross the ocean's purple rim,
With Him you'll tread the awful fields
Where Life to Death rich harvest yields—
He walks beside you there!
What though from thence He bid you fare
Beyond man's ken to Otherwhere,
There is no place outside His care.
Long have you served Him, faithful, true—
Shall He not keep this word to you,
"Lo I am with you always?" So
With Him I bear to let you go.
A deep, deep glance, a clasp of hand,
No need of speech to understand.

I will not say "goodbye," dear heart,
It is a word
So often heard
It means too little when we part—
I will not say "goodbye," dear heart.

(11) Charles McClay Culbertson studied for the ministry, but lost hearing. Moved to Madison, Ind., and engaged in farming.

(59) Chas. McClay C., his son, was a self-made man. Left home at fourteen years of age and entered a store as a clerk. After some years went into merchandising and pork packing, in partnership with Daniel A. Jones, at Newport, Ind. The firm moved to Chicago, Ill, in 1857, and engaged in packing. This firm was dissolved later, and the firm of Culbertson & Blair formed. Charles remained in active business until 1878, and in 1896 removed to his farm at Newman, Ills., and engaged in the breeding of Hereford cattle. Here he had a stock farm of 4000 acres and the finest Hereford cattle, it is said, in the United States.

Was a member of the Chicago Board of Trade for some years. It is said he was the largest breeder and importer of Hereford cattle in the United States. His daughters reside in the most aristocratic part of Chicago, and are married to prominent men.

(55) Elizabeth McClay Culbertson was a beautiful woman and a woman of great brain. Both of her husbands were prominent and wealthy men. Her daughter, Kate Scott, (149), was a fine singer and musician. Studied music in Milan. Another daughter, Mary Belle (148) was a singer but turned her attention to literature, particularly that of translation of the Italian contemporaneous literature. While engaged in this work, she met and married the Count Uda, a man of some note in literature.

(56) Josephine Culbertson mar. Rev. John Black, Presbyterian minister, born in Pa., who was first a carpenter; next studied divinity, and assumed pastorate of the Fifth Pres. Church, of Pittsburg, Pa. Later was in Miss., and Ky. Was a man of great power and eloquence. His son (51) Gen. John Charles Black, born in Miss., was in college when the war broke out. He was the first man to enlist in the Co., which became Co. 1, of the 11th Ind. Zouaves, and on the same day his brother, Wm. P. (152), joined the same Co. and served three months. After this they entered the 37th Ill. Regt. for three years. At the organization of the 11th Ind. John was made the Sergeant-Major, and Wm. was made Corporal. At the organization of the 37th Ill., at Chicago, he was elected Major. Upon his election as Major his brother was elected Capt. of Co. K, in which capacity William served for three years, being mustered out Sept. 30, '64. During this time John had been promoted to Lieut. Col., then

Col. of the Regt. He served until the close of war and was in command of a brigade, and as Brig. General, led the charge upon the Blakely Batteries at the Capture of Mobile, the last general engagement of the war. Was in Texas a short time and mustered out in summer of 1865. Wm. Black was a noted lawyer in Chicago. John was Commissioner of Pensions under Cleveland's first administration, and was one of Chicago's most noted lawyers. He was seriously crippled while in the army. He at one time resided at Urbana, O., and later at Danville, Ills. The mother of these men was a beautiful woman, and a woman of brain. He was also Congressman-at-large from Illinois. There were no lawyers in Chicago with greater reputations than these two men.

(156) James McKemey Culbertson was a dry goods merchant, and at his death left most of his fortune to a church. He was a handsome man and a great favorite in society.

The second wife of Chas. McC Culbertson (11) was living at the advanced age of ninety-four years in 1892-the oldest of the name—and in a remarkable state of preservation.

(62) Samuel Culbertson was a contractor. Also Deputy U. S. Marshal. His son (164) Charles W., received a college education. He then became a carpenter; later, a ticket agent; telegrapher, and last, assistant cashier of the First Natl. Bank, at Shelbyville, Ind. He is a leader in the Prohibition party and was nominated Lieut-Gov. on that ticket (1892).

(219) Tingle Woods Culbertson, son of John D. Culbertson of Wheeling, W. Va., served in World War in A. E. F. in France, Co. H., 318 Regt., 80 Div.

CHAPTER XXII

FIFTH GENERATION

(II) Col. Robert Culbertson of Bedford Co., Pa. Made a quit claim deed to his brother Samuel, March 4, 1770, then residing in Lurgan Tp., Cumb. Co., Pa. In his father's estate he chose his own guardian in 1758 showing he was 14 years of age or over. This would denote he was born 1742-44. He must have married before or by 1770 because the Census of 1790 for Bedford Co., Pa. gives himself and wife; 3 sons over 16; 1 son under 16; and four daughters. With three sons over 16 in 1790 the youngest of the three must have been born by 1774. The age of 4 daughters in 1790 is not indicated in Census. His wife (if married in 1770) is not on deed, Mar. 4, 1770.

Eagles History of Pa. says, "He was one of the first Commissioners of Bedford Co."

He moved to Bedford Co. in 1770 together with his brother, James and brother-in-law Col. Chas. Cessna. He was called "Robert of Bloody Run" because he lived on the stream of that name, so called because of the battle of "Bloody Run" or Sideling Hill was fought (1756) there. There was no Robert Culbertson killed in this battle. He and his brothers, James and John, and sister Elizabeth took up their claim in Bedford Co., of 150 acres each, coming to them in settlement of their father's estate in 1770 (John did not move to Bedford). Robert paid tax 1772 in Cumb. Valley Tp., Bedford Co. In 1776 he is taxed in this Tp. with 150 acres (40 improved), 3 horses and 2 cows. Had 50 acres in Providence Tp., in 1779 and 1802. Also his son, John, taxed same Tp., 1802.

Most of his children went to Miami Co., Ohio, but his youngest son, Samuel, born 1799, went to Maryland, so say family reports. Reports do not say where Samuel lived in Maryland. Col. Robert did not move to Miami Co., Ohio, at least court and family records show he did not move there. The Oath of Death, Will and Administration Records show he did not die in Bedford Co., or if he did left no property. Census of Md. 1800, 1810 does not give him. Miami Co., O., taken off of Montgomery Co., Jan. 16, 1807. Troy, Ohio., founded in 1807.

The family records given me in 1892 are incomplete and only three of his children's dates of birth were given. Their record gave by first wife: Joseph, Henry W., Robert, Mary, Nancy. Second wife: Samuel, John and Aseneth. These are wrong as Census of 1790 proves (i. e. checking up dates of birth of several as taken from a Family Bible).

His Revolutionary Record is as follows: "Commissioned Major, Dec. 10, 1777, in Col. Wm. Parker's Batt'n of Bedford Co., Pa. Ass'rs. Commissioned Sub. Lieut. (Lt. Col.) of Bedford Co. Troops, May 18, 1781." (Pa. Arch. by Bruce p. 149). This was an important office he being the officer to buy arms, drill, discipline, collect fines, etc., and was paid at value of 1½ bu. of wheat per day.

We do not know the names of either of his wives or date of marriage. Descendants state that John was his youngest son. I am now positive that this is incorrect and that

John was by the first wife and probably the eldest son. John appears in same Tp. 1802. In 1807 he does not appear in this Tp. Only other John found 1807 was John Esq. of Hopewell Tp. This was land only and was John of Mifflin Co., the fuller, and no relation and whose estate was settled and this land sold 1812.

After a most exhaustive search I am now positive that Col. Robert moved to Dayton, Ohio, with all of his children in 1802-03. D. C. Cooper was giving away lots to settlers in Dayton at that time which attracted many there—so says a history of Montgomery Co., Ohio. I have not been able to find any deed to or from Col. Robert at Dayton, nor have I been able to find any will or administration of him. It is possible that some old church in Dayton may have record of his membership or of his death which may yet be discovered. The State Librarian at Columbus, O., informs me he has searched carefully state records of burial places of Revolutionary soldiers in Ohio but cannot find him.

Census 1800, 1810 of Ohio destroyed in 1812 by British. Census of 1820 for Montgomery and Miami Counties, Ohio, does not give him. Howe's Hist. of Ohio says D. C. Cooper located there in 1798 and laid out Dayton. History of Piqua, Ohio, says, "Henry Culbertson was an apprentice of Squire Brown, a saddler, and an early postmaster of Troy, O. Miami Co., Ohio, formed 1807 off Montgomery Co. Joseph Culbertson had come to Troy in 1808. He was a poor boy but brought to Troy a trade that flourished from the first. He was a hatter. Joseph was a soldier from Piqua in War 1812.

Beers Hist. Miami Co., Ohio, "The Culbertson brothers originally came from Cumberland Co., Pa., five brothers and located in Miami Co., O., in 1807, viz. Joseph, Robert H., Henry W., Samuel and John." It will be noted above that Joseph was a hatter. Probably learned trade with his brother, John of Dayton. Am inclined to think that John of Dayton was a hatter also. In personal estate was "flat-iron", probably a hatter's iron.

Probate and Common Pleas Court Records of Montgomery Co., O., give no other Culbertson, save Robert and John. Census of Bedford Co., Pa., 1800, 1810, 1820, does not give Col. Robert or his children. It is probable he was overlooked in 1800. No deeds for his property in Bedford. I think he was poor and moved to Dayton and either died there or in Miami Co., O., after 1807. He is not on Census 1820 Montgomery or Miami Co., His children (or part of them) were quite young when he went to Dayton. Apparently his wife (second) survived him and probably died at Troy. The females given in 1820 Census which were not children of the brothers given were no doubt their sisters and nieces, and possibly one was their mother.

Col. Robert was given in the old Culbertson Genealogy as being an inn-keeper at Bedford up to 1820. This is wrong. He was not an inn-keeper. The inn-keeper was Robert, son of Col. Samuel Culbertson, of Culbertson Row, Pa. He afterwards moved to Md. There was no executor or administrator appointed for any John Culbertson in Miami Co., Ohio, between 1807 and 1820 and as there is no John Culbertson on Census of 1820, either in Montgomery Co., Ohio, or Miami Co., Ohio, it proves conclusively that John Culbertson who died at Dayton, Ohio, in 1805 was a son of Col. Robert Culbertson of Bedford Co., Pa. I have had the Court Records of Miami Co., Ohio, examined thoroughly and the Probate Judge at Dayton, Ohio, writes me, "I personally examined the records for an estate of Robert Culbertson, deceased, but could find no such record. I did, however, find an estate of John Culbertson, dec'd, in which it is apparent that Robert Culbertson is an heir. The papers are so old that the writing is almost illegible. As near as I am able to decipher, the letter of administration was issued Aug. 29, 1805. The inventory consisted of personal property—'$150, and the estate was insolvent. I find marriage license of Robert Culbertson and Mary Culbertson, married Aug. 16, 1805, by Jos. Ryburn, J. P."

The County Recorder at Dayton, writes, "the only deed is Robert Culbertson and Mary his wife, conveyed to David Lindley, lot so and so, in Dayton, Ohio, Jan. 30, 1817. Residence Miami Co., Ohio. Witnessed by Hon. McClung and Nancy McClung. Our records do not show how he acquired this property. D. C. Cooper laid out Dayton and it is my opinion he got it from him."

Now the above shows that Robert son of Alexander Culbertson lived in Dayton for a time.

John was the eldest son of Col. Robert of Bedford, Pa., and it was he who died in Dayton in 1805. Family records say he lived in Miami Co., Ohio, and had three children. It was either his cousin Robert, son of Alex of Guilford Tp., who administered his estate, or his father.

Col. Robert's son John was married but his wife evidently died before he left Pa. or shortly after. He moved to Dayton, Ohio, in 1802, and was the John who died in Dayton,

Ohio, in 1805, and whose cousin(?) Robert (second cousin), was appointed administrator of his estate in 1805. Family records say John lived in Miami Co., Ohio, and had three children. His children no doubt were raised by relatives in Miami Co., Ohio. (See descendants of Alexander, son of Irish Samuel of the Row for further data in regard to John's death at Dayton, Ohio.) My arrangement of Col. Robert's children would be:

Issue:
1. John, b. ——; d. Aug., 1805, at Dayton, Ohio.
2. Name unknown (son). It is possible that he had a son James. There was a James went to Maryland near Havre-de-Grace and died about 1815 (See end of book for James who mar. Elizabeth Stillings).
3. Son, name unknown. Either died young or moved away.
4. Daughter, b. before 1790.
5. Mary, b. 1775 or before.
6. Nancy, b. before 1790.
7. Daughter, b. before 1790. Name unknown.
8. Joseph, b. 1787, in Bedford Co., Pa., d. Miami Co., O.

Col. Robert Culbertson married second.

Issue:
9. Robert H., b. 1794 in Bedford Co., Pa.; d. Miami Co., Ohio, Nov. 28, 1884.
10. Henry W., b. 1797; d. Miami Co., Ohio.
11. Aseneth, b. ——; d. Miami Co., Ohio.
11½. Samuel, b. Apr. 14, 1799; d. Apr. 26, 1876. Miami Co., Ohio.

SIXTH GENERATION

1. John Culbertson mar. ——. John probably married before 1800. Moved to Dayton, O., before 1805. Wife died before him. His children were raised in Miami Co., by their uncles.

Issue:
12. George E. Lived at E. Liverpool, Ohio.
13. Amanda (Mrs. I. Miller).
14. Pearson.

(5) Mary Culbertson moved to or near Dayton, Ohio, before 1805 and married her second cousin, Robert Culbertson, son of Alexander Culbertson and grandson of Irish Samuel of the Row. On Aug. 16, 1805 in Montgomery Co., Ohio, by Squire Reyburn. They resided in Dayton, O., until

1817 when Robert and wife Mary deeded land in Dayton, Jan., 1817, and moved to Miami Co., Ohio. Her husband died there in 1825 and his widow renounced right of administratrix and brother-in-law, H. W. Culbertson, was appointed Admin'r Nov., 1825. Robert, Census 1820, Troy, Ohio. Males of 26 and under 45 years, one; males under 10, one; females of 10 and under 16, two; of 16 and under 26,. two; of 45 and upwards one.

As both were married in 1805 and neither had been married before they could not have had children of their own that old, therefore the two girls of 16 and under 26 must have been the orphans of Mary's deceased brother John, who died in Dayton in 1805 and whose wife died before him. Above also shows Mary 45 years old (older than husband by several years).

Issue:
15. Hester. Married.
16. Anna Maria, d. 1875. Married
17. Joseph, d. young. } Twins.
18. Nancy, d. infancy. } Twins.
·19. Mary Jane, d. Married.
20. Eliza, d. young.
21. Sarah, d. young.
22. Martha A. Married.

(6) Nancy Culbertson mar. A. McDonald. Lived in Miami Co., Ohio. It seems was married twice as she witnessed a deed in 1817 in Miami Co., of Robert Culbertson for property in Dayton. Witnesses were Hon. McClung and wife Nancy.

Issue:
23. James McDonald.
24. Maria (Mrs. Robert Douglas).
25. Henry.
26. Archibald.
27. Joseph.

(8) Joseph Culbertson moved to Miami Co., Ohio, before 1808. Served in Capt. Francis Patterson's Co. Militia, Ohio, Sept. 12, 1812. (Pension Records). Merchant at Troy, O. Married Mary Hamer, May, 1812. On Census 1820, Troy, O. Self over 26. (No wife), one male over 16, two males under 10; 2 females under 16; one female over 45 years. This was either his mother-in-law or his sister. One of the males was no doubt George, son of his brother John.

Issue:
28. Henry H.
29. Nancy J., d. 1878. Auburn, Neb. (Mrs. Jas. Bilger).
30. Mary H., d. 1852. (Mrs. Cloyd McClung).

(8) Joseph Culbertson mar. second Eleanor Cecil.
Issue:
31. Barbara Eleanor. Unmar.
32. Elizabeth L., d. infancy.
33. Eliz. Roe, Unmar.
34. Wm. H., d. infancy.
35. Sarah G., d. infancy.
36. John T., d. infancy.
37. Joseph F.

(8) Joseph Culbertson mar. third Rebecca Harker, Sept. 14, 1839. No issue.

(10)- Henry W. Culbertson mar. Maria Coleman, Feb. 25, 1819. Moved to Troy, Ohio, in 1808. Was then an apprentice saddler (Hist. Miami Co., O.) Was also Mayor of Troy, Ohio.
Issue:
38. Cordelia, d. 1840.
39. John N., Troy, Ohio.
40. Hezikiah H., b. Aug. 10, 1825. Versailles, Ky.
41. Nancy Mariah.
42. Clara F. (Mrs. J. L. Abbott,. Fremont, Neb.)
43. Henry, d. 1881. Served Civil War 10 Ohio Vol.
42. Horace Coleman.
43. Mary I, d. young.
44. James Fergus, d. young.

(9) Robert H. Culbertson. Moved to Miami Co., Ohio, in 1807. Served in Capt. Francis Patterson's Co. in war 1812. (Pension records applied 1877 in which he said he was born 1794 in Bedford Co., Pa.). Mar. Sept. 30, 1818 to Miss Rhoda Lampson of Greene Co., O. Census 1820 Troy, O., self 26 years and wife under 26 years; one female over 45. This must have been Robert's mother. Wife b. 1801; d. Mar. 24, 1881.
Issue:
45. Charles.
46. Caroline (Mrs. E. Parsons of Granville, Ohio). June 12, 1821; d. Aug. 8, 1888.
47. Joseph C., was bank cashier at Troy, Ohio.
48. Emma (Mrs. Marvin Munson).

49. Henry.
50. William mar. and lived in Pa.
51. Mary J. (Mrs. S. Smith, Piqua, Ohio).

(11½) Samuel Culbertson moved to Maryland on or before 1820, married to Miss Mary B. Hedge of Maryland in 1823. Then moved to Miami Co., O.
Issue:
52. John W. (Dr.) b. Dec. 1, 1827; d. Nov. 12, 1888. Richmond, Ind.
53. Charles H. (Judge) d. 1892. Troy, Ohio.
54. Samuel S. (Major U. S. A.).
55. Nancy (Mrs. Geo. Kerr) Miami Co., O.
56. Joseph (mar. Mary Drake).
57. Hester (Mrs. A. Grovener).
58. Aseneth (Mrs. Kerr).

⟍ SIXTH GENERATION

(15) Hester Culbertson mar. Wm. Gahagan. Lived near Troy, O.
Issue:
59. Anna Maria (Mrs. Thos. Cory).
60. Mary (Mrs. Alex. Peterson).
61. Wm. Harrison.
62. Emma H. (Mrs. Jas. T. Moorehead).
63. Jane (Mrs. Wm. Peterson).
64. Thomas, d. young.

(16) Anna Marie Culbertson mar. H. S. Mayo, of Troy, Ohio.
Issue:
65. Edward Hanson.
66. Anna Maria (Mrs. U. F. Shalter).
67. Lucy Jane (Mrs. W. D. Lawrence).
68. Chas. Telford.
69. Henrietta Culbertson (Mrs. Chesebrough).
70. Alice Evilena.
71. George Walter.
72. Mary Elizabeth (Mrs. M. W. Goss).

(19) Mary Jane Culbertson mar. S. Worrell.
Issue:
73. Florence (Mrs. J. W. Barry).
74. Mary E.
75. Theresa (Mrs. McKnight).
76. Rufus Lindsay.

77.   Anna, d. young.

(22) Martha Culbertson mar. W. H. H. Dye of Troy, O.
Issue:

78.   Laura Lamb (Mrs. Livingston Singer).
79.   Elizabeth (Mrs. Hall).
80.   Josephine (Mrs. Jerome Weller).
81.   Charles R.
82.   Nancy A.
83.   Martha Hester (mar. Robt. H. Marsh, Oct. 8, 1879).
        Issue: Martha Cornelia (Mrs. Guy Hagerty, Peo-
        ria, Ills.) ; Nancy Eleanor (Mrs. Bernal Dyas).

(28) Henry H. Culbertson mar. cousin Susan V. Worrell.
Merchant. Troy, Ohio.
Issue:

84.   Eliza (unmar.).
85.   Sarah (mar. cousin H. H. Weakley, editor and prop'r
        Dayton Herald in 1892).
86.   Mary Ellen.
87.   George.

(37) Joseph F. Culbertson mar. first Anna Worth. No
issue. Mar. second Helen Walker. Widow lived at Columbus, O., in 1892. Was secy-treas. of R. R. Conductors'
Ass'n.
Issue:

88.   Daughter.

(38) Cordelia Culbertson mar. S. D. Bayliss.   Died 1840.
Issue:

89.   Osee (Mrs. S. Thompson, Columbus, O.)
90.   Mary, d. 1852.

(39) John N. Culbertson mar. Eliz. G. Foster in 1846.
Issue:

91.   Edward, b. 1847. Omaha, Neb. (unmar.).
92.   Mary F., b. 1849. (Mrs. Young).
93.   Mary E. (Mrs. Eddy).
94.   Arthur T., b. 1855.
95.   Lina Cordelia, b. 1858 (Mrs. W. S. Becker).
96.   Sue Bilger, b. 1862.

(40) Hezikiah H. Culbertson mar. Susan Kincaid. Moved
to Woodford Co., Ky., in 1848. Stock raiser. Know nothing
of issue.

(41) Nancy Maria Culbertson mar. J. V. Curtis. Lived at Auburn, Neb.
Issue:
97. Daughter (Mrs. Gilmore). Auburn. Neb.

(46) Caroline C. Culbertson mar. Ebenezer Parsons in 1841 at Troy, Ohio. Husband b. Suffield, Conn., Apr. 25, 1810; d. ——. Judge at Troy, Ohio.
Issue:

99. Clarisse Jane Parsons, b. Nov. 30, 1842. Living. Mar.
      Martin Luther Temple, Troy, Ohio, 1864. No
issue.
100.Emma Fannie, b. July 15, 1845; d. Apr. 2, 1913. Mar.
      at Troy, O., 1876 to J. G. Detmer of Brooklyn, N. Y.
      Issue: Caroline mar. in Brooklyn, N. Y., to St.
      John Wood, Apr. 1895. No issue. Justice G. Det-
      mer.
101. George Fitch, b. Dec. 29, 1847; d. Apr., 1911. Troy,
      Ohio.
102. Caroline Culbertson Parsons, b. July 13, 1850. Mar.
      1869 at Troy, O., to Lieut. E. B. Thomas, U. S.
      Navy. Died 1896-7. No issue.
103. Robert Hovey, b. Dec. 12, 1852; d. Sep. 28, 1918.
      Troy, Ohio.
104. Laura Belle, b. Feb. 12, 1855; d. July 8, 1921. Mar.
      Oct., 1882 at Troy, O. to Miles G. Nixon. Issue:
      Mary Caroline Nixon, Troy, Ohio.
105. Estella Kate, b. Jan. 15, 1858. Troy, Ohio.
106. Mary, Jr., June 18, 1861. Mar.

(52) Dr. John W. Culbertson mar. Mrs. Elizabeth Ashman of Bath, Eng. Richmond, Ind.
Issue:
107. Mary (Richmond, Ind.) Artist.

(53) Charles H. Culbertson mar. Elizabeth Stewart. No issue.

(54) Major Samuel S. Culbertson mar. Mary Hill.

EIGHTH GENERATION

(92) Mary F. Culbertson mar. J. H. Young.
Issue:
107. Anna Goodrich Young, b. June 8, 1872
108. James Wilson, b. Nov. 6, 1876.
109. Lillie Abbott, b. Oct. 16, 1878.

(93) Maria E. Culbertson mar. Frank G. Eddy, May 13, 1875.

Issue: Paul Goodrich Eddy, b. Nov. 7, 1876.

(95) Lina Cordelia Culbertson mar. Wilson S. Becker. Husband d. March 6, 1885. No issue.

(96) Sue Bilger Culbertson mar. Robert C. Enders, Nov. 1885. Troy, Ohio.

Issue:

110. Henry Culbertson Enders.
111. Lina G.
112. Arthur Edward.

(106) Mary Parsons, Jr. mar. Charles Converse West. Lives at Mt. Clair, N. J.

Issue:

113. Charles Parsons West, b. Apr 9, 1888; d. June 16, 1889.
114. Helen Copland, b. June 9, 1894. Mar. Apr. 19, 1919, John M. Chapman, Jr. Issue: Helen W., b. June 9, 1920, d.; Mary Parsons, b. Nov. 27, 1921. Caldwell, N. J.
115. George Parsons, b. Dec. 29, 1896. Mar. Florence L. Farish. Issue: Chas. Converse (2nd) b. Feb. 3, 1921. Plainfield, N. J.
116. Robert Culbertson, b. Sep. 20, 1903.
117. Converse Dittmar, b. Sep. 3, 1890. Mar. Katherine Carr, Apr. 6, 1909. Issue: Mildred, b. Dec. 3, 1909; Katherine b. Sep. 29, 1912.

(107) George Parsons West volunteered for service in World War July 4, 1917. Entered 112 H. Field Art'y. Sent to Sea Girt, N. J. Made Sergt. Sent to Anniston, Ala. Sent to officers' training camp. Made Lieut. Studied Art. Radio College, Park, Md. Sent as Instructor to San Diego, Cal. Discharged Dec., 1918.

PROMINENT DESCENDANTS OF COL. ROBERT CULBERTSON OF BEDFORD CO., PA.

(8) Joseph and his brothers, Henry W., and Robert, together with Henry H., organized the firm of Culbertson & Bros., about 1836, and did a large dry goods, pork packing and milling business for many years. Their cousin, Robert, was also associated in business with them.

(11½) Samuel Culbertson moved from Bedford Co., Pa.,

to Maryland and, in 1823, moved to Troy, O., being one of
the early settlers of that place, and contributed to the development of that village and the advancement of the interests of the community. In 1837 he moved to a farm in
Miami Co., O., where his son, Dr. John W., was born. This
son, Dr. J. W., was raised here and at the age of fourteen
entered McCurdy's Academy. Here he qualified himself
for the vocation of teacher. He became a teacher, earning
in this way the money to pay for his medical education. He
studied under Dr. Sabin, of Troy, T. Graduated at the Ohio
Medical College, Cincinnati, O., and located at Troy, O. He
soon decided to make the eye and ear his specialties and
with this object in view became a private student of Dr. G.
B. Woods, of Allegheny, Pa. He then took up the practice
of his specialty in Richmond, Ind. He was of an inventive
turn of mind, and originated a painless treatment for gran-
ulated eye lids, which obviates the excruciating tortures of
cauterization; benefits accruing from the treatment being
manifest at once. He likewise invented an artificial fluid
ear drum (a bulb filled with liquid) easily adjusting itself
to the opening in tympanic membrane. He performed over
two thousand operations for straightening crossed eyes. He
had an eye hospital in Indianapolis to which people went
from several states. He had the Culbertson build and possessed the indomitable energy and will, which is a characteristic of the Culbertsons. His wife married first, Rev.
Ashman, an Episcopal clergyman, of England, and had by
him one son, Dr. Edward H. The god-father of Dr. Culbertson's daughter, Sir Thomas Blake, has published a
book of poems and songs, some of which are dedicated to
Mrs. Dr. J. W. Culbertson.

His daughter, Mary, is a prominent artist. A writer in
Demorests Magazine on the "Society Leaders of Indiana,"
says of her: "If one were writing a sketch of the women of
Indiana, who are distinguished for rare talent, he would
place at the top of the list Miss M. E. B. Culbertson; and
yet she is equally entitled to a place among the beautiful
society favorites, for nature and her own efforts have
fitted her to adorn the sphere of both. Young, handsome,
talented, wealthy, on the maternal side, Miss Culbertson
belongs to the family of the Duke of Rutland. Her mother
was the daughter of Major Kilbourne, a celebrated naval
officer, and is a prominent figure in the book of English
beauties, with the Duchess of Southerland and other noted
women. Her only daughter, the subject of this sketch, was

a god-child of Sir Thomas Blake; a member of the historic
Carlton Club. At his death he left her a ward in Chancery,
with a fortune that enables her to follow her own sweet will
in study, travel, and the pursuit of the aesthetics of life.
After her father's death she went to Paris and entered the
famous studio of Julian, where the unfortunate Marie Bash-
kirtseff was once a pupil. Here, under such teachers as
Constant and Bouguereau, she threw her whole soul into
the work. For two years she lived in the Latin Quartier;·
ignoring the young and gay society of the French capital,
and devoting all her time and energy to art. Like all artists,
her ambition was to have a picture accepted by the French
Salon. Steadily and faithfully she toiled, and finally finished the picture and sent it to the august tribunal. To her
inexpressible joy it was one of fifteen hundred which were
accepted out of six thousand. In France this means fame,
and is an almost incredible honor for a young American
girl. While in the studio, Miss Culbertson was intimately
associated with Amelia Rives Chanler, and the warmest
friendship exists between them; indeed there is a great
similarity in their characteristics. Miss Culbertson's pictures cover a wide range of subjects, and in all there
breathes the spirit of a remarkable genius."

"She has traveled extensively in Europe, both for pleasure and to increase her knowledge of art and her ability to
execute. The subject of her picture which was accepted by
the Salon was that of the escaped nun, Maria Monk. This
picture now hangs in the Gallery of Honor, in the Woman's
Building, at the World's Fair, at Chicago. A picture of
Miss Culbertson, painted by herself, hangs in the Indiana Building, at the World's Fair. Her picture of 'The
Burial of a Monk', a copy of the celebrated painting by Leon
Benouville in the new French Salle at the Louvre, is considered as strong and bold as the original. It is of the Rem-
brandt school. Her copy of the head of a famous dog, the
original by Gricault, was complimented by C. Duran, the
finest portrait painter of the age.

She has copies which she made of two very old paintings,
"The Drinker", and "The Reader,,' made by the Flemish
artist Vanostade. They exhibit her conscientiousness as a
copyist, for she has not only copied, but followed the ancient
style of coloring, mellowed by age and changed by smoke.

A sculptor of renown made and presented to her a bas-
relief, in memory of her salon success. It represents Literature and Art. The head is that of Miss Culbertson. She

is also a sculptor of great ability and is now at work on a bust of her father. She is also writing a book, entitled: 'Among the Art Students of Paris'. The author of the projected work, 'Distinguished Women of the Century', has asked Miss Culbertson's consent to include a sketch of her in his work."—Newspapers (1892).

(54) Major Samuel S. Culbertson "was appointed from Army, 2nd Lieut. 19th Inf., Nov. 20, 1861; Ist Lieut., June 30, 1863; Capt., Sep. 26, 1865. Transferred to 28th Inf., Sep. 21, 1866. Transferred to 19th Inf., Mar. 31, 1869. Mustered out Jan. 1, 1871. Brevet Rank:—Bevet Capt., Apr. 2, 1865, for gallant and meritorious service at Battle of Selma, Ala. Brevet Major, Apr. 2, 1865, for gallant and meritorious service during the war." (Army Reg.)

(53) Charles H. was a Judge and prominent lawyer at Troy, Ohio.

CHAPTER XXIII

(IV) "Baron James" (Capt.) son of Capt. Alex of Lurgan (Died Dec., 1805). In 1774 lived in Cumb. Tp., Bedford Co., Pa., as shown by quit claim. Paid tax Bedford, 1776 to 1779 in Cumb. Tp. and Coleraine Tp. This was a warrant his father took out. He afterwards moved to Fannettsburg, Franklin Co., Pa., where he died. We do not know why he received the appellation of "Baron", probably to distinguish him from "Gentlemen James". Mar. Ann ——. (From administration; children from family records.) His (James) widow and James McMordia were adm'n'rs of his est. and settlement was made and they were released by court in 1812 in Franklin Co., Pa. Census 1790 gives him and six sons under 16, wife and one daughter (Southhampton Tp. "Row") Letterkenny Tp., 1799 (Tax). Married 1773-4? See end of Chapter for Revolutionary Record.

Issue:
1. John, d. in army.
2. James, b. Sept. 3, 1779; d. Sept. 3, 1836. (Hatter).
3. Joseph, b. Dec. 20, 1780; d. 1852.
4. Alexander, d. Bachelor.
5. Wm. B., d. 1841.
6. Samuel, d. 1819. Moved to Ohio.
7. Robert, d. at Fannettsburg, Franklin Co., Pa.
8. Margaret, d. (Mar. cousin "Devil Alex."); born 1774.
9. Pauline, d. Mar. Stephen Wilson.

SIXTH GENERATION

(2) James Culbertson mar. Miss Cassandra Jamison, of Franklin Co., Pa., daughter of Col. David Jamison, who at one time lived at York, Pa., and was an officer as well as surgeon, both in the French and Indian War and the Revolution. It was he (D. Jamison) who was in the battle of Bloody Run, in 1756. James Culbertson moved to McKeesport, Pa., and later to Zanesville, O., in 1805, being one of the early settlers of that place. Then moved to Columbus, O., and remained a short time; then returned to Zanesville, where he died. Wife b. 1782; d. Aug. 17, 1852.

Issue:
10. Elizabeth, b. Mar. 17, 1802; d. Mar. 3, 1861.
11. James, b. July 10, 1804; d. Apr. 2, 1862.
12. Emily, b. June 1, 1807; d. Apr. 10, 186—.
13. Jane, b. Feb. 20, 1809; d. Mar. 15, 1852.
14. David Jamison, b. June 8, 1811; d. May 1, '63.
15. Samuel, d. young.
16. Harriett J., b. July 15, 1815; d. young.
17. Horatio Perry, b. July 16, ——; d. Sept, 2, 1871.
18. Nancy, b. July 4, 1820; d. infancy.
19. Joseph, b. Dec. 25, 1821; d. Aug. 3, '64.
20. William, b. Dec. 17, 1824. (carpenter) Zanesville, O.

(3) Joseph Culbertson mar. Martha Walker, of Burnt Cabins, Cumb. Co., in 1805 (now Fulton Co.), Pa. Moved first to Washington Co., Pa.; then to Meigs Tp., Muskingum Co., O., in the thirties. Mar. by Rev. McGinley.

Issue:
21. David, d. 1877, aet. 71. Washington Co., Pa.
22. James, d. 1877, aet. 68. Muskingum Co., O.
23. Alexander, d. 1844. (bachelor) Musk. Co., O. Salt Creek Tp.
24. Mary, d. young.
25. John W., b. 1812. Macon Co., Ills.
26. Eliza, b. 1815. Minnesota.
27. Samuel, b. June 21, 1821; d. Oct. 22, 1882.

(5) Wm. B. Culbertson, Fannettsburg, Franklin Co., Pa., mar. Elizabeth——. Moved to Meigs tp., Muskingum Co., O. Moved from Franklin Co., in 1812. No issue. Left property to wife and nephew B. Hamer. His brother Joseph Culbertson and nephew, James Culbertson, witnessed his will.

(6) Samuel Culbertson moved from Fannettsburg, Pa.,

to Ohio. See end of this chapter.

(7) Robert Culbertson made a deed for land in Metal Tp in 1807. No wife on deed. We do not know what became of him after this. There was a Robert died in 1814 in Franklin Co., Pa. and a Jos. Culbertson app ad'm'n. Do not know if this was his estate.

(8) Margaret Culbertson mar. cousin "Devil" Alex. See descendants of Col. Samuel (I).

SEVENTH GENERATION

(10) Elizabeth Culbertson mar. Cadwalader Dickerson, of Philadelphia, Sep. 7, 1820. Lived at Zanesville, O. Was one of the first silversmiths of that place.
Issue:
28. Harriet Dickerson (Mrs. P. Berry). Moulton, Ia.

(11) James Culbertson mar. Miss Sarah Cliffton, of Zanesville, July 25, 1826.
Issue:
29. James, d. 1863.

(12) Emily Culbertson mar. Washington Jeffries, of Zanesville Feb. 5, 1829, whose mother was a daughter of Col. Crawford, of War of 1812, who was burned at the stake by the Indians.
Issue:
30. Emily Jeffries, d. Apr. 10, 1867. Lancaster, O.

(13) Jane Culbertson mar. Thos. H. Patrick of Zanesville, O. Husband d. Sep. 18, 1881.
Issue:
31. Jamison Patrick, d.
32. James Harvey, d.
33. Perry, d.
34. Elizabeth Ellen, d.
35. Catherine Brown (Mrs. Dr. Slater). Aurora, Ills. Dead.
36. Harriet Jane (Mrs. J. C. Harris). Zanesville. Dead.
37. Asa Peters, d.
38. Thomas Adams, d. Issue: Thos. and Nathan (Dr.) dead.

(14) David Jamison Culbertson mar. Mary Ellen McLeary of Zanesville, Oct. 19, 1841. Capt. in Union Army, Ohio Vols.

Issue:
39. Susan, mar.. Lived at Peru, Ind.
40. Elizabeth, mar. Lives at Peru, Ind.

(20) Wm. Culbertson mar. Miss Margaret Bonham Bell, daughter of Dr. Bell of Zanesville, O., Apr. 21, 1853. Wife d., 1893. (Carpenter) Zanesville.
Issue:
41. Lillie. Zanesville (unmarried). Lives Zanesville, O.
42. Harry Jameson. Zanesville: Dead. Mar. Phoebe ——.
     Issue. Lives Zanesville.
43. James Clifford. Zanesville. Dead. Bachelor.
44. Wm. Edward, d. young.
45. Charles Goddard. Bellaire, O. (Ex-Mayor).
46. Wm. Edward, d. young.

(25) John Walker Culbertson, mar. Eliza James in 1855. Moved to Macon Co., Ills. Wife b.—'; d. May, 1852.
Issue:
47. David James. Died in Civil War; b. 1838; d. 1865.
48. George Smith, b. 1841; d. 1918.
49. Joseph Benjamin, b. 1845; d. 1906.
50. Griffith James, Lincoln, Neb., b. 1848; living Lincoln, Neb.
51. William Henry, b. 1850. Mar. Emma Lietzel.
52. Mary, d. 1837, in infancy; b. 1837.
53. Martha Eliza, b. July 31, 1840 (Mrs. Kennard).
54. Nancy Jane, b. 1833; d. 1921. (Mrs. Knoop).
54¼. Alice A. Culbertson, b. 1861. Unmar. Lives Macon, Ills.
54½. L. Florence Culbertson (Mrs. Clarence Wise, Macon, Ills.) These daughters of (25) John Walker Culbertson were by second wife, Margaret Gibson of Cumberland, Ohio to whom John Walker Culbertson was married in 1855.

(27) Samuel Culbertson mar. March 13, 1845, to Miss Celinda Amanda Matson; lived at High Hill, Muskingum Co., Ohio. (b. June 7, 1825. Wife d. July 2, 1915.)
Issue:
55. Sarah Ellen Culbertson, b. Feb. 21, 1846; d. Nov. 18, 1914.
56. William Alex. Culbertson, b. Nov. 21, 1847; living.
57. Mary Eliza Culbertson b. June 14, 1851; living.
58. Niry Jane Culbertson, b. March 17, 1853; d. Jan. 21, 1878; unmar.

59. James Willis Culbertson, b. March 11, 1855; d. May 4, 1914; unmar.
60. Theodore Walker Culbertson, b. Feb. 2, 1858; d. Aug. 10, 1899.

EIGHTH GENERATION

(36) Harriet Jane Patrick mar. John C. Harris, a promi‐ nent merchant of Zanesville, Ohio.
Issue:
61. Ralph, d. infancy.

(38) Thomas Adams Patrick, mar. ——.
Issue:
62. Thomas mar. Issue, daughter. Lives at Chicago.
63. Nathan (Dr.) d.

(48) George Smith Culbertson, mar. 1866 to Lucy Cona‐ way.
Issue:
64. Altah.
65. Ethel.
66. Hazel.

(49) Joseph Benjamin Culbertson, mar. 1869 to Eliza Lane.
Issue:
67. Wynona.

(50) Griffith James Culbertson, mar. 1872 to Lydia Peeper. Wife b. Oct. 21, 1848; d. Nov. 26, 1921.
Issue:
68. Hannah Gertrude (Mrs. S. J. Bell), b. Apr. 8, 1874.
69. Jesse Carrol, b. Nov. 25, 1882. Unmarried.
70. Harold Griffith, b. Oct. 9, 1884.

(53) Martha Elizabeth Culbertson, mar 1861 to Mr. Wm J. Kennard. She is living at McArthur, Ohio.
Issue:
71. Daughter.
72. Daughter.

(54) Nancy Jane Culbertson mar. Mr. Wm. Knoop, 1865 Live at Grand Island, Neb.
Issue:
73. Oscar Culbertson Knoop, Stonington, Ill.s.
74. ——
75. Alice Almeda Knoop. Unmar. Macon, Ills.
(51) Wm. Henry Culbertson, Grand Island, Neb. Mar

1874, to Emma Leitzel.

(55) Sarah Ellen Culbertson, mar. Lewis McClelland, Apr. 4, 1863.
Issue:
76. Mary Maude, d. childhood.
77. Fred d. when young man; mar. Clarkie Hunter. Issue, Paul and Fred.

(56) Wm. Alexander Culbertson. Lives at Cumberland, Guernsey Co., Ohio, R. F. D. Married first, Martha Criss.
Issue:
78. Claude R. who married —— and had issue seven children; was a Presbyterian minister in Pennsylvania and a fine young man.

(56) Wm. Alexander mar. second to Jennie Cubbison.
Issue:
67. Eleanor Francis, b. 1913.

(57) Mary Eliza Culbertson, mar. Monroe Thomson. No issue. Husband died. She remarried to Perley B. Sevall who died several years ago. Widow lives in Zanesville, O.

(60) Theodore Walker Culbertson, mar. Alice McCracken, Apr. 1, 1880 (wife b. Jan. 28, 1861; d. Dec. 20, 1915).
Issue:
79. Perley Francis, b. Sept. 12, 1880. Mar.
80. Carrie Maude, b. Dec. 24, 1881.
81. Harry Willis, b. Nov. 10, 1883.
82. Fred Darwin, b. Jan. 16, 1886.
83. Howard Vaughn, b. June 20, 1888.

NINTH GENERATION

(68) Hannah Gertrude Culbertson mar. Samuel J. Bell. Lincoln, Neb. May 11, 1899.
Issue:
84. Marjorie Culbertson Bell, b. Aug. 13,1902.

(69) Jesse Carroll Culbertson, Muskogee, Okla.; wealthy oil producer. Unmarried.

(70) Harold Griffith Culbertson, mar. July, 1916, to Anna Cantwell. Live at South Minneapolis, Minn.
Issue:
85. Wayne Keith, b. June 24, 1919.
86. Robert Griffith } Twins, b. Oct. 28, 1920.
87. Gene Allen

(79) Perley Francis Culbertson, mar. Lives in Zanesville, O.

(80) Carrie Maude Culbertson, mar. E. H. Waller.

(81) Harry Willis Culbertson, mar. Louella F. Van Dyne, July 8, 1905.
Issue:
88. Gladys Culbertson, b. March 4, 1906.
89. Willis D., b. Aug. 25, 1907.

(82) Fred Darwin Culbertson, mar. Fronie Mae Paisley, Jan. 4, 1905.
Issue:
90. Herbert Malcolm, b.

(83) Howard Vaughn Culbertson, mar. Sept. 3, 1913.
Issue:
91. Mary Louise, b. July 22, 1916.
92. Robert Wm., b. July 25, 1918.

NOTE: Just before going to press I received a letter from a descendent of (6) Samuel, son of "Baron" James Culbertson. As I could not rearrange my forms I will take up this Samuel's children and number them where I left off with number in above chapter.—(Editor).

* * * * *

SIXTH GENERATION

(6) Samuel Culbertson mar. Hannah Trousdale in 1805, in Path Valley. Mar. by Rev. A. A. McGinley. Wife b. 1785; d. Nov. 14, 1864. The family moved to Ohio, where Samuel died. The widow then moved back to Path Valley, Franklin Co., Pa., where she died. Widow app. adm'trix Nov. 23, 1819, Franklin Co., Pa.
Issue:
93. Eliza, b. Apr. 4, 1808. Unmar.
94. William, b. Feb. 26, 1809.
95. James, unmar.
96. Stephen, b. June 19, 1813.
97. Jane, b. Nov. 4, 1816. Unmar.
98. Margaret, b. Mar. 19, 1818.

SEVENTH GENERATION

(94) William Culbertson mar. Margaret Scott in 1835. She died shortly after. He remarried to Polly Dunkle in 1837

Issue:
99.   James.
100.   Mary, d. aet 15 years.

(96) Stephen Culbertson mar. Margaret McCune, Apr. 5, 1838.
Issue:
101.   Mary Anna, b. Jan. 5, 1839; d. Apr. 6, 1906.
102.   James Barkley, b. May 22, 1841; d. Jan. 7, 1904.
103.   Samuel, b. Oct. 11, 1844.
104.   McGinley, b. Mar. 27, 1847.
105.   Sarah Elizabeth, b. Oct. 17, 1849 d. Dec. 8, 1906.
106.   David Isaac, b. Dec. 17, 1852.
107.   William West, b. Mar. 26, 1854
109.   Margaret Ellen, b. July 22, 1857.
110.   Albert Ross, b. Oct. 20, 1861.

(98) Margaret Culbertson mar. Stephen McGinley Skinner, Mar. 26, 1840.
Issue:
111.   Calvin M. Skinner (mar. Mrs. Johnson in 1879).
112.   Isaac Skinner (wife's name unknown).
113.   Drucilla (mar. Dr. Campbell).
114.   James W. Unmar.
115.   Daniel M. (mar. Blanche McKim).
116.   Maggie S. (mar. J. Mac Wolff).
117.   West C. (mar. Emma Stitt).

EIGHTH GENERATION

(99) James Culbertson, mar. Jane L. Rogers.
Issue:
118.   Minta (mar. James Rolls).
119.   William (mar. Mary Mowers). Homestead, N. D.

(101) Mary Anna Culbertson mar. Simon Stewart, Apr. 24, 1867. Issue: Ella M. (Mrs. F. M. McGee); Annie R. (Mrs. A. W. Ekenrode); Alden L.

(102) James Barclay Culbertson, mar. Margaret Stewart, Dec. 31, 1863.

(103) Samuel Culbertson mar. Ann Jane Culbertson, Oct. 13, 1870.

(104) McGinley Culbertson mar. Evaline McVitty, Dec. 27, 1870; mar. second Mary Ann Fegan, Dec. 9, 1873.

(106) David Isaac Culbertson mar. Emma Sherer, Dec. 29, 1881. Lives York, Pa.

Issue:
120. Bessie S., b. 1883.
121. Ella Mabel, b. 1885.
122. Ralph T., b. 1891, Mar., has one daughter, Doris Fay.
123. A. Newlon, b. 1893. Mar., has six children.
124. Raymond Eugene, b. 1899.

(107) Wm. West Culbertson mar. Ida M. Piper, May 9, 1907. No issue.
(109) Margaret Ellen Culbertson mar. Wm. A. McVitty.
Issue:
125. Dwight.
126. Carrie (Mrs. Clark P. Craig).

(110) Albert Ross Culbertson mar. Orpha Ann Piper, Nov. 30, 1886.

(102) Stephen B. Culbertson was an Elder of Path Valley Church (Franklin Co., Pa.) and in 1876 built a church for the Amberson District. Was Elder for 35 years. Was also a veteran of the Civil War.

* * * * *

*(IV) CAPT. JAMES CULBERTSON AND PROMINENT DESCENDANTS.

Capt James ("Baron James") moved from Bedford Co., Pa., in 1779. Is not found in tax records of Franklin or Cumb. Co. from 1779 to 1785, but is found on the Census of 1790 in Southhampton Tp., Franklin Co. (Row). A deed in 1791 shows him residing in and a member of the school-board of Southhampton Tp. He must have been a tenant or renter as I could find no deed from him. Moved to Fannettsburg before he died. The Pa. Archives gives his service "Was commissioned Capt. of the Third Co., 4th Batt'n (Col. Samuel Culbertson) of Cumb. Co., Ass'rs., May 10, 1780."

(36) Mrs. Dr. Slater was a prominent physician of Peoria, Illinois.

(50) Griffith James Culbertson of Lincoln, Neb., is a prominent real estate man and one of Nebraska's brainy and successful men. His son (69) Jesse Carroll Culbertson is a wealthy oil producer at Muskogee, Okla. Another son (70) Harold Griffith is a prominent business man of Minnesota (Minneapolis).

*His son Alex (4) may have moved to Washington Co., Pa., but no court record of him there or in Muskingum County, Ohio.

CHAPTER XXIV

FIFTH GENERATION

(V) **Capt. Alexander Culbertson** mar. Mary Sharp, dau. of Capt. Jas. Sharp. Was a tanner. Lived at Strasburg, Franklin Co., Pa. Afterwards moved to Zanesville, Ohio. On Census of 1790, self and wife, 4 sons under 16, 2 daughters. First on tax lists in Letterkenny Tp., in 1772, 88 acres. War. 10 acres clear, 1 horse, 1 cow. First on tax lists Cumb. Tp., Cumb. Co., 1770; this land was in Bedford Co., 1771, and was on a warrant taken out by his father in 1762.* Wife Mary Sharpe, daughter Capt. Jas. Sharpe.

Issue:

1. James, d. Nov. 1821 (tanner), Zanesville, Ohio.
2. Margaret, b. 1773; d. 1834. Franklin Co., Pa.
3. Elizabeth, b. 1779; d. 1845. Zanesville, O.
4. Samuel W., b. 1780; d. 1840. Zanesville, O.
5. Alexander d. 1823 (May). Zanesville O.
6. William d. Apr., 1833. Wash. Tp., Musk. Co., O.
7. Robert, d. 1860. Wash Tp., Musk. Co., O.
8. John, d. 1860. Perry Tp., Musk. Co., O.
8½. Mary (Mrs. Col. Steph. Willson) Franklin Co., Pa.

SIXTH GENERATION

(1) James Culbertson mar. Miss Huey at Zanesville, Ohio. Moved to Zanesville about 1812.

Issue:

9. Samuel, d. Tanner at Zanesville. (Know nothing of).
10. Alexander, d. Tanner at Zanesville.
11. Ellen, d. (Mrs. Reeves).

(2) Margaret Culbertson mar. Judge Wm. McClay, of Path Valley, Franklin Co., Pa., Dec. 22, 1789.

Issue:

12, 13, 14, 15, 16, 16.
18. Ellen McClay (Mrs. Cyrus D. Culbertson).

(3) Elizabeth Culbertson mar. Jacob Cassel, of Strasburg, Pa., and later of Zanesville, Ohio. Jacob Cassel, b. 1775; d. 1841.

Issue:

19. Joseph Cassel, d. Zanesville, Ohio.
20. Wm. Culbertson, d. Miller, Zanesville, Ohio.
21. Elizabeth Culbertson, d. (Mrs. Brotherton).

*See end of this chapter for Revolutionary Record.

22.   Alexander, d. Issue: Wm. C., Tupper Cassel, Zanesville,
       Ohio.
22½. James Wilson, b. 1815; d. 1850. Zanesville. Issue:
       Florence, Leila (Mrs. Gibbs). Douglas (Comman-
       der U. S. N.).
23.   ——, d.

(4) Samuel W. Culbertson mar. Nancy Boyd, daughter of
Samuel Boyd of Philadelphia, Pa. Moved to Zanesville, O.,
about 1810. Lawyer. Wife b. Mar. 8, 1789; d. Mar. 31,
1860; mar. April, 1804. Issue:
23½. Alex. Samuel Boyd, b. 1805; d. 1856. Lawyer.
24.   Wm. Boyd, b. 1807; d. 1861.
25.   Sidney A., b. July 2, 1813; d. Sept. 5, 1884. Never
       married. Zanesville, O.
26.   Mary E., b. Dec. 31, 1809; d. Sept. 7, 1854.

(5) Alexander Culbertson mar. Annauche Cassel. Moved
to Zanesville, O., in 1810 and lived on River Road just back
of where Merkle's Brewery stood. No issue. Left money
to wife and niece, Margaret Annauche Culbertson (28).
(Annauche Cassel was an aunt of one Ferree, who died in
Zanesville 1813. Soldier War 1812.)

(6) Wm. Culbertson mar. first a daughter of Francis
Campbell, Jr., Jane Campbell of Franklin Co., Pa. Moved to
Washington Tp., Muskingum Co., O. Buried in Wash. Tp.,
Musk. Co., O., probably on farm. (Jane Campbell's grandfather, Frances Campbell, wounded at "Bloody Run Battle",
1756. Shippensburg home.)
Issue:
27.   Sarah, b. 1817; d. Aug. 20, 1841 (Mrs. Louis Henry
       Dugan).
28.   Margaret Annauche, b. Feb. 20, 1813; d. June 2, 1881.
       (Mrs. Lloyd Dillon).
29.   Mary Jane (Mrs. R. P. Robinson).
30.   Rebecca, b. 1819. (Mrs. Dunn of Zanesville).

(6) Wm. Culbertson mar. second Mrs. Martha Marple,
Dec. 29, 1825. No issue.

(7) Robert Culbertson mar. Alice Johnson, moved to
Washington Tp., Muskingum Co., Ohio. Farmer.
Issue:
31.   George W., d. Muskingum Co., O.
32.   James, d. 1892. Bachelor. Muskingum Co., O.
33.   Jane, d. Mar. No issue.

34. Mary, d. Never married.
35. Margaret (Mrs. Walters).
36. Elizabeth. (Mrs. Burwell).

(8) John Culbertson mar. Miss Beavers of Virginia. Moved to Perry Tp., Muskingum Co., O.
Issue:
37. Edward Cassell, Delavan, Ills.
38. John. Editor. Delavan, Ills.
39. Wm. Flood Beatty, d. in California. (Bachelor).
39½. Cecelia, d. young.
40. Jane, d. young.
41. Sydney, d. young.

(8½) Mary mar. Col. Steph. Wilson of Strasburg, Pa. (tanner). A daughter Mary married Thos. Pomeroy (tanner) at Roxbury, Pa. Col. Wilson and wife, Mary, had issue 6 boys and 3 girls.

SEVENTH GENERATION

(10) Alexander Culbertson mar. April 16, 1832, to Ann Haslett. Tanner in Second Ward, Zanesville; afterwards moved to farm near Dresden, Ohio.
Issue:
42. Mary Haslett, b. 1833; d. 1892. (Mrs. Paul Egan), Zanesville, Ohio.
43. Elizabeth Ellen, b. 1837. (Mrs. Lynn). Belmont, O.
44. Sarah Jane, b. 1841. (Mrs. W. T. Voris).
45. Margaret, b. 1846. (Mrs. Dr. Geyer). Norwich, O.
46. Frank Samuel, b. 1847. Mo.
47. Robert Morton, b. 1850. Mo.
48. James, d. in Army at Port Hudson, 1862.
49. Daughter, d. young.

(23½) Alexander S. B. Culbertson mar. Dec. 4, 1828, Sophia Tupper, daughter of Gen. Tupper of War of 1812, and granddaughter of Gen. Rufus Putnam. Was a lawyer at Zanesville, Ohio. No issue.

(24) Wm. Boyd Culbertson mar. Louisa B. Moody of Baltimore, Md., who was a sister of the fighting Parson Moody. Lived on River Road near Zanesville, in Wayne Tp., five miles south.
Issue:
50. Samuel W., b. 1836; d. 1861, near Zanesville.
51. Wm. M., d. Feb. 26, 1892.

52. Harriet A.
53. Alexander Keith. Kansas.
54. Sidney E.
55. Ida L.
56. Granville, d. young.
57. Louisa, d. young.
58. Stilman, d. young.
59. George V. N., b. 1853; d. Dec. 31, 1877.

(26) Mary E. Culbertson mar. Joshua Mathiot of Newark, O., a lawyer.

Issue:
60. Ann Eliza (Mrs. Rev. Theo L. Cuyler of Brookyln). d.
61. Sidney L. (Mrs. Arthur B. Proal of Brooklyn).
62. George C., d. young. June 15, 1853.   `
63. S. W. Culbertson, d. young. July 16, 1840.
64. Culbertson K., d. young.

(27) Sarah Ann Culbertson mar. Louis Henry Dugan of Muskingum Co., O., April 19, 1836.

Issue:
65. James Dugan, d. young.
66. John, d. young.
67. Caroline (Mrs. Wm. Fillmore of Zanesville), b. Sept. 5, 1840. Issue of Barbara Caroline (Dugan) and Wm. Fillmore: Annie (Mrs. Douglas Blandy, issue Marie (Mrs. T. B. Trainer) ; Arthur; Harry L., of Columbus; William, mar. Kitty Harris, and Ralph. (Harry L. mar. Ida Marshall, issue Helen and Robert; Helen mar. Ralph W. Yingling; Robert mar. Mary Mehling. Issue: Harold Louis, Wm. Fillmore.

(28) Margaret Annauche Culbertson was adopted by her Uncle Alexander Culbertson, Jr., and his wife Annauche, being named after her aunt. When her uncle Alex. died he left one-half of his estate to his wife to dispose of as she pleased and the other half he left to his niece, Margaret Annauche Culbertson. She married Apr. 3 1832 to Lloyd Dillon of Zanesville, O., and later moved to Sterling, Ills. Her children were prominent people of central Ills. Her son Washington M. Dillon was a Civil War officer and became a wealthy iron-master of Sterling, Ills. Lloyd Dillon, Sr., b Baltimore Md., Feb. 2, 1803; d. June 2, 1881.

Issue:
68. Ellen Annauche Dillon, b. Feb. 15, 1834.

69. Mary Price, b. Mar. 7, 1836; d. May 16, 1867
70. Loyd Haynes Dillon, b. Dec. 18, 1838; d. June 18, 1898
71. Washington Morehead Dillon, b. July 2, 1842; d. Jan 12, 1920.
72. Moses Dillon, b. Sept. 19, 1845.

(29) Margaret Annauche (Culbertson) Dillon mar. second, her deceased sister's (Mary Jane) husband, R. P. Robinson. Issue: 72¼, George, Sterling, Ills; and 72½ Samuel. Her son Samuel mar. Miss Herron of Pittsburg, Pa. and had issue: Maude (Mrs. King of Chicago) and Maizie (Mrs. Melvin).

(30) Mary Jane Culbertson mar. R. P. Robinson of Zanesville, O., and Sterling and Dixon, Ills., a wealthy iron and hardware man.
Issue: Sarah, Samuel, Frank of Morrison, Ills., Lloyd Aarabella, Robert and William.

* * * * *

Issue of (71) Washington M. Dillon, son of Margaret An nauche and Loyd Dillon who mar. May 8, 1873 to Sarah Jane Martin. Resided at Sterling, Ills. Issue: Mary Cath erine (Mrs. D. P. Wild) ; Margaret Annauche (Mrs. H. F. Eshelman of Lancaster, Pa.) ; Dr. John Dillon; Paul Dillon.

* * * * *

(31) Geo. W. Culbertson mar. ——, Washington Tp., Mus-kingum Co., O.

Issue: 73, Sophia; 73½, Sydney; 74, Cyrus; 75, Mathiot; 76, Howard M.; 77, Cuyler; 78, Wm.; 78½, Joshua M.; 78¾, Geo. W. K. (See Addenda for 76-78).

(35) Margaret Culbertson mar. Mr. Walters of Wash. Tp., Musk. Co., O.
Issue: 79, Lydia; 80, Amanda; 81, Anna; 82, Samuel.

(36) Elizabeth Culbertson mar. Joseph Burwell of Wash. Tp., Musk. Co., O.
Issue: 83, Robert; 84, Alice; 85, Mary Jane.

(37) Edward Cassel Culbertson mar. Ruth Caroline Sheets. Lived at Delavan, Ills.
Issue:
86. Wm. Joseph.
87. Maurice Edward.
88. Elizabeth Ann.

89.   John Thomas.
90.   Mary Belle.
91.   Ruth Caroline.

(38) John Culbertson mar ——. Was an editor at Dela van, Ills.
Issue:
91.   Cecelia Blanche.
92.   Ella Augusta.
93.   Sarah A. (Ertie.)

EIGHTH GENERATION

(43) Elizabeth Ellen mar. Mr. Lynn of Belmont, Ohio.
Issue:
94.   Charles Culbertson Lynn.
95.   Howard Voris.
96.   Nellie May.
97.   Anna Bell (McKisson).
98.   Maggie Hazlett (King).

(46) Frank Samuel Culbertson, lived in Mo. In tobacco business.
Issue:
Know nothing about.

(47) Robert Morton Culbertson lived in Mo.; in tobacco business.
Issue:
Know nothing about.

(51) Wm. M. Culbertson mar. Kate B. Welch of McConnelsville, O. Widow lives at Lawrence, Kan.
Issue:
99.   Howard D., d. 1870.
100.   Francis, d. 1878.
101.   Chas. W.
102.   Katherine W.

(52) Harriet A. Culbertson mar. Alfred Fillmore, of Zanesville, O. Widow lived at Brooklyn.
Issue:
103.   Wm. Culbertson Fillmore. Brooklyn. Mar. Issue.
104.   Margaret E. Brooklyn (unmar.).

(52) Alexander Keith Culbertson mar. Drury Davis. Lived in Kansas. Wife died 1905.
Issue:
105.   Wm. Boyd, d. 1895.

106.   Sidney Brooks. Living Omaha, Neb.
107.   Berryman Keith. Atlanta, Ga.

(54) Sidney E. Culbertson mar. Jefferson Van Horne of Zanesville, O. Husband dead. Living in Chicago.
Issue:
108.   Bernard Van Horne d. unmar.
109.   Wm. C. mar. Captain in World War.
110.   Keith. Mar.
111.   Ida Louisa, mar. Chas Upjohn. New York .
112.   Clifford. Mar.
113.   Mary. Mar.

(55) Ida L. Culbertson mar. Albert Lyman of Muncie Indiana.
Issue:
114.   Louisa Sidney. Lives at Muncie, Ind.

(60) Ann Eliza Mathiot mar. Rev. Theodore L. Cuyler the great Presbyterian minister of Brooklyn, N. Y.
Issue:
115.   Mary E. Cuyler, mar. Dr. Wm. Cheeseman of N. Y.
          No issue.
116.   Louisa L. Cuyler, d.
117.   George M., d.
118.   Theodore L. Cuyler mar. Helen ——, of Brooklyn
          Issue, one child; mar. second, his cousin Mary S.
          Proal. No issue.

(61) Sidney L. Mathiot mar. Arthur B. Proal of N. Y.
Issue:
119.   Arthur B.
120.   Mary Sidney.

(73) Sophia Willis Culbertson mar. Mr. Washington Hardy. Living at Columbus, Neb., age 80 years (widow). Mar. Dec. 17, 1861.
Issue:
121.   Elizabeth Annie, b. Mar. 30, 1862.
122.   Leota May, b. Dec. 1, 1864.
123.   George Byron, b. Dec. 1, 1865.
124.   Elmer Elsworth, b. Apr., 1868.
125.   Clarence Clinton, b. Jan. 1, 1873.
126.   Laura Gertrude, b. Apr. 9, 1874.
126½.   Albert Howard, b. May 6, 1876.
126¾.   Ethel Ellen, Nov. 1, 1878.

(73½) Sydney E. Culbertson mar. Mr. Atkinson.
Issue:
127. Pearl Atkinson. Lives Zanesville, Ohio.

(78½) Joshua M. Culbertson mar. ——.
Issue:
128. Helen, b. 1904. Lives at Cambridge, Ohio.
129. Cora.
130. Chester.
131. Elmer.

(78¾) George W. K. Culbertson mar. ——.
Issue:
132. Walter R., b. 1894. Lives at Columbus, O. Clerk
      Ohio Road Commission.
133. Douglas Cassel, b. 1896.
134. Claude, b. 1901.

(86) Wm. Joseph Culbertson mar. Ruth Shurts.
Issue:
135. William Edward. Champaign, Ills. Stock broker.
136. Albert Ludlum.

(87) Maurice Edward mar. Florence H. Duncan.
Issue:
137. Grace Harriet, d. age 5.

(88) Elizabeth Ann Culbertson mar. Wm. Culbertson
Duncan.
Issue:
138. Ed Culbertson.
139. Helen Ruth.

(89) John Thomas Culbertson mar. Jennie McKinstry.
Issue:
140. John McKinstry.

(91) Cecelia Blanche Culbertson mar. H. C. Meeker.
Issue:
141. Clyde Earle.
142. Ellen Marie.

NINTH GENERATION

(106) Sidney Brooks Culbertson mar. ——. Lives at
Omaha, Neb.
Issue: Data not given.

(107) Berryman Keith Culbertson mar. Leila King, of
Oklahoma City, July 28, 1909. Living at Atlanta, Ga.

Issue:
143. Katharin, b. Apr. 13, 1910.
144. Mary Marjorie, July 15, 1912.
145. Carolyn Keith, b. May 28, 1922.

(IV) CAPT. ALEXANDER CULBERTSON AND PROMINENT DESCENDANTS.

Capt. Alexander was a tanner at Strasburg, Letterkenny Tp., Franklin Co., Pa. at the foot of the Tuscarora Mountains. In this business he accumulated considerable wealth and was a man of influence. He belonged to the "Row." I first find him spoken of as Capt., on a deed in 1807, so he must have been a Captain after the Revolution. Moved to Zanesville in 1807. "Capt. Alex" in pew (1794).

(1) James, his son moved to Zanesville, O., about 1810, where he owned a large tannery which occupied two squares in the Second Ward, being the largest in that section of the country. It was afterwards run by his sons.

(2) Margaret Culbertson mar. Judge Wm. McClay of Path Valley, Franklin Co., Pa., who was a member of the House of 14th and 15th Congress.

(4) Samuel W. Culbertson was one of Zanesville's most eminent lawyers. He was educated in Pa. and received a thorough education. He was admitted to the bar at Chambersburg, Pa., in 1805, and very shortly after moved to Zanesville, O. He studied law at the University of Pa., at Philadelphia. He at once took up the practice of law at Zanesville and soon won distinction and wealth. He was not only noted as a criminal lawyer, but was also well versed in the technicalities of law. He founded the town of Marysville, Ohio, named in honor of his daughter, Mrs. Mathiot.

(IV) His children who moved with him to Musk. Co., O., were Alex. (Jr.), Sam. W., William, James, Robert, John and Elizabeth (Mrs. Cassel). His wife died in Pennsylvania. She was a Miss Mary Sharpe, daughter of Capt. James Sharpe, a member of old Rocky Spring and a captain in the Revolutionary War. Her mother was a Miss McConnell, daughter of Robert McConnell. In 1810 he bought a store of Ebert & Wood on the Corner of Fourth and Main streets, Zanesville, where he resided. He gave this property to his son, Alex., Jr. In 1810 he and his son, James, owned a large tannery in the Second Ward, Zanesville.

In 1812 he bought of the United States much land in Muskingum Co. This he divided among his children. He died 1822 and was buried on High School Hill Cemetery. His son Alex owned one of the first glass works in southeastern Ohio, and made considerable in real estate. He was worth about $40,000 at his death. His brother William lived in Washington Tp., not Blue Rock. Samuel W. Culbertson in 1828 built on the corner of Fifth Street and Fountain Alley what for many years was the most palatial residence in Zanesville. He owned much valuable real estate in Zanesville, and 1,500 acres of land in Muskingum county, and at his death was worth $75,000, at least. It was his son William who owned the old homestead at Brush Creek bridge.

S. W .Culbertson's son-in-law Joshua Mathiot was Congressman from Licking county for many years.

(5) Alexander Culbertson moved to Zanesville about 180£ and purchased large tracts of land about Zanesville. Ʈ owned land in Washington, Wayne and Zanesville townships. He owned land in what was called "Culbertson's Addition", Sixth Ward, which was sold for a good price. He was one of Zanesville's wealthiest citizens at his death. His old home, on a hill overlooking the "blue Muskingum" river is still standing. He owned a glass works on the river road, the first in eastern Ohio. His father lived here also.

(6) Wm. Culbertson lived in Washington Tp., Musk. Co., O. His father-in-law (first wife) was Francis Campbell, Jr., of Franklin Co., Pa. and merchant and wealthy and prominent in Pa.

(37½) John Culbertson was a prominent politician and editor and proprietor of the Delevan, Ills., Advertiser. He was a self-made man, having begun life as a compositor at Zanesville and from thence arisen to the top.

(60) Mrs. Ann (Mathiot) Cuyler was the wife of Rev. Theo. L. Cuyler one of America's most eminent Presbyterian divines, who was many years pastor of the most fashionable Presbyterian church in Brooklyn, N. Y.

(20) Wm. Cassel married Lydia Martin, was a prominent miller at Zanesville, O. One of his daughters,. Leila,. married Lieut.-Col. Kline of the 9th U. S. Inf. (now Major-General) ; another, Kate, mar. George Stewart, Cashier of the First National Bank of Zanesville, O. Another daughter, Hannah, mar. Col. Anson Mills, of the 10th U. S. Cav., in·

ventor of the Mills cartridge belt. A Major General. Living at Washington, D. C., 1921. Several years ago Gen. Mills published his autobiography which is extremely interesting. Another daughter, Lizzie mar. Mr. T. C. Orndoff, of Worcester, Mass., the inventor of the typewriting machine for the blind and other inventions.

Generals Mills and Kline are officers of high standing in the army.

(22½) James Cassell, son of Jacob and Elizabeth (Culbertson) Cassel had a son, Douglas Cassel, who was a Lieut. Commander, U. S. Navy. Served in Navy all through the Civil War. Shortly after the war he was granted a six months leave of absence and accepted the command of the Japanese navy during the war between Japan and Formosa. At the close of this war he returned home and soon after died of the Japanese fever.

He brought from Japan many rare and expensive curios. He was a man of tall and commanding figure and very handsome; beloved by his fellow officers and all who knew him The Japanese government paid his mother for her son's services.

* * * * *

Revolutionary Service of Alexander Culbertson (tanner) of Strasburg, Pa. "A class roll of the Fourth Batt. of Cumberland Co., Pa. Militia, Capt. John McConnel; Lieut. Col. Samuel Culbertson, gives Alexander Culbertson, private, Aug. 10, 1780. Service same Aug. 23, 1781." (Pa. Arch.) Same 1782. Wife b. about 1747, d. Franklin Co., Pa., Aug. 24, 1799. A daughter of Capt. James Sharpe of Cumb. Co., Pa., who was in French and Indian War.

(136) Albert Ludlum Culbertson, son of (86) Wm. Joseph Culbertson was a major in A. E. F., World War, in France. (Newspaper statement during the war.)

CHAPTER XXV
FIFTH GENERATION

(VI) "Capt." John Culbertson, son of Irish Alexander of "Culbertson Row", Pa. As before mentioned make a quit claim deed Dec. 24, 1774, then residing in Letterkenny Tp., Cumberland Co., Pa. Tax lists of Letterkenny show him 1775 to 1779. "John mountain") Tax List 1780 to 1782, his name does not appear. I can find no deed from him in

Cumb. or Franklin Co., Pa., after 1774. John Culbertson (residence not given in Warrant) received a warrant for 100 acres, Sept. 25, 1781, in Lincoln Co., Va. (now Kentucky) on Bauls Fork, a branch of Paint Lick Creek. Issued to him as assignee of Will Miller. Survey was made and patent was issued Dec. 2, 1785. This land was in territory about present Girard Co., Ky., or Madison Co. as warrant says land is next to Estill patent. John must have moved to Kentucky in 1779, because he served with Ky. Militia "Feb. 21, 1781, his name is found on payroll of Capt. Jos. Kinkcaids Co. of Light Horse, who were ordered from Lincoln Co. by Col. John Bowman for the defense of Fayette Co., Feb. 21, 1781, entered Mar. 3, discharged Mar. 28, 1781." Also "May 4, 1782, private in Capt. John Snoddy's Co., under Col. Benj. Logan, May 4 to June 4, 1782." Also "July 10 to Aug. 10, 1782, private in Capt. John Wood's Co., Col. Benj. Logan, stationed at Estells Station." (See Ills. Papers D. 124, D. 81; D. 162. Richmond). Also service "Lieut. in Capt. Samuel Culbertson's Co.; 5th Batt'n., Col. Jos. Armstrong, Dec. 8, 1776." (Pa. Arch.). In battles of Trenton, Princeton, etc. Have not been able to find service with Pa. troops after this date. I have written the various counties that at that time made Lincoln Co., Ky., but there is no deed or record from John. There is no John Culbertson in Census 1790 in Bedford Co., Pa. Nor in any county in Pa.

A history of Muehlenburg Co., Ky., says that old Capt. John Culbertson first lived in the country about Fayette Co., shortly after the Revolution but the Indians were bad and he left this country and went to the country about Hartford (Ohio Co.) but after several years moved to Muehlenberg Co., being one of the first settlers of the latter county. I find a deed to him for 400 acres in 1796 in Logan Co. on Nelson Creek. This territory afterwards went into Muehlenburg Co., Ky. He lived in Kentucky when it was "A dark and bloody ground." The great Daniel Boone had made his final stand in Ky. only five or six years before John Culbertson located in Ky. Otto Rotherts History of Muehlenburg Co., Ky., p. 50 says: "John Culbertson and Wm. Cessna were on the first grand jury (July 28, 1799) of Muehlenburg Co., Ky." This Wm. Cessna may have been a son of John Cessna, Sr., of Shippensburg, Pa., brother of Col. Charles and Major John Cessna of Bedford Co., Pa. Wm. Cessna sold his farm in Letterkenny Tp., Cumb. Co., Pa. to A. Winger for £650 in 1790. Deed recites that land was conveyed to Wm. Cessna by John Cessna (his father) and that land was conveyed to John Cessna, Sr. Feb. 26, 1755. Wm. Cessna not in 1790 Census of Pa. Evidently was overlooked as deed shows him there Oct., 1790. (See Part Third, Section Second, for Elizabeth, daughter of Irish Alexander of the Row in regard to Col. Chas. Cessna). Robert Cessna was one of the first Justices of the Peace of Muehlenberg Co., Ky. (Rothert's Hist.) This Robert Cessna married Elizabeth, daughter of John Culbertson. John Culbertson also purchased 200 acres on the Green River in 1800. We do not know whether he attained the title of Capt. in Ky. He died 1844. Appraisement of his estate in 1847 shows his estate consisted of ten slaves. He deeded land to his children before his death. Died intestate. His wife died before him most likely in Ky. In 1837 he deeded land on Green River to his son Samuel living in McCracken Co., Ky. Old (Capt.) John last on tax records (land only) Bedford Co., Pa., 1779. His son, Joseph, received a warrant for 300 acres in Logan Co., south side of Green River Oct. 13, 1796, pat'd June 3, 1797. This was Capt. John's son and shows Joseph was the oldest son and was born about 1777. Samuel Culbertson, son of Capt. John, received a warrant for 300 acres, Sept. 17, 1798, in then Harden (now Ohio Co.), Ky., at the junction of Big Clifty and Rough Creeks. Patented June 10, 1799. This would tend to show that Samuel was the second son and born 1776-7.

Alexander Culbertson received warrant for 40 acres in Muehlenberg Co., Ky., 1800. Born 1779(?).

Robert Cessna received a warrant for 200 acres in Logan Co. (Later Muehlenberg Co.) 1796. This would indicate he was born 1775. County Clerk of Ohio and Harden Counties, Ky., says no record of any of these parties on their records. Capt. John was a deacon from 1800 until his death in the Mt. Zion church near Greenville, Ky. Census 1820, self over 45; 3 males between 26 and 45. Census 1830, self, bet. 70 and 80, one male 40 to 50.

Issue:

FIFTH GENERATION

1. Joseph, b. Mar. 31, 1777; d. about 1818.
2. Samuel, b. 1776-7; d. Nov. 4, 1865(?). Bachelor, lived McCracken Co., Ky.
3. Alexander, b. 1778-9; d. before 1845. Bachelor. River Trader.
4. Robert, b. 1780-81; d. before 1845. Bachelor.

5. ——, Mrs. Nelson Sharp of Muehlenberg Co., Ky.
6. Joannah (Mrs. Samuel C. Long) of Muehlenberg Co.,
   Ky. Died 1850.
7. Elizabeth (Mrs. Robert Cessna), Muehlenberg Co., Ky.
   born between 1770-1780.

Court records of Muehlenberg, Ohio, Harden, Scott, Lincoln, Logan, Fayette, Bourbon, Franklin, Madison, Girard, Nelson counties, do not give marriage record of Robert Cessna and Elizabeth Culbertson.

Rothert's Hist. of Muehlenberg Co., Ky. says that "Robert (4) Culbertson served in Capt. Lewis Kinchloe's Co., of Ky. Militia (pr.) in War of 1812 and was in the battle of the Thames."

SIXTH GENERATION

(1) Joseph Culbertson married Miss Rebecca Beck of Ky. Wife b. Mar. 10. 1787. Moved to near Sprigfield, Ills.

Issue:

8. Alexander Beck, b. Jan. 10,. 1816; d. 1855-6. Bachelor,
   conveyed his interest in estate to his brother, lived
   in Knox Co., Ind. in 1845.
9. John Beck, b. Sept. 3, 1813; d. Aug. 16, 1872.
10. Mary (Mrs. Metcalf) merchant, b. Jan. 8, 1806.
11. Ann Ella (Mrs. Rev. Council) Methodist. Iowa, b.
    Sept. 17, 1810.
12. Elizabeth (Mrs. Judge R. B. Ewing), b. Apr. 27,. 1808.
    The Widow of Joseph remarried to a Mr. Garrett.

(7) Elizabeth Culbertson married Robert Cessna of Muehlenberg Co., Ky., about. 1800. (Robert Cessna died about 1815). Census 1830 gives Elizabeth bet. 50 and 60 years; one girl and two boys between 15 and 20.

Issue:

13. Mary Cessna (Mrs. Quisenberry of Ky.).
14. Nancy (Mrs. Thos. Kirtly of Ky.).
15. Joannah (Mrs. Rev. Adlai Boyd of Ky.), b. Feb. 2,
    1803; d. 1882. Several children.
16. Sarah (Mrs. J. C. Berryman), b. 1808; d. 1846.
17. Charles, d. young.
18. Robert J. C. Cessna.
19. Margaret (Mrs. T. N. Berryman).
20. Elizabeth (Mrs. John Milligan).

SEVENTH GENERATION

(9) John Beck Culbertson married Eliabeth Berryman (his cousin) dau. of (19) Thomas Newton Berryman and Margaret Cessna. Mar. Nov. 26, 1846. Moved to Ohio Co., Ky. about 1846.

Issue:

21. Margaret Cessna, b. June 15, 1848,. died June 6,. 1878,. mar. Mr. Murphy. Had issue.
22. Romulus B., b. Nov. 8, 1850; living at Central City,. Ky. Married Jennie Addington, b. Oct. —, 1855; d. July 20, 1894.
23. Cathrin or Kate, b. April 13, 1852; d. April 19,. 1879; married Robert M. Cessna. Had issue.
24. Thomas Robert, b. Oct. 22, 1853; d. Jan. 20, 1876. Unmarried.
25. Annie, b. Oct. 17, 1855; d. Oct. 10, 1874. Unmarried.
26. John J., b. Mar. 13, 1857, d. Mar. ——, 1905, married Laura Benton, one issue, Jessie L., who married John Burk (issue).
27. S. Erskin, b. June 17, 1858; d. Aug. 10, .1911,. married, had issue.
28. Joseph K., b. Sept. 2, 1860; d. Feb. 6, 1901. Unmarried.
29. Gerard B., b. Oct. 18, 1862; d. Aug. 16, 1863.
30. Nannie, b. Sept. 8, 1864; d. Aug. 10, 1892, married. No issue.
31. Edmonia, born June 7, 1867; living at Eldorado, Ills. Married twice. Married first Eaves, then Dibble, both dead. Issue by both.
32. Lillian, born Nov. 24, 1870, living at Hillside, Ky. Married twice; first Goode, then Hoard; issue by Goode.

(16) Sarah Cessna, married Jerome Causin Berryman of Ky., October 4, 1831 (husband born 1810; d. 1906).

Issue:

33. Girard Quisenberry Berryman, b. Sept. 22, 1835; d. 1895.
34. Emily G., b. 1837; d. 1921 (mar. Giles Russel about 1867).
35. John W. Berryman, b. 1839, living. Lives at Biloxi, Miss.
36. Elizabeth, b. 1844; d. 1897. (Mrs. Warren B. Peck).

(18) Robert J. C. Cessna mar. Angeline Calvert. Many

descendants living in Muehlenberg Co., Ky. Had issue, a descendent, Dr. James Bailey, ex-service man, lives Greenville, Ky.

(22) Romulus B. Culbertson married Jennie Addington.
Issue:
37. Harry M., b. Oct. 15, 1880; living at Central City, Ky. Married Tillie Martin, have issue.
38. Hubert B., b. May 15, 1882; d. Nov. 29, 1912. Unmarried.
39. Mary Dee, b. Aug. 24, 1883; d. July 10, 1906. Unmarried.
40. John C., b. April 11, 1885; living, unmarried; Central City, Ky.
41. Jesse R., b. May 21, 1887, living Central City, Ky. Married to Miss Whitmer; one issue, son. Jess served in late war.
42. Annie, b. May 21, 1889; d. Sept. 22, 1916. Married to Mr. Hodge. One issue, William Culbertson Hodge. She and son both dead.
43. Thomas Alexander, b. May 29, 1891, living. Came from Fance a nervous wreck. Unmarried. This boy was big and stout, went to France in U. S. service, came home a wreck.

EIGHTH GENERATION

(33) Girard Q. Berryman mar. June 15, 1869 to Minerva Woods, b. Sep 15, 1844; d. 1892.
Issue:
44. Jerome W. Berryman living at Ashland, Kans. Is a prominent and wealthy banker and stock grower. b. March 12, 1870.
45. Wm. S. Berryman, b. Arcadia, Mo., Apr. 16, 1871. Mar. 1912. Issue: Lloyd P. and Mary E.
46. Sarah C. Berryman.
47. Emily Berryman.

(34) Emily G. Berryman mar. about 1867 to Giles Russel.
Issue:
48. Jerome; 49, Thomas; 50, Pitkin; 51, Gordon; 52, Arch S.; 53, Trevis; 54, John G; 55, Addie; 56, Dupuy.

(35) John Wesley Berryman mar. first Laura Matthews; second Jennie ———. No issue. Lives at Biloxi, Miss.

(36) Elizabeth Cessna Berryman mar. Warren B. Peck.
Issue:
57. Ella (mar. Chas. Shinn of Russellville, Ark.). Mar.
    second Capt. Fred E. Barrow. Issue, son, 58, Ed-
    ward, Farmington, Mo.

NINTH GENERATION

(44) Jerome W. Berryman mar. June 8, 1898 to Nancy
Annette McNickle.
Issue:
59. Dorothy Berryman, b. Sep. 6, 1899.
60. Jerome C. Berryman, b. May 2, 1901.
61. James W. Berryman, b. Mar. 2, 1908.
62. Virginia Berryman, b. Sept. 15, 1910.
63. George A. Berryman, b. Mar. 6, 1912.

(39) Sarah Chandler Berryman mar. 1899 to Wm. Madison Price of El Paso, Tex. Now state senator and banker
at Emporia, Kan.
Issue:
64. Gerard Price, b. 1900.
65. Lloyd Price, b. 1905.
(34) Martha Emily Berryman mar. 1903 to W. L. Roberts
of Ashland, Kan. Died Mar. 14, 1917. No issue.

* * * * *

(5) Mrs. Nelson Sharp's husband and (6) Mrs. Samuel C.
Long's husband were sons respectively of Irish Samuel Culbertson's (of Pa. Row) daughters Agnes (Mrs. Wm. Long)
and Joannah (Mrs. Sharp) of Cumb. Co., Pa., the latter who
went to Muehlenberg Co., Ky., and whose descendants now
live in aforesaid county in Ky. Wm. Long and wife (Agnes) lived in Fayette Co., Ky.
Note: There was a deed made in Cumb. Co., Pa., in
1779, in which Robert Chambers of Shippensburg, Pa., con-
veys land in Shippensburg to John Culbertson of Shippensburg. This land was conveyed the same year to Robert
Donovan by John Culbertson and wife Jean, of Shippensburg. John Culbertson of Erie Tp., Allepheny Co., Pa.,
lived before that date in Southhampton Tp., Franklin Co.,
Pa., and paid taxes in the latter township, but it is possible
he may have lived in Shippensburg for a short time, or it
may be that John, son of Irish Capt. Alex, may have lived
in Shippensburg for a short time and then moved to Ky.
If this were the case then we could prove that his wife's
name was Jean, also.

John, son of Oliver, did not sell or leave his farm in
Southhampton Tp., Franklin Co., until 1799 and it does not
seem at all likely that he would own his farm and home in
this township and go and live in Shippensburg in 1779 or
before, and buy property there. Letters of Administration
were issued Sept. 10, 1803, to Samuel W. Culbertson of
Chambersburg, Pa. (an attorney of that place), in the
estate of Mary, wife of John Culbertson. No account or other papers on file there. I can find no John Culbertson in
Franklin Co., Pa., at this time to whom this ad'm'n belonged
and I am inclined to believe it was for some one living away
from there and that either she or her husband had land in
Franklin Co. I never found deed of Capt. John Culbertson
of Ky., for any land he had in Franklin Co., Pa. Did not
look to see if Samuel W. Culbertson conveyed this for him.
Indications are that Capt. John's wife died about this time.
I could find no deed in Ky. from John in which his wife participated.

PROMINENT DESCENDANTS OF JOHN (VI)·
CULBERTSON

(44) Jerome Woods Berryman was born at Arcadia, Mo.,
March 12, 1870, had a common school education in the public schools and one year at the Belleview Collegiate Institute
at Caledonia, Mo. In 1887 he went to Kansas taking a position in the Elk City Bank and in 1888 was elected cashier
and put in charge of the bank, in 1891 he removed from Elk
City to Medicine Lodge, Kan., taking a position with the
Citizens Bank of that place. When the Cherokee Strip in
Oklahoma was thrown open to settlement in 1893, he made
the "run" from Hennesey, Okla. to the new townsite of Enid
but getting nothing satisfactory there he moved on to the
Government townsite of Round Pond in "L" now Grant
County, Okla., where he established the Bank of Pond
Creek and conducted it for several years, serving two terms
as Mayor of the City of Pond Creek and in various
other public capacities. In 1897 he disposed of a
part of his Oklahoma interests and returned to Elk
City, Kansas, to again take charge of the Elk City Bank
at that place, removing a few years later (1900) to Ashland, Kansas where he now resides and is President of the
Stockgrowers National Bank of that place and largely interested in banking, lumber yards, ranching, etc. He was married June 8, 1898, to Nancy Annette McNickle at Cortland,

Neb., and they have five children, Dorothy, now a Senior at Washburn College, Topeka, Kan.; Jerome Charles, now in his Sophomore year at Centre College, Danville, Ky., where he has already won signal honors in scholarship and athletics and is Student Business Manager of the famous "Praying Colonel" football team and other athletics of the college. The other children born in the order named, James Woods, Virginia and George Albert are yet in the public schools at Ashland. Jerome W. Berryman has taken an active part in the business, social and political life of the state of which he has, for the greater part of his life, been a resident, has served as President of the Kansas Bankers Association, on numerous banking and corporate boards, as a member of the Executive Council of the American Bankers Association, the Cattle Raisers Association of Texas, mayor two terms of Pond Creek, Okla., mayor and member of Council several terms Ashland and Elk City, member of the Kansas Legislature four times and in other public capacities, including President of the Board of Education at Ashland, in which capacity he has served a number of terms. He has been a Mason since 1891 and a member of all the Masonic bodies, Scottish and York Rite, Shrine, O. E. S. etc. Is financially interested in the First National Bank of Wichita, Kansas, and the Red Star Mills, and other Wichita enterprises.

His grandfather, Jerome C. Berryman, was a Methodist minister and a pioneer missionary among the Indians in Kansas in 1833.

(G) PART FOURTH
Irish Samuel of Culbertson Row

(G) PART FOURTH

(G) **Samuel Culbertson** who emigrated from "Culbertson Row", Antrim Co., Ireland, and with his brother, Alexander, settled in Lancaster Co., Pa., in what afterwards became Lurgan Twp., Cumberland Co., and still later became Greene Twp., Franklin Co., Pa., and called their settlement "Culbertson Row." The first official mention we find of him is in the Pa. Colonial Archives, New Ser., by Bruce, which gives him as "Sergeant-Major in Col. Hugh Mercer's (Third) Battalion of Pa. Provincial Troops, in 1758. Col. Mercer was in the Forbes Expedition in 1758." Col. James Burd says in a letter in the Pa. Arch., dated Dec. 2, 1758: "I have the pleasure to inform you, that on Friday last, our Army being within fourteen miles of Ft. Duquesne, the enemy thought proper to blow up the Fort, and went off bodily in their battoes. They entirely destroyed the works and rendered everything useless."

We know from the Pa. Archives that Samuel was still in the service in 1759. He was stationed for a while at Ft. Duquesne under Col. Mercer. We cannot find any record of his military services after 1759. His term of enlistment was for "three years, or until the close of the war."

I obtained the names of his children from his will, probated in Franklin Co., Pa., Oct. 15, 1789.

Samuel's son, Robert, married his cousin, Elizabeth Lindsay. This shows that either Elizabeth Lindsay's mother was a Culbertson, or Jennet Shield's (Samuel Culbertson's first wife) mother was a Lindsay.

Irish Samuel Culbertson of Pa. "Row" was a very wealthy and prominent man. Owned at one time nearly 2000 acres.

Before his death he gave (1785), his sons, John, Alexander, James and Joseph 200 acres each. He gave Robert land prior to 1777 as he did also John. He gave in his will: Samuel, £400; John 5 shillings; Robert (dec'd) portion given during his lifetime. Son-in-law, Thos. McKean (son of Eleanor) £500., silver spurs to grandson, Samuel Culbertson McKean; son Alex, coat and grey mare; daughter, Agnes (Mrs. Wm. Long) £60; Martha £60, Joannah (Mrs. Sharp) £60; Mary £50; Jennet (Mrs. Guthrie) £50 (each child also got a negro or negress slave). To son James he left the use of his farm for seven years providing he pays above bequests and maintenance money to his widow

Eleanor. Should James refuse or fail to carry out this provision then, he directs ex'rs to sell this land and give James one-half of the amount arising from such sale.

Samuel Sr. married his second wife in 1782 (Eleanor W. McKean, of Frederick Co., Md.) Made a prenuptial agreement with her Aug. 20, 1782. No children by this marriage. In 1802 she gave a quit claim to the executors of Samuel's est. in consideration of $1050 and released all right of dower. Samuel, Sr.'s son, John, died 1797, and his children sued the Exrs. for their share in the estate, £21. Samuel in his will named Executors Counsin Joseph son Joseph and Cousin or Nephew Samuel. Will made Oct. 9, 1789; probated Oct. 15, 1789. This will establishes the fact that Joseph, he mentions as his cousin, was Irish Joseph of Culbertson "Row"—whom everybody supposed was his brother—was in reality his cousin.

The appraisers were Col. Joseph and Col. Robert Culbertson and John Brackenridge.

The second account from 1797 to 1801 was filed by Col. Samuel Culbertson and (son) Joseph Culbertson, surviving executors of Samuel Culbertson, Sr. His cousin Joseph (Irish) had died in 1794. The final acc't was filed 1804 by surviving ex'rs. Col. Samuel and Col. Joseph Culbertson. His son, Joseph, had died in 1801. First account filed June 4, 1794, it shows "pd. ex'rs. Samuel (Col.), Joseph (Cousin) and Joseph (son) £36 for services." They sold his home farm, 1803, to Adam Harbison, Dec .22, 1803, for £4716, 16s. —450 acres.

The bequests made to the daughters do not equal the value of land deeded to his sons. He must have paid them in money prior to his death. There is one peculiar thing, that a Samuel Culbertson (residence not given) was granted 3000 acres of land in Ky. (then Va.) in 1781-85 I have searched many counties in Ky., but cannot find any record of this land and no deeds from him or his executors for this land. Some of the land was on Harrods Creek, near Louisville, some in Ohio county, and some in Muehlenberg Co., Ky., on Big Caney and Little Clifty. This is in the same territory in which the Sharps and Longs settled and I thought it might be possible that this Ky. land to Samuel Culbertson might have been granted to his married daughters who went to Ky., but can find no deed for it. It was not a military grant.

Samuel's first wife was Jennet Shields, dau. of David Shields of Letterkenny Tp., Cumb. Co., Pa., to whom he must have been married about 1736-38. (David Shields was in French and Indian War; d. 1773) (David Shields pr. Aug. 7, 1755, French and Indian War).

David Shields, father of Jennet (Shields) Culbertson, made his will in Cumb. Co., Pa., May 27, 1766, probated May 8,. 1773. In it he devises to daughter, Jennet,. wife of Samuel Culbertson, Sr.

The inventory of chattels of Irish Samuel's estate was filed Oct. 21, 1789, and totaled £1046, 2 s., 1d. The first account from June, 1794 to 1804 totaled £908, 12.s, 6d.

The account from 1797 to 1802 totaled £2669, 12s, 6d. The bequests amounted to over £1240, outside of amounts in prenuptial agreement, £200, were paid widow in 1802 for release of dower. If we take the value of the farms which he gave his sons at what they sold them for (i. e. John 424 acres for £1485; Samuel £1750; Robert £400—not counting money given Robert's heirs during his lifetime—Alexander £1500; Joseph £1550). Total in farm values to sons £5885; add this to total of disbursements of executors, not including bequests (i. e. £3577). Total £10,312 or $51560—a huge sum for those days.

There must be added to this the amount ($15,000) which the farm of 195 acres in Montgomery Tp., Franklin Co., Pa. (which was given "Gentleman James by his father in 1785, and which James sold in 1795). There must also be added to this the value of a farm of 244 acres in Letterkenny Tp., which was deeded by Samuel, Sr., to his son Joseph, in 1785, then valued at £300; also farm in Letterkenny Tp. of 200 acres, which Samuel, Sr., deeded for $1 to son Alex. in 1785, valued at least £400. These two would add $3300. This would give a total estimate of Samuel's financial standing of $70,460.

He stated in his will that if there was any surplus in his estate above all costs and bequests that then said surplus should be equally divided among my daughters then alive.

FOURTH GENERATION

Issue of Irish Samuel and wife, Jennet:
  I.   **Samuel,** b. 1738-9 ?; d. 1814 (Chapter XXVI) Westmoreland Co., Pa.
  II. **John,** b. 1739-40 ?; d. 1797 (Chapter XXVII), Westmoreland Co., Pa.
  III. **Robert,** b. 1741-2 ?; d. 1777-8 (Chapter XXVIII) Cumberland Co., Pa.

IV. **Eleanor,** b. 1742-3?; d. before 1789 (Mrs. Thos. Mc-
Cane of Franklin Co., Pa. Census 1790 shows she
was not living; husband given with 3 sons over 16;
2 sons under 16; 4 daughters. One son's name
Samuel C.

V. **Joseph,** b. ——; d. 1801; (Chapter XXIX), Shippensburg, Pa.

VI. **Alexander,** b. 1747?; d. 1790 (Chapter XXX) Franklin Co., Pa.

VII. **Agnes,** b. 1749; d. —— (Mrs. Wm. Long of Franklin
Co., Pa.) Census 1790, Wm. Long, self and wife,.
one son over 16 4 sons under 16, and 3 daughters.
Married 1770. Moved to Fayette Co., Ky. Issue:
Nine children. One son Samuel C. married Joannah, daughter Capt. John Culbertson of Muehlenberg, Co., Ky.?

VIII. **James,** b. 1750?; d. 1812. "Gentlemen James" (Chapter XXXI, of "Culbertson Row").

IX. **Martha,** b. ——; d. ——. (unmarried) Culbertson
Row.

X. **Joannah,** b. ——; d. ——. Lived first Cumb. Co.,
Pa., *later moved to Ky.* Census 1790, Pa., Joannah
Sharp, 2 sons under 16, one daughter. Husband
died before 1790. One son Nelson married a
daughter of Capt. John Culbertson of Muehlens-
berg Co., Ky.?

XI. **Jennet,** b. ——; d. ——. Franklin Co., Pa. Married
James Guthrie. Issue: (Seilheimer's report)
James Guthrie; Wm. Guthrie; John Guthrie (all
three and James Sr. Census 1790, Westmoreland
Co., Pa.) ; Archibald; Esther (Mrs. Paul Morrow).

XII. **Mary,** unmarried, b. ——; d. ——. Culbertson Row.

* * * * *

Irish Samuel was most too old (about 58 years) at the beginning of the Revolution to have served. The tax records
from 1776 to 1782 give only four Samuel Culbertsons and
none are thereon designated Col. but one and he was Irish
Alexander's son. One Samuel is designated on tax list as
Irish Samuel (or Samuel Sr.), one Col.; one Sam of "Creek",
one Samuel Jr. (son of Irish Samuel). There were four
Sams from what is now Franklin Co., Pa. in military service
at the same time, and one Sam from Cumb. Co., at same
(Sam of Silverspring Tp.).

CHAPTER XXVI

FIFTH GENERATION

(I) **Samuel Culbertson,** eldest son of Irish Samuel, of Culbertson Row, Pa., was raised in Letterkenny Tp., Cumb. Co., Pa. and moved in 1785-6 to Westmoreland Co., (now Indiana Co.) Pa., four miles from Blairsville. His name appears on tax lists of Lurgan in 1762,. therefore, he must have been born about 1740 or before this (tax lists before 1762—except 1750—are not available, hence he may have paid tax before 1762). Deeded property in Lurgan Tp. in 1778 to M. Kiner, £1750 being part of land conveyed him by M. Karr, said land adjoining Joseph Culbertson's land. In May, 1778, sold some land in Westmoreland Co., Pa., his residence then being Cumb. Co. Wife's name in deed, Mary. Family records say he was married twice. Second wife, Mary Wiley. (Samuel and wife Mary deeded land in Letterkenny to A. Burkholder, June 1, 1769). Samuel is on tax list in Letterkenny Tp., 1770, designated "widower." Paid tax on this land in 1782-85. According to D. A. R. Reports (Vol. VIII, pg. 204) "Was Quartermaster of Cumb. Co., Pa., troops." Service not given. I am of the opinion that he was married by 1760. Census 1790: males (including self) over 16, four; males under 16, three; females, four including wife. (West'moreland Co.). The Census of 1800, Westmoreland Co., Pa., gives him Derry Tp., self over 45; males of 16 and under 26, four; males of 26 and under 45, one; females over 45, one; females of 16 and under 26, one; females 10 years and under 16, one; of 10 years, one.

This shows his son, Alexander, was by second wife. Therefore the third Alexander with Revolutionary record in Cumberland Co., Pa., was not this Alexander. Was not old enough to serve.

Revolutionary Service of Samuel (I), eldest son of Irish Samuel of "Row". "Samuel Culbertson, Jr., pr. 4th Battn, 3rd Co., Col. Samuel Culbertson, Cumb. Co., Pa., Aug. 30, 1780" (Pa. Arch. 5th. Ser.). "July 21, 1781, Lt. Samuel Culbertson, 4th Co., 4th Batt'n. Col. John Scott." (Pa. Arch., Vol. VI, 5th Ser., page 293). In Capt. John Orbison's Co.

* * * * *

(I) Samuel. Samuel's making a deed June 1, 1769, with wife Mary, and being on tax duplicate 1770 "widower", would indicate that his first wife's name also was Mary.

Issue: (by first marriage).

1. Robert, married an Indian woman. Was a trapper. Had several children and lived on the Winnebago Agency in Nebraska. Left home in early life because he did not like his step-mother (Mary Wiley). Left home after 1790.

2. John Culbertson (a hunter). Not liking his step-mother left home.

3. James Culbertson, Hempfield Tp., Westmoreland Co., Pa. "He served in the Frontier Rangers from Cumb. Co., Pa., 1781-2" (Pa. Arch.) James signed a release in Feb., 1823, on his father's estate, but wife, if living, did not sign. No deeds to him and no ad'm'n or will in Westmoreland Co. Do not know where he went.

(1) Samuel Culbertson married second, Mary Wiley, daughter of Hugh Wiley, of Cumb. Co., Pa. (Wife born before 1775; died Dec., 1827.)

Issue:

4. Alexander Culbertson, Westmoreland Co., Pa. Bachelor. His brothers and sisters signed a release with him in 1823 but no wife signed with him although the other wives signed.

5. Joseph, d. 1824. Westmoreland Co., Pa.

6. Hugh (Judge). Wooster, Ohio.

7. Margaret (Mrs. John Huey), b. 1779; d. 1842. Westmoreland Co., Pa.

8. Keziah (Mrs. Thos. Rees). Washington Co., Pa.; later Wayne Co., O.

9. Esther (Mrs. Samuel Culbertson). Holmes Co., Ohio.

10. William (unmar.), d. 1814. Westmoreland Co., Pa.

SIXTH GENERATION

(2) John Culbertson, descendants say, mar. Miss Martha Craig. Living with father in 1790, but not in 1800

Issue: (given by relatives). Widow moved to Slippery Rock, Lawrence Co., Pa. None of descendants there now.

11. John.

12. William.

(3) James Culbertson. Have not names of his children. He is given in his father's will 1814. On release 1823 his residence is given Westmoreland Co., Pa.

(5) Joseph Culbertson married Miss Agnes Dickson, lived near Blairsville, Pa. Soldier in War 1812.

Issue:

13. Samuel, d. 1866. Bachelor. St. Louis, Mo.
14. William, b. 1806; d. 1872.
15. Isaac, b. ——; d. 1850.
16. James, b. ——; d. ——. Bachelor. Piqua, Ohio.
17. Maria, b. ——; d.
18. Eliza, b. ——; d.
19. Margaret, b. —— d. —'. Never married.
21. Joseph, b. '—; d. young. Dwarf.
22. Samuel, b. ——; d. Unmarried.

(6) Judge Hugh Culbertson married Jane ——. Lived at Wooster, O.

Issue:

23. Samuel ⎫
24. Mary D. ⎬ Twins; d. near Wooster O.
25. Margaret, b. 1805.
26. James G., d.
27. John Welch. b. July 3, 1809; d. 1883.
28. Betty. d. Never married.
29. Drusilla. d. ⎫ Twins.
30. Susan. d. 1892 ⎭
31. Wm. G., dwarf.
32. Jane W., d. at 20; unmar.
33. Hugh M. Living near Wooster.
34. Eli B., d.

(7) Margaret Culbertson, born in Row in 1783-4, Apr. 14. died at Washington, Pa., February 11, 1861, or October 11, 1860. She married Brigadier-General John (not William) Huey.

Issue:

35.   a. Mary Wiley, born April 3, 1809; died June 7, 1880-81; unmarried.
35¼.   a. Lucy, born May, 1810; died July 2, 1891-2; married Dr. John Alexander, of St. Clairsville, O., May 26. 1842; no issue.
35½.   a. Eliza Jane, born October 9, 1811; died April 10, 1891 married Hon. Alex. Murdoch, of Washington, Pa., December 5, 1844. Issue: Rebecca, John (married), Margaret, Lucy (Mrs. A. Donnan), Elizabeth.
36.   a. Samuel Culbertson Huey, born July 21, 1813, in Indiana Co., Pa. died at Enterprise. Fla., Feb-

ruary 11, 1886. Married Ann Scott Baird of Pittsburg, Pa., August 24. 1836.

Issue:

b. John Baird, born May 20, 1837; died April, 1839.

b.Robert Culbertson, born September 11, 1839; died August 9, 1847.

b. Samuel Baird, born January 7, 1842; married June, 1868, Mary E. Abrams, of Philadelphia. He lived at Philadelphia. Was lawyer to Bell Telephine Co. and Edison Electic Light Company and was one of the most eminent corporation lawyers of that city. Was Secretary of Union League Club a number of years; an elder in Walnut Street Presbyterian Church and Superintendent of Sunday School Was a paymaster in U. S. Navy during the Civil War. Both he and his father are spoken of in histories of Philadelphia, as being among the eminert men of that city.

b. Emma Harvey Huey, born January 7, 1842; died April 4, 1858.

b. Harriet J. Baird Huey, born April 27, 1849 lived at Philadelphia.

b. Robert S., born 1820; died October 6, 1890. Married Miss Friend.

b. John Thompson, born 1821; died August 20, 1864. Married.

b.William Culbertson, born 1822-5; died 1873. Married.

(b) Samuel Baird Huey mar. Mary Elizabeth Abrams (wife b. 1845; d. 1919) ; married 1868.

Issue:

c. Arthur Baird, b. 1870. Mar. Ellen Cadwallader Smith (b. 1875). No issue.

c. Wm. Abrams, b. 1872; d. 1878.

c. Emma Harvey, b. 1874. Mar. 1906 to Alexander Wister Jr. (1865). Issue: Eleanor W. Wister, b. 1907; Deborah Gaynor Wister, b. 1910. Philadelphia, Pa.

c. Samuel Culbertson Huey, b. 1877. Unmarried. A prominent corporation lawyer. Philadelphia, Pa.

c. Malcolm Sidney, b. 1880, mar. 1919 to Emily McAllister Hibbard (b. 1884). Issue: Sidney McAllister Huey, b. 1920.

(c) Malcolm S. Huey was a Major in the Ordnance Dept. (World War) and saw service in France. (Phila.)

c. Howard Hunt Huey, b. 1885; d. 1889.
Unmar ied.
c. Mary Dorothy Huey, b. 1889. Lives at Philadelphia.
(8) Keziah Culbertson mar. Mr. Thomas Reese. Moved to Wayne Co., Ohio.
Issue:
37. Samuel.
38. Rush.
(9) Esther Culbertson mar. her cousin, Samuel Culbertson. Lived at Millersburg, Holmes Co., O. Engaged in merchandising. First wife d., and then remarried. Do not know which children by first wife. She died after 1823, when she signed a release.
Issue:
39. Louisa, d. unmar.
40. Margaret. Mar. Dr. Stephen Norris.
41. William. Birmingham, Iowa.
42. Smith. Birmingham, Iowa.
43. Robert (?) d. single, 1819.

SEVENTH GENERATION

(14) William Culbertson mar. Mary Ann Coe, daughter of Rev. Jas. Coe. Moved to Miami Co., Ohio. Later to Butler Co., Ohio. He died on his farm near Middletown, O.; wife living 1893.
Issue:
44. James Coe (M. D.) Cincinnati, Ohio. b. Dec. 19, 1840; d. June 4, 1908.
45. Joseph Washington, b. July 13, 1843; d. Jan. 29, 1909.
46. Eliza Agnes.
47. Mary Bell.
48. Anna Margaret, d. young.
49. Francis Jane.
50. William Lowry.
51. Etta Maria. Unmar. Blue Ball, Ohio.

(15) Isaac Culbertson mar. Mary McChesney, moved to Ohio.
Issue:
52. Agnes.

(17) Maria Culbertson mar. Jos. Thompson, of Indiana Co., Pa. Both dead.
Issue:
53. Wm. Thompson, mar.
54. John, d.

55. Joseph, lawyer, Quincy, Ills.
56. James, unmar.
57. Samuel, unmar.
58. Nancy, b. 1820, living in 1892. (unmar.). Kent, Ind. Co., Pa.
59. Margaret, d.
60. Maria (Mrs. Davisson).
61. Rachel, d.
62. Eliza Culbertson mar. John Devining of Ind. Co., Pa. (both dead).
63. Wm. Culbertson, d.
64. Amanda (Mrs. Stewart Davis). Blairsville, Pa. Issue: John, Leroy, Archie.
65. Mary A. (Mrs. R. D. Wilkinshaw, Lebanon, Mo.).

(19) Margaret, mar. Allen Wilson, lived on farm near Nashville, Holmes Co., Ohio.
Issue: Several children.

(23) Samuel Culbertson mar. Rebecca Richey, Aug. 11, 1825. Widow at Allegheny City, Pa., in 1892.

Issue:

66. John R. Lived Jefferson, Ia., 1892.
67. Dan. d.
67½. Dan D.
68. Mary Douglas Culbertson mar. Col. Jacob Beam. Lived at Sioux City, Iowa. 1892.
69. ——,. Mrs. Langley, Chicago, Ills.
70. Son.
71. Son.

(25) Margaret Culbertson mar. Mr. Bigham. Lived at Niobrara, Neb.
Issue:

72. William. Lived at Sioux City, Ia.

(26) James G. Culbertson. Lived at Lawrence Co., Pa. Married Miss Bell.
Issue:

74. Sarah (Mrs. Bigham).
75. Anna. (Mrs. Hon. Kelly W. Frazer, DeKota, Neb.).
76. Joseph B. Grand Rapids, Wood Co., Ohio. Farmer.
77. Eli E. Grand Rapids, Wood Co., A. Farmer.
78. Louisa S. (Mrs. Ryan). Bryan,. Ohio.

(27) John Welch Culbertson mar. Elizabeth A. Eagle of

Mohican Twp., Wayne Co., Ohio. Wife b. 1811. Living (wife) at Fairfield, Iowa, 1892.
Issue:
79. W. Benton, d. lawyer. Lived at Burlington, Ia.
80. Edward B., d. Farmer.

(29) Drusilla Culbertson mar. Rev. ——, a Methodist minister, who was a foreign missionary. Had a family, but know nothing about them. (1892).

(30) Susan Culbertson mar. Mr. Fenton.
Issue:
81. Norman, d.
82. ——, son, d.

(33) Hugh M. Culbertson mar. first, Margaret Sanderson, of Wooster. Wife died.
Issue:
83. Benjamin Byers. Homestead, Pa.
84. John Lawyer. Peoria, Ills. Married, died; wife re-married.
85. Robert S. Wooster.
86. Helen, mar. Wooster.
87. Harry W. Editor, Chicago, Ills.
88. Frank.

(33) Hugh M. mar. second——. Issue not known.

(34) Eli B. Culbertson mar. Catherine ——. Husband dead. Soldier in Mexican War in Col. Curtis Regt.
Issue:
89. Alice, mar. (Davenport, Ia.).
90. Eli, killed in R. R. accident in Tex., 1883. Widow re-married. Mr. Cavan, lived Tuscaloosa, Ia., in 1892.
91. Aaron S., residence unknown. Soldier in Union army.
92. Mrs. James Early, Guernsey Co., O.

EIGHTH GENERATION

(44) Dr. James Coe Culbertson, mar. first 1865 to Virginia Clark. Wife died. No issue. Mar. second Sarah Pogue, Apr. 10, 1873, died 1884. Wife from Cincinnati, O.
Issue:
93. Henry Coe, b. at Cincinnati, O., July 11, 1874.
94. James Clark. Cincinnati, O., unmarried.
95. Margaret Elizabeth.

(44) Dr. J. C. Culbertson mar. third Sophia Braun of

Ripley, Ohio, 1888. No issue. Wife living (Ripley, Ohio).

(45) Joseph W. C. Lived at Blue Ball, Ohio. Married Henrietta Allison. (Wife b. Mar. 31, 1840; d. Mar 19, 1909.)
Issue:
96. Belle (Mrs. W. B. Forman), Franklin, O.
97. Mary L., b. Aug. 14, 1866; d. Aug. 16, 1906.
98. Martin A., d. Mar. 10, 1891; b. Oct 28, 1867

(46) Elizabeth Agnes Culbertson mar. Mr. Mitchell. Lives near Blue Ball, Ohio.
Issue: 99-103.

(47) Mary Belle Culbertson mar. Mr. Hunt, of Lytte, O.
Issue: ·

(49) Francis Jane mar. W. A. Eudlay, a prominent lawyer of Cincinnati, Ohio.

(50) William Lowry C. mar. Lives Blue Ball, Ohio.
Issue:
104. Frank B., Middletown, O.
105. Daughter.

(52) Agnes M. Culbertson mar. Theodore Clarke Miller, M. D., a prominent physician of Massilon, Ohio. Civil War veteran. Died 1923, aged 80 years.
Issue:
106. Clarke Culbertson Miller.
107. Charles Rush.
108. Thomas Culbertson.
109. Clara.
110. Mary Garvin.

(66) John R. Culbertson mar. Sarah R. DeWitt, dau. of Col. Joseph DeWitt. Lived in Wayne Co., O. Then moved to Iowa.
Issue:
111. Edward D. Y. Jefferson, Ia.
112. William.
113. Harry.
114. Verner.
115. Anna Mary.
116. Gertrude.
117. Blanche.

(74) Sarah Culbertson mar. Rev. Bigham. Widow lives at Plain Grove, Lawrence Co., Pa.

(79) W. Benton Culbertson mar. first——. Wife d.
Issue:
118. Frank O., d. Married. Had a son, Frank Seymour.

(79) Hon. W. B. C., mar. second——.
Issue:
119. Boy, d. young.
120. Boy, d. young.

NINTH GENERATION

(93) Henry Coe Culbertson mar. Mabel D. Freeman of Chicago, March 14, 1900. Lives at Chicago, Ills.
Issue:
121. Eleanor Pogue Culbertson, b. Apr. 1908.
122. Margaret Freeman Culbertson, b. June, 1913.

(95) Margaret Elizabeth Culbertson mar. John F. Wheeler. Lives at Portland, Oregon. Mar. June 5, 1907.
Issue:
123. Wm. Egbert Wheeler II, b. July 31, 1908.
124. Mary Elizabeth, b. May 25, 1911.
125. John Pogue, b. Apr. 27, 1915.
126. Margaret Knox, b. May 10, 1920.

(96) Belle Culbertson mar. W. B. Forman. Lives at Franklin, Ohio.
Issue: ——.

(97) Mary L. Culbertson mar. John P. Harkrader, Oct. 14, 1885. Husband born Jan. 16, 1860.
Issue:
127. Mabel Alberta Harkrader, b. Aug. 17, 1888; d. Apr. 27, 1889.
128. Roy Culbertson, b. Nov. 14, 1889. Married to Harriet Wetmore Miller, of Oxford, Ohio, June 16, 1914. No issue. Lives at Cincinnati, O. (Dentist)
129. Florence Mary Harkrader, b. Oct. 25, 1891; mar. to A. E. Wittenberg of Toledo, O., June 27, 1922.
130. John Myron Harkrader, b. Dec. 30, 1893; d. July 22, 1912.
131. Edwin Forrest, b. July 5, 1890.
132. Joseph Allison, b. Apr. 18, 1896.
133. Margaret Elizabeth, b. Mar. 18, 1902.
134. Marion Coe Culbertson, b. Aug. 5, 1906; d. Apr. 16, 1907.

PROMINENT DESCENDENTS OF SAMUEL (1) CULBERTSON OF WESTMORELAND CO., PA.

(1) Robert Culbertson and (2) John Culbertson not liking their step-mother, Mary Wiley, ran away from home when quite young, and Robert became a hunter and trapper in the far West. One of these brothers, Robert married an Indian. Mrs. Hon. Kelly W. Frazier, while teaching in the government school in the Winnebago Agency, Neb., heard of his descendants and visited them. She said they were educated, culture.d and refined, and that they told her that "their father, not liking his step-mother, Mary Wiley, left home."

(13) Samuel, (14) Wm., (15) Isaac, and (16) James, in early life were engaged as contractors on Public Works, building a large part of the Miami and Erie Canals north of Troy, and the Wabash Canal in Indiana. They were all noble and upright men, beloved by all who knew them. William erected mills and pursued this business for a time in Miami Co., O,. and for the last twenty-eight years of his life was a farmer. His son was (44) Dr. J. C. Culbertson, of Chicago and Cincinnati.

(44) James Coe Culbertson, M. D., born December 19, 1840, Miami County, Ohio. Died June 4, 1908, Cincinnati, Ohio. When Fort Sumter was fired on April 12, 1861, there was a prompt response to the call to arms from thousands of young men, who were then students in various literary, technical and medical schools of the country. Professional careers were thrown aside and ignored in the feeling of patriotism which filled the hearts of these young men. Dr. James Coe Culbertson was one of those patriotic young men. When the war broke out, he was a medical student in Cincinnati, but he enlisted as a private in Co. D., 5th O. V. I. April 19, 1861. Soon after his regiment entered West Virginia he was detailed to act as Assistant Surgeon by Col. Dunning. He served in that capacity until Nov., 1861, when he was ordered to Romney, Va., Dec. 5th to Wheeling, W. Va., to act as Hospital Steward, April, 1862, to Cumberland Md., and placed in charge of medical stores at that point. September 13, 1862, mustered in as Hospital Steward, U. S. A. In October, 1862, was ordered to Washington for duty in Emory General Hospital. He remained there until October, 1863, when he was ordered to the Marine, Hospital, Cincinnati. In February, 1864, he was discharged on certificate of disability, resulting from an attack of Typhoid

fever. In May, 1864, he was commissioned Assistant Surgeon 137 O. V. I. with which command he served in charge of Post Hospital at Fort McHenry until mustered out, on expiration of term of service of the regiment.

In autumn of 1865, Dr. Culbertson passed a competitive examination and was admitted as an Assistant in Bellevue Hospital, New York. While there he attended lectures in Bellevue Hospital Medical College and received the degree of Doctor of Medicine in March, 1865. In the fall of the same year he began the practice of medicine in Cincinnati. During his long and useful career in our city, he was better known as an editor than as a practitioner. In 1873 he purchased the Lancet and Observer, a monthly journal owned by Dr. E. B. Stevens. In 1878 he purchased the Clinic, a young weekly medical journal, founded by one of our Companions, the late Dr. J. T. Whittaker. The merger of the two journals was called the Lancet and Clinic, and as such it still exists. As editor he achieved marked success. It was his ambition to publish a weekly medical journal, and his opportunity had come. Under his care the Lancet and Clinic grew in strength and influence, and became a financial as well as literary success. His editorials were strong and vigorous, but characterized by a spirit of fairness on disputed questions. He had broad views of the function of a medical journal, and advocated measures to improve the health as well as the morals of the community. As a member of the Board of Education, he was particularly interested in the education of the children who lived in the densely settled portions of our city. His efforts for better education were not limited to the public schools. The University of Cincinnati owes him a debt of gratitude for his work in its behalf. It could not expand, located as it was on the side hill on McMicken Ave.; it needed room. In May, 1889, Dr. Culbertson, then a member of the Council introduced an ordinance for the occupancy of sixty acres of Burnett Woods for University purposes. He advocated the passage with great vigor and wrote numerous editorials in its behalf. The ordinance passed in September of the same year. In 1891 he was called to Chicago to edit the Journal of the American Medical Association, a position which he held for about two years. From 1893 until it closed its doors, he was Professor of the Principals and Practice of Medicine in the Cincinnati College of Medicine and Surgery.

In appreciation of his literary work, the American Social Science Association elected him a member, an honor which he highly prized. All in all Dr. Culbertson lived a very useful and successful life, a good soldier, a good citizen, a devoted member and Elder of the Presbyterian Church.

He was married three times, his wife and three children survive him, Rev. Henry C. Culbertson, Mr. James C. Culbertson and his daughter, Mrs. John Wheeler. (From In Memoriam by Drs. S. C. Ayres, C. L. Bonifield and Byron Stanton, committee of Commandery Military, Order of the Loyal Legion of the U. S.)

(7) Judge Hugh Culbertson moved to Wooster, O., about 1824. Here he was a noted lawyer and judge. He owned a farm just outside of Wooster. His hospitable home was always open, and no family was more universally respected than his.

(27) John W. Culbertson first engaged in mercantile business in Wayne Co., O.; in 1828 moved to Gilead, Wood Co., O., engaging in same business, and was appointed Postmaster by Van Buren. In 1840 he settled on what is now Fairfield, Ia. He was a Democrat of pronounced type. Was a member of the first Legislature of Iowa, representing Jefferson Co. two terms. Also held minor township and county offices. In 1856, he was appointed Receiver of Public Moneys, at Fairfield, by President Pierce. He also served three terms as Clerk of Court, Jefferson Co., Ia. The latter part of his life was spent on his farm of 500 acres, adjoining the town of Fairfield. His wife, who was of an old Virginia family, was a well-preserved old lady of eighty-two years in 1892, and her letters are very interesting. Their son (79) "Hon Wm. Benton Culbertson was a student at Howe's Academy, Mt. Pleasant, Ia. He read law with Chas. Negus, of Fairfield, Ia. and then entered Yale Law School and graduated in 1857-8. He then engaged in practice of law at Fairfield. In 1882 he removed to Burlington, Ia. As what is generally called "a jury lawyer", Mr. Culbertson stands at the head of his profession. As a jury lawyer he has gained more than statewide celebrity. His thorough knowledge of the law, quick perception, and indomitable energy makes him sought after by both rich and poor, the latter especially, knowing his generous mind and sympathetic feeling toward them. He is a Democrat in politics. In 1880, he was Democratic candidate for Congress in the First Dist.—a strong Republican district—and yet he ran 1400 votes ahead of his own party ticket, a thing without a precedent in this state. He was elected to the Legislature in 1883." (From Iowa Review of 1884).

(93) Culbertson, Henry Coe, college pres., b. Cincinnati, O., July 11, 1874, son of Dr. J. C. and Sarah (Pogue); A. B. Univ. Cin., 1895 studied Columbia Law School 1896-8; B. D. Univ. Chicago 1900; (D. D. Lenox Col. 1910) mar. Mabel D. Freeman of Chicago, Mar. 14, 1900; Asst. Pastor Presb. Ch. Lake Forest, Ills., 1901-2; ordained 1902; pastor Iola, Kan. 1902-7; pres. Coll. Emporia, Kans., May, 1907. Mem. Beta Theta Pi. Progressive Club, Emporia, Kans. (From Who's Who in America). The mother of H. C. Culbertson was a daughter of the wealthy Mr. Pogue, merchant of Cincinnati, Ohio.

(36) Samuel C. Huey, President of the Penn. Mutual Life Insurance Company for thirteen years. Was a member of Union League Club of Philadelphia; a director of several insurance companies; an elder in a Presbyterian church of Philadelphia many years. He was in the manufacturing business in Philadelphia before the war, later President of the Black Heath Coal Company. After this he was in partnership with his brother William-in agricultural implement business at Winona, Minn., after this he accepted the presidency of the Penn Mutual Life Insurance Co.

CHAPTER XXVII
FIFTH GENERATION

(II) John Culbertson, second son of Irish Samuel Culbertson of the "Row" mar. to Margaret ———. Paid taxes in Letterkenny Tp. in 1762. Born between 1740-41. In his father's will he cut John off with five shillings. Just why we do not know but it is most likely that he had given John land and money in sufficient amount before death to compensate him; but this lead to a law suit and in 1809 his son Samuel of Westmoreland Co., Pa., gave power of att'y to his brother Alex, to bring suit in his name, as administrator of John against the administrators of (Irish) Samuel, to make demand and to sue to recover a legacy left by said (Irish) Samuel of Letterkenny Tp., Cumb. Co., Pa. John and wife Margaret sold 424 acres in Letterkenny Twp, for £1485 in 1786. Recites that land was given to him by his father Samuel Culbertson in 1785 and that said land was sold to his father in 1760. He then (1786) moved to Hempfield Tp., Westmoreland Co., Pa. purchasing part of the land on which Hannastown (the first county seat) was located (about 400 acres). Died intestate and letters of administration were issued Mar. 28, 1797 to wife, Margaret, and son, Samuel. At this date all of the children were given of age save Martha and Alexander over 14 years and Margaret under fourteen. "John Culbertson, pr. 3rd Co., 4th Batt'n, 2nd Class, Cumb.Co., Pa. Ass'rs. Col. Samuel Culbertson, Aug. 30, 1780. (Pa. Arch., 5th Ser., page 279). Census 1790, Westmoreland Co., Pa.: 3 males over 16 (including head) males under 16, three; females, including wife, three. Also "Revolutionary Service, pr. in Capt. Sam Culbertson's Co., Col. Jos. Armstrong, Dec. 8, 1776 (Pa. Arch.)

Issue:
1. Samuel.
2. Esther (Mrs. Wm. Thomas) Census 1790, self and wife, 1 son under 16; 2 daughters.
3. Nancy (Mrs. John Dewitt) 1790 Census, self and wife.
4. Robert, d. Apr. 19, 1357, Beaver Co., Pa.; born 1771. (tombstone).
5. John, Wayne Co., Ohio.
6. Martha (Mrs. David Rankin).
7. Alexander, .Wayne Co., Ohio.
8. Margaret (Mrs. John Conor).
   All were of age in 1803.

SIXTH GENERATION

(1) Samuel Culbertson lived in Westmoreland Co., Pa., as late as 1809. There was a Samuel Culbertson bought land in the county (Allegheny Tp.) in 1826 and sold it in 1826. No wife signed the deed so I presume he was unmarried.

(4) Robert Culbertson married first Elizabeth Thomas before 1800 in Westmoreland Co., moved to Beaver Co. Pa., where he died. Wife born 1781; d. Aug. 5, 1833. Deeded his share of est. Oct. 31, 1798. No wife signed deed.

Issue:
9. William, b. 1800, d. June 8, 1835. Warren, Pa.
10. John, b. 1802; d.——. Beaver Co., Pa.
11. Isaac, b. in Beaver Co., Pa.; d. ——. Warren Co., Pa.
12. Alexander, b.——, Beaver Co., Pa.; d. ——, Warren Co., Pa.
13. Robert, b.——, Beaver Co., Pa.; d. ——, Bachelor at New Orleans.
14. Armstrong, b.—— Beaver Co., Pa.; d. young.
15. Esther b. 1811 Beaver Co., Pa., married Mr. Reed; Issue, John Q. Reed, b. 1836, living.

16. James, b. ——, Beaver Co., Pa.; d. young.
17. Ruel, b. ——, Beaver Co., Pa., mar. no children; d. Mobile, Ala.
18. Wilson, b. ——, Beaver Co., Pa.; d.——, Green Co., Ind.; 4 children.
19. Clark, b. ——, Beaver Co., Pa.; d. ——, Green Co., Ind.; 4 children.
20. Margaret, d. young.
21. Elizabeth, d. ——, Beaver Co., Pa.; Mar. no children.

(4) Robert Culbertson mar. second Abigail Edwards. (Robert rec'd pension $40 year for Indian War Services, 1792-4 beginning Jan. 1, 1852.)

Issue:

22. Parker, b. ——, Beaver Co., Pa.; d.——, Alliance, O., 3 children.
23. Joseph, b.——, Beaver Co., Pa.; d. ——, Alliance, O., 3 children.
24. Samuel, b. Beaver Co., Pa.; Left home, never heard from.
25. Esther, b. ——, Beaver Co., Pa.; taken to Iowa when young; never heard from.

(5) John Culbertson was mar. by or before 1798 to Jane Sloan. He and wife Jane sold land at Hannatown, West-moreland Co., Pa., in Oct. 1798. He moved to Venango Co., then to Beaver Co., Pa. and lastly to Wayne Co., Ohio. Pd. tax Irwin Tp., Venango Co., Pa., 1805.

Issue:

26. John.
27. Joseph.
28. William.
29. Sloan.
30. Alexander.
31. Margaret.
32. Ellen (Mrs. Dunham or Duncan).
33. Hetty.
34. Polly.
35. Jennie.
36. Elizabeth.

(7) Alexander Culbertson mar. Margaret Sloan, moved to Venango Co., Irwin Tp. (tax 1805), a.nd Beaver County, Pa., then to Wayne Co., Ohio, where he died.

Issue:

37. John, b. 1805.

38.   Samuel.
39.   Andrew.
40.   Alexander.
41.   Margaret.
42.   Jane.
43.   Ellen.

SEVENTH GENERATION

(9) William Culbertson mar. Miss Nancy Mohr. Kept a hotel at Sharpsburg, Pa., in 1856. Wife b. Mar. 25, 1805; d. Nov. 4, 1845.

Issue:

44.   Jackson.
45.   James.
46.   Robert.
47.   Elias, b. Apr. 19, 1833.
48.   William Wallace, b. Mar. 25, 1839; d. July 9, 1846.

(9) William Culbertson mar. second Miss Jane Strong.

Issue:

49.   Nancy Jane (mar. cousin Robert, son of Alexander). b. May 3, 1854; d. Jan. 30, 1899.
50.   Minnie (Mrs. Chas. Knapp). Warren, Pa.

(10) John Culbertson mar. Miss Elizabeth Thompson; wife died aged 96 years.

Issue:

51.   Mary Elizabeth, living 1922, Oakdale, Alle. Co., Pa.
52.   Samuel.
53.   Robert.
54.   Joseph.

(11) Isaac Culbertson mar. Miss Mary Shirley. No issue. Died in Warren Co., Pa.

(12) Alexander Culbertson mar. Lucinda ——. Died Warren Co., Pa.

Issue:

55.   Isaac, d.
56.   Robert, b. 1845; d. Sept. 5, 1891; Warren Co., Pa.
57.   Alexander.
58.   John, d.
59.   Esther, d.
59¼.   Nancy, d   59½. Wm., b. 1839. Living at Kinzua, Pa.

(15) Esther Culbertson mar. Mr. Reed.

Issue:

60.   John Quincy Reed, b. 1836, living.

(17) Ruel Culbertson mar. ——. No issue. Died at Mobile, Ala.

(18) Wm. Culbertson mar. ——. Died Greene Co., Ind.
Issue: 61, 62, 63, 64.

(19) Clark Culbertson mar. ——. Died Greene Co., Ind.
Issue:65-69.

(21) Elizabeth Culbertson mar. ——. No issue.

(22) Parker Culbertson mar.——. Married in Beaver
Co., Pa. Died Alliance, Ohio. Issue: 70-71.

(23) Joseph Culbertson mar. ——, Alliance, Ohio.
Issue 72-75.

(26) John Culbertson mar. his cousin, Miss Dorcas Thomas, of Wayne Co., Ohio., Aug. 25, 1825.
Issue:
76. John.
77. William.
78. Alexander, d. 1885. Loudonville, O.
79. Milo, Lyons, Kans.
80. Levi, d. 1863. Unmarried.
81. Jane (Mrs. Roth), Shreve, O.
82. Esther (Mrs. Case), Orrville, O.
83. Ellen (Mrs. McIntire).
84. Matilda Ann, d. 1879.

EIGHTH GENERATION

(37) John Culbertson mar. ——. Lived in Wayne Co., O.
Issue:
85. Alexander.
86. Jacob.
87. William, b. 1835. Lived at Akron, Ohio, in 1892.

(44) Jackson Culbertson mar. Miss Tilly. Living in Minnesota. Issue: 88-89.

(45) James Culbertson mar. Miss Ella——. Issue, two
grandchildren, Bolivar Co., Miss, i. e. Miss Luella Soloman
and Mrs. Betty Roberts, 138-139.

(46) Robert Culbertson mar. Lizzie ——. No issue.

(47) Elias Culbertson mar. first Miss Harriet Marsh.
Lived at Oil City, Pa.
Issue:

90. Almon Elias, b. Mar. 27, 1856. New York City.
91. Orie, b. Sept. 19, 1860; d. Apr. 10, 1919, in Russia.

(47) Elias Culbertson mar. second Miss Lizzie Mohnkern. Wife b. Oct. 27, 1851.
Issue:
92. Warren L, b. Nov. 4, 1879. Lives at Oil City, Pa.
93. Eva, b. Feb. 13, 1876. (Mrs. Evan Dickson), Oil City, Pa.
94. Lawrence B., b. June 30, 1886. Lives at Oil City, Pa.

(50) Minnie Culbertson mar. Chas. Knapp.
Issue:

95. Ralph Knapp.
96. Goldie.

(51) Mary Elizabeth Culbertson mar. Philis Bradshaw. Widow living at Oakdale, Pa.
Issue:
97. Margaret Bradshaw.
98. Robert
99. John R.
100. Joseph.
101. Eva E.
102 Mabel (Mrs. Dr. Clark Denny), Oakdale, Pa.
103. William.

(56) Robert Culbertson mar. his cousin (49) Nancy Jane Culbertson, daughter of Alex (12).
Issue:

104. Wm. M., b. Apr. 5, 1876; d. Jan. 30, 1899.
104¼. Ward B., b. Oct. 3, 1877; lives at Grand Valley, Pa.

(59½) Wm. Culbertson mar. ——. Lives at Kinzua, Warren Co., Pa.
Issue:

105. Belle (Mrs. McArthurs), Kinzua, Pa.
105½. Alexander, b. 1851. Lives at Kinzua, Pa., is married. Issue: 136, Fred; 137, Harry; Kinzua, Pa.

(76) John Culbertson mar. Mary Lovett. Lived at Akron, Ohio.
Issue:

106. Josephine.
106½. Laura.
107. Addie.

(77) Wm. Culbertson mar. Miss Fullerton, of Wayne Co., Ohio.

Issue:

108. Frank.
109. Ed.
110. Henry.

(78) Alexander Culbertson mar.——

Issue:

111. Milton, Loudonville, Ohio.

(79) Milo Culbertson mar. ——.

Issue:

112. Francis Rolland. Kans.
113. Annie May. (Mrs. L. Banker).
114. Alvin E. Lyons, Kans.

(81) Jane Culbertson mar. Mr. Roth, of Shreve, O.

Issue:

115. Albert.
116. Nora (Mrs. J. D. Banker), Russell, Kans.
117. William.

(82) Esther Culbertson mar. Mr. Case of Orrville, O.

Issue:

118. Horace.
119. Wm .A.

(83) Ellen Culbertson mar. R. B. McIntire. Live at Butler, Bates Co., Mo.

Issue:

120. L. O. McIntire, Lawrence, Kans.
121. Harry R. Butler, Mo.

NINTH GENERATION

(90) Almon Elias Culbertson born in Warren Co., Pa. About forty years ago moved to Russia. During the World War moved to United States, New York City. Married in Russia to Xenia Rogozny. Wife born in Russia June 28, 1856, w.ife died in America.

Issue:

122. Pavel.
123. Julia.
124. Milie.
125. Evan.
126. Evgenie.

127. Elie.
128. Saisha (Alexander), b. Dec. 29, 1893. Lives in N. Y.
City.

(91) Orie Culbertson born Warren Co., Pa., died in Russia. Mar. Miss Georgia Mott (widow lives Philadelphia, Pa.)
Issue:
129. Elie, Philadelphia, Pa.
130. George,. Philadelphia, Pa.

(92) Warren Culbertson, Oil City, Pa., mar. Mar. 19, 1913, to Miss Edna Verda Gartner, who was born April 3rd, 1880. No issue.

(93) Eva Culbertson Dickson, Oil City, Pa., mar. Sept. 5,. 1900, to Mr. Evan Dickson, who was born Dec. 6, 1866.
Issue:
131. John Dickson, only child, born June 3, 1904.

(94) Lawrence B. Culbertson, Oil City, Pa., mar. Oct. 30, 1907, to Miss Minnie McKim, who was born April 17, 1886.
Issue:
132. William, only child, born Feb'y 4, 1915.

(104¼) Ward B. Culbertson mar. Clara B. Marsh of Warren Co., Pa. (Wife b. Nov. 16, 1886).
Issue:
133. Nancy A., b. at Russell, Pa., March 23,. 1907.
134. Martha, b. at Russel, Pa., Jan. 29, 1909.
135. Robert H,. b. at Russel Pa., July 16, 1918.

PROMINENT DESCENDANTS OF (II) JOHN CULBERTSON.

(90) Almon Elias Culbertson and (91) Orie Culbertson were mining engineers and oil producers who went to Russia forty years ago and came back to America during the World War.

(128) Sasha Culbertson, the great Russian Violin Virtuoso, now making New York his home; was raised partly near the Carpathian Mountains in Russia and early learned the wierd and beautiful strains of gypsy, Russian and Cossak music. His mother was a fine musician and his father musical.

His first teacher was a Cossak (Prof. Sevcik). Later attended the Imperial Conservatory at Rostov. In 1905 he went to Prague, Bohemia to study for three years. In 1906 Dr. Borecky of Prague wrote "What this young artist accomplishes today borders on the incredible—the impossible." In Vienna in 1908 Dr. Max Kalbeck wrote "Sasha Culbertson made his debut with a cycle of gigantic concerts and carried off the honors over all his colleagues who have appeared upon the concert platform this season. He is the Rubenstein of the violin, not only by virtue of his outward appearance, but that he possesses absolute mastery of the fingerboard, etc., etc." Berlin, London, Rome and New York critics give equal lauditory criticisms. He has also played at the Vatican in a private audience with the Pope of Rome and His Holiness had a medal made for him in honor of this in 1910. His violin is a Joseph Guarnerius, bearing date 1732, having cost $10,000 and formerly belonged to Count Cessoli and intimate friend of Paganini and this violin was greatly admired by Paganini.

Sasha last year was doing concert work in America and playing for the Vocalian Record Co. Will tour Europe 1923 in concert. These records show his marvelous execution and depth of feeling and the wondrous beauty of his violin. Saisha played with the Y. M. C. A. throughout the World War in France, to the sick and wounded and was demobilized in Aug. 1919. Elie, his brother was an interpreter in the army in France and Eugene served two and a half years in the French Heavy Art.

(51) Mrs. Mary Elizabeth (Culbertson) Bradshaw has a granddaughter, Ruth Bradshaw of Denver, Col., who (I am so informed) was awarded the prize in 1922, of being the most beautiful woman in America, as per decision of readers of the American Magazine offering said prize. The photos were shown in the August number of The Metropolitan and the readers voted Miss Bradshaw the winner. Her picture was again shown in the Dec. '22 number of this magazine. She has won several beauty contests in Denver.

Note: Would state that some of Saisha Culbertson's records in the Vocalion are, 70001 "Dance of the Goblins" (Bazini); "Meditation" from Thais (by Massenet); also 52041 "Scherzo Tarantelle"; "Serenade" No. 60001, and "Waltz in A Major"; also Slavonic Dance.

CHAPTER XXVIII

(III) **Robert Culbertson, son of Irish Samuel,** of the Row, (G). Mar. his cousin, Elizabeth Lindsay of Cumberland (now Franklin) Co., Pa. First owned a farm in the "Row", then in 1773 sold his farm, 300 acres in Letterkenny Tp., and moved to Brownsville, Pa., where he lived for a year. He then tried to repurchase his farm in the Row, but failing in this bought a farm at the foot of South Mountain, Franklin Co., Pa., (several miles from Row) where he died. Letters of administration issued to his wife, Feb. 11, 1778. (Lived in Guilford Tp.) Later she married Mathew Sharp and he was appointed administrator. Sale bill returned March, 1778, showed bonds and Congress Money valued at £1180. In final acct. filed 1783 it states that the bonds were used to purchase the property of the heirs. They purchased property in Westmoreland Co., Pa., in 1789. They sold the Guilford Tp. farm in 1792 when they moved to Allegheny Co., Pa. Robert owned a farm in Letterkenny Tp. (Row) as it was on the tax list Cumb. Co., 1779 as "Elizabeth, widow and 1782-85 Roberts heirs." Descendants say that Robert was killed at the Battle of Brandywine (fall of 1777) but I hardly believe this can be true as administrator was not appointed until Feb., 1778. He might have been wounded there and death resulted therefrom.

There were only three Robert Culbertsons of military age in Aug., 1776, in territory embraced by Cumb. and Franklin Counties, hence he was the "private in Capt. Samuel Culbertson Co. of Col. Jos. Armstrong's Batt'n. (First) of Cumb. Co., Pa. Ass'rs., Dec. 8, 1776" (Pa. Archives). Robert's wife was a reigning belle of Franklin Co., Pa. She is given Elizabeth Sharp on Census of 1790 in territory embraced in Row, self and 2 males over 16 years old; one male under 16 (a Sharp?) and 5 females. Before 1792 they had moved to Guilford Tp. Family records say that she lived in Franklin Co., after her third marriage and is buried with her husband, Robert Peoples, near Shippensburg, Pa.

Issue:
1. Esther, b. ——; d. ——.
2. Elizabeth, b. ——; d. ——.
3. Jane, b. ——; d. ——.
4. Samuel, b. —— d. Apr. 1800.
5. Agnes, b. 1774; d. Nov. 1836.

Children obtain from a deed and family records.

After the death of Robert Culbertson, his widow mar. Mathew Sharp, the founder of the town, Sharpsburg, Pa.
Issue:
6. Rosanna Sharp, mar. John Liggett and had three sons and three daughters. A grandson of (6) is Sidney B. Liggett.
7. Mary, d. unmarried.
8. James, d. 1861. Mar. twice; had eight children, one of whom is Mrs. E. L. Clark, of Sharpsburg, Pa.
After the death of Mathew Sharp (died 1786), his widow, Elizabeth, married Robert Peebles, a prominent man of Franklin Co. Pa., and nephew of Col. Robert Peebles.

SIXTH GENERATION

(1) Esther Culbertson mar. her cousin, Andrew, son of Col. Robert, of Columbus Ohio. See descendants of Andrew son of Col. Robert Culbertson of Columbus, O. She died after husband who d. Apr., 1826.
Issue:
9. Alexander.
10. Elizabeth (Mrs. Dill, Andrew). Columbus, O.
11. Isabella (Mrs. Emick, John). Columbus, O.
12. Rebecca (Mrs. Smith, Nathaniel W.). Columbus, O.
13. Mary (Mrs. Shannon, Wm. W.). Columbus, O.
13½. Robert, Gilman, Ills. (See descendants of Andrew, son of Col. Robert, of Columbus, O.).

(2) Elizabeth mar. cousin, Wm. Lindsay, and settled in Kentucky.

(3) Jane mar. John Hancock, an English gentleman.
Issue:
14. Crawford C. Mar. Charlotte Peters, of Pittsburg and had issue: John, Lewis and Jane. John served all through the Civil War and was a Major. Lived at Pittsburg.
15. Robert, d. young.

(4) Samuel Culbertson mar. Miss Elizabeth Work. Lived in Allegheny, Pa. (from will). No issue.

(5) Agnes Culbertson mar. James B. Clow of Pittsburg, Pa., Dec. 25, 1794.
Issue:
16. Samuel Clow, d. infancy.
17. Eliza, d. infancy.

18.James, d. infancy.
19.   James L. (Dr.) Mar. first, Miss Nina Clark; second,
      Miss Brown.
20.   Samuel Culbertson (N. Sewickly, Pa.).   Mar. first
      Sophia Rusk; second L. Weihl.
21.   Sarah Ann, b. 1803; living 1893.   Mar. W. B. Clark,
      lawyer, Pittsburg.
22.   Ellza Jane, d. 1858.
23.   John H., d. 1836.
24.   Edward S., mar. Margaret Fleming.
25.   Mary Sharp, mar. G. B. Boyd.
26.   Agnes, mar. R. P. Marshall.

SEVENTH GENERATION

(12) Rebecca Culbertson mar. Nathaniel Smith of Pittsburg and afterwards moved to Wheeling, W. Va.
Issue:
27.   Mary (Mrs. McConahey).   Pulaski, Pa.
28.   Esther (Mrs. Hawkins). Sharpsburg, Pa.   Had issue:
      Dau. Mrs. A. H. Jones, of Pittsburg.
29.   Martha.
30.   Culbertson Smith.

(19)   Dr. James L. Clow mar.
Issue:
31.   James C. Clow, d. 1857.
32.   Agnes Clow mar. Amos Lusk, M. D.
33.   Robert.
34.   Maria V., mar. D. H. Metzgan.

(20) Samuel Culbertson Clow mar. ——.
Issue:
35.   James B. Clow, founder of the great James B. Clow &
      Sons, manufacturers of plumbers supplies, etc.
      One of the big iron corporations of the U. S.
36.   Maria. 37, Milton. 38, Emma. 39, Mary. 40, Win-
      field. 41, Mary. 42, Lois. 43, Grace. 44, Annie.
      45, John. 46,——. 47 ——.
48.   Sarah Ann mar. Wm. B. Clark, an eminent attorney
      of Pittsburg, Pa. Issue: Jennie P. (Mrs. Ed Sul-
      livan) ; Agnes; Wm. Francis; Sarah Mina.
49.   Eliza Jane, d. 1858.
50.   John H., d. 1856.
51.   Edmond S. mar. (five children).
52.   Mary Sharp (Mrs. T. B. Boyd), 6 children.
53.   Agnes Ewalt (Mrs. R. P. Marshall) 8 children.

(3) Jane Culbertson was one of the reigning beeles while in Philadelphia. It is said that one of her pictures hung in one of the Art Galleries of Philadelphia for some years. Her grandson, John Hancock, was a Major in the Civil War.

(6) Rosanna Liggetts grandson, Sidney B. Liggett, was a secretary of the Pa. R. R. Lines West of Pittsburg, with headquarters at Pittsburg. Jennie A. Clark, daughter of (48) Sarah Ann Clow of Pittsburg, mar. first Mr. Arthurs, a wealthy iron manufacturer of Pittsburg; no issue. He died and she afterwards maried Ed Sullivan of Zanesville, Ohio. She died first and her husband died recently and left large bequests for Presbyterian and Methodist churches and other charitable bequests.

CHAPTER XXIX

(V) **Joseph Culbertson, son of Irish Samuel.** His father conveyed to him in 1785 for £300. (244 Acres) in Letterkenny Tp. Also 32 acres in Shippensburg and 187 acres in Southhampton Tp., Cumb. Co. Joseph and wife, Margaret, sold the Shippensburg property in 1790 to Geo. McCandless for £162. Joseph died in 1801 in Jan. (ad'm'n Feb. 2, 1801, to S. W. Culbertson). Robert of Southhampton and John Calwell shortly after were app. administrators, and later by order of the court deeded a lot in Shippensburg to Dr. Simpson (1801). Later C. Clippenger was appointed administrator. In petition to court for sale Shippensburg lot, Robert C. and John Caldwell state "that Joseph Culbertson of Southhampton, deceased, died in 1801, leaving a widow, since married to David Reynolds, and five children the eldest not being over 12 years of age, we do hereby petition court to sell lot in Shippensburg to pay debts, made 1801." Administrators released by court on distribution of £118, 1801.

In 1811 by decree of Orphans Court, "Samuel Culbertson, eldest son of Joseph Culbertson, deceased, late of Southhampton Tp., Cumb. Co., there became vested in said Samuel right and interest of his said father's in land in aforesaid tp., containing 137 acres, subject to certain recognizances entered into by him with his brothers and sisters, viz.: Robert, Joseph and James Peoples, and Esther, his wife. Samuel hereby gives notes to pay for their share with interest from Aug. 19, 1811."

Issue: Joseph and Margaret Culbertson:

1. Samuel, b. 1787-8.
2. Esther (Mrs. James Peoples), b. 1789-90.
3. Robert.
4. Joseph.
5. Child, d. young.

There was an administrator appointed for a Joseph Culbertson of Shippensburg, Mar. 19, 1839. (Item Cumb. Co. No. 253). There is no inventory or acc't filed. This may or may not have been the Joseph of this family.

Irish Samuel also deeded to his son, Joseph, 137 acres in Southhampton Tp. I could not find his deed or administrator's deed for the 244 acres in Letterkenny. Must have overlooked it. Above items show that Samuel bought his brothers and sisters' interest in the estate. What became of them I know not. I find no deed from Samuel to show that he sold this land. Census 1790 gives him in Shippensburg (Hopewell Tp.) one male (self) one son under 16 and wife and one daughter. "Served in Cumb. Co., Pa. company of Frontier Rangers." (Pa. Archives).

CHAPTER XXX

(VI) **Alexander Culbertson**, son of Irish Samuel, married Janet Lindsay. Col. LaBree (a Ky. genealogist) claims he was born 1748. He first appears on the tax lists of Letterkenny Tp., Cumb. Co., Pa., as "freeman" 1768.. Appears in Guilford Tp. list 1772, 190 acres. Revolutionary Service: "Was enrolled Aug. 10, 1780, in Capt. James Young's Co. of Col. Jas. Johnson's Batt'n. Cumb. Co. Militia, and in same Batt'n Aug. 21, 1781." (Pa. Arch.) His father deeded him 200 acres (pat. to Samuel, Sr., 1743) in Letterkenny for $1.00. Sold this before his death. Also deeded him 195 acres in Guilford Tp., 1785. Said land pruchased by Samuel in 1770. This farm embraced a part of land on which Chambersburg was built. He made his will Apr. 17, 1790, will probated June 1, 1790. The Census of 1790 was started in March, 1790. His name does not appear thereon but his widow does appear thus: "Jean Culbertson head, males over 16, one (this was her son Samuel) ; males under 16, three; females 7 including self." In his will he mentions son-in-law, James Lindsay and widow Jean, as executors. A genealogist in Ky. claimed that Alex and family moved to Kentucky in the spring of 1790 with Wm. Long and died shortly after. The probating and making of his will in Pa. proves

he died in Pa., as does also the fact that his widow appears
with his famiily in Pa. in 1790 Census. Her brother (Lindseys of Fayette Co., Ky.) Jos., James, Henry and William
went to Kentucky in 1775. (Courier Jour. Genealog. Notes).
His widow died intestate in 1794 and James Lindsay was appointed administrator in Franklin Co., Pa. In Alex's will
he devised that if his wife remarried before his youngest
child attained his majority, then she (widow) should get
one-third of his estate; but that she was to get her income
from his estate if she did not remarry. Should she live until their youngest child attained his majority, then she
should get one-ninth of his estate. She did not remarry.
The youngest child became of age in 1810,, at which date
she was married and lived in Ky. Maria born after her
father's death, 1790. The children are given in will in following order: Esther, Elizabeth Agnes, Jane, Martha, Robert, Samuel, John, Prudence. Co. Clerk of Fayette Co., Ky.,
says there are no records of them. They went to Scott Co.,
Ky. Records of that county were destroyed by fire in the
thirties. It is my opinion that they went to Ky. in 1795,
probably with "Samuel of the Creek" and the Lindsay family. Prudence told her daughter that they moved to Ky.. in
1802. Franklin Co., Ky., Court Records do not give them.
The estate was settled by deeds. These deeds—or part of
them—were made in Ky. and the witnesses to all of them
save one—that of John Adams and wife of Washington Co.,
Pa.—were made and witnessed by Bernard and Christian
Wolff. John's deed says "late of Westmoreland Co., Pa.,"
showing he was in Ky. date deed was made, Dec. 26, 1806.
Robert's deed says residence "Montgomery Co., Ohio, Jan.
18, 1810." No wives signed on these two deeds. Martha
Culbertson and Esther Lindsay deeded in 1803 from Scott
Co., Ky. Clerk of Franklin Co., Ky., says no Culbertsons
on his records. Other heirs deeded in Franklin Co., Ky.
Deeds made by balance of heirs in 1810, state that Samuel
and Martha had died prior to that time, unmarried.

(1) Robert Culbertson lived in Montgomery Co., Ohio, in
1810 as shown by a deed. (For descendants see Chap. on
Col. Robert of Bedford.) (2) Samuel died young. (3) John
Culbertson lived in Westmoreland Co. Pa., prior to 1806 as
shown by a deed, then moved to Ky. (4) Esther Culbertson married James Lindsay, her cousin, and moved to
Franklin Co., Ky. (5) Elizabeth married George McCandless and died in Ohio. (6) Agnes ("Nancy") married her
cousin, John Adams, and moved to Franklin Co., Ky. (7)

Jane married Mr. John Adams and lived at Washington Co.,
Pa. (8) Maria married Mr. Adams, Scott Co., Ky. (9) Mar-
tha, unmarried. (10) Prudence left Pennsylvania when 12
years old. Was 90 years old when she died. She was married July 24, 1810 to Benjamin Hensley, Esq., of Scott Co.,
Ky. Issue: Jane, d. young; Maria Antoinette (Mrs. Lyne
Starling, of Frankfort, Ky., living 1896, aged 84 years);
Alexander Culbertson, a distinguished surgeon in Mexican
War—in Sixteenth U. S. Regulars—and Surgeon-in-Chief of
Louisiana troops (Confederates), killed at New Orleans during war; Benj. Hensley, Lucien Hensley, and Harry Hensley
were three surgeons of note; Charles Hensley and Alfred,
lawyer and civil engineer; Edward Hensley, accountant and
insurance agent; Wilkinson, died aged 17 years; John Culbertson Hensley died 1856; Elizabeth Love (Mrs. George
Morgan Woodbridge, a son of Dudley Woodbridge), of Marietta, O; Laura Genevieve (Mrs. Torrance). The last named
married, first Jordon A. Pugh, of Cincinnati, O. Then was
a widow for sometime, and in 1875 married Hon. Mr. Justice
Torrance, one of the Judges of the Superior Court of Canada, who subsequently died. She lived in Montreal, Canada
(1896).

(4) Esther Culbertson (Mrs. James Lindsay). Issue: William, unmarried; Janet (Mrs. Leaven Cooper); Polly (Mrs.
Louis Cooper); James (married Lucy Cooper), all of Galla-
tin Co., Ky.; Nancy (Mrs. Newman, of Owensboro, Ky.);
Eliza (Mrs. Dr. Lilly, of Corydon, Ind.); Patty (Mrs. Patterson, of Fayette Co., Ky.); Juliana (Mrs. Ford). (Mrs. James
Lindsay no doubt eldest child of Alex.).

(5) Mrs. George McCandless, had one son.

(6) Agnes (Mrs. John Adams). Issue: Alexander, unmarried; William, married; Robert, unmarried; David, married, lived at Hawesville, Ky.; James.
Of the children of (10) Prudence Culbertson and Benjamin Hensley (b. 1780; d. Nov. 5, 1849), one daughter, Elizabeth Love Hensley, who was born Sept. 1, 1820; d. Jan. 23,
1899. Married May 10, 1844, to George Morgan Woodbridge of Marietta, Ohio.
Issue:
Maria P. Living. Marietta, O.
Laura, b. Sept. 7, 1849, married Frank A. Gallaher, April
        4, 1877. Issue: Elizabeth (Mrs. Frank Farring-
        ton); Maria Woodbridge (Mrs. Dr. J. B. Penrose),
        d. Aug. 23, 1882.

Dudley Morgan, b. Aug. 30, 1853; mar. Miss Lizzie Anderson. Issue: Elizabeth Dudley.

George Morgan, b. July 4, 1858. Mar. Miss Julia Warner. Wife born July 4, 1858. Wife living at Seattle, Wash. Issue: (a) Dudley Warner Woodbridge, Jr. born Feb. 24, 1896 (he married and had issue— wife, Ruby Mendenhall)—(b) Hensley C. Woodbridge, born Feb. 6, 1923); (a) Laura F. Woodbridge, mar. Henry C. Peeples (issue (b) Cicely Frances, born Aug. 27, 1918 and Mary Belle, born March 12, 1922).

Dudley Warner Woodbridge was in 31st Div. and served in hospital at Le Mans, France, in World War.

Lyne Starling Woodbridge, b. Jan. 30, 1860. Mar. Cora May Holroyd, Apr. 20, 1887. Issue: Lucy Starling, Laura Elizabeth, Jessie Louise.

CHAPTER XXXI

FIFTH GENERATION

(VIII) "Gentleman" or "Beau James" Culbertson first appears on the tax lists of Letterkenny Tp. in 1771 as "James son of Samuel." This would lead to the inference that he was born 1750 or before that. He lived in the Row and his farm was next to that of Col. Samuel Culbertson. He erected a magnificent stone mansion (do not know the year this was built), which is still standing. The Author visited this mansion in 1922. It has many large rooms in it, finished in beautiful wood (same he put in it) and the house is well kept by the present owners. Gentleman James was a princely entertainer and many a sociable gathering was held in this stately mansion. James was a great dresser; kept hounds and was very fond of hunting. Besides this farm, he was in a land company which owned 3400 acres of land in Toboyne Tp., Cumb. (now Perry) Co., Pa., and he sold his interest in this in 1795 for $1783. His father in 1785 deeded him a farm in Montgomery Tp., Franklin Co., Pa. He sold this in 1795 to Abraham Smith and Wm. Irwin, for £3000. Deed recites that this land was deeded to him in 1785 by his father, Samuel Culbertson, Sr. He was "Commissioned Cornet, May 10, 1780, in Capt. John Johnston's Troop of Light Horse, from Cumberland (now Franklin) Co., Pa. Wm. Sharpe was a Lieut. in this Co. This Co.

marched to Lancaster, but their services were not needed."
(Pa. Archives). A copy of Scott's Bible Commentary
which belonged to his wife, is in possession of a descendant,
Mrs. Martin of Springfield, O., and in it is written "Margaret Culbertson, wife of James Culbertson." She was Margaret Smith, a daughter of Robert Smith, grandson of
Wm. Smith, who laid out Mercersburg, Pa. Robert Smith's
first wife was Grizell Newell and second wife, Elizabeth,
daughter of Archibald Irwin.

Irish Samuel Culbertson in his will left the plantation on
which he lived to his son, James, under the following conditions: That owing to his obligations to me, bearing date
herewith, I have ordered him to pay by my assignments on
said obligations for some of my heirs, and in order also to
enable him to give and pay to my aforesaid wife the support
and maintenance bequeathed to her annually during her life,
which I allow him to pay quarterly to my ex'rs, for benefit
of my widow; which support aforesaid I here subject my
son, James, to pay as long as he enjoys the use of said plantation, providing my wife lives so long. If at the end of
seven years it appears to my ex'rs that he has paid my
widow the proper sums for her support then my son shall
have the power to dispose of said farm and keep all the
proceeds of said sale. But if he has failed to fully carry out
all stipulations of my will then my executors shall sell my
farm seven years after my decease and shall give my son
James one-half of the proceeds of such sale, and the other
half shall be equally divided among my sons and daughters
then alive.

The accounts filed by Samuel, Joseph and Samuel Culbertson (1794-1800) ex'rs of Irish Samuel Culbertson show that
he only paid $50 to the widow, therefore he did not carry
out the provision in his fathers will, hence he got only one-half of the proceeds arising from the sale of his father's
farm. Census 1790 gives him in Green Tp. Males over 16
years, 2; males under 16, 1; females 5. The latter included
wife and step-mother. This shows James had one son over
16 years (Samuel). Therefore he must have married by
or before 1772. Still resided in Greene Tp., 1799 (taxes). In
Row. "Gentleman James'" magnificent stone mansion is
still standing in Culbertson Row and in excellent repair.

"Baron" James died in 1812, intestate and his widow and
Alexander McCoy were appointed administrators, Sept. 23,
1812. They sold his home farm. I could find no inventory
or account of his estate. The widow lived in Mercersburg

in 1816 as shown by deed of Power of Att'y to Wm. Irwin by James Smith and wife of Hamilton Co., Ohio, and Jennet Campbell of Rockbridge Co., Va. for land in Mercersburg, Pa., to Margaret Culbertson for $200, July, 1816.

In Margaret Culbertson's Bible Commentary it says, "Robert Culbertson, son of Samuel, died Oct. 24, 1819." The presumption is that this is a grandson of Gentleman James.

Mathew Patton was appointed Administrator of Margaret Culbertson in Franklin Co., Pa., Nov. 28, 1822. In a sale bill, 1832, of this estate the heirs are the same as given in Genealogy, but Robert is not given. Mathew Patton filed his final account and same approved in 1846.

Issue of James and Margaret:

1. Samuel, was living in Millersburg, Holmes Co., O., in 1839 as shown by a deed from him and wife, Francis, for land in Franklin Co., Pa. Born before 1775.

2. James, unmarried (?) lived in Chambersburg, Pa., and kept a hat store for a time. Later he edited the Anti-Masonic Gazette which he sold in 1828. (See McCauley's History of Franklin Co., Pa.). Rev. Nevin's work on Churches of the Cumb. Valley states that "in 1826 James Culbertson and Alexander McCoy were added to the session of the Mercersburg, Presbyterian Church." Mrs. Martin states that after his mother's death, he went west to near Peoria and died there, unmarried. Investigation of Court Records of Peoria shows that on "Nov. 19, 1846, a certain attorney petitioned court for sale of household goods of James Culbertson, late of Chillicothe, Ills. (Peoria Co.), deceased; that he died Aug. 28, 1846 and his widow Louisa is the only person mentioned." Would infer from this he had no children. I believe this is Gentleman James' son, although Mrs. Martin's story does not corroborate this. Court records of Tazewell Co., Ills., do not give him; nor do court records of Peoria Co., Ills. I can find no court or Bible records to show that "Gentleman" James had a son Robert.

3. Robert (?).

4. Esther Culbertson, b. ——; d.——. (Mrs. J. R. Sharon).

5. Jane, b. ——; d. ——. (Mrs. Alex. McCoy).

SIXTH GENERATION

(1) Samuel Culbertson moved to Millersburg, Holmes Co., O. Mar. first, his cousin, Esther Culbertson, dau. of his uncle Samuel. Was a merchant.

Issue:

6. Louisa, d.
7. Margaret (Mrs. Dr. S. Norris).
8. Robert d. Oct. 24, 1819.

(1) Samuel Culbertson mar. second, Francis ———. Moved to Madison or Keokuk, Ia. after 1840. (Lived at Peoria, Ills., for a while.)

Issue:

9. Wm. Birmingham, Ia.
10. Smith. Birmingham, Ia.
May have been others.

(4) Esther Culbertson mar. Rev. James Russell Sharon, who for thirty-five years was pastor of the churches of Derry and Paxtang, Dauphin Co. Pa.

Issue: ·

11. Harriett Newell (Mrs. A. S. McCoy, of Mercersburg)
    Issue: Mary (Mrs. Oscar T. Martin of Springfield, Ohio) ; Mrs. John Reynolds of Dayton, Ohio; Alexander W. McCoy, M. D., Philadelphia, Pa.; James McCoy, New York City.
12. Elizabeth, Tiffin, Ohio. (Mrs. McMeen).

(5) Jane Culbertson mar. Alexander McCoy,. of Franklin Co., Pa.

Issue:

13. Abraham Smith (mar. 11 of this chapter).
14. Sarah Jane McCoy, b. Feb. 5, 1812 d. May 24, 1849; buried Presbyterian churchyard at Millerstown, Pa. Married Rev. Geo. Dougal Porter, May 12, 1840. Issue: Mary Dougal Porter* (Mrs. Wm. F. Spangler) ; Alex. M. Porter; Ann M. Porter (Mrs. A. Spangler) ; Geo. D. Porter; Thos. C. Porter.

---

*A son, Geo. Spangler, is a prominent attorney at Peoria, Ills., and his wife furnished me much information on this family as well as the McCune family.—(Ed.)

SECTION SECOND
PART FIFTH
Irish Robert (H) of Peters Tp., Cumberland County, Pa.

(Younger Brother of Alexander Culbertson and Samuel
Culbertson of Culbertson Row, Pa.)

(H) PART FIFTH

IRISH ROBERT OF PETERS TP., CUMBERLAND COUNTY, PENNSYLVANIA.

Took out a warrant for land in Peters Tp. in 1743 (then in Lancaster Co., Pa.). Supposed to have come to America at the same time his brothers, Alexander and Samuel came over. Paid taxes in Peters Tp. in 1750. He died in 1763. On October 19 of this year, John Clark, Margaret Culbertson and Hannah Clark were appointed administrators of his estate. In 1764 Margaret Clark, late Culbertson and relict of Robert Culbertson of Peters Tp., deceased, was appointed guardian of minors: Thomas, Mary, Ann, James, Robert and Margaret, and the court issued an order to sell the real estate consisting of 120 acres. This sold for £64 and return made to court and distribution made. Nothing further appears on court records of Cumberland or Franklin Counties from the administrators or Margaret Clark as Guardian. We presume this is the date at which John Clark and wife and step-children moved to Shermans Valley, Perry Co., Pa. They lived there, we presume, in 1788 as shown in James Culbertson's will in Staunton, Va. John G. Orr (80 years old in 1920) says that Robert's wife Margaret, was a Breckenridge. Thomas G. Culbertson of Wheeling, W. Va., in 1892 (who lived in the Row until 30 years old) and who was 87 years old in 1892, said that she was a Breckenridge and that Robert was the third Row brother. Capt. James of Staunton, Va., gives all his brothers and sisters in same order as given in guardianship application of Margaret, widow of Robert of Peters Tp., save that he does not mention Thomas.

FOURTH GENERATION

Issue:

I. Thomas, b.——; d. young.
II. Mary.
III. Ann.
IV. James (Capt.), d. 1788, Staunton, Va. Bachelor. (Chapter XXXII.).
V. Robert, b. ——; d. ——. Shermans Valley.

VI. Margaret. Lived Shermans Valley Pa. 1788.

I have had the tax records of Cumberland and Bedford Counties thoroughly examined by an attorney and fail to find John Clark or Thomas Culbertson, in the territory in these counties in what was Shermans Valley (Toboyne Tp.). Find a Robert Culbertson, "renter" in Toboyne in 1784. This was Robert, son of Robert of Peters Tp. Find no deeds in Cumberland from either Thomas or Robert. Capt. James' will establishes the fact that they lived in Shermans Valley, Pa., in 1788.

There is positively no court record to show that they lived in the Row after 1764. John Clarke (step-father) may have moved into Shermans Valley after sale of Robert of Peters Tp. farm 1763-4. Robert of Shermans Valley must have come of age about 1780-81. This Robert (V) served in (McCauley's Hist. Franklin Co., Pa., says that Col. Abraham Smith was from what is the present Cumb. Co. and not Franklin—page 78 McCauley's Hist.) "Col. Abraham Smith's Regt. (Eighth) in 1779 and in Capt. Joseph Culbertson's Co. of Fourth Batt'n 1781 of Cumb. Co., Pa., Ass'rs." (Pa. Arch.). Part of the Eighth Regt. was from Cumb. and Perry and part from the present Franklin Counties. (McCauley's Hist. Franklin Co.). Irish Robert Culbertson of Peters Tp. took out first land warrant on Mar. 31, 1743 (No. 212) Lancaster Co., Pa. (present Franklin Co.).

(H) Robert (Irish) of Peters Tp. sued several parties on notes in Augusta Co., Va. (See Chalkley Papers, Augusta Co., Va., abstract). Also records of same county in Oct., 1755, and judgment rendered to him in Pa. money, one judgment for £11 and one for £8, 5s. States "Robert Culbertson of Pennsylvania."

Vol. 2, p. 100, Apr. 15, 1806, Complainants John B., Thos. M., Chapman, Wm., Jane, Ann Johnson, Patrick Machie and wife Dorothy, late Johnson. In 1802 Chapman Johnson administered the estate of Thomas Johnson, when he found that James Culbertson had been dead a considerable time. In his will he speaks of 4000 acres of military land, etc., and mentions heirs brother and sisters (before mentioned) of Shermans Valley, Pa."

I gather from this that Thomas Johnson married a sister of Capt. James Culbertson, perhaps Anne Culbertson, daughter of Irish Robert of Peters Tp., Cumb. Co., Pa.

Thomas, brother of Capt. James Culbertson of Staunton, Va., does not appear on Capt. James' will, and there is no trace of him on Va. or Pa. tax records and I am positive he died young. For a time I had him confused with Thomas of Westmoreland Co., Pa., but a Power of Attorney from Thomas and Robert on file in New Castle, Del., proves these Westmoreland brothers to have come from Delaware.

* * * * *

(V) Robert of Shermans Valley not on Census 1790 Toboyne Tp., Cumb. Co., Pa. (Shermans Valley). He might have been overlooked in the enumeration. Not on Census 1790 or 1800 of Westmoreland Co., Pa. Robert Culbertson of Shermans Valley, Pa., signed a deed (residence not stated) which is recorded in Staunton, Va., in 1805, as one of executors of his brother James' estate. We have no further court data in regard to him. It is my belief that he went to western Pennsylvania and the descendants given below of Robert Culbertson (whom descendants say died in Venango Co., Pa.) are, I believe, the descendants of Robert of Shermans Valley, Pa. A descendant of party below wrote me in 1892 that her grandfather Robert came from Culbertson Row.

THIRD GENERATION

(V) Robert Culbertson lived in Westmoreland Co., Pa., until 1812. Moved to Beaver Co., Pa., then to Venango Co., Pa. where he died. Mar. (no court record Venango Co.). From data sent by family in 1892.
Issue:
1. Samuel, d. about 1853-55.
2. John, d. 1865.
3. Mary, d. 1870 (Mrs. Sloan).
4. Isabel, d. 1872 (Mrs. Walker).

FOURTH GENERATION

(1) Samuel moved to Venango Co., Pa., to Butler and then Clarion Co., Pa., where he died. Mar. first ——.
Issue:
5. Andrew, d. about 1782.
6. Alexander Hamilton, whereabouts unknown.
7. Martha (Mrs. John Dunbar).
8. Matilda (Mrs. Geo. Platt).

(1) Samuel Culbertson mar. second Miss Nancy Dixon.
Issue:
9. John S., b. 1842, Seneca, Venango Co., Pa. (Soldier Civil War three years).

10. Jane Venice, d.
11. Ann Phoebe, d.
12. ——, daughter, d.

(2) John Culbertson moved to Venango Co., Pa., after his marriage moved to Butler Co., Pa.; about 1844 moved to Clarion Co., Pa. and later to Venango Co., Pa. Mar.
Issue:

13. Robert, whereabouts unknown. Riverman.
14. Daniel, b. 1832. Lived at Bradford Pa.
15. Rachel, b. 1832. (Mrs. S. Stover). Fertigs, Pa.
16. Lavinia, b. 1836. (Mrs. Thos. Perry).
17. Rebecca, b. 1836 (Mrs. Thomson McKisic).
18. Emma, d. (Mrs. John Stevens).

(3) Mary Culbertson mar. Mr. Sloan of Salem, Pa.
Issue: not known.

(4) Isabel mar. Wm. Walker of Mariasville, Pa.
Issue:

19. Amos.
20. John. Killed battle Gettysburg.

(5) Andrew Culbertson mar. America ——. Lived at Harlansburg, Lawrence Co., Pa., where he owned an iron furnace. His widow gave me data in 1892. She was then a grandmother. Her husband's grandfather was Robert. Counting present (1923) generation this would make six generations not counting Irish Robert of Peters Tp., Cumb. Co., Pa.
Issue:

21. John.
22. William.
23. Samuel.
24. Charles.
25. Ella.
26. Margaret (Mrs. J. C. Hunt), Slippery Rock, Pa.
27. Melissa (Mrs. S. Burnside), New Castle, Pa.
28. Emma (Mrs. W. S. Amberson) Harlansburg,. Pa.
29. Electa, d.
30. Elizabeth (Mrs. J. P. Caldwell), New Castle, Pa.

(8) Matilda Culbertson mar. Geo. Platt of Algona, Ia. Live Lu Verne, Ia.
Issue:

30½. Samuel Culbertson, editor Des Moines Valley News.

(9) John S. Culbertson, soldier Pa. Vols. 3 years Civil War. Mar. Issue: 31-38.

(14) Daniel Culbertson mar. Issue: 39-47.

(16) Livinia Culbertson mar. Thos. Perry. Issue: 48-57.

(17) Rebecca Culbertson mar. Thomson McKisic. Issue: 58-66.

(18) Emma Culbertson mar. John Stevens. Issue: 67-73.

CHAPTER XXXII

(IV) Capt. James of Staunton, Va., moved to Virginia before the Revolution.

Was commissioned 2nd Lieut. in the 9th Va. Line Regt. Mar. 16, 1776. Capt. Lt. Nov. 17, 1776, transferred to 1st Va. Line Sept. 14, 1778, and Capt. 5th Va. Line, Feb. 12, 1781. I have his will and in it he states he was Commissary, Quartermaster and Forage Master to Pulaski's Legion for which he says he was not paid. Also that he was Commissary for the prisoners stationed at Staunton, of Burgoyne's Army for which he was not paid. He was given a bounty land warrant by the government of 4000 acres of Military Land north of the Ohio, near the mouth of the Miami river, but he willed all of this to his various creditors. He was an all round popular man in Staunton. He willed the balance of his property, if any (there was none) to his brothers and sisters: Robert, Molly, Ann and Margaret of Shermans Valley (Perry Co.), Pa. His brother, Thomas, was not named in the will. Robert was named one of the executors. Will made in April, 1788; probated June, 1788.

SECTION SECOND
PART SIXTH
Irish Joseph (J) of Culbertson Row, Pa.

(A First Cousin of the Three Pennsylvania "Row"
Brothers.)

(J) PART SIXTH

FOURTH GENERATION

(J) **Joseph Culbertson** (Irish) was always supposed to have been one of the three brothers of "Culbertson Row," Pa. He lived and died in the Row, whereas the third brother lived in Peters Tp., Cumb. Co., Pa. He came to America with his cousins between 1728 and 1742. He received a warrant for his land in Lancaster Co., Pa. (No. 255), issued Feb., 1744, Pat. ret'd 1752, made his will in Letterkenny Tp., Franklin Co., Pa., Dec. 12, 1784; probated Jan. 1, 1795; wife died 1791. He was a first cousin of the three "Row" brothers. Samuel (Irish) of the Row calls him in his will "Cousin Joseph." His daughter, Margaret, at the time he made his will, was married to a Duncan but before 1794 Duncan had died and she had remarried to a Breckenridge, as shown by Settlement Record of Franklin Co., Pa. of estate of Joseph's daughter, Martha, as in this it says, "Paid £24 to each brother Samuel, Joseph, Robert, Mary Breckenridge (no doubt a niece and daughter of Mary), Margaret (Breckenridge), James and Elizabeth Breckenridge. This Martha died intestate 1793.

Irish Joseph married Mary Breckenridge (according to John G. Orr), who was a sister to James Breckenridge, who was born in Ireland in 1710, so it is probable that she was of age by 1730-35. She was related to the great Breckenridge family of Va. and Ky. John G. Orr, an eminent historian of Cumb. Co., Pa., still living aged 80 years, is a descendant of the Breckenridge's and from Irish Andrew Culbertson of Shippensburg, Pa. Joseph Culbertson and Mary Breckenridge.

Issue: (Taken from will but not in order given therein.)
I. **Samuel**, Capt., b. before 1746; d. in Scott Co.; Ky. (Chap. XXXIII).
II. **Joseph**, b. 1753(?); d. Nov. 1818. (Capt.) Franklin Co., Pa. (Chap. XXXIV).
III. . **Robert**, b. July 23, 1755: d. July 26, 1801. (Col.) "Row" (Chapter XXXV).
IV. **Martha**, d. 1793. Unmarried.

V. **Margaret**, mar. first Mr. Wm. Duncan second John Breckenridge of Cumb. Co., Pa.

VI. **Mary**, d. before 1784 (Mrs. Samuel Breckenridge) of Cumb. Co., Pa. Had a daughter, Mary, who married Percival Adams.

VII. **Elizabeth** (Mrs. James Breckenridge).

Joseph may have mentioned daughters first through courtesy. James and Samuel Breckenridge were on a school board in 1763. Samuel Culbertson was on tax records of 1775 designated "Samuel Creek". Irish Joseph's wife's will was probated in 1791. Samuel was on tax records of Cumb. Co., Pa., in 1770, designated "Samuel, son of Joseph." Census for 1790, Letterkenny Tp., Cumb. Co., Pa., gives Samuel, males over 16 three (including self), males under 16, one, females including wife, three. This is "Samuel of the Creek" who went to Scott Co., Ky.

Census of 1790 gives Irish Joseph and one son over 16 (Col. Joseph), and 2 males under 16 (grandchildren), and 7 females (daughters and granddaughters). Two unrelated males (help) and 2 slaves. Greene Tp.

CHAPTER XXXIII

(I) **Samuel Culbertson** ("of the Creek"), son of Irish Joseph "was commissioned Captain Dec. 8, 1776 in the 5th Cumberland County Penna. Militia, Col. Joseph Armstrong" (see Penna. Arch.). This regiment was in service in the Battles of Trenton and Princeton in Dec., 1776, and in other engagements. We do not know whether he was a captain before this date as Col. Joseph Armstrong was a colonel of the 5th Batt'n in July, 1776. We have not been able to find any service for this Captain Samuel among rosters of June, 1777, and the presumption is that he did not serve any longer. Col. Samuel, son of Irish Alexander, was a captain in July, 1776, but he was commissioned Lieut. Colonel, Dec. 8, 1776, showing that he was a captain in the fall of 1776 and that on date of Dec. 8, 1776 he was a Lieut. Colonel in the 4th Batt'n while Capt. Samuel was in the 5th Batt'n.

Irish Samuel's son, Samuel, evidently did not enter the service before 1780 as he was spoken of in the Rosters 1780 as Samuel Culbertson, Jr., showing that he was Irish Samuel's son.

Samuel "of the Creek" was the Captain Samuel in the 5th Batt'n, in Dec. 8, 1776. The probabilities are he did not serve any longer. Possibly he was wounded and could not serve.

Samuel Culbertson ("Creek) is given Census 1790, Letterkenny Tp., Franklin Co., Pa., males over 16 (including self), three; males under 16, one; females five (including wife). Slaves one.

FOURTH GENERATION

Samuel Culbertson ("of the Creek") lived in Franklin Co., Pa., between Culbertson Row and Strasburg in Letterkenny Tp. The tax lists designate him "creek." I find him on tax lists of Cumb. Co., Pa., 1770-1785, but is not on tax lists of Franklin Co., Pa., in 1799. Cumb. Co., Pa., tax list 1770 gives him Sam'l, son of Joseph (Irish). Paid pew rent 1794 Rocky Spring. Same pew as brother Capt. Robert. On Oct. 6, 1794, Samuel Culbertson and wife, Martha, of Letterkenny Tp. deeded his farm to Samuel Nicholson. They then moved to Scott Co., Ky.; relatives in Indiana claimed they moved to Bourbon Co., Ky., but court records there give no trace of them. I found them in Scott Co., Ky. in this way: Descendants in Indiana said they had moved to Ky. before 1800 and that Samuel's sons, Joseph, Alexander and Robert had moved to Indiana after 1800. Court records of Marion Co., Ind., gave no trace of any of them save Joseph. Joseph's descendants gave his birth March 27, 1767, and in 1892, a daughter of his stated that Joseph came from or near Shippensburg, Pa. The Scott Co., Ky., court house was burned in the thirties and most of the records were destroyed. Could find no undamaged deeds but a will partly destroyed by fire was found which I herewith copy.

"Whereas, I Martha Culbertson of the County of Scott and State of Kentucky, being on the decline of life, and at the———————————————————— as she at this time is pregnant ———————— child the child is to belong to my ———————— give to my daughter Esther half of all ———————— kind and one-third of all my money ———————— and goes to her and her heirs forever ———————— I give to my ———— Martha in addition ———— to Sib's unborn child one-third ———— money —————————— to her and her heirs forever.

I do appoint my sons, Alexander and Robert as my exctrs.

to this my last will and testament. In witness whereof, I have hereunto set my hand and seal this 11th day of May, 1816. —————— In the presence of us"

"John Mathews   "Martha Culbertson" (Seal)
"Alexander Culbertson

From this it will be seen her husband was dead; Sib was evidently a favorite slave. Esther and Martha are each given one-half of her estate. As she left Alexander and Robert nothing, she naturally would not have mentioned Joseph. There is no further record in Scott Co., Ky. Because of destroyed records cannot get Samuel's will or administration. John G. Orr says that Irish Joseph's eldest son was Samuel. This is undoubtedly true as Joseph, his son, was born 1767.

FIFTH GENERATION

Issue of Samuel and Martha Culbertson:
1. Joseph, b. March 27, 1767; d. Feb. 11, 1850. Marion Co., Ind.
2. Alexander, d. 1833. Fayette Co., Ky. Bachelor(?)
3. Robert, relatives claim went to New Orleans.
4. Esther.
5. Martha.

The County Clerk of Court of Scott Co., Ky. writes me that there was a deed made in 1906 by J. B. Finnell to C. S. Culbertson and Mary E. Culbertson (therefore not property inherited from Culbertson's) and they deeded this property in 1916. All other records, save the above will were destroyed by fire.

Relatives claimed in 1892 that Robert (2) and (3) Alexander settled in Indianapolis, Ind., and that Robert afterwards went to New Orleans. Court Records at Indianapolis give no record of these two men and I do not believe they ever lived there.

In the Settlement of Alexander Culbertson's estate in Fayette Co., Ky. (1833) John Clarke Adm'r there is one item of payment of an order to Robert Culbertson $89. No relationship given. No mention is made to whom bal. in hand was paid. Whether this item referred to his brother, I know not. Robert Culbertson, grandson of Irish Sam of Miami Co., Ohio, who married his cousin Mary at Dayton, O. died in 1825. In matter of Martha Culbertson estate in Scott Co., Ky., Alexander Culbertson and Robert Culbertson signed ex'rs. bond for $1500 in August, 1816. Alexander evidently was a bachelor. Scott and Bourbon Counties adjoin and Bourbon Co. may have been taken off Scott Co.

* * * * *

SIXTH GENERATION

(1) Joseph Culbertson moved from Franklin Co., Pa., to Bourbon Co., Ky., before 1800, so say descendants. Moved to Marion Co., Ind., six miles north of Indianapolis, being one of the early settlers of that county. Washington Tp. Married.

Issue:
6. Samuel, b. Apr. 21, 1799; d. Oct. 10, 1874. Major.
7. Mary ("Polly"), d. before 1850.
8. Joseph, b. 1804; d. 1870. Marion Co., Ind.
9. James McClure, d. (Bachelor).
10. Alexander, d. June 20, 1839.
11. Robert, d. Feb. 21, 1863.
12. William, d.
13. Martha ("Patsy").
14. Elizabeth, d.
15. Esther (Mrs. Lorenzo Vansyock).
16. John M., d. after 1840. Moved to Calaway Co., Mo.

SEVENTH GENERATION

(6) Samuel Culbertson (Major of Militia), moved from Bourbon Co., Ky. when a boy with his father and settled six miles north of Indianapolis. Mar. Miss Sarah Sutton, May 24, 1822. Lived in Rush Co., Ind. Sarah Sutton b. Aug. 2, 1803. Died at Knightstown, Ind. Oct. 4, 1862.

Issue:
17. Elizabeth Jane.
18. Mary Katherine, b. Jan. 8, 1834; d. Nov. 9, 1906.
19. Martha Ann (Mrs. Holloway), Indianapolis; b. Dec. 3, 1834; d. May 25, 1915.
20. Sarah Margaret.

(7) Mary Culbertson mar. John Martin of Ky., moved to Rush Co., Ind., and later moved to Calloway Co., Mo. Court records in 1850 in settlement of her father's estate name "John Jones in right of his wife Mary, formerly Mary Culbertson." This shows that she was mar. twice.

Issue:
21. Abel.
22. Thomas. Calloway Co., Mo.
23. Armbras, Kansas City, Mo.

24. James, d. Indiana.
25. ———, son.
26. Elizabeth d.
27. Martha (Mrs. Purdy). Centralia, Mo.
28. Caroline. Calloway Co., Mo.

(7) Mary Culbertson mar. second John Jones.

(8) Joseph Culbertson mar. ———. Lived in Marion Co.,
Ind. Born in Ky. Married in Ky. in 1829 to Sallie Ann
Griffith. Moved from Marion Co., Ind. to Calloway Co., Mo.
before 1840.
Issue:
29. Joseph Culbertson.
30. James.

(10) Alexander Culbertson moved to Indiana in 1829.
Mar. in Ky. Lived on farm, Marion Co., Ind.
Issue:
31. Martha, d.
32. Mary E.
33. Dr. Joseph, d.
34. Samuel.

(11) Robert Culbertson mar. Isabel Dawson, a neighbor
and settled on a farm near his father in Marion Co., Ind.
Issue:
35. Alexander. Lives on farm, Marion Co., Ind.
36. James. Lives on farm, Marion Co., Ind.
38. Pricilla J. d. ⎰
37. Lucullus M. ⎱Twins,. Knightstown, Ind.
39. Mary C., d. youth.
40. Isabella E., d. youth.

(12) William Culbertson mar. Eliza Goble and moved
from Ky., to Marion Co., Ind. Lived on farm,. Marion Co.,.
Ind.
Issue:
41. Elizabeth C.
42. James McClure.
43. Wm. Doud (Dr.). Indianapolis.
44. Clarinda A.
45. Helen Mary.

(13) Martha Culbertson mar. Mr. Shaw of Xenia, O.

(14) Elizabeth Culbertson mar. Uriah Dawson, of Marion
Co., Ind.

Issue:
46. Elvia.
47. Mary.

(15) Esther Culbertson mar. Lorenza Van Syock. Lived in Indiana, but in 1892 lived in Maryland, at which date she stated that her father went from near Shippensburg, Pa. to Ky.

EIGHTH GENERATION

(17) Elizabeth Jane Culbertson mar. first Dr. Robt. D. Moffitt. Husband died.
Issue:
48. Sarah Isabella Moffitt.
49. Mary C.

(17) Elizabeth J. Moffitt mar. second, Dr. Abner C. Dillon.
Issue:
50. Josephine, d.
51. Elizabeth Evalyn, d.
52. John Samuel, d.
53. Jefferson C. (Dr.).

(18) Mary Catherine mar. Henry Ball, March 6, 1845.
Issue:
54. Erastus Samuel.
55. Sarah Isabel, b. Oct. 15, 1847; d. Sept. 1, 1905..

(19) Martha Ann Culbertson mar. Elisha B. Holloway of Indianapolis, Ind., May 4, 1852. He was b. Nov. 4, 1823; d. Feb. 34, 1908.
Issue:
56. Eddy Fletcher, d. infancy.
57. Olin E. Holloway (Dr.) Knightstown, Ind.; b. Apr. 19, 1856, at Richmond, Ind.

(20) Sarah Margaret mar. John Furgason.
Issue:
58. Rose Emma.

(24) James Culbertson mar. ———. Indiana.

(27) Martha Culbertson mar. Mr. Purdy. Lived at Centralia. Mo.

(29) Joseph Culbertson, Jr. mar. Frances Smith. Lived at Ladona, Mo.

Issue:
59. Joe Edward Culbertson.
60. Charles.
61. James.
62. Laura (Mrs. Fred Read).
63. Rosa.
64. Anna.
65. S. Price.

(30) James Culbertson mar. Sarah Selby in 1856. (Wife b. 1838; d. 1888.)
Issue:
66. William.
67. Albert, b. 1861.
68. Ida, b. 1863 (Mrs. C. F. Richmond). Issue: Albert Richmond, Selby, Frank, Angie, Wm. V., Ida B., Gene.
69. Walter Culbertson.
69⅛. Mary.
69¼. Sarah.
69⅜. Amanda.
69½. Thomas.
69⅝. Samuel.
69¾. Rosella.

(34) James Culbertson. Lives on farm Marion Co., Ind. Know nothing of.

(35) Lucullus M. Culbertson mar. Alice A. Alspaw of Knightstown, Ind. (Hardware merchant, Knightstown.)
Issue:
70. Edward H.
71. Charles F.
72. Lora B.
73. Augusta L.
74. Altha.
75. Pearl.

(41) Dr. Doud Culbertson. Lived at Indianapolis, Ind.

(42) Col. James Culbertson of 80th Ind. Vols. in Civil War belonged to this family.

NINTH GENERATION

(53) Sarah Isabella Ball mar. James Armstrong Sargent, Oct. 31, 1871. Lived at Seymour, Ind. Husband b. Sept. 10, 1843, Warren Co., Ohio; d. Baltimore, Md., Jan. 29, 1920.

Issue:
76. Florence Mary Ball, b. Oct. 6, 1877. (Mar. Rev. Loren
    McLain Edwards, D. D., in Seymour, Ind., Sept.
    14, 1905; husband b. Rising Sun, Ind., Nov. 14,
    1877). Issue: Justin Sargent, b. Apr. 7, 1908;
    Mary Elizabeth, b. Feb. 22, 1910, died same date.

77. Henry Hurst Ball, b. Feb. 18, 1879. 77½. John
    Thomas, b. Dec. 11, 1883; d. Nov. 21, 1887.

(57) Dr. Olin E. Holloway, mar. Maude Ferguson dau. of
Samuel W. and Mary (Muzzy) Ferguson, Oct. 22, 1884.
Wife born Sept. 3, 1858.
Issue:
78. Agnes, d. infancy.
79. Jean Samuel, b. May 30, 1888; married Apr. 17, 1912,
    to Miriam Wright, dau. of Chas. S. and Lulu U.
    Wright of Greensboro, Ind. (Wife b. Oct. 27, 1887)
    Issue: 79¼, J. Samuel, Jr. 79½, Susan June.

(66) Wm. Culbertson, mar. Gene ——.
Issue:
80. Townley Culbertson, Kansas City (banker).
81. Hallie Belle.

(67) Rev. Albert B. Culbertson mar. Ann Elizabeth Harrison in 1891. (Wife b. 1860.) Prominent Methodist minister, Mexico, Mo.
Issue:
82. James B., b. 1892.
83. Dulcinea, b. 1893 (Mrs. Robt. Campbell).
84. Harrison, P., b. 1894.
85. Sarah Selby, b. 1896.
86. Albert B. b. 1898.
87. Wm. T., b. 1901.

(69) Walter Culbertson, mar. Blanche Quisenberry.
Issue:
88. Phillip Culbertson, mar. Linnie Schooler. Issue: 94,
    Lee Culbertson.
89. Frank Culbertson.
90. Imogene (Mrs. Chambliss).
91. Richmond, b. 1920.

(69⅛) Mary Culbertson (mar. Frank Baker). Issue:
Faris Baker, Lena Baker, Irene, Frank, Will, Mary. 95-100.

(69¼) Sarah Culbertson mar. John Provines.

(69⅜) Amanda Culbertson mar. John Martin.

(69½) Thomas Culbertson mar. ——.

(69⅝) Samuel Culbertson mar. ——.

(69¾) Rosella (Mrs. Allen). Issue 101, Joseph; 102 Luella.

PROMINENT DESCENDANTS OF (I) SAMUEL "OF TEE CREEK" CULBERTSON.

(6) Was called Major but I have not been able to ascertain his service. Was a prominent citizen of Marion Co., Ind.

(43) Dr. Dowd Culbertson was a prominent physician of Indianapolis, Ind.

(19) Martha Ann (Culbertson) Holloway's husband, Elisha B. Holloway, was a prominent citizen of Indianapolis, Ind. Their son (57) Olin E. Holloway and his son are prominent physicians at Knightstown, Ind.

(67) Rev. Albert B. Culbertson has been a prominent Methodist minister of Missouri for years.

(82) Served through World War in Chemical Div. Edgewood Arsenal.

(84) Harrison P. Culbertson, World War, in Machine Gun Div. Camp Lewis and Augusta, Ga.

(91) Richmond Culbertson served in Machine Gun Dep. 35 Div. in France. -

(80) Townley Culbertson is a prominent banker in Kansas City, Mo. Director in Federal Reserve, etc.

CHAPTER XXXIV
FOURTH GENERATION

(II) Col. Joseph Culbertson, son of Joseph (F), mar. first Elizabeth Wiley, of Franklin Co., Pa. Lived and died in "Row", Green Twp. Children obtained from his will and family records. Census 1800 males (self) over 45, wife, one son under 26, 2 males over 10 and under 16, 2 daughters under 16, 2 daughters under 10. Green Twp.

In list of Col. Joseph Culbertson's children given in the first edition of the Culbertson Genealogy, his son Joseph was given "died young unmarried". This list was given me by Rev. John N. Culbertson and he obtained it from his brother in 1855. This is an error as the will of Col. Joseph proves. He made his will Oct. 9, 1817, will probated Nov. 17, 1818. In it he mentions daughters Mary (Mrs. John Breckenridge) Elizabeth, Sarah and Martha. Sons Hugh, John, Joseph.

Issue: Col. Joseph (first wife).

1. Joseph, b. after 1775; d. 1830-31.
2. John.
3. Margaret, intermarried with John Breckenridge of Franklin Co., Pa.
4. Elizabeth never married.
5. Sarah, never married. b. 1800.
6. Martha (Mrs. Duncan). Two children.
7. Hugh, b. July 12, 1792; d. Mar. 29, 1876.

(II) Col. Joseph Culbertson mar. second Mrs. Margaret Finley (d. 1839), who had a son, Wm. A. Finley, when he married her. No issue by second wife.

FIFTH GENERATION

(1) Joseph Culbertson. On tax Southhampton Tp., Franklin Co., Pa., 1799, "freeman". A deed in 1804 from D. McConaughy and wife Prudence for land left by Andrew Thompson, to Jos. Culbertson and wife Jean. Also deed in 1802 from Jos. Culbertson and wife Jean, of Fannett Tp, and sister Elizabeth Thompson for land left by their father, Andrew Thompson; land in Hopewell Tp. to Joseph, Sr. 260 acres. Joseph later lived in Southhampton Tp. (Row) and was related to the Johnstons. Joseph died intestate and John Johnston app. Ad'm'r. Jan., 1831. Estate was not settled until 1840 when surviving heirs gave release to John Johnston. John Thompson and wife in 1824 sold 150 acres for $3762 in Southhampton Tp. to Jos. Culbertson and wife Jean. They were married 1800-01.

Issue:

8. Sarah.
9. Joseph d. 1839 (unmar.).
10. George J. This Geo. J. and sister in 1841 bought of Wm. Johnston 100 acres for $9400 partly in Green and partly in Southhampton Tps. Found no will or administration of either of them, either in Cumb. or Franklin Counties.

(7) Hugh Culbertson mar. first Sallie Witherow of Adams Co., Pa., June 15, 1815. Wife b. May 7, 1793; d. 1835.

Issue:
11. Joseph.
12. Rebecca, d. Feb. 9, 1817. (Mrs. Witherspoon).
13. Samuel W. Lived near Fairfield, Adams Co., Pa.
14. John.
15. William E., d. Aug. 15, 1865, born 1838.
16. Chas. McClain.

(7) Hugh Culbertson mar. second Jane M. McClelland of Roxbury, Franklin Co., Pa., Jan. 31, 1837. Wife b. Nov. 1799; d. Jan. 30, 1885.

Issue:
17. Susan.
18. Martha (Mrs. A. Musser, Shippensburg, Pa.)
19. Catherine H. Shippensburg. (unmar. in 1892).
20. Thomas, b. June 25, 1843; d. July 24, 1865. Served 6 months in 21st Pa. Cav. Civil War. One year 209 Pa. Inf. in skirmishes at Bermuda Hundred; Ft. Stedman; charge and capture of Petersburg. Discharged, May 1865.

(2) John Culbertson mar. Catherine Wiley. Lived in Row.

Issue:
21. Edgar.
22. Joseph.
23. Mary.
24. Sarah.
25. Margaret.
26. John.
27. Catherine.
28. Laura.
29. Michael.
30. Elizabeth (Mrs. Wm. B. Walker).
Also two other children.

SIXTH GENERATION

(12) Rebecca Culbertson mar. David C. Witherspoon of Franklin Co., Pa. In 1895 she was the only Culbertson living in "Culbertson Row". Before her death she resided a number of years with her nephew, Albert, of Adams Co., Pa. Issue: 28, son; 29, a daughter.

(13) Major Samuel W. Culbertson of Gettysburg, Pa., mar. Mary Belle McGinley.
Issue:

31. Samuel Albert, Gettysburg, Pa. Mar. Feb. 26, 1920, to Helen Margaret McCullough.

32. Blanche (mar. Mar. 6 1920, to James Witherspoon Moore of Fairfield, Adams Co., Pa.)

* * * * *

(II) Col. Joseph Culbertson born and raised in the "Row," nicknamed "red-headed" Joe. "Was in Capt. Samuel Culbertson's Co. of Col. Jos. Armstrong's Regt. (5th) of Associaters, of Cumb. Co., Pa. at date of December 8, 1776.

Commissioned Capt. of 5th Co. of Sixth Batt'n (Col. Sam Culbertson's) of Cumb. Co. Associaters, July 31, 1777. Capt. of Fifth Co., Sixth Batt'n (Col. Sam Culbertson's) May 14, 1778." (See Pa. Arch.) His commission as Lieut-Col. does not appear in Pa. Archives. In his election as Poor House Director, in 1807, he was spoken of as Col. Joseph. I believe he was a Col. of Militia after the War. Records show he was not in the War of 1812. His farm stood at the head of the Row, on the east. Fort Culbertson stood almost in front of his house. His granddaughter, Mrs. D. C. Witherspoon, lived on part of his farm and was the only Culbertson descendant living in the Row in 1896. Col. Robert's house was long since pulled down. Col Joseph's farm adjoined Col. Robert's.

CHAPTER XXXV

(III) **Col. Robert Culbertson** of Greene Tp. He is found in a deed made by "Captains Joseph and Robert Culbertson of Letterkenny and James Breckenridge of Lurgan of first part to Col. Robert Culbertson of Hopewell Tp., Cumb. Co. second part 300 acres in Lurgan for £3000, bounding land of Daniel Duncan, etc. Date made Dec. 4, 1779." In deed "made 1798 Samuel Nicholson to Capt. Robert Culbertson of Greene Tp. land at Greenvillage at crossing of Chambersburg and Strasburg Roads." This was sold in 1802 by administrators of Capt. Robert Culbertson.

McCauley's History of Cumberland Co., says "Col. Jos. Armstrong Batt. (5th) was from Hamilton, Lurgan and Letterkenny Tps., it had in it Capt. Robert Culbertson." In membership of Rocky Spring Church he is given as "Capt. Robert Culbertson." For a long time I thought he had not attained a higher rank than Capt. in the Revolution. By a most exhaustive search of tax records, Census 1790, and deeds, I have ascertained positively that he was a Lieut. Col. in the Revolution. I thought for a long time that Robert of Shermans Valley, Pa. (son of Irish Robert of Peters Tp.) was the second Lt. Col. But here is the proof he was not. When his mother went into Orphans Court in 1764 and gave names of her children, Robert was given as next to youngest. Thomas given eldest. This would make Robert of Shermans Valley born about 1760-61. Therefore in 1776 he could not have been over 16 years old—too young to have held commission of Capt. and in 1777-8 too young for Major. The only other Robert Culbertson in Cumb. Co. during Revolutionary period was Col. Robert of Shippensburg or Hopewell Tp. Also Robert, private, died 1778 (Guilford Tp.)

Service Col. Robert of Rocky Spring. Amer. Archives show Capt. "stationed at Philadelphia, Aug. 27, 1776 in Col. Jos. Armstrong's Reg't (Fifth) Cumb. Co., Pa. Militia. Paid in advance Capt. pay ($750) Aug. 17, 1776 (Am. Arch.) Lt. Col. Second Batt. Sept. 16, 1777, John Davis Col.; Robert Taylor, Major. July 14, 1778, Col. John Davis; Lt. Col. Robert Culbertson; Major Robt. Taylor. Appointed Major and Wagonmaster of Cumb. Co., Aug. 10, 1780. Pa Arch. show an account filed and signed by him in 1782 as Master-Wagonmaster (Pa. Arch.) The tax lists of Franklin Co., 1799, gave him "wagon m'r." He was nicknamed "curly-headed Bob." He loaned the Government money during the Revolution which was refunded long after the war. His farm was the middle one in the Row and on his farm was the boiling spring.

Stryker's Battles of Trenton and Princeton state that "Capt. Robert Culbertson of Col. Joseph Armstrong's Batt'n (5th) of the Cumb. Co., Pa., 'Flying Camp' was in Philadelphia Aug. 16, 1776, where he drew knap-sacks and 50 cartridge boxes for his company. This regiment took part in the Battles of Trenton and Princeton." Col. Jos. Armstrong was commissioned Col. of the 5th Cumb. "Flying Camp" July 1, 1776. Capt. Robert's service dates from July 1, 1776.

The Flying Camp regiments of Pa. were brigaded under Gen. Ewing at the Battle of Trenton.

FIFTH GENERATION

(III) Col. Robert Culbertson, mar. May 6. 1778, to Miss Annie Duncan, of Middle Spring, Franklin Co., Pa. Wife b. 1755; d. Mar., 1827; wife a dau. of Capt. Wm. Duncan.
Issue:
1. Joseph, b. Feb. 27, 1779; d. July, 1858.
2. William, b. Sep. 15, 1780; d. Aug. 1785.
3. Robert, b. July 16, 1782; d. August 1864.
4. Alexander, b. 1784; d. Apr. 1809. Unmar.
5. Samuel Duncan (Dr.), b. Feb. 26, 1786; d. 1865 (Aug. 25).
6. William, b. Dec. 12, 1787; d. July 12, 1824.
7. Stephen, b. Jan. 15, 1790; d. June, 1854.
8. John Craighead (Capt.), b. Sep. 19, 1791; d. 1860.
9. Mary, b. Apr. 9, 1793; d. 1852.
10. Daniel, b. Apr. 15, 1795; d. Dec. 1808.
11. Anne, b. Apr. 18, 1797; d. Feb., 1867.
12. James b. Oct. 12, 1799; d. Feb'y, 1873. (Col.)

SIXTH GENERATION

(1) Joseph Culbertson mar. first, Mary Finley, daughter of Capt. James Finley, of Revolution—of Chambersburg, Pa. Mar. Apr. 12, 1804 Hotel proprietor, at Chambersburg, Pa. (Wife d. Apr. 2, 1817; born Jan. 13, 1781).
Issue:
13. Robert, b. Apr., 1805; d. 1882. Tanner. Cincinnati.
14. James Finley, b. May, 1809; d. 1878.
15. Alexander, b. May, 1809; d. 1878.
16. Cyrus Duncan, b. 1812; d. 1870. Pork packer.
17. William, b. Oct. 1814; d. June, 1857. (Dr.).
18. Mary, d. Oct. 2, 1817.

(1) Joseph C., mar. second Francis Stewart, at Fairview Farm, near Harrisburg, Pa., Apr. 21, 1818. Wife b. Feb. 16, 1785; d. Nov. 27, 1867.
Issue:
19. Michael Simpson, b. Jan. 18, 1819; d. Aug. 25, 1862.
20. Joseph, b. 1821; d. 1830.
21. Thaddeus Ainsworth, d. Sept. 1850; aet. 27. Unmar.
22. Anna Mary, b. 1827; d. Feb. 1858. Unmar.

(3) Robert Culbertson, mar. Nancy Breckenridge, a daughter of Sarah Breckenridge, who was a daughter of Irish Andrew Culbertson, of Shippensburg, Pa. Married Feb. 1, 1803. Wife also called Agnes. Lived at Amberson, Franklin Co., Penna.

Issue:

23. Annie,. b. Oct. 1, 1803; d. Aug. 15, 1858, mar. John McVitty.
24. Sarah, b. Apr. 4, 1805, d. May 10, 1861. Mar. John Harvey.
25. Samuel b. Feb. 12, 1808; d. May 28, 1809.
26. John, b. Feb. 9, 1809; d. Nov., 1885; mar.
27. Joseph, b. Mar. 31, 1811; d. ——. Mar. Mary McGhee.
28. Agnes Purviance, b. July 9, 1816; d. ——. Mar. John Stake.
29. Frances Stuart, b. Feb. 27, 1818; d. ——. Mar. John McVitty.
30. Benjamin, b. July 1, 1821; d. ——. Mar. Martha McGee.
31. Wilson Hays, b. Feb. 4, 1824; d. Dec. 1878. Mar. Mary A. Duncan.
32. Jeannette, b. Oct. 27, 1831; d. ——. Mar. Cyrus Hazlett.
33. ——.
34-36. d. young.

(5) Col. Samuel Duncan Culbertson, M. D. Physician at Chambersburg, Pa. Mar. Nancy Purviance; wife b. 1786. Issue:

37. Edmund (Dr.) b. 1812; d. 1883.
38. Augustus H., d. 1839; aet 16 years.
39. Albert, b. 1818; d. 1878.
40. Ferdinand, b. 1823; d. 1863.
41. John P., b. Aug. 26, 1827; d. Aug. 23, 1900.
42. Elizabeth, d. 1891; b. 1814.

(6) Wm. Culbertson, of New Market, York Co., Pa., mar. Julia Stuart of Palmyra, Dauphin Co., Pa. (Wife b. 1787; d. 1857.) Mar. Dec. 25, 1810. Wife a daughter of Wm. Stuart Quartermaster to Gen. Sullivan. Issue:

43. Mary Ann,. b. Oct. 3, 1811; d. Oct. 6, 1880.
44. Wm. Stewart, b. Feb. 4, 1814; d. June 25, 1892.
45. Robert, b. May 16, 1816; d. Dec. 4, 1825.
46. John Craighead, b. Jan. 20, 1819; d. 1890.
47. Julia De Witt, b. Jan. 1, 1822; d. Nov. 1822.
48. Julia, b. May 15, 1824; d. Nov. 1828.

(7) Stephen Culbertson, mar. Jan. 9, 1810, Mary Hays, of Shippensburg and moved to Philadelphia in 1848; (wife b. 1789; d. 1858).

Issue:
49. Henrietta b. Nov. 26, 1810; d. Oct. 15, 1815.
50. Robert, b. Aug. 28, 1812; d. July 1833.
51. David Hays, b. Jan. 23, 1815; d. Aug. 11, 1895.
52. Joseph, b. Oct. 12, 1816; d. Oct. 25. 1837.
53. Anette, b Sep. 21, 1818; d. Sep. 3, 1852.
54. James, b. Oct. 24, 1820; d. 1904-5.
55. Mary, b. Nov. 10, 1822; d. July 8, 1845.
56. Jane, b. July 28, 1824; d. Aug. 19, 1839.
57. Samuel, b. Mar. 2, 1827; d. Oct. 11, 1839.
58. Elizabeth, b. July 29, 1829; d. Oct. 11, 1839.

(8) Capt. Jchn Craighead Culbertson, mar. first Margaret Hamilton, of Lancaster, Pa. Capt. U. S. A.; also banker, etc. Cincinnati, O.
Issue:
59. Josephine. (Mrs. Heighway).

(8) Capt. J. C. Culbertson mar. second, Jane Moody, of Shippensburg, Pa.
Issue:
60. John M.
61. Joseph A.
62. Samuel D.
63. William, c. 1889. Bachelor.
64. Robert C.
65. Henry Clay. Cincinnati (Bachelor). In Civil War, 137 O. V. I.
66. Mary.
67. Libbie.
68. Anna.
69. Frank.

(9) Mary Culbertson mar. Wilson Hays, of Shippensburg, Pa.
Issue:
70. Robert Hays, d.
71. David.
72. Hamilton.
73. Martha Ann (Mrs. J. Briscoe).

(11) Anne Culbertson mar. Alex. McCreight, of Springfield, Ohio.
Issue:
74. —— Mrs. Blount. Issue: Wm. Blount.
75. —— Mrs. Wilson.

(12) Col. James Culbertson moved to Palmyra, Mo., Mar. ——.

Issue:

76. James (Dr.), b. 1827; d. 1889. Waco, Tex.
77. Jeremiah, d. young man.
78. William, d. 1886.
79. Anne.

By second wife Col. James had:

80. Stephen, d. 1851.

SEVENTH GENERATION

(13) Robert Culbertson, of Cincinnati, O., mar. Mary Peebles. Was a tanner. No issue.

(14) James F. Culbertson mar. Elizabeth B. Wallace.

Issue:

81. Joseph A., d.
82. Frances L. Mar.
83. Cyrus J., d. in California in 1851.
84. Anna M. Unmar. d. May 21, 1903.
85. Ella A. (Mrs. W. Kennedy). No issue.
86. Thaddeus W. Killed in R. R. accident, 1863.
87. Emma I.
88. Robert S. Merchant. Ft. Benton, Mont.
89. Ferdinand A., d. Unmar.

(15) Alexander Culbertson (Major) mar. first Natawis-chicksina (also called Natawista), daughter of the Chief of the Blood or Blackfeet Indians (See Prominent Descendants at end of chapter). Lived at Peoria, Ills. about 1853 on a farm. Had lived in the far west prior to this.

Issue:

90. Maria. Mar. Jos. Kipp, a missionary.
91. Janie. Mar. Wm. Hunt.

(15) Major Alexander Culbertson mar. second ——. Lived at Ft. Benton, Mont. (Culbertson, Neb., named after him.)

Issue:

92. Julia (Mrs. Geo. Roberts), Boise, Idaho.
93. John A. d.
94. Fannie (Mrs. L. S. Irvine).
95. Joseph. Poplar, Mont.
96. ——.

97. Joseph, d.
98. Mary F.
99. Ellen Bell.

(19) Michael Simpson Culbertson, mar. Mary Dunlap,
May 16, 1844. W. d. Sep. 30, 1888.

Issue:

100. Helen Anna, b. Jan. 15, 1847.
101. Frances Cornelia, b. Dec. 25, 1848; d. Mar. 28, 1877.
102. Walter Lowrie, b. 1850; d. 1852.
103. Mary Josephine, b. May 4, 1852. Artist at Brook-
     lyn, N. Y. (Unmar.)
104. Emma Barbara, b. 1854; d. 1855.
105. Laura, b. 1857; d. 1858.
106. Lilly Fitch, b. 1858; d. 1860.
107. Alice Julia, b. 1859; d. 1860.

(26) John Culbertson mar. Hannah McVitty, daughter
     Ed. McVitty, in 1831.

Issue:

108. Denton D., b. Feb. 9, 1832.
109. Mary Elizabeth, b. Jan'y 23, 1833; d. (Mrs. Knox).
110. Hanna Jane, b. May, 1835; d. Sept., 1851. Unmar.
111. Cyrus, b. 1837; d. 1876.
112. Edward Hudson, b. 1839; d. 1843.
113. John N. (Rev.), b. Aug. 22, 1841.
114. Wm. F. Breckenridge, b. June 4, 1844, d.
115. Harriett Newell, b. Aug. 5, 1846; d. Mar. 19, 1913.
116. Martha Ann, b. Sept. 2, 1848; d.
117. Pauline V., b. June 28, 1850.
118. Robert Mason, b. June 28, 1850.
119. Rebecca Jane, b. May 7, 1853; d.

(30) Benjamin J. Culbertson, of Amberson's Valley,
Franklin Co., Pa. Was a soldier in Civil War. Mar. Martha McGhee.

Issue:

120. ——, d.
121. Margaret d.
122. Robert A.
123. James B., d.
124. Adam J.
125. Wm. C., d.
126. Samuel C.

(31) Wilson Hays Culbertson mar. Mary A. Duncan,

Aug. 4, 1844. Wife born Cumb. Co., Penna., Feb. 24, 1825; d. Winona, Minn., May 25, 1875.

Issue:
127. David, died when a child.
128. Albert Culbertson, b. Feb. 14th, 1847; d. May 12, 1922.
129. William D. Culbertson, b. May 27, 1848; d. Oct. 9, 1913.
130. Josephine Culbertson, b. Dec. 30, 1851; still living.
131. Robert Culbertson, b. Nov. 26, 1854; d. Oct. 25, 1886.
132. Edgar Hays Culbertson, b. Apr. 30, 1857; never married.
133. Mary Ann Culbertson, b. June 26, 1859; d. June 25, 1918.
134. Hugh Culbertson, b. Aug. 30, 1864; d. Dec. 4, 1864.
135. James Calvin, b. Dec. 9, 1861; d. Apr. 18, 1863.

(37) Dr. Edmund Culbertson, Chambersburg, Pa. mar. Miss Kennedy, May 4, 1844.

Issue:
136. Lucy A., d. young.
137. Samuel D.
138. Emma S.
139. Nannie P.
140. James K.

(39) Albert Culbertson, mar. E. Brown, of Pittsburgh, Pa. Paper man'f'r at Monongahela, Pa.

Issue:
141. Samuel Duncan, Gen. Freight Agent, Youngstown.
142. Mary.
143. Nannie.
144. James.
145. Bessie.

(40) Ferdinand L. Culbertson, mar. first, Lavinia Culbertson. Husband died, and widow mar. S. W. Hays.

Issue by first mar.:
146. Herbert.
147. Nannie.
148. Lewis H.

(41) John P. Culbertson mar. first Miss Mary Bell Watson. No issue. Wife d. Mar. second, Bird. Sturgeon.

Issue:
149. Richard, d. infancy.

(41) Mar. third, Julia E. Wonderlich. Lumber merchant Chambersburg, Pa. Wife b. Sept. 12, 1849; d. Jan. 30, 1913.
150. John P., b. Nov. 4, 1870.
151. Charles, b. Aug. 19, 1872.
152. Wm. A., b. July 16, 1874, Chambersburg, Pa. Un-married.

(42) Elizabeth Culbertson mar. Capt. E. D. Reid.
Issue:
153. Samuel Reid, d. 1867.
154. Edmund C., d. May, 1861.
155. Helen (Mrs. Stenger). Philadelphia.
156. Anna (Mrs. Dr. B. Bowman of Chambersburg, Pa.)

(43) Mary Ann Culbertson mar. Daniel Snively, of Greencastle, Pa., Jan. 24, 1833.
Issue:
157. Wm. Andrew Snively, b. Dec. 6, 1833. (Rev.) mar. and has issue.
158. Joseph C. (Dr.), b. Jan. 17, 1836; d. 1885. Mar. Miss Strickland.
159. Daniel Duncan, b. Mar. 1838; d. 1862. Texas.
160. Julia Francis, b. Apr. 30, 1840. (Mrs. Wm. H. Lewis of New Albany, Ind.), d. May, 1887.
161. Anne Mary, b. Sept. 3, 1843 (Mrs. F. Colton, of Washington, D. C.).
162. John C., b. Sep. 28, 1845. Mar. Miss Eyster. (Crete, Neb.)
163. Summerfield E., b. Jan. 10, 1848. (Rev.)
164. Thaddeus A., b. Feb. 1, 1851. (Rev.) Mar. E. Crosby.

(44) Wm. Stuart Culbertson, of New Albany, Ind., mar. first Eliza Vance, of Corydon, Ind., Feb. 19, 1840. (Wife b. 1822; d. 1865). Banker.
Issue:
165. Wm. A., b. 1841; d. June, 1885. Banker, St. Paul, Minn.
166. John Vance, b. March 1843; d. Aug., 1843.
167. Mary Julia, b. Jan., 1847; d. Sep., 1867. Unmarried.
168. Frances Stuart, b. Feb., 1849; d. Aug., 1851.
169. Charles Stuart, b. Apr., 1852; d. Feb. 26, 1901. Un-married.
170. Joseph Simpson, b. Nov., 1855; d. March, 1904. Un married.

171.   Anna Vance, b. July 24, 1859; d. Apr. 8, 1910.
172.   Samuel Alexander, b. Aug., 1862.   Banker.

(44) Wm. S. Culbertson, mar. seconl, Mrs. Cornelia Warner Eggleston, Jan. 10, 1867. Wife b. at Pennyan, N. Y.
Aug. 27, 1832; d. Oct. 18, 1880.
Issue:
173.   Walter Stewart, d. July, 1868.
174.   Blanche Warner, b. Sep., 1870.

(44) Wm. S. Culbertson mar. third Mrs. Rebecca K.
Young, of Paris, Ky.   No issue; widow living, Louisville
Ky.

(46) John Craighead Culbertson mar. Mary Pintard
Bicknell.   Widow lives at Santa Barbara, Calif.
Issue:
175.   Emma Bicknell, b. 1854; d. (Dr.) Unmar.   Boston,
          Mass.
176.   Florence Stewart, b. July, 1856; d. Jan., 1861.
177.   George Augustus, b. Aug., 1861.   California.

(51) David Hays C., mar. Mary Linn, Dec. 20, 1843, and
settled at Germantown, Pa.; moved to Blair, Pa., in 1845;
to Philadelphia, in 1848; to Carlisle, Pa., in 1858; to
Princetown Ia., in 1866 where he resided.   Widow d. Mar.
15, 1902.
Issue:
178.   Wm. Linn, b. Dec. 20, 1844; banker, d. Oct. 19, 1908.
179.   Stephen D., b. Oct. 6, 1846.   St. Louis, Mo., d. July 9,
          1921.
180.   Augustus J., b. Apr. 29, 1849.   Gleden, Ia.   d.
181.   Mary, b. Mar. 17, 1854.
182.   Robert, b. Nov. 14, 1851.; d. May 9, 1904.
183.   Henry, b. May 19, 1856.   Unmar.   Princeton, Ia., d.
184.   Elizabeth, b. May 17, 1859.   Unmar.   Princeton, Ia.
185.   James C., b. Feb .17, 1852.   Greenfield, Ia.   d.
186.   Julius A. d.

(53) Annetta Culbertson, mar. Robert Young, of Me-
chanicsburg, Cumberland Co., Pa., May 22, 1838.

(54) James Wilson C. mar. Mar. 15, 1842.   Lives at
Monmouth, Ills.   Served three years in Civil War.
Issue:
187.   Joseph Shrom, b. Dec. 19, 1842; d. Jan. 7, 1918.
          (Neb.) Served two years in Civil War.

188. Stephen Robert (California), b. Jan. 11, 1848; d. Feb. 3, 1915. Los Angeles.
189. Mary Hays, b. Oct. 1, 1844. Santa Monica, Calif.
190. Annie. Los Angeles, Calif.
191. Nettie.

(55) Mary Culbertson mar. S. I. Henderson, of Shippensburg, Pa., Aug. 20, 1840.

(58) Elizabeth Culbertson mar. James Clark, of Harrisburg, Pa., Dec. 20, 1859.
Issue:
192. George Clark.
193. Edward Clark.
194. James Arthur Clark.
195. Helen Culbertson Clark.
196. Hays, d.
197. Boy, d. in infancy
197½. Boy, d. in infancy.
198. Elizabeth, d.

(60) John M. Culbertson mar. ——. Lives at Glenwood, Ind. (Stock Farmer).
Issue:
199. Catherine E.
200. Mary J.
201. Alice C.
202. John M.
203. Robert A.
204. Margaret J.
205. Henry C.
206. Charles E.
207. Ann E.

(61) Joseph A. Culbertson mar. ——. Lives at Milford Center, Union Co., Ohio. (Stock Farm).
Issue:
208. Samuel.
209. Walter M.

(62) Samuel D. Culbertson mar. ——. Lives at Milford Center, Union Co., O. (Stock Farm).

(64) Robert C. Culbertson mar. Edith Knight, of Cincinnati, Ohio. Wholesale tobacconist, Cincinnati. (Wife d. 1878).
Issue:
210. Mary Knight Culbertson.

(66) Mary Culbertson mar. J. W. Kilbreth. Live at Southhampton, N. Y.
211. Edith J., d. Young.
Issue:
213. Mary Kilbreth (unmar.).
212. John C. Kilbreth.
214. Wm. Kilbreth.

(67) Libbie Culbertson mar. Rev. John Annan, pastor of First Presbyterian Church, of Cincinnati, O.
Issue:
215. Alice.
216. Helen.

(68) Anna Culbertson mar. Carl Adae, of Cincinnati, O.
Issue:
217. Marie Adae.
218. Anna Belle Adae.
218½. Carlotta Adae.
219. Carl Adae.

(69) Frank C. mar. Florence Moody, daughter of Rev. Moody, of Shippensburg, Pa. Banker, San Angelo, Tex.
Issue:
220. Eleanor Catherine.
221. Florence Edith.

(76) Dr. James Culbertson mar. ———. Moved to Waco, Tex. from Ralls Co., Mo. Was a graduate of Jefferson Med. College, Philadelphia, Pa.
Issue:
221½. Mary H., d. 1869.
222. Emma S., Waco, Tex. Teacher. Unmarried.
223. Virginia L., mar. 1889.
224. Minnie V., Waco, Tex., Teacher. Unmarried.
225. William J., Waco, Tex. Unmarried.
226. Irene M., Waco, Tex. Unmarried.
227. V. L. Walker, Waco, Tex. Unmarried.

(78) Wm. Culbertson. Know nothing of.

(79) Ann E. Culbertson mar. Mr. Biggs.
Issue:
228. Rebecca (Mrs. Hawkins) Bowling Green, Mo.
229. Emma (Mrs. Moffett) Mexico, Mo. And four others.

EIGHTH GENERATION

(82) Frances L. Culbertson. See (40).

(83) Cyrus J. Culbertson mar. ——. No issue.

(87) Emma I. Culbertson mar. first Theodore Pinkey. Husband died.
Issue:
230. Alexander C. Pinky.
She (87) then mar. Wm. Clark. No issue.

(88) Robert S. Culbertson mar. Lydia Smith. Merchant. Lives at Ft. Benton, Mont.
Issue:
231. Helen.
232. Mabel.
233. Robert.
234. Esther.
235. Mollie.
236. John.
237. William.
238. Frances.

(95) Joseph Culbertson,. mar. a daughter of Major Mossman.
Issue:

239. Samuel Culbertson. In World War. Married.
Issue:
Two daughters.

(96) Margaret Culbertson mar. P. C. Bartlett, of Peoria, Ills.
Issue:
240. Sue Herron Bartlett.
241. Nannie Bartlett.
242. Edward P. Bartlett. Mar. Miss Beardsley.
243. Lucy E. Bartlett.
244. Wm. C. Bartlett.

(98) Mary F. Culbertson mar. John S. McIlvaine, cashier of National Bank, Chambersburg, Pa.
Issue:
245. Nellie Bell McIlvaine (Mrs. Chas. Hoopes).
246. Wm. McIlvaine, b. Oct. 29, 1867; d. Apr. 1868.

247. George Duffield. Mar. Lives at Pittsburgh, Pa.
248. John S., Jr.

(99) Ellen B. Culbertson mar. Wm. Hopkins, of Syracuse, N. Y.
Issue:
249. Nannie Hopkins.
250. Harriett Hopkins.
251. Edward Hopkins.

(100) Helen Anna Culbertson, mar. Leonard Wm. Kip, of N. Y., a missionary to China, June, 1865.
Issue:
252. Alice Mabel, b. 1867 (Mrs. Alex. S. Van Dyck, missionary to China).

(101) Frances Culbertson, mar. Dr. Samuel Whitall of N. Y. City.
Issue:
253. Frances Culbertson Whitall, b. 1872; d. 1874.

(108) Denton Dun Culbertson, mar. Mary Sly, 1851.
Issue:
254. Mary, b. ——. Mar. Mr. Wheeler.
255. Wm., d. young.

(109) Mary Elizabeth Culbertson mar. Samuel Knox, M. D. of Adams Co., Pa.
256. Mary Knox, b. June, 1852. Physician, Adams Co., Pa. Unmar.
257. Mary E. Knox, mar. —— Meadley, a civil engineer. No issue.
258. James Mason Knox, d. young.
259. Samuel Knox, d. unmar.
260. Chas. Knox, mar. lives in Montana—a ranchman.

(111) Cyrus J. Culbertson mar. Rachael Doty, July 4, 1858.
Issue:
261 One son.
262 to 267. Five daughters.

(113) John Newton Culbertson (Rev.). Soldier in Civil War. Mar. Jan'y 9, 1880 to Belle Caldwell of Wheeling, W. Va., in Bangkok, Siam. Prin. of Harriet House School for Girls.
Issue:
268. Keren Whittier, b. Oct. 16, 1881.
269. John Travis, M., b. Sept. 21, 1883.
270. Helen Duncan, b. Oct. 16, 1888; d. in infancy.
271. Robert Caldwell, b. Jan. 9, 1891; d. June 17, 1897.

272.   Gladys Isabel, b. June 17, 1897; unmar.

(114) Wm. F. Breckenridge Culbertson. Died (unmarried) of wounds received in the Battle of Prairie Grove, Ark., in Civil War.

(115) Harriett Newell, mar. John Osborn, a soldier of the Civil War, Aug. 14, 1866.
Issue:
273.   Wm. Denton Osborn, b. July 12, 1867.
274.   Richard Leon, b. Oct. 14, 1868.
275.   Florence Iola, b. Oct. 4, 1870.
276.   Bessie Henderson, b. ——.
277.   John Culbertson, b. ——.
278.   Bernice H.
279.   Ruby A.
280.   Leslie McVitty.

(116) Martha Ann Culbertson, mar. Horace Wycoff.
Issue:
281.   Josephine Wycoff.
282.   Culbertson.
283.   Joseph.
283½.   June.

(117) Pauline V. Culbertson mar. Wm. Powell, a soldier in Civil War.
Issue:
284.   Wm. Court Powell, b. Dec. 12, 1870.
285.   Lena Powell, b. May 9, 1872.
286.   Alberta, b. Oct. 16, 1874.

(118) Robert Mason Culbertson, mar. Miss —— Wilson, of Stuart, Ia.
Issue:
287-8.   Two daughters.
289-90½.   Three sons.

(119) Rebecca Jane Culbertson mar. ——, Woodley, M. D. Husband died. No issue. She married second, Herbert Wood.
Issue:
292.   May Wood, mar. and lives near Calgary, Can.

(128) Albert Culbertson, mar. Emma Jane Canefield, May 8, 1872. No issue; have adopted son, born Feb. 1, 1892, and named Robert W. Culbertson. Emma Jane Canefield died July 8, 1912. Albert Culbertson mar. second wife, Anna Mary Jorpeland, Sept. 3, 1913.

Issue:
292. Annie Jeannette Culbertson, b. July 11, 1914.
293. Albert Duncan Culbertson, b. Mar. 16, 1916.
294. Mildred Ann Culbertson, b. Dec. 3, 1918.

(129) William D. Culbertson mar. Nettie Canfield, Dec. 10, 1872.
Issue:
295. Elsie May Culbertson, b. July 21, 1873.
296. Ruth D. Culbertson, b. Aug. 18, 1878.

(130) Josephine Culbertson, b. ——, 1852; mar. Charles A. Abbott (Charles A. Abbott died ——).
Issue:
297. Maud Abbott.
298. Mollie Abbott.
299. Vaughn Abbott.
300. Robert Abbott.
301. Gertie Abbott.
302. Clinton Abbott.
303. Lincoln Abbott.
304. Florence Abbott.

(131) Robert Culbertson, mar. Carrie Olson, Jan. 2, 1876,
Issue:
305. Letitia Culbertson, b. Feb. 14, 1876; d. Oct., 1918.
306. Robert Wilson Culbertson, b. Sept. 3, 1878.
307. Effie Culbertson, b. Dec. 13, 1871; d. Aug., 1883.
308. Harvey D. Culbertson, b. Dec. 22, 1882.
309. Albert Hays Culbertson, b. Mar. 23, 1885.
310. Edgar William Culbertson, b. Dec. 26, 1886.

(132) Edgar Hays Culbertson; unmar. lives at 423 Court St., Albert Lea, Minn.

(133) Mary Ann Culbertson, b. June 26, 1859; d. June 25, 1918; mar. to James Ferrier, Nov. 6, 1879.
Issue:
311. Jeanette Evangeline Ferrier, mar. Robert Bain.
312. Blanche Ferrier, mar. Neil Bain; no issue.
313. John Ferrier, mar. Hazel Patterson; no issue.
314. Josephine Farrier, mar. Frank Root, 3 children.
315. James Farrier, mar. Hester ——.
316. Evelyn Ferrier, unmar.

(138) Emma S. Culbertson, mar. Chauncey Ives, Chief Engr. of Cumberland Valley R. R. Lived at Chambersburg, Pa.

Issue:
317. Charles Ives.
318. Chauncey, Jr.
319. Nellie (Mrs. Wentworth Hart, of Hood River, Oregon.) Issue: Charlotte (Mrs. John Putnam, of Norristown, N. J.).

(139) Nannie P. Culbertson mar. Daniel H. Wingerd, Oct. 19, 1876.
Issue:
320. Margaret Wingerd, d.
321. Edmund Wingerd.

(137) Samuel Duncan Culbertson, mar. Miss Cook. (General Freight Agent, P. & W. R. R.)
Issue:
322. Emily C., d. 1878.
323. Elvira H.
324. Lillie Cook.
325. Jacob W. C.
326. Clara W.

(150) John P. Culbertson, mar. May Ellen Sharp. Lives at Carlisle, Pa.

(151) Chas. A. Culbertson, mar. Amelia Birkhead Hanway at Aberdeen, Md.

(157) Wm. Andrew Snively mar. Ella Pirtle of Louisville, Ky. Both d.
Issue:
Jane Snively, d. young. Theodore, unmar. Atty. at Law at
　　　　Louisville, Ky.; Elsie (mar.).

(158) Dr. Joseph C. Snively, mar. Miss Strickland. Both died many years ago.
Issue:
Edith (Mrs. Henry Sanford). Issue: Culbertson Sanford;
　　　　Edith Sanford.

(160) Julia Frances Snively, mar. Wm. Henry Lewis at new Albany, Ind., Oct., 1861. Husband died May, 1906.
Issue:
a. Edward Mann, b. Dec. 10, 1863 (Gen.) Mar. at Evanston,
　　　　Ills., Hattie Russel Balding, June 12, 1888. Issue:
　　　　Henry Balding, b. May 8, 1889; Adelaide Palmer,
　　　　b. July 22, 1895. (Mar. Arthur D. Newman, Major
　　　　of Cav. Had issue Edward L. Newman, b. Apr. 9,
　　　　1919; Frank McCoy Newman, b. Oct. 12, 1920);
　　　　Thomas Edward Lewis, b. Oct. 16, 1898.

b. Wm. Andrew Lewis, b. Mar. 30, 1867.
c. Arthur Henry, b. Mar. 13, 1869.
d. Adelaide Louisa, b. Feb. 12, 1880; mar. in 1906, Harry
     Heffrin; lives at Kittanning, Pa. (Issue: Emma
     Josephine; Harry Lewis; Adelaide Sara; Frances
     Snively.)
e. Frances Snively, b. Aug. 24, 1876.

(161) Mary Ann Snively, mar. F. Colton, of Washington,
D. C.

(162) John C. Snively, mar. Miss Eyster; lived at Crete,
Neb.

(163) Rev. Summerfield E. Snively, mar. Ida Selleck, of
New York. She died years ago; he died a few years since,
when he was rector of an Episcopal church at Nice, France.
     Issue:
De Forrest, an Episcopal clergyman at Westfield, Mass.
Margaret (mar. Bernard Pratt, an Englishman) County
     Kent, Eng. Issue: Several children.
Ethelwyn (Mrs. Edward Cosbey, Asst Rector at St. Marks-
     on-Bowery, N. Y.) Issue: Edward, Robert C.,
     Kenneth Tryon, Ethelwyn.

(164) Thaddeus Snively, mar. Lily Crosbey, of Troy, N.
Y. He d. 1912.
     Issue:
Schuyler Snively, Alexander Snively; both officers Cana-
     dian regiments World War.

(165) Wm. Arthur Culbertson, mar. Olive Glover of
Evansville, Ind. Was a banker at St. Paul, Minn. Wife
living in 1923 at San Angelo, Tex.
     Issue:
327. Glover Culbertson.
328. Arthur Percy, San Angelo, Tex.

(171) Annie Vance Culbertson, mar. Francis Bailey
Semple, Nov. 15, 1883. Moved to Minneapolis, Minn. Husband died.
     Issue:
329. Rebekah, b. Dec. 18, 1884.
330. Wm. Culbertson Semple, b. Sept. 1887. During
      World War gave his yacht to U. S. and served on
      it as member of the crew.

(171) Annie Vance Culbertson mar. second, Alonzo Rand
of Minneapolis, Minn. (No issue).

(172) Samuel Alexander Culbertson. Is a banker at Louisville, Ky. Served in Remount Service during the latter part of the World War. Mar. Louise Craig of Pee Wee Valley, Ky., Feb., 1886.

Issue:

331.   William Stuart, b. Aug. 1887, who served on his cousin's yacht in World War.; mar. Effie Bagnall of St. Louis. No issue.

332.   Louis. No issue.

332½.   Alexander Craig, b. 1889.

(174) Blanche Warner Culbertson, mar. Leigh French of Minneapolis, Minn., June 27, 1893.

Issue:

333.   Leigh French, Jr., b. March 17, 1894.

334.   Cedric French, b. Sept. 22, 1895.

335.   George Franklyn French, b. July 24, 1897. New York City.

(177) George Augustus Culbertson, mar. Margaret Moore, lived at Santa Barbara, Calif.; died years ago.

Issue:

336.   George Augustus, mar. had a daughter.

337.   John Thomas.

338.   Henry.

339.   Emita (Mrs. Benj. Rowan), Los Angeles, Calif.

340.   Francis.

(178) Wm. Linn Culbertson; mar. Ruth Olivia Johnson, of Carroll, Ia., June 5, 1873; wife b. Jan. 13, 1853; banker Carrollton, Ia. Widow living (1923) at Worland, Wyo.

Issue:

341.   Mary Wood, b. May 4, 1874, at Carroll, Ia. (Unmar..)

342.   Ralph Wm., b. Feb. 5, 1878; d. 1886, at Carroll.

343.   Rober Goodwin, b. June 14, 1881, Worland, Wyo.

344.   Wm. Linn, Jr., b. Feb. 20, 1884, U. S. N.

(179) Stephen D. Culbertson, mar. Mary E. Hess, of Princeton, Ia., Feb. 2, 1872. Lived at Glidden, Ia., now at St. Louis, Mo. Jeweler.

Issue:

345.   Robert Hays, b. July 14, 1873.

346.   Cornelia May, b. July 19, 1875.

347.   Stephen Roy, b. Aug. 24, 1877.

348.   Ethel Burchard, b. Nov. 11, 1882.

349.   Rolla McLosky, b. Oct. 19, 1884.

350.   Linn Nichols, b. Mar. 16, 1890.

(180) Julius Augustus Culbertson, mar. Jane Hunter, Feb. 15, 1877. Lives at Glidden, Ia. (Dry Goods Merchant).
Issue:
351. Faye Belle, b. Nov. 8, 1880.
352. Robert Coe, d. infancy.
353. Hays, b. July 1, 1885.

354. Margaret Emma, b. Dec. 17, 1888.
(181) Mary Hays Culbertson mar. John E. Darrah, of Indiana Co., Pa., Apr. 23, 1879. (Dry goods merchant, Greenfield, Ia.).
Issue:
355. Cora L. Darrah, b. May, 1880.
356. Ernest Hays, b. Aug. 9, 1882.
357. Olive Estelle, b. Jan. 11, 1893.

(182) Robert Y. C. mar. Henrietta Bell at Princetown, Ia. Mar. 16, 1876 Live at Carroll, Ia
Issue:
358 Frederick Hayes, b. May 16, 1879.
359. Frank, b. May 20, 1881; d. July 20, 1886.
360. Clara Bell, b. June 5, 1887.

(183) James C. C., mar. Ada E. Bennett, Dec. 15, 1889. (Dry goods merchant, Greenfield, Ia.). Widow lives Des Moines, Ia.
Issue:
361. C. Linn, b. Sept. 29, 1890.
362. Fern.

(187) Joseph Shrom Culbertson, d. about Jan. 7, 1918 at Edgar, Nebraska. His only wife, Nancy Daniels, survived him until about Jan. 9, 1922.
Issue:
363. Laura Belle, b. Oct. 4, 1869, still living.
364. Robert William, b. Mar. 16, 1871 in Warren Co., Ia. Living.

(188) Stephen Robert Culbertson was born Nov. 1, 1848, Shippensburg, Pa. d. Mar. 2, 1915, at Los Angeles, Calif. Mar. Mary Estelle Downer in Nebraska, Mar. 5, 1876. Wife living; address Claremont, Calif.
Issue:
365. Elnora May Culbertson, b. Dec. 12, 1876, in Nuckolls Co., Nebraska.
366. James Downer, b. Apr. 17, 1882, in Superior, Nuckolls Co., Neb.

367. Sarah Rebecca, b. Apr. 17, 1882, in Superior, Nuck-·
     olls Co., Neb.
368. Mary Catherine, b. May 19, 1886, Davenport, Neb.
369. Stephen Robert, b. July 24, 1888, Davenport, Neb.
370. John Talmage, b. Feb. 24, 1891, Angus, Neb.
371. Augustus Culbertson, b. March 20, 1894.
372. Opal Estelle, b. Oct. 1, 1895, at Bloomington, Calif.

(189) Mary Culbertson mar. Dec. 21, 1869 to Wm. T.
Black. Between 75 and 80 years old; living at Santa Monica, Calif.
Issue:
374. Roy Black; mar. Cora Hanford. No issue. Lives
     Santa Monica, Calif.
375. James Black.
376. Wm. C. Black, mar. 1917 to Hattie Hall. Lives at Los
     Angeles, Calif.
377. Jessie Black (mar. John Hossack, 1903). Issue: two
     sons; lives at Ventura, Calif.
378. Fannie Black, mar. Anderson T. Finney; Issue: one
     daughter, one son; lives Yellow Springs, Ohio.
379. Mollie Black, mar. Apr. 1, 1905, to Louis R. Kohl.
     Issue: Two daughters, one son; Belleville, N. J.

(190) Nettie Culbertson mar Harry Flemming at Monmouth, Ills. Issue: Linnie Flemming (Alone).

NINTH GENERATION

(245) Nellie Bell McIlvaine mar. June 7, 1887, to Chas.
Stockton Hoopes.
Issue:
380. Helen Hoopes.

(247) George Duffield McIlvaine mar. Sara Leightcap of
Easton, Pa., Jan'y 5, 1888; lives Pittsburgh, Pa. Sec'y
National Pipe & Supplies Co. Pres Nat'l Phi Kappa Society; Pres. LaFayette Alumnae, etc.
Issue:

381. John Stauffer (3rd), b. Dec. 2, 1888; enlisted Dec.,
     1917, in Coast Art. Corps. Trained Ft. Scott and
     San Francisco. Went overseas May, 1918 in Coast
     Art. Corps (42nd.). Discharged Sept. 10, 1919. Was
     wearing three sleeve stripes and service ribbon on
     which are two bronze stars for major operations
     and one silver star, reg. cit., for bravery in action.

Mar. Susanne Celestine Chappe in Nancy, France, Nov. 20, 1919.

(248) John Stauffer McIlvaine, Jr. Jr. mar. Bessie Mc-Gowan, Oct. 4, 1904.
Issue:
382. Alice Chambers McIlvaine.
383. Mary Culbertson.

(268) Karen Whittier Culbertson mar. Arthur J. Baker of Birmingham, Eng. Live at Toledo, O.
Issue:
384. Robert Baker, b. Apr. 12, 1909.

(269) John Travis McVitty Culbertson, mar. Feb. 12, 1911, to Miss Ivy Phelps. (b. Oct. 4, 1881, Stevensville, N. Y.)
Issue:
385. John Phelps, b. Apr. 21, 1912, at Great Falls, Mont. John Travis Culbertson connected with reclamation work in arid west.

(295) Elsie May Culbertson mar. John Weldon, Dec. 11, 1891.
Issue:
386. Gladys, b. July, 1892; d. Oct. 8, 1893.
387. Phyllis, b. Oct. 10, 1893 (mar. Douglas Brower, Oct. 5, 1917; later mar. Frank Weller, Oct. 23, 1922).
388. Gwendolyn, b. Feb. 26, 1895 (Mar. to Warren Hamilton Sept. 9, 1920. Issue: Gwendolyn W. Hamilton, b. July 1, 1921).

(296) Ruth D. Culbertson, mar. Neil Currie, Jan. 25, 1896.
Issue:
389. Earl W. Currie, b. Jan. 18, 1897 (mar. July 1, 1921 to Nina Karlsbrotin).

(305) Letetia Culbertson, mar. Edward H. Straw, Oct. 21, 1896.
Issue:
390. Robert Henry and Leslie Edward, b. July 13, 1897; Leslie Edward died Set. 29, 1897.
391. Gladys Rosemond, died Feb. 5, 1901.
392. Oaka Carrie, born Aug. 27, 1904.

(390) Robert Henry Straw, mar. Florence May Terry, Dec. 29, 1920; I.ssue, one son born Feb'y 9, 1923.

(392) Oaka Carrie Straw, married Verne S. Lewis, Dec. 5, 1922.

(306) Robert Wilson Culbertson, mar. Nellie Henry, Sept. 20, 1905.
Issue:
393. Paul Robert Culbertson, b. Oct. 22, 1906.
394. Francis Henry Culbertson, b. June 1, 1913.

(308) Harvey D. Culbertson, mar. Sarah Ann Primrose, Primrose, Neb., Sept. 30, 1914.
Issue:
395. Thelma Ione Culbertson, b. Aug. 19, 1917.
396. Harvey Rex Culbertson, b. Aug. 29, 1919.
397. Robert Edgar Culbertson, b. Mar. 24, 1921.
398. Willis James Culbertson, b. Set. 12, 1922.

(309) Albert Hays Culbertson mar. Elma De Etta Lien, Albert Lea, Minn., Aug. 8, 1918.
Issue:
399. Albert Hays Culbertson, Jr., b. Aug. 1, 1919.

(310) Edgar William Culbertson mar. Jan. 25, 1912, Edna B. Anderson, Albert Lea, Minn.
Issue:
400. Sydney Edgar Culbertson, b. July 31,1913.

(321) Edmund Culbertson Wingerd of Chambersburg, Penna. Attorney and former Mayor of Chambersburg. Mar. Miss Margaret F. Coleman, Nov. 12, 1914.
Issue:
401. Edmund Culbertson Wingerd, b. Apr. 4, 1916.
402. Joseph Coleman, b. Nov. 11, 1917.
403. William Noble, b. Jan. 5, 1920.

(328) Arthur Percy Culbertson of San Angelo, Tex., mar. Hazel Hershey, of San Angelo, in 1920.
Issue:
404. Wm. Semple Culbertson, b. ——.

(329) Rebecca Semple married Allen West of St. Louis, Mo. Prominent society and club woman.
Issue:
405. Allen West.
406. Annie West.
407. Rebecca West.

(332½) Alexander Craig Culbertson mar. Florence Mc-

Fatrick of Chicago, Ills. Served in World War as Commander of Cadets at Omaha Balloon School.

Issue:

408. Samuel Alexander, Jr.
409. Florence.

(333) Leigh French, Jr., mar. Phyllis Wildes Brown, Apr. 13, 1918, at Dobbs Ferry, N. Y. Lives at Ardsley on Hudson.

Issue:

410. Leigh French (3rd) b. Oct. 18, 1920.

(343) Roger Goodwin Culbertson, mar. Sept. 7, 1909, to Annie C. Cummins, Des Moines, Ia.

Issue:

411. Jane Culbertson, b. June 11 1911.

(344) Wm. Linn Culbertson, Jr., graduate Annapolis. In U. S. Navy. Mar. Sept. 12, 1906, at Fairfield, Conn., to Lisa Winchester Heighe.

Issue:

412. Wm. Linn, Jr., b. July 1, 1908.

(347) Stephen Roy Culbertson, mar. June 1, 1914, to Olive Outten. Lives St. Louis, Mo.

Issue:

413. Olive Mary, b. Oct. 30, 1916.

(350) Linn Nichols Culbertson served with Headquarters Detachment of 35th Div. in France. Returned safely. Lives St. Louis, Mo.

(351) Faye Belle Culbertson mar. March 28, 1913, Luther Ridenour; lives Plentywood, Mont.

Issue:

414. Jane Ellen Ridenour, b. Nov. 22, 1915.
415. Alice Margaret, b. Dec. 25, 1918.

(353) Dr. Hays Culbertson. Served in World War; lives Driggs, Idaho.

(354) Margaret Emma Culbertson mar. Harry A. Mcgill; widow lives at Alameda, Calif.

Issue:

416. Son.
417. Son
418. Son.

(358) Frederick Hayes Culbertson, mar. Marian Edith Park, June 16, 1909. Resides Carroll, Ia.
Issue:
419. Helen Adelaide, b. March 26, 1910.
420. Frederick Park, b. Jany. 5, 1912.

(360) Clara Belle Culbertson, mar. Fern H. Cooney, June 16, 1920. Resides Carroll, Ia. Husband member of Co. L, 131st Inf. Cited for bravery in Gressaire Wood, Aug. 10, 1918.
No issue.

(361) Charles Linn Culbertson. Unmarried. Served in World War; returned safely. Lives Des Moines, Ia.

(362) Fern (Mar. Glen Eastburn).
Issue:
421. Ruth Emily. Des Moines, Ia.

(363) Laura Belle Culbertson, mar. Timothy Kane, retired farmer, Edgar, Neb.
Issue:
422. ——, d. at birth.

(364) Robert Wm. Culbertson, mar. about 1897 to Ethel White of Iowa.
Issue:
423. Fay (mar. Homer Mallory, 1918. Issue: Wilma and Wm. Jr., twins, three years old; Wanda, 1 year. Live at Edgar, Neb.)
424. Cleo.
425. Joseph Shrom.
426. Daughter, d. .

(365) Elnora May Culbertson, mar. George E. La Gaye, a rancher. Husband d. 1912. Widow lives at Claremont, Calif. Teacher; Grad. State Normal.
Issue:
427. Virginia May, b. Apr. 23, 1909.
428. Marie Estelle, b. May 11, 1911.

(366) James Downer Culbertson; grad. as B. A. from Pomona College, Calif., 1904. Mar. Bertha Mabel Eldridge, Aug. 8, 1908 Lemon grower and Assistant Field Mgr. of Limoneria Co., a corporation owning and operating some 1500 acres lemons and 240 acres English walnuts, Santa Paula, Calif.
Issue:
429. Helen Jean, b. Sept. 12, 1909.

439. Barbara Eldridge, b. Apr. 30, 1914.
431. James Downer, Jr., b. Apr. 24, 1919.

(367) Sarah Rebecca Culbertson. Mar. June 30, 1901, at San Bernardino, Calif, to James Russell, merchant, San Bernardino, Calif.
Issue:
432. George Vernon, b. July 4, 1905, at San Bernardino, Calif.

(368) Mary Catherine Culbertson. ·Graduated from San Diego State Normal, taught school 5 years. Mar. Rolland C. Springer, an attorney of San Diego, Calif., about Sept. 29, 1914, at San Bernardino Calif.·
No issue. Address 3351 29th St., San Diego, Calif.

(369) Stephen Robert Culbertson. Born Davenport, Ia. Married Dec. 1, 1909, to Myrtle Revill at San Bernardino, Calif. Lemon grower and manager for Santa Paula Lemon Co., Santa Paula, Calif.
Issue:
433. Grace Marie, b. Dec. 31, 1910.
434. Lloyd Revill, b. Aug. 7, 1912.
435. Clearence Leon, b. Sept. 11, 1915.
436. Robert Junior Culbertson, b. July 25, 1919.

(370) John Talmadge Culbertson. Mar. at Los Angeles, Calif., about Nov. 1, 1912, to Selma Leonore Drott. Lemon grower and manager Cascade Ranch Co., nurseryman and poultryman. San Fernando, Calif.
Issue:
437. Hazel Marie, b. June 1, 1915.
438. Ruth Louise, b. Mar. 19, 1917.
439. John Talmadge Culbertson, Jr., b. Aug. 19, 1921.

(371) Augustus Culbertson.

(372) Opal Estelle Culbertson, mar. June 8, 1920, to Fred L. Wilkinson, lemon grower and poultryman of San Fernando, Calif. Opal grad. Los Angeles State Normal; formerly public school teacher.
No issue.

PROMINENT DESCENDANTS OF (III) COL .ROBERT CULBERTSON

(5) Col. Samuel D. Culbertson, M. D., raised in "Row", was educated at Canonsburg College, Pa. Studied medicine and practiced many years in Chambersburg. In 1812,

he gathered a company and, as Lieut. marched them to Buffalo, and was appointed Bridgade-Surgeon. In 1814, he raised a company and, as Captain, marched them to defend Baltimore against the British, and was again appointed Brigade-Surgeon. Rev. A. Nevin says of him: "The love of country which warmed the bosoms of the Culbertsons in the days that tried men's souls and which glowed in the ardent heart of their illustrious descendant in the vigor of his manhood, suffered no cooling amid the infirmities of his age. When the wicked Rebellion massed its hosts for the overthrow of the government, he gave no equivocal support to the earnest, strenuous prosecution of the war for national existence, but uttered a full voiced advocacy of prompt, decided, unremitting action. In medicine he was a remarkable diagnostician, as well as a skillful surgeon and obstetrician. The great Prof. Chapman, of Philadelphia, spoke very highly of him. He was engaged in a number of business enterprises, among them paper manufacture, in which he massed a large fortune. He practiced medicine until 1831, when he retired from practice. His son (37), Dr. Edmund, was a surgeon of great skill and reputation at Chambersburg. His son (39) Albert, owned the first paper mill west of the Alleghenies that used steam rolls.

(42) Elizabeth Reid's daughter, Helen (155), mar. Hon. W. S. Stenger, who was congressman from Franklin Co., in 1878. Was also District Attorney of that county for three terms. Was a prominent lawyer of Philadelphia.

(8) Capt. John C. Culbertson was born and raised in "Row". After the breaking out of the War of 1812, he entered the army as Ensign in the 22d U. S. Inf., 17th of March, 1812. Commissioned 2nd Lieut., Mar. 13, 1813; 1st. Lieut., Oct. 1, 1813. Transferred to 8th U. S. Inf., May 17, 1815. Captain, June 1, 1819." (U. S. Army Register). Disbanded June 1, 1821.

"After leaving the Army he went to the Frontier, engaging for a time in the Santa Fe trade. His career in trading in the West, laid a broad foundation for his fortune, that became assured after his settlement in Cincinnati in the year 1828. A few years after his establishment in Cincinnati he organized the Franklin bank and gave a large share of his attention to its management. When the bank surrendered its charter, Capt. Culbertson associated with M. Grosbeck and Mr. Kilgour, as successors of the

Franklin bank, in private banking, and continued this association for many years. The rigid will, sturdy resolution and courage that were the prominent characteristics of Capt. Culbertson, were doubtless the basis of his successful business career. Socially, he was a genial and generous liver, his home being perhaps more thoroughly patrician in style than any in the city." (From a Cincinnati Paper.) His fortune at his death was estimated at $500,000. His sons were wealthy and influential men and his daughters married prominent men, one of these being Rev. John Annan, pastor of the First Presbyterian Church, Cincinnati. Capt. J. C. Culbertson married the daughter of Rev. John Moody, who preached for fifty-three years at Middle Spring Church, Cumberland Co., Pa.

(15) Alexander Culbertson was in the Battle of Ft. McKenzie, Aug. 28, 1833 (Indian battle). Maximiiian, prince of Wied of Austria, visited America at that time and admired Major Culbertson very much. Lauds him highly in his book of Travel in America. Major Culbertson's picture hangs in the Public Library at Ft. Benton, Mont. Also a picture of the Indian battle with Culbertson thereon— above mentioned.

(16) Cyrus D. Culbertson was a wealthy packer of Baltimore and Cincinnati.

(21) Thaddeus A. Culbertson wrote a Journal of an Expedition to the Mauvais Terres (Black Hills), published by Smithsonian Institute, 1850.

(19) Michael Simpson Culbertson was one of the most brilliant of the family. "Entered Military Academy, at West Point; was appointed Second Lieut., First U. S. Art'y July 1, 1839. Resigned April 15, 1841." (Army Register). Rev. A. Nevin says of him:"After resigning from Army, he entered the Theological Seminary at Princeton, N. J., and graduated from there in 1844. He was licensed at Carlisle, and ordained as a foreign missionary to China. Before sailing he married Miss Dunlap, of N. Y. State. His career as a missionary was marked by extraordinary devotion and ability. In the midst of his labors, was taken with cholera and died after a short illness. Among his fellow students were Halleck, McDowell, Beauregard, all of whom afterwards wore the insignia of Major Generals. In the progress of his course, he was appointed drill officer with title of Captain, and served for a time as Professor of Mathe-

matics. When two cadets were chosen to go to France, at the Government's expense to complete their education at the school that had produced Napoleon Bonaparte, Culbertson was the first selected; and obtained suffrages of all the electors.

At West Point he earned for himself the beatitude of peacemaker. Engaged to act as a second to the afterwards famous Magruder, in an affair of honor, he adjusted the difficulty and prevented a probably fatal encounter. He labored in connection with the late Dr. Bridgeman, for several years, with assiduity and perseverance, in preparing a revised translation of the Bible in the Chinese language, a labor of love which he regarded as the great work of his life, and it was a source of especial consolation to him, just before his departure, that God had enabled him to complete it. He also wrote a work entitled "Darkness in the Flowery Land." His daughter Josephine (103) was an artist of prominence in Brooklyn (1892).

(44) William Stuart Culbertson was born at "Fairview Farm," near the little town of New Market, and a few miles from Harrisburg. He was but ten years of age when his father died. Upon the settlement of the estate, it was found that the security notes, which he had signed for others would leave only a small property for the widow.

Young William, felt so strongly that he must help his mother, that at the age of fifteen he entered a mercantile establishment at Harrisburg, where he remained until he was twenty-one and then left for what was the "West" in those days—Indiana. He settled in the thriving little town of New Albany, just across the river from Louisville, Ky., and there he lived for the rest of his long life. For many years he was a wholesale merchant and a banker; later only a banker. He was much interested in banking in the Northwest, especially in Minneapolis and St. Paul. His ability as a merchant and banker was widely recognized.

William Stuart Culbertson, like all his ancestors, was a Presbyterian. No doubt influenced by the example of his mother, who was much given to hospitality and very charitable, he excelled in both these virtues. Naturally, in most cases, his "right hand knew not what the left hand" gave, but in two instances at least it was impossible to keep the benefactions from public knowledge. These two benefactions were "The Old Ladies Home," and the "Cornelia Memorial Orphans Home." The latter, on completion, Mr. Culbertson turned over to the trustees for a permanent dwelling for the children, who until then had lived in rented quarters. The "Old Ladies Home'" however, was quite another affair; as long as he lived, he maintained it and gave, with the other members of the family, personal supervision. He endowed it generously and at this writing, it is still a flourishing and much needed institution. We would add that the mother of Wm. Stuart Culbertson was a wonderfully intelligent and interesting woman as were also his wives.

(171) Mrs. Annie Vance Culbertson (Mrs. F. B. Semple) was a charming woman and a highly gifted singer. She was a woman of great charity and the poor and the unfortunate and the fallen of Minneapolis long had cause to remember her kindness and charity, and when she passed away the poor and down-and-out thronged to her home to take one last look at her kind and beautiful face.

(174) Blanche Warner Culbertson, born Sept. 15th, 1870, Married Leigh French of Minneapolis, Minn., June 27th, 1893. In the Spanish War, Dr. French served as Major in the Third Volunteer Regiment of Cavalry under Colonel Grigsby. In the World War he was given the commission as Captain in the Air Service. Residence New York City. Practiced Medicine until 1898. Children: Leigh, b. March 17th, 1894. He was given the commission of Lieutenant in the Ordnance Corps, during the World War. He trained at Plattsburg, the summer of 1917, serving at Camp Hancock, Georgia, and Camp Raritan, N. J.

Cedric Culbertson, born Sept. 22nd, 1895. Williams College. Trained at Plattsburg Camp in 1917. Commissioned Second Lieutenant of Field Artillery. Later in a competitive examination chosen for the Balloon Corps and sent to Fort Omaha· Balloon School. Went overseas with his regiment, the 307th Field Artillery, May 25th, 1918. Regiment stationed at Vannes in Brittany, where he acted as interpreter until sent to the front with the 43rd Balloon Co., Fourth Army Corps, early in August, 1918. Was in the St. Mihiel and Meuse-Argonne offensives. Landed in New York, June 1st, 1919.

George Franklin, b. July 24th, 1897. Enlisted in World War. 10th Oct., 1917. Trained at Ground School, Cornell University, and at Ellington Field, Texas. Commissioned Second-Lieutenant U. S. Air Service. Instructor at Ellington Field in High Altitude Bombing and Acrobatic Flying until Nov. 11th; Instructor in Aerial Gunnery at Taliaferro Field,

Texas, until December 19th, 1918. Graduate of Massachusetts Institute of Technology. Residence New York City.

(157) Rev. Wm. A. Snively was rector of Grace Episcopal Church, one of the largest and most fashionable churches in Baltimore, Albany and Trinity Church, New Orleans.

(148) Dr. Joseph C. Sniveley was a prominent physician of Brooklyn.

(160) Julia F. Snively, married Edward H. Lewis, who was secretary and treasurer of the Monon R. R., with headquarters at Chicago.

(163) Rev. Summerfield E. Snively, M. D., a graduate of Dickinson College, Pa. (as were his brothers); afterwards graduated from Medical Dept. of University of Penna., in 1872. Was a physician in the Catharine Street Hospital for a year. He afterwards studied medicine in Gottingen and Darmstadt. Before this he practiced medicine for two years in Brooklyn. After returning from Europe he studied at the Divinity School, Middletown, Conn., and was ordained in 1879, and accepted the Rectorship of St. Paul's Church, Flatbush, L. I. Warden of the Burd Orphan Asylum, Philadelphia, Pa. (1892).

(164) Rev. Thaddeus A. Snively was Asst. Rector of St. John's Church, Troy, N. Y., and Rector at Qiuncy, Mass. Western Theological Seminary, Chicago, Ill. (1892).

(175) Dr. Emma B. Culbertson, daughter of (46), was one of Boston's most prominent surgeon's. She spent several years in Europe studying languages, history, etc.; entered Vassar College in 1873, and graduated there in 1877, taking the degree of A. M. in 1881. Her medical degree was taken in 1881 at the Woman's Medical College, Philadelphia. During the next two years she occupied her time in hospital work in Boston and Zurich, Switzerland. On returning to Boston, in 1883, was put on the staff of the New England Hospital, with which institution she is now connected as Surgeon and Gynaecologist. Was a member of Mass. State Med. Soc.; New England Med. Society, and the American Academy of Medicine. Her father was a man of wealth and traveled extensively abroad. (1892). Also given in Who's Who in America, 1917. Died since then.

(165) Wm. A. Culbertson enlisted in Aug., 1862, in Co. G., 20th Iowa Inf., and served three years. From March to

July, 1864, was prisoner at Camp Ford, near Tyler, Texas. In 1869, he removed from Scott Co., to Carrol Co., Iowa, where he engaged in farming for two years. In December, 1870, he was elected Auditor of Carroll Co., and served in that office three years. Was then elected County Treasurer, and served two years. In 1876, he engaged in the banking business and has been President of the Bank of Carroll ever since. In 1886-7 he represented Carroll Co. in the Legislature. Is an Odd Fellow and member of G. A. R. (1892).

(95) Joseph Culbertson married a daughter of Major Mossman. Issue: Samuel Culbertson who was in World War. Is married and has two daughters. Joseph (95) living 1921. Is the oldest living Indian Scout. Was with Gen. Miles in Indian Campaigns. Has 32 honorable discharges from the army.

(113) John Newton, son of John and Hannah McVitty,. born August 22, 1841, Franklin Co., Pa. Served over 3 years in the Civil War, Co. C, 7th Kansas Cav. Educated for the ministry. Served 9 years in Bangkok, Siam, a missionary of the Presbyterian church and 5 years a Home Missionary in South Dakota, and for 32 years was employed in the Interior Department, Washington, D. C. Married Miss Belle Caldwell, Principal of the Harriet House Academy, Bangkok, Siam, Jan'y 9, 1880. Miss Caldwell was born in Wheeling, W. Va., Feb. 23, 1857. To them were born 5 children: Keren Whitier, married Arthur J. M. Baker of Birmingham, England, live at Toledo, Ohio; John Travis, married Miss Ivy Phelps of Sterling, Ills.; Helen Duncan, deceased; Robert Caldwell, deceased, and Gladys Isabel. Arthur J. M. Baker is a high salaried engineer (mechanical) in an automobile factory at Toledo, Ohio.

(26) John McVitty Culbertson, father of Rev. John N. Culbertson, of Washington, D. C., was born in Franklin Co., Pa. Removed from this county to Scott, Co., Ia., in Oct., 1849, where he took a prominent part in business, being senior member of "The Flour and Lumber Co., of Culbertson, Russell and Fordyce", of Princeton, Ia.

CONDENSED MILITARY RECORD OF MAJOR GENERAL EDWARD M. LEWIS, SON OF (160) JULIA F. SNIVELY AND WM. H. LEWIS.

Appointed to U. S. M. A., West Point, N. Y., from Indiana. Graduated in 1886.

Served as Brigadier General and Major General National Army throughout the World War. Commission as Major General continued until June 30, 1920, when all temporary commissions lapsed. Appointed Brigadier General Regular Army, January, 1920. Major General, Dec. 2, 1922.

GENERAL'S COMMANDS HELD.

13th Provisional Division, Camp Llano Grande, Texas, 1916-17. 76th Brigade and 38th Division, Camp Shelby, Miss, 1917. U. S. Troops in Paris, France, December 1, 1917, to May 5, 1918. Third Brigade of Second Division, May 5, 1918, to July 15, 1918. 30th Division, July 18, 1918, to its departure for the United States, March, 1919. Fifth Division and Camp Gordon, Ga., July to December, 1919. Douglas, Arizona District, December, 1919, to January, 1920. Third Division and Camp Pike, Arkansas, January, 1920 to September, 1921. Second Division and Camp Travis, Texas,. to November 1922. Since that date in command VIII Area. At various times in command for short periods of the VI Corps Area and the VII Corps Area.

Participated throughout the Cuban Campaign as Adjutant 20th Infantry. Present at El Caney on July 1, 1898 and throughout siege of Santiago.

Participated as Adjutant 20th Infantry in Philippine Insurrection February 23, 1899 to September, 1901. Personally accepted surrender of General Aglipay in Illocas Norte.

WORLD WAR

Commanded 76th Brigade and 38th Division at Camp Shelby, Miss. Commanded U. S. Troops in Paris. Commanded 3rd Brigade, Second Division in Defensive Sector in front of Verdun and throughout the operations at Chateau Thierry, May 31 to July 15, 1918. During this period the 3rd Brigade was continually in the front line which it advanced twice, capturing the village of Vaux on July 1, 1918. Commanded 30th Division in Belgium and France which captured Vermosele and Lock 8 in the Canal District in front of Ypres. This Division under his command served with British First, Second, Third and Fourth Armies. Broke the Hindenburg Line at Belliecourt on September 29, 1918, and in subsequent battles ending October 20, captured many towns and advanced against strong opposition, twenty-four miles. After departure of 30th Division retained at G. H. Q. in office of Chief of Staff. President of Infantry Board to study lessons of the war as regards infantry equipment and organization.

HONORS AND DECORATIONS

Commended for gallantry by Regimental Commander at El Caney, Cuba, 1898. Recommended for brevet for gallantry Cuban Campaign and Philippine Insurrection. World War: United States, Distinguished Service Medal (Congress).

Great Britain: Knight Commander Order of Saint Michael and Saint George.

France: Commandeur Legion of Honor, Croix de Guerre with two palms.

Belgium: Commandeur Order of Leopold, Croix de Guerre.

Montenegro: Grand Officier Order of Daneloler.
LLD. DePauw University, 1919.

SECTION THIRD

The Delaware Families

PART FIRST (K)

Robert of Mill Creek Township

(CHAPTER XXXVI)

PART SECOND (KK)

John Culbertson of Pencader Twp.

Relationship of These Two Not Known, But Probably Were Brothers.

PART FIRST

SECTION THIRD

CHAPTER XXXVI

FIRST GENERATION

(K) Robert Culbertson died about 1766-67 and his wife was made executrix as per will. This will is not on record in New Castle Co., Del., and court officials there tell me it was probably destroyed by the British, during the Revolutionary War, at Chester, Pa., where the records were kept for a time. The said will is referred to in settlement of Robert Culbertson's estate (Settlement Record D-1-346, New Castle, Del.) "Joseph Barton and wife, Sarah, (late Sarah Culbertson, relict of Robert Culbertson) of this county said Sarah, executrix of Robert Culbertson, hereby files account with court. Amount £190, etc., etc., disposed of as per will of Robert Culbertson, deceased. Account approved by court, 1772."

Also see Deed Book, W-1-131, New Castle Co., Del. "Dec. 14, 1762,. Chas. Bryan of St. Georges Hundred and Mary (Campbell) his wife to Robert Culbertson of Mill Creek Hundred. Recorded Feb. 14, 1763. Witnesses John Bryan, Chas. Bryan, Jr."

The author is under the impression that Mary (Campbell) Bryan was an aunt of Robert Culbertson.

Also see Deed Book Y-1-421, New Castle, Co., Del. "Jan. 15, 1768, Sarah Culbertson, widow of Mill Creek Hundred, to Alex Bryan. Said Sarah Culbertson being a daughter of Sarah Murphy and the latter was a daughter of John Campbell. Land in Mill Creek Hundred."

Also Guardian Record E-1-5 "Andrew J. Bryan appointed guardian for Alexander and Robert Culbertson, minor heirs of Robert Culbertson, deceased, being 15 years of age."

Robert's widow married Joseph Barton as the following deed shows (See Deed Book G-2-46): "Dec. 14, 1786, Joseph Barton of Mill Creek Hundred, New Castle Co., Del., leases land on London Line to Sarah Barton (his wife) and Thomas Culbertson, both of Mill Creek Tp."

The following Power of Attorney shows that Robert's sons, Thomas and Robert, went to Westmoreland Co., Pa., in 1787. "Thomas Culbertson of Derry Tp., Westmoreland Co., Pa., and Robert Culbertson of Salem Tp., Westmoreland Co., Pa., do hereby appoint, etc., Joseph Barton of Mill Creek, Tp., New Castle Co., Del., to recover debts, etc." (See Deed Book R-2-p. 46, Wilmington, Del.) Robert Culbertson, Sr., married Sarah Murphy. Issue:

SECOND GENERATION

I. Thomas, b. 1754; d. Aug. 12, 1823. Westmoreland Co., Pa. (Chapter XXXVII).

II. Robert,, b. 1758-9; d. 1835, Westmoreland Co., Pa. (Chapter XXXVIII).

III. Alexander, b. 1760(?); d. 1833. Westmoreland Co., Pa., and Wayne Co., Ohio. (Chapter XXXIX).

*   *   *   *   *

CHAPTER XXXVII

THIRD GENERATION

(I) Thomas Culbertson of Mill Creek Tp., New Castle, Tp., Del. took the Oath of Allegiance Jan. 9, 1778." (See Del. Archives, Vol. II).

Thomas Culbertson of Del. does not appear on Cumb. or Franklin Co., Pa. court records, or tax lists. In Census, 1790, he is given in Hempfield Tp. Westmoreland Co., Pa.: 3 males over 16 years, including self; wife and one daughter. Census 1800 Derry Tp., same county :males under 10 years, 3; males between 10 to 16 years, 1; males 16-26 years 1; females of 26 and under 45, 1; females over 45, 1. The census of 1790 shows he had then 2 sons, 16 or over, therefore married by 1772-3 If age of wife, Nancy Ogle, is correct and Census 1790 correct, then he must have married twice as Nancy Ogle born 1758 would have only been 15 years old in 1773. Census of 1800 shows that enumerator had either put Thomas' age wrong or left him out as item shows in census males over 45, none. Dr. Geo. Culbertson of Greensburg, Pa. in 1892 wrote me that he was buried in cemetery of Unity Presbyterian Church, near Latrobe, Pa., and that he died Aug. 12, 1823, aged 69 years. Nancy, his wife, died Feb. 18, 1838, aged 80 years. In the first letter he said he had written the minister of Unity Church who had not replied, and Dr. George in a later letter gave above dates and did not state whether he had gotten them from tombstone. Made his will Aug. 19, 1819. His grand-son, Thos. of Nankin, Ashland Co., O., in 1892 wrote me that Thos., Sr., married Miss Nancy Ogle of near Wilmington, Delaware.

Examination of records of Unity Church recently and of tombstones there fails to reveal name of Thomas Culbertson or his wife.

Issue:

1. Alexander, b. 1788; d. 1852.
2. Moses, d.
3. Thomas, b. 1793; d. 1838. Wheelwright and teacher..
4. Margaret, b. ——; d. —— (Mrs. John Thorn).
5. Anna, b. ——; d. Feb. 14, 1864. (Mrs. J. Bell).
6. Elizabeth, b. ——; d. —— (Mrs. W. Bell).

FOURTH GENERATION

(1) Alexander Culbertson mar. Miss Livinia Sloan. Lived in Unity Tp., Westmoreland Co., Pa.,where he died.

Issue:

7. Thomas, b.
8. John, b. ——; d. ——; No heirs. Married Mariah ——.
9. Alexander, Jr., b. 1819; d. 1871.
10. James, d.
11. Jane. (Mrs. Clark).
12. Lucy. (Mrs. Anstraw).
13. Lavinia, b. ——; d. May 5, 1852. Unmar.
14. George, b. ——; d. May 18, 1849. No issue.

(2) Moses Culbertson mar. Jane Dunlap. No issue. Moved to Wayne Co., Ohio.

(3) Thomas Culbertson mar. Elizabeth Craig of Westmoreland Co., Pa. Lived in Westmoreland Co., Pa., Derry Tp. (Wheelwright and school teacher).

Issue:

15. Franklin, b. ——; d. 1853. Derry Tp., Westmoreland Co. Pa.
16. George W., Nankin, Ashland Co., Ohio.
17. Joseph C., b. ——; d. 1852.
18. Nancy, b. ——; d. ——.
19. Elizabeth, b. ——; d. ——.
20. Margaret, b.. ——; d. ——. Unmar.

(4) Margaret Culbertson mar. John Thorn.

Issue:

21. Craig Thorn. Clarion Co., Pa.
22. Culbertson Thorn (Rev.), St. Louis, Mo.
23. Elizabeth Thorn (Mrs. Thompson).
24. Livinia (Mrs. Donaldson).

(5) Anna Culbertson mar. James Bell, of Westmoreland Co., Pa.

Issue:

25. Nancy Bell. Unmar. Lives near Latrobe, Pa.
26. Eliza J., d. single, Feb. 6, 1859.
27. John, d. single, Dec. 5, 1852.
28. Maria, d. single Nov. 10, 1852.
29. Milton H., d. Jan. 7, 1851 (single) at Canonsburg College, Pa.
30. Columbus Bell, d. Aug. 1874. Banker at Blairsville.
31. Lavinia (Mrs. McLaughlin). Latrobe, Pa.
32. Annie M., d. 1869. (Mrs. Bott).
33. Alexander Culbertson. New Alexandra, Pa.

(6) Elizabeth Culbertson mar. Walter Bell of Westmoreland Co., Pa. Later moved to Indiana Co., Pa.

Issue:

34. Thomas Bell, Miller (Black Lick, Indiana Co., Pa.).
35. Jackson, d. 1892. Black Jack, Douglas Co., Kan. Was a guide and scout on plains; served in Rebellion, and was a captain.
36. Martha (Mrs. Geo. Stauffer).
37. Julia (Mrs. Raugh).
38. —— (Mrs. Moorehead).
39. Moses, d. single.
40. James, d. single.
41. Walter Bell (M. D.), d. Altoona, Pa. Issue: Fred, Chas., Walter, Ralph.
42. John. Lives near Black Lick, Pa.

FIFTH GENERATION

(9) Alexander Culbertson, Jr., mar. Amanda Giffin, of Greensburg, Pa.

Issue:

43. Edward, b. June 8, 1845.
44. Evaline, b. July 10, 1847; d. May 22, 1851.
45. Lavinia, mar. Mr. Hershay. Issue: dau. Mrs. Alex. McConnell, Greensburg, Pa.

46. Mary (Mrs. P. M. Hill). Issue: Craig Hill, married.
47. Giffin.
48. George, dentist.
49. Ella, d. Mar. 24, 1871, aet 4 years.
50. Alexander J., Bassano, Alberta, Canada. Mar.——.
    Issue:
51. William, d. infancy.

(10) James Culbertson mar. Lived in Mt. Pleasant Tp.
in 1849, Westmoreland Co., Pa.
Issue:
52. Albert.
53. Alex., d.
54. Ella. Unmar.
55. Elizabeth. Unmar.

(11) Jane Culbertson mar. Mr. Clark. Know nothing
about.

(12) Lucy Culbertson mar. Mr. Anstraw. No issue.

(15) Franklyn Culbertson mar. Narcissa Craig of Westmoreland Co., Pa. Wife living at Mt. Vernon, Ohio (1892).
Issue:
56. Thomas, d. 1877, unmar. Attorney Mt. Vernon.
57. W. C. Mt. Vernon, Ohio.

(16) George W. Culbertson mar. Rosannah Goodman.
Lives at Nankin, Ashland Co., O. Moved from Westmoreland Co., Pa., to Ohio in 1856. Served in Ohio Vols. in the
Rebellion.
Issue:
58. Thomas.
59. Sloan.
60. Margaret.
61. Della.
62. James.

(17) Joseph Culbertson mar. Martha Waugh.
Issue:
63. Joseph. Lived at Tarkio, Mo.

(18) Nancy Culbertson mar. Alex. Nelson.
Issue:
64. Margaret Nelson, d.
65. Thomas Nelson,. d.

(19) Elizabeth Culbertson mar. Hunter Corbett and they
went to China as missionaries.

Issue:
66. Fannie Corbett. Lives in China.
67. Merlie, drowned.
68. Bessie. Clarion Co., Pa.
69. Ross.

SIXTH GENERATION

(43) Edward Culbertson mar. Cynthia Newman(?) first wife now living, at Park Dale, Oregon.
Issue:
70. Ella G.
71. Emma J.
72. Mary A.
73. Thomas Alexander.
74. Todd Baird.

(45) Lavinia Culbertson mar. Mr. Hershey of Greensburg, Pa.

(46) Mary Culbertson mar. P. M. Hill of Greensburg, Pa.

(47) Giffin Culbertson mar. Margaret Hope. Lives at Long Island, Kan.
Issue:
75. Lloyd (married). Lives at Long Island, Kan.

(48) Dr. George Culbertson mar. Sarah Jane Smith. Dentist, Greensburg,. Pa. Later of Emporia, Kan. (both deceased.)
Issue:
76. William S., b. Aug. 5, 1884. Washington, D. C.
77. Alexander Edward, b. Jan. 19, 1888.
78. Robert Hill, b. Jan. 31, 1890; d. June 20, 1900.
79. George Giffin, b. Oct. 23, 1892.
80. Paul Trauger, b. Apr. 11, 1897 (Unmar.).

(52) Albert Culbertson mar. in 1871 to Fannie Moats. Lives at Washington, D. C. Wealthy oil producer.
Issue:
81. Mary (Mrs. J. S. Brothers of Oil City Pa.).
82. J. W. Culbertson, Wichita Falls, Tex. Oil Producer.
83. J. G. Culbertson, Wichita Falls, Tex. Oil Producer.
84. H. J. Culbertson, Tulsa,. Okla. Oil Producer.
85. O. H. Culbertson, Clarion, Pa.

(58) Thomas Culbertson mar. first Elizabeth Cole. Wife died.
Issue:

86.   Jennie, d. young.
87.   Harry, d. young.

(58) Thomas Culbertson mar. second, Helen Cook.
Issue:
88.   Grace.

(31) Della Culbertson mar. S. D. Umbaugh.
Issue:
89.   Bessie May.

SEVENTH GENERATION

(76) William S. Culbertson mar. Dec. 28, 1911, to Mary
J. Hunter of Pratt, Kan.
Issue:
90.   Junia Wilhelmina, b. Dec. 9, 1912. Washington, D. C.
91.   Margaret Jane,. b. Dec. 16, 1914.

(77) Alexander Edward Culbertson mar. Vivian Hedlund.
Live at Pasadena, Calif.
Issue:
92.   Ruth Jane.

(79) George Giffin Culbertson mar. Florence Braming.
Issue:
93.   Robert Braming.
94.   Vivian Eunice.

PROMINENT DESCENDANTS OF THOMAS (I)

(9) Alexander Culbertson, Jr., was educated for the ministry.   When a young man, in 1840, he made a trip to the
Falls of St. Anthony, Wis., for his health.   Made a trip by
boat and kept a journal of his travels.   This journal is very
interesting.   I have read other letters written by him,
which show that he was a man of great intellect and of a
poetical temperament.

(50) Alexander J., is a prominent citizen of Washington,
Pa.

(21) Rev. Alexander Thorn was a prominent Presbyterian minister of one of the largest churches in St. Louis,
Mo., where he received a salary of $5,000.

(57) Wm. C. Culbertson is a prominent attorney at Mt.
Vernon, Ohio.

(52) Albert Culbertson, millionaire oil producer, Washington, D. C.

(48) Dr. George Culbertson was a prominent and skillful
dentist of Greensburg, Pa. For many years he here practiced
his profession of dentist and where all their children were
born. He moved in 1897 to Phillips County, Kansas, and for
a number of years engaged in cattle raising and farming. In
1902 he moved to Emporia, Kansas, where he lived until
his death. He was a trustee of the College of Emporia (Kansas) from June, 1903, to the time of his death. During this
time he served as treasurer of the College for three years,
from June, 1906, to June, 1909. His wife was a daughter of
William Smith, born in 1820 and died Sept. 3, 1877. His
son (80) Paul Trauger Culbertson was eighteen months in
service overseas (World war) with A. E. F. Decorated with
French Croix de Guerre. Is now a senior at Yale College.
From Who's Who in America, 1922-23:

(76) "Culbertson, William Smith, lawyer, tariff com-
mr.; b. Greensburg, Pa., Aug. 5, 1884; s. George and Jennie
(Smith) C.; A. B., Coll. of Emporia, Kan. 1907; A. B., Yale,
1908, Ph. D:, 1911; special studies Univs. of Leipzig and
Berlin; (LL. D., College of Emporia, 1918); m. Mary J. Hunter, of Pratt, Kan., Dec. 28, 1911. Examiner for U. S.
Tariff Bd., 1910-12, and prepared 1st vol. of its report on
the wool tariff, entitled, "Glossary on Schedule K"; practiced law in Washington, D. C., 1812-15; mem. McLanahan,
Burton & Culbertson, 1914-15; rep. Federal Trade Commn.,
studying trade conditions and the tariffs in Brazil Uruguay,
Argentina, Ch.ile, Peru and Panama, 1915-16; spl. counsel
and memb. Bd. of Review of Federal Trade Commn, 1916-
17; mem. U. S. Tariff Commn. since March 23, 1917, by
appt. of President Wilson and reapptmt for term of 12 yrs.
beginning Mar., 1921, by President Harding, v. chmn, since
Jan. 15, 1922. Overseas sec. Y. M. C. A., 1918, Mem. of
exec. faculty and lecturer* on commercial treaties and policies,. Georgetown University, Sch. of Foreign Service, Oct.
1919; chmn Economic Liaison Com. U. S. Govt., 1921—;
tech. adviser in charge of economic questions, Am. Delega-
tion, Conf. on Limitation of Armament, 1921. Capt. U. S. A.
R. C. Republican. Presbyn. Mem. Am. Econ. Assn., Phi
Beta Kappa, Phi Alpha Delta, Delta Phi Epsilon (natl.
pres., 1922). Clubs: Cosmos (Washington, D. C.); Chevy
Chase Club (Washington, D. C.); Current (Emporia, Kan.);

*Since this was published was chairman of the round table on
International Commercial Policies, Institute of Politics, Williams-
town, Mass., summer of 1922.

Rotary. Author: Alexander Hamilton, an Essay, 1911; Commercial Policy in War Time and After, 1919. Contbr. to mags. Home: Emporia, Kan. Address U. S. Tariff Commission, Washington, D. C.

CHAPTER XXXVIII

THIRD GENERATION

(II) Robert Culbertson, son of Robert of New Castle, Co., Del. Census 1790 Westmoreland Co., Pa., Hempfield Tp., gives him with 3 sons under 16; wife. Census 1800 gives him with 2 more sons and 2 daughters in Salem Tp., Westmoreland Co. His age given under 45, wife under 45. Bought farm Salem Tp., Westmoreland Co., Pa., in 1798 (Deeds). He sold his farm in 1816 and bought a farm in Allegheny Tp., same county, .where he died in 1835. Mar. first ——. Issue: Obtained from deeds and administration. His son, Robert Barton Culbertson, of Hart Co., Ky., was evidently his eldest son, born 1783. The middle name being Barton, shows he was named after his step-grandfather. "Robert Culbertson appears on the rolls for Delaware Militia among those who presented vouchers for payment for services June 9, 1778 and Nov. 16, 1779 respectively. Services not given" (Del. Arch. Vol. II). Moved from Delaware to Westmoreland Co., Pa., 1786-7.

(II) Robert Culbertson mar. first ——.
Issue:
1. Robert Barton, b. 1783; d. Oct. 3, 1865.
2. Alexander b. 1788; d. 1848.
3. Elizabeth (Mrs. Thos. Campbell).
4. Son, d. young.

(II) Robert Culbertson mar. second Mary ——.
Issue:
5. David.
6. Thomas.
7. Margaret.
8. Nancy.

FOURTH GENERATION

(1) Robert Barton Culbertson. I was informed in 1892 by descendants of his brother Alex. that he had moved to

near Mammoth Cave, Ky. A letter in 1922 from Robert's descendants in Kansas enabled me to trace out Robert's history. A grandson in 1922 says that Robert B. when he (Wm. B.) was a child told him of Culbertson Row and about Zanesville and a David Culbertson and a sister, Mrs. Campbell, near Zanesville. Says that Robert B. not liking his stepmother ran away from home as did his sister (Elizabeth) and they lived near Zanesville, O. (This was evidently with his brother Alex. who came to Zanesville in 1810). That Robert B. first went to the Carolina's and later went to probably Christian Co., Ky. Christian Co. records do not show him. He later moved to Hart Co., Ky (this adjoins the county in which is located Mammoth Cave). There he married Elizabeth Cook, an English girl. He must have been twenty-seven years of age by that time (after 1810) and settled on the Green River. He died in Hart Co., Ky., aged 82 years.

Issue:

9. Theodore, b. Nov. 9, 1819,. died in Mexican War 1846. Unmar.
10. Harriet M. A., b. Mar. 30, 1821, d. infancy.
11. William A., b. Sept. 16, 1824,. was in Mex. War; later returned to Ky., and was in Civil War. Unmar.
12. Emeline, b. May 21, 1826, d. Dec. 28, 1826.
13. Rachel, b. June 30, 1828; d. infancy.
14. Joseph, b. June 18, 1830; d. Nov. 13, 1906.
15. Robert Emmett, b. July 2, 1832; d. Nov. 19, 1906. Born Hart Co., Ky.
16. Clarissa Jane, b. June 21, 1834; d. infancy. b. Hart Co., Ky.
17. James Alexander, b. Nov. 2. 1836; Killed in battle in Tenn., Civil War. Born Hart Co., Ky.
18. Sarah Ann, b. Nov. 7, 1838; d. a few years ago in Ky. Unmar.
19. Mary Elizabeth, b. July, 1840; d. Mar. 24, 1917 in Ky. Unmar.
20. Hester, b. Apr. 3, 1843; d. infancy.

(2) Alexander Culbertson mar. Alcey Mason, of Muskingum Co., Ohio., Sept. 8, 1814. He moved to Falls Tp., Muskingum Co., Ohio, in 1810 and lived on the National Pike, three miles from Zanesville where he owned a farm and grist mill. Release signed by them 1836 Alexander and wife Alcey, of Muskingum Co., Ohio.   e

Issue:

21. David M., d.

22. Lewis, d.
23. Aurelius, b. 1819; d. 1908.
24. Edwin.
25. Eliza Jane, d.

(3) Elizabeth Culbertson mar. Mr. Thomas Campbell, of Morgan Co., O. Know nothing of issue. She and her husband signed release in their father's estate in Jan., 1836. States "living in Ohio."

(5) David Culbertson moved to Perry Co., O., and lived there three years; then moved to Columbiana Co., O. He lived in Columbiana Co., O., in July, 1835, as Deed Records show. He still lived there in 1852, but did not die in Columbiana Co., as Will and Administration Records show. He signed a release in 1836. His half-brother, Robert B., did not sign this release in their father's estate. The probabilities are they did not know his whereabouts at that time.
Issue:
Mary. Know nothing as to the other issue.

(6) Thomas not mentioned on release in 1835. Most likely dead.

FIFTH GENERATION

(14) Joseph Culbertson mar. May 4, 1855, to Laura S. Patton (b. Apr. 26, 1831; d. Dec. 5, 1885). Moved to Iola,. Kan., then to Springfield, Ills., and back to Iola.
Issue:
27. William Byron, b. Apr. 21, 1858, at Springfield, Ills.
28. James Alexander b. Mar. 4, 1864; d. Sept. 15, 1892. Unmar. Iola, Kan.
29. Elizabeth Margaret, b. Oct. 4, 1866 in Hart Co., Ky.; d. Mar. 1892, Pasadena, Cal.
30. Richard T., b. Aug. 4, 1868; d. Feb. 17, 1869. Ky.
31. Claude Simpson, b. Feb. 20, 1870 in Ky.
32. Robert Emmett, b. Oct. 12, 1871 in Ky.; d. Dec. 17, 1915, in New Mexico.

(15) Robert Emmett Culbertson mar. June 9, 1861, to Fidelia Ellen Smith (wife b. Nov. 3, 1842). Living Rose, Kan.
Issue:
33. M. J. Alice, b. Mar. 8, 1862; d. Jan 1893. Mar. at Humboldt, Kan. to Robert Crook. Issue: Beulah Clara Crook, b. Apr. 8, 1890.. Mar. to Walter Cox, Lees Summit, Mo. Issue: Homer Clarence Crook, b. Sept. 30, 1883, mar. and lives at Iola, Kan.

34. James B., b. July 28, 1863; d. Mar. 7, 1884. Unmar.
35. Anna, b. Feb. 1865; d. infancy.
36. George W., b. Sep. 21, 1868 at Humboldt, Kan.
37. Sherman, b. May 3, 1875; born Oakland, Ore.
38. Harry Emmet, b. June 23, 1877. Oakland, Ore.
39. Elizabeth, b. May 5, 1882; d. Sep. 10, 1883.

(21) David M. Culbertson mar. Sept. 26, 1839, first Miss Woodside. No issue. Mar. second, Sarah Sypes.
Issue:
40. Samuel.
41. Mary.

(22) Lewis Culbertson mar. Jane Galigher.
Issue:
42. Alexander.
43. Ida, d.

(23) Aurelius Culbertson mar. Margaret Galigher. Lived on farm in Falls Tp., Muskingum Co., O., until ——, when he moved to Chariton, Ia., where he resided on his farm (1892). Wife b. 1822; d. 1900.
Issue:
44. John.
45. Louis Alexander.
46. Howard.
47. Alsia Jane.
48. Sarah, b. 1855.
49. Mary Adelaide, d.
50. Martha Elizabeth.
51. James William, d. Jan. 30, 1905.
52. Izette Dare.

(24) Edwin Culbertson mar. Caroline James. Moved to Falls Tp., Muskingum Co., O., to Iowa, and later to Freeman, Cass Co., Mo.
Issue:

53. Mary (Mrs. Henderson Halloway).
54. Rosilla (Mrs. Geo. Marvin; 2nd G. M. Wright).
55. Lewis, mar. Mary Turner.
56. Robert. Farmer. Mar. Sarah Jetton.
57. Charles. Farmer. Mar. Ella Thomas.
58. John. Farmer. Mar. Dessie Longeor.
59. George. Unmarried..
60. William. Unmarried.
61. Etta. Unmarried.

(25) Eliza Jane mar. Chas. Johnson of Falls Tp., Muskingum Co., O. Family now at White Cottage, Muskingum Co., O.

Issue:

62. James Theodore, d. Jan., 1877.
63. Robert A., Martinsville, Ill.
64. John F., White Cottage, O.
65. Wm. E., White Cottage, O.
66. Louis A., White Cottage, O.
67. Rosswell M., White Cottage, O.
68. Sadie (Mrs. S. H. Allen), White Cottage, O.

SIXTH GENERATION

(27) Wm. Byron Culbertson mar. Oct. 11, 1883, to Adda McGee at Iola, Kan. (b. Aug. 11, 1861). Lives Scott City, Kan.

Issue:

69. Mary L., b. Aug. 26, 1884, at Yates Center, Kan. Living Kansas City, Mo. Unmarried.
70. Lena, b. May 4, 1887. Larned, Kansas. Unmarried.
71. Lulu, b. Dec. 19, 1889 at Larned, Kansas. Mar. Ross A. Stewart. Live Dallas, Texas.

(31) Claude Simpson Culbertson mar. Maude Holden, June, 1901. Lives at Seattle, Wash.

Issue:

72. Ruth, b. Sept. 5, 1905.
73. Robert Emmett, b. June, 1909.

(36) George W. Culbertson mar. Apr. 26, 1911, to Ida Geddes of Humboldt, Kan. Live at Iola, Kan.

Issue:

74. Velma Pearl, b. Jan. 2, 1914.
75. Vincent, b. Dec. 15, 1916.
76. George Kenneth, b. Dec. 15, 1921.

(37) Sherman Culbertson mar. Leila Foushee at Newton, Kan., Jan. 14, 1904. Lives Wichita, Kan.

Issue:

77. Roberta E., b. June 11, 1909.
78. Sherman, Jr., b. June 13, 1916.

(38) Harry Emmet Culbertson mar. Nov. 22, 1897, at Emporia, Kan., to Almira L. Galutia. Lives Emporia, Kan.

Issue:

79. Roy Lee, b. Nov. 19, 1898; d. Aug. 2, 1900. Born at Humboldt, Kan

80. Jesse Ray, b. June 9, 1900., Born at Humboldt,. Kan.
81. Melvin Edward, b. Apr. 1, 1903. Born at Humboldt, Kan.
82. Viola Leota, b. Apr. 12, 1912. Born at Medina, Kan.
83. Leda Fidelia, b. Sep. 30, 1914. Born at Emporia Kan.

(40) Samuel Culbertson mar. ——. Lived at Newark, O. Not there now. Know nothing of issue.

(41) Mary Culbertson mar. R. Mitchell of Norwalk, O. Doesn't live there now. Know nothing of issue.

(42) Alexander Culbertson, lives at Pleasantville, Ia.

(44) John Culbertson. A banker at Chariton, Ia. in 1892. Mar. first Angie Irwin. Wife died.
Issue:
84. Lee I. (Married Miss Ida Reece. Issue: 118, Robert; 119, John. Live at Spokane, Wash.
85. Edward A. (mar. Florence Helen Doyle. Issue: 120, Ralph. Live at Salt Lake City, Utah. Banker.).
86. Angie (Mrs. A. L. Champlin). Issue: 121, Lewis Champlin.

(44) John Culbertson mar. second Clara Hollinger.
Issue:
86½. Charles Calvin, unmar. Prof in Agriculture College, Ames, Ia.

(47) Alsia Culbertson mar. James Alexander. Live at Chico, Calif.
Issue:
87. William.
88. Maggie.
89. Ralph.
90. Harry.
91. Louis.
92. Mary.
93. Coral
94. Andrew.
95. Etta.
96. Lizzie.

(45) Louis A. Culbertson mar. Ida Barnes, dau. of Hon. T. H. Barnes, M. D., of Waukon, Ia., Oct. 1883. Provo, Utah.
Issue:
97. Mary,. b. 1885.
98. Howard, d. young.

99. Lulu, b. 1889.
100. Benjamin Ely, b. 1891.

(46) Howard Culbertson mar. ——. Lives at Chariton, Ia.
Issue:
101. Joseph B.
102. Nellie.
103. Francis.
104. Ralph.

(48) Sarah Culbertson mar. Geo. Champlin of Derby, Ia. in 1873. Living at Chariton, Ia.
Issue:
105. Albert Louis, lives Ames, Ia., b. 1874, mar. Angie Culbertson 1906.
106. George, b. 1876. Unmar.
107. John Champlin, b. 1877. Red Deer, Alberta. Mar. Anna Smith, 1902.
108. Inez, b. 1878, mar. John H. Conner, 1899.
109. Mary F., b. 1880, mar. Gene Wright 1902.
110. Dr. Howard W., b. 1884; mar. Jean Mullen 1913. Chicago, Ill.
111. Mabel, b. 1886. Unmar. Ames, Ia.
112. Eleanor, b. 1887, mar. Clell H. Fulton of Derby, Ia., in 1920.
113. Florence, b. 1889, mar. Orrin McGinnis, 1916. Waterloo, Ia.
113½. Ada, b. 1892. Unmar. Chariton, Ia.

(50) Elizabeth Culbertson mar. Jesse Snedaker of Mt. Ayr, Ia.
Issue:
114. Mabel Izette, b. Oct. 31, 1888.
115. Howard Evarts, b. Nov. 29, 1890.

(51) James W. Culbertson mar. Hattie Patterson. Wife died Oct. 28, 1919. Lived at Chariton, Ia.
Issue:
116. Charles H. (mar. Florence Darner, Oct., 1907).
116½. Leonard C., d. June 30, 1904.
117. Fred A., d. Oct. 9, 1918, on board ship Geo. Washington. Member of Med. Dept. 605th Engineers
118. Mae (mar. William M. Osler, Jan. 15, 1920. Live at Chariton, Ia.).

(52) Izetta Dare Culbertson mar. —— Granville. Live at Chariton, Ia.

PROMINENT DESCENDANTS OF (II) ROBERT CULBERTSON

(44) John Culbertson of Chariton, Ia., is a prominent citizen and banker of that place.

(85) Edward A. Culbertson graduated Parsons, Col., Fairfield, Ia., 1902; has been in banking business Salt Lake City for past twenty years with the Nat'l Bank of the Republic, being President of that bank when the Continental National Bank consolidated with the National Bank of the Republic. Since the consolidation he has been Vice-President of The Continental Bank of Salt Lake City.

CHAPTER XXXIX

(III) Alexander Culbertson bought land of Alex. Guthrie of Delaware in 1787 in Hempfield Tp., Westmoreland Co., Pa. He sold part of this in 1807 to Thomas Culbertson of Derry Tp., and balance of land in Westmoreland Co. in 1813. Wife's name Ruth, moved to Wayne Co., Ohio, in 1813-14. Family records say he moved to Millbrook, Wayne Co., Ohio. His son stated in 1855 that his father was in the Revolution. Could find no Revolutionary service for him in Del. Arch. His will was made in 1830, died in 1833 in Plain Tp., Wayne Co., Ohio. It is my opinion that Alexander left New Castle Co., Del. in 1778; went to Cumberland Co., Pa. I find an Alexander Culbertson was "taxed in 1782-3 in Newton Tp., Cumb. Co., Pa. with one horse and one cow—Trade 5." This township abutted Teboyne and probably formed from it. It is my opinion that this Alexander was the Alexander Culbertson who "served in Capt. Noah Abraham's Co., 8th Batt'n, Col. James Johnson, Aug. 10, 1780." (Vol. 23, 3 Ser., p. 699 Pa. Arch.)* No further record is found of him in Cumb. Co. after 1783. He evidently was only a renter in this county. After 1775 he does not appear on records of New Castle Co., Del., although Thomas appears there in 1786. Does not appear on Deed Records of Westmoreland Co. until 1787. There were absolutely only three Alexander Culbertsons of military age in 1780 in Cumb. Co., Pa. Alexander is given in 1790 Census, male over 16 (self) one, males under 16 three,. females wife and 2 daughters (Westmoreland Co.) Census 1800 gives Alex's

---

*McCauley's Hist. Franklin Co., Pa., says, "Noah Abraham and his Co. was from Path Valley. (Newton Tp. adjoins their section.)

age between 26 and 45. Wife ditto. Had five more children than he had in 1790. Residence Derry Tp. Probably married about 1780. Could not give names of other children. They must have died young as they are not mentioned in his will. Married Ruth——. Tax lists Westmoreland Co. 1776-1800 Lost.

THIRD GENERATION

Issue: (From will dated Aug. 30, 1830. Prob. 1833. Final acct. 1835 at Wooster, Ohio).
1. Robert, b. ——; d. Feb. 25, 1815.
2. Thomas, d. Feb. 25, 1815. Coshocton Co., Ohio.
3. John. Probably died single Wayne Co., Ohio
4. Alexander, b. about 1800.
5. Sarah (Mrs. Jones) Auburn, Ind.
6. Ruth (Mrs. Hague), Auburn, Ind.

Note: Alexander, Sr., according to his son, Alexander, made a statement in 1855 "that his father served with the Cumb. Co., Pa. troops and that he had received a certificate from the Auditor General of Penna., that the state had allowed him £6, 10s. for military services in the Revolution."

FOURTH GENERATION

(1) Robert Culbertson moved in 1812 to Coshocton Co., Ohio, and settled on the right bank of the Tuscarawas River, on White Eyes Plains, four miles from Coshocton, O. Mar. Nov. 17, 1808 to Mary Peoples of Westmoreland Co., Pa., dau. of John Peoples. Robert was in Capt. Adam Johnston's Co., of Ohio Militia in War of 1812. After Robert's death Feb. 25, 1815, his widow remarried to a Mr. Henderson and later becoming a widow, remarried to a Mr. Jones. Robert Culbertson and Mary Peoples, wife died Story Co., Iowa.

Issue:
7. Alexander, d. 1852. Coshocton Co., Ohio.
8. Robert, lived Auburn, Ind. Mar. Margaret Brown.
9. Wm. Peoples moved to Fulton Co., Ohio; b. Apr. 4, 1813; d. June 4, 1896.

9½. Jane (Mrs. Thos. F. Jones, Wayne Co., O.), d. about 1850.

(2) Thomas Culbertson died at Shreve, Wayne Co., Ohio. Married ——.

Issue:
10. Thomas.
11. Samuel (mar. Cousin Esther Culbertson).
12. —— (Mrs. Smith), Delaware, Ohio. (Issue: Thos.).
13. —— (Mrs. Harvey), Wayne Co., Ohio. (Issue: C. Harvey).
May have been others.

(4) Alexander,. lived south of Haysville, Ashland Co., O. Buried at Millbrook. Mar. Nancy Cahill.
Issue:
14. Abraham.
15. —— (Mrs. Shelly) Plain Tp., Wayne Co., O. May have been others.

FIFTH GENERATION

(7) Alexander Culbertson of Coshocton Co., O., mar. Elizabeth Wilson of the same county in 1829.
Issue:
16. Anna J. (Mrs. S. L. Waggoner, later Mrs. T. F. Jones).
17. Mary (Mrs. Lewis Fletcher).
18. Robert W. Served in Union Army.
19. Thomas W., Isleta, Coshocton Co., O. Mar. twice.
20. Margaret, d. 1859.
21. James H. Living in Ia. Served in Union Army.
22. David R., West Lafayette, Coshocton, Co., O. Served in Union Army.

(8) Robert Culbertson mar. Margaret Brown of Wayne Co., O., and moved to DeKalb, Ind.
Issue:
23. Zephaniah, killed in Battle of Shiloh.
24. Mary Jane (Mrs. Owen).
25. James.
26. Emily (Mrs. Welch) Issue: son. Remarried name not known.
27. Hugh. Lives at Auburn, Ind.

(9) William Peoples Culbertson mar. Sarah Jewell, Nov. 1836, in Wayne Co., Ohio. Later lived in Fulton Co., Ohio. (Wife b. Nov. 16, 1816, Wayne Co., O.; d. Apr. 12, 1856.)
Issue:
28. Benjamin Franklin, b. May 30, 1838; d. Jan. 16, 1909 Lived in Cleveland, Tenn. Mar. Issue: (Judge) Wm., dead; Cora (nurse) d.; Mae (teacher) dead.
29. Ithamar (had one adopted son, Glenn); b. Sep. 20, 1840; d. Oct. 1,. 1916.

30.   Enoch, b. May 8, 1842; d. Jan. 3, 1875.

31.   Merilla, d. infancy; b. Dec. 6, 1843; d. Nov. 12, 1844.

31½. Orville, b. Aug. 18, 1845; d. Apr., 1872.

32.   Mary R. (Mrs. R. C. Hood, Joplin, Mo.). Mar. DeWitt C. Hood in Iowa, 1881. Issue: a, Margaret May mar. John Gilbert Robbins of Washington, D. C.; b, Olive Belle mar. A. J. Dearing of Joplin, Mo. Issue: b, Olive Eleanor, Clint E., Joplin, Mo.

33.   Wm. Newton Culbertson died 1911 in Colorado and left a widow. He was born Feb. 2, 1850. Issue: 2 children dead and 9 living.

34.   Sarah Jane Woolson, b. May 22, 1853; d. Feb. 6, 1920. Mar. Wm. Allen. Issue: several sons, prominent men living near Mt. Vernon, Ohio.

(9) William Peoples Culbertson mar. second Ann Pocock Robinett of Shreve, Ohio, Jan. 6, 1867. (Wife b. Jan. 6, 1826; d. near Pettisville, O., April 13, 1893.)

Issue:

34¼. Harriet Ellen (mar. John P. Braughton, Sep. 25, 1888. Issue: a, Minnie Maud Braughton, who mar. Arthur Gossuch and had issue: Wm.; Warren; Gene; b, Vera Agnes mar. Wm. McDermott, Feb. 22, 1913, and had issue: Eileen, Betty).

(9½) Jane Culbertson mar. Thos. F. Jones of Wayne Co., O. Lived at Shreve, O.

Issue:

35.   Richard, 36, George; 37, Margaret; 38, Esther; 39, Sallie b. Feb. 6, 1843; 40, 41, 42, 43, 44, 45.

SIXTH GENERATION.

(22) David R. Culbertson, mar. Mary E. Gordon. Lives at Columbus, O. Served in Civil War, Ohio. Vols.

Issue:

47.   Laura B. (Mrs. J. S. Norman), Seattle Wash. No issue.

48.   H. E.

49.   Harry A. No issue.

50.   Nellie M. (Mrs. Will Williams).

51.   Roland R.

52.   Helen (Mrs. Will Mulvane).

(28) Benjamin Franklin Culbertson, mar. Ella E. ——; widow living at Cleveland, Tenn.

Issue:

53.   William (Judge) d.

54.   Cora, d.

55.   Mae, d.

SEVENTH GENERATION

(39) Sarah S. Jones born at Shreve, O. Mar. in 1860 to Pierson Brown, who was killed in the Civil War in 1862.
Issue:
56. Mary, deceased.

(39) Sarah S. Jones mar. second Thomas Benton Hammond, who died in 1880 at Meadville, Pa.
Issue:
57. Maud L. (Mrs. Chas. J. Swift,. Cleveland, O.) Issue: Alice S. Warner; Marion Hammond, deceased.
58. Ralph Keeler, mar. Kate Leete of Barberton, O. Issue: Fred, Ruth E., Benton Ives.
59. Grace, married Arthur Holmes of Ypsalanti, Mich. Now living at Canton, O.

(48) H. E. Culbertson mar. Henrietta Foster. Live at Cleveland, O. Was for a time a Civil Engineer on Penna R. R. and is now a prominent Highway Engineer and Contractor.
Issue:
60. Florence L. (Mrs. S. A. Frolking), Cleveland, O.
61. Mary Jane. Unmar.

(50) Nellie M. Culbertson mar. Will Williams of New Comerstown, Ohio.
Issue:
62. Dorothy Williams.
63. Francis.
64. David.

(51) Roland R. Culbertson lives at Cleveland, Ohio.
Issue:
65. Donald.
66. Jean.
67. Roland.

(52) Helen Culbertson mar. Will Mulvane of New comerstown, O.
Issue:
68. Beatrice Mulvane.
69. Mary.
70. Myron.

(53) Judge William Culbertson mar. ———.
Issue:
71. Harry Floyd, b. Aug. 15, 1897. Was Capt. of officers' boat, Bonsecour, 1918, in World War.

PART SECOND

OF SECTION THIRD

(K. K.) John Culbertson of St. George's Hundred, Delaware.

PART SECOND

(K. K.) JOHN CULBERTSON OF ST. GEORGES AND PENCADER HUNDRED, NEW CASTLE CO., DEL.

John Culbertson, present at Old Drawers Church, 1748, owned property in St. Georges and Pencader Hundreds, New Castle Co., Del., deceased before May 19, 1763. Wife Elizabeth Culbertson, mentioned Orphans' Court Records, Wilmington, New Castle Co., Del., Book D, Vol. 1, page 322, 1772, children 9.

Deed Book U-1-457, Thomas Dunn, Sheriff to John Culbertson of Pancader Tp., New Castle County, Del., one hundred acres adjoining John Culbertson's land. Land deeded belonging to E. David. Date of Deed, November 18th, 1762.

The following records were examined by F. E. Kempton at Wilmington, Delaware, in 1920.

Orphan's Court, Wilmington, Newcastle County, Delaware

	Book	Vol.	Page	Year
Culbertson, John, choseth a guardian	D	1	83	1763
Culbertson, John, order for annual valuation of father's estate....	D	1	167	1765
Culbertson, John, order for settlement of father's estate............	D	1	174	1767
Culbertson, John, return of annual valuation of estate, 2 farms, 4 parcels......................	D	1	177	1768
John Culbertson, Attch for administrator	D	1	211	1768
John Culbertson, Attch for administrator			213	1768
			222	1769
			230	
John Culbertson, annual return of valuation	D	1	316	1771
John Culbertson, settlement of estate	D	1	322	1771
John Culbertson, settlement of estate	D	1	323	1772
			336	1772
John Culbertson, order to lay one-third of his estate, order court	D	1	402	1773

			416	1773
			445	1773
			478	1773
			479	1773
			498	1773
Order to divide estate	D	1	511	1774
Order for petition cont'd	D	1	526	1774
Orderfor petition cont'd	E	1	2	1775
Order for petition cont'd	E	1	13	
			18	
		•	41	
			54	
			68	1775

SECOND GENERATION

   I. **Robert,** eldest son who died without issue prior to 1773. (Chapter XL).
  II. **William,** wife Ann was living on father's plantation in Pencader Hundred, 1771. Supposedly our ancestor (Chapter XLI).
 III. **John** (probably born Jan. 10, 1748) 15 years old, Jan. 10, 1763 from Record D 1 page 323. (Chapter XLII).
  IV. **Mary** choseth a guardian April 21, 1767, also mentioned in 1772 (XLIII).
   V. **Benjamin,** mentioned in record Jan. 21 and 22, 1772 (assessment sheets in St. Georges Hundred, 1794, and 1797 mentioned a Benjamin Culbertson). Census 1800 Newcastle Co., Del., page 262 Benjamin Culbertson, 8 in family (Chapter XLIV).
  VI. **Samuel** for whom John Hyatt was appointed guardian Oct. 17, 1771, and who later in same year chose another guardian (Chapter XLV).
 VII. **David,** John Hyatt appointed guardian Oct. 17, 1771. Census of 1790, Elk Neck Hundred, Cecil Co., Md., himself, wife, 1 boy under 16 and 2 girls. Census 1800, pages 234-237 Newcastle Co., Del., D. Culbertson, 6 in family (Chapter XLVI).
VIII. **Sarah,** mentioned as married to Wm. Flynn sometime prior to 1773 (Chapter XLVII).
  IX. **Jane,** John Hyatt appointed guardian Oct. 17, 1771. Later listed with same brothers as Jean (Chapter XLVIII).

Each of the families of the issue of John Culbertson of New Castle County, Del., that is the second generation will be referred to as follows: I. Robert, II, William, etc. If little or no information is at hand but one mention will be made of others. Taking the family of William, II William, the third generation will be referred to as a.1. Ann, a.2. David, a.3. Jean, etc. This method may not be adhered to closely for all generations but will be the general plan. Other references pertaining to this, some of which may have been included above are:

Culbertson, Jane (John Hyatt appointed guardian of Samuel, David, and Jane, children of John Culbertson, deceased)	D	1	314	1771
Culbertson, Samuel, choseth a guardian	D	1	322	1771
Culbertson, Samuel, et al ordered to valuation estate of John	D	1	406	1773
Culbertson, order court			433	1773
			466	1773
			476	1773
			482	1773
Culbertson, Mary, choseth a guardian				1767

Mary Culbertson also mentioned in a record, 1772.

Culbertson, Benjamin, mentioned in record Jan. 21, 22, 1772.

On page 332, D. 1772 Elizabeth Culbertson says that John Culbertson left a widow and 9 children, Robert the oldest, who since died without issue, John, Benjamin Samuel, David Mary, Sarah, married to Wm. Flynn and Jane.

You will note that she mentions only 8 but in these series of records, William is mentioned D. 1., 316, 1771, as living on the plantation situated in Pencader Hundred, which was valued at that time at £3 per acre, while the mansion plantations in St. George's Hundred was valued at £4 per acre.

Estates, Page 402, D. 1, 1773. Petition of Elizabeth Culbertson of St. Georges, widow of John Culbertson, 4 parcels of land with improvements, two of which lie together and contain 216½ acres of St. Georges Hundred, adjoining the lands of E. David, Thomas Hyatt and James James, deceased, and the other two parcels of land also lie together and contain 250 acres situated in Pencader Hundred, adjoining the lands of Richard Griffith, John Cazier, James James, Thomas David.

Left widow and 9 children. 1. Robert, eldest who is since

dead without issue. 2, John; 3, Benjamin; 4, Samuel; 5, David; 6, Mary; 7, Sarah, married to William Flynn and, 8, Jane. William, another son is not mentioned here, but in earlier references to John Culbertson's estate he is mentioned as living on his father's plantation in Pencader Hundred and later he deeds a part interest.

My uncle W. B. Elwood and myself, F. E. Kempton, visited at the same time Old Drawers Church, southwest of New Castle near Odessa, Del., we found a record mentioning John Culbertson as an attendant in 1748. We also visited various churches and cemeteries but found no other record of him and his family nor any grave stones.

My uncle found at Baltimore, Maryland, Historical Society in History of Holy Trinity (Old Swede's Church) of the marriage of a Wilmington, Del. Mary Culbertson on Sept. 15, 1794, to Michael Mueller at Holy Trinity (Old Swede's Church) Wilmington, Del. (While surmises are hazardous in this work). She may have been the daughter of John, mentioned by Elizabeth in the records of the settlement of the estate and who choseth a guardian in 1767. Of course she may not be that Mary as the first mentioned would no doubt be 42 years old in 1794 if she was 15 in 1767 for Delaware records indicate that guardians could be chosen at that age.

Note: Mr. Kempton has not discovered whether John Culbertson, Sr., came from Ireland or Scotland, nor has the Author, but it is my opinion and belief that they came from North Ireland. At this early date (1746) I have never found any Scotch Culbertsons or Cuthbertsons who emigrated direct to America, save the Cuthbertsons of Mecklenberg Co., N. Car., probably about 1765.

CHAPTER XL

(I) ROBERT CULBERTSON

Robert Culbertson, referred to in settlement of the estate of John Culbertson, New Castle County, Delaware, as being the son of John Culbertson, record of Orphans Court, Wilmington, New Castle Co., Delaware, Book D, Vol. 1, Page 332, 1772, Elizabeth Culbertson says that John Culbertson left a widow and 9 children, Robert, the oldest who is since dead without issue, etc.

CHAPTER XLI

(II) WILLIAM CULBERTSON.

William Culbertson. He was married and living on his father's plantation in Pencader Hundred, in 1771 (father, John Culbertson, mother, Elizabeth Culbertson). A number of references as to Revolutionary War activities of what appears to be 3 different William Culbertsons were examined. The only records which seems to apply to this William is as follows:

Captain Isaac Lewis' Company—Capt. Isaac Lewis, Lieut. David Howell. 60 names are given. John Culbertson, No. 36, William Culbertson No. 38.

I do hereby certify that the above and foregoing lists are the names of the officers and privates which were with me on the Expedition to Thorough Fair Neck and at the taking of the several vessels in Duck Creek, in Nov. 1777, which were afterwards libeled in my name and condemned as prizes and sold by James Booth, Esq., marshall of Admiralty for the Delaware State in the month of June, 1778 or thereabouts.

Witness my hand 4th Sept., 1789.

ISAAC LEWIS.

Other names appearing on this list are common in old records for Pencader and St. Georges Hundreds, Wilmington, New Castle Co., Del.

The name of William Culbertson has been inscribed along with that of his brother, John Culbertson, on a bronze tablet placed on the monument erected in Rocky Spring Church Cemetery near Chambersburg, Pa., to Culbertsons who served in the Revolutionary War and earlier wars.

As to the family affairs of Wm. Culbertson, I have the following which was procured by my uncle, W. B. Ellwood, Altovista, Virginia while. I·was procuring the records given for the family of John Culbertson. County records Newcastle Co., Wilmington, Del., Deed Book B, 2, 372, May 17, 1775. (It was not clear whether this was a mortgage or a deed).

(Record procured by Dr. L. R. Culbertson). William Culbertson and wife to James for two hundred pounds, a one-eighth interest in 204 acres in St. George's Hundred aforesaid land having been deeded by the Sheriff in 1762 to his father, John Culbertson. Also twelve acres in Pencader Hundred. Date of making deed, May 17, 1775. Witness

John Dodd and John Culbertson.

Note: Mr. Kempton says he could not find William's Will at Wilmington. I found this will and also have a full copy of same sent me by court official in 1892. It is found in Will Book No. M-1-219 New Castle Co., Del. Will made March 16, 1786; recorded Sept. 16, 1786. Devisees: Ann, John, David, Jean, William, Robert, Francis, Thomas. Wife Ann, executrix. Witnesses Jacob Cazier and Israel Ashton. Residence of Testator Pencader Hundred, New Castle Co., Del.—Editor.

From these records the following can no doubt be deduced: William Culbertson, father John Culbertson, mother Elizabeth Culbertson, wife Ann.

An obituary in the family of Robert Culbertson, the son of William, says that William Culbertson married Nancy Thorton, who was born on the Atlantic Ocean, of Scotch parents as her parents came to Delaware in 1757. The mother went to Bourbon County, Ky., about 1802; and that four sons raised families. (Nancy and Ann seems to have been used to designate the same person in different branches of this family.)

Note: The above referred obituary would corroborate the evidence that the John Culbertson who died in Clark Co., Ky., in 1807, was a son of William of Pencader Tp., New Castle, Co., Del.—Editor.

What is known of William Culbertson and of each of the generations of his children will be recorded, referring to these numbers as: 1. a., Ann; 2. b., John, etc.

(II) WILLIAM CULBERTSON CONT'D
THIRD GENERATION

(1. à.)   Ann, died young in Delaware, according to family rumor through the family of Robert Family 6. (Chapter XLIX).

(2. a.)   John, family rumor says he died without family. One cannot tell from records which applies to him and which to his uncle John who was in the Revolutionary war. Records of marriage licenses issued by Clerk of Cecil County, 1777. to 1840 give, John Culbertson to Sarah Foster, May 8, 1799, Rev. McCosden. These families will be referred to later. (Chapter L).

(3. a.) David records of Elkton, Md., show that on Dec. 21, 1800, he married Clarissa Brevard. Tax records Pen. Hun. Newcastle Co., Del. 1798 and 1801 give a David Culbertson. He is known to have moved to Clark Co., Ky by 1814, to Wayne Co., Ind., about 1820. Later to Grant Co., Ind., where he died. (Chapter LI).

(4. a.) Jean, married Frederick Ellsbury about 1797. Have been unable so far to locate the record of marriage; issue 7. He was killed at celebration of a victory of United States by explosion of a cannon. Later she married Samuel Chesnut, issue 4. (Chapter LII).

(5. a.) William, probably the one recorded as being in Delaware Militia, Third Co., Third Regiment, First Battalion, 1799, Middle District, St. George's Hundred. William Frazier, Captain. No further record. (Chapter LIII).

(6. a.) Robert, was born March 27, 1781, died May 13, 1875. Married Rebecca King, 1809, Ky., who was born Feb. 1, 1793,. and died July 18, 1857. Issue 13 children. Census 1810, Bourbon Co., Ky. Page 93. (Chapter LIV).

(7. a.) Francis Culbertson, Census record 1810, Bourbon Co,. Ky. In 1820 he was living in Wayne Co., Ind. on a farm that he owned near Centerville, Ind. Issue 2 daughters, names not known. One married a Mr. Burke Cincinnati Ohio. Francis and his family was known to have lived in Cincinnati Ohio, in 1850 (Chapter LV).

(8. a) Thomas. Married his first wife Anna Beall in Bourbon Co., Ky. Census Record Bourbon County, Ky.,page 93. Later came to Wayne County, Ind, as shown by census records of 1830 and and 1840. Issue 4 children, Jane, James, William and Roxann. He was married a second time. Had one child, Thomas Newton, of which we know nothing. (Chapter LVI).

CHAPTER XLII

(III) JOHN CULBERTSON

John Culbertson, Orphans Court Record, Wilmington, New Castle County, Delaware, Book D, Vol. 1, page 83, 1763, John choseth a guardian, May 19, 1763, being 15 years of age, Jan. 10 last. Other records of the settlement of the estate of his father, John Culbertson, deceased, give his name. His service record in the Revolutionary War follows:

Captain Isaac Lewis' Company—Capt. Isaac Lewis, Lieut. David Howell. 60 names are given. John Culbertson, No. 36, William Culbertson No. 38.

I do hereby certify that the above and foregoing lists are the names of the officers and privates which were with me on the Expedition to Thorough Fair Neck and at the taking of the several vessels in Duck Creek, in Nov., 1777, which were afterwards libeled in my name and condemned as prizes and sold by James Booth, Esq., marshall of Admiralty for the Delaware State in the month of June, 1778, or thereabouts.

Witness my hand 4th Sept., 1789.

ISAAC LEWIS.

Other names appearing on this list are common in old records of Pencader and St. Georges Hundreds, New Castle County, Del., at Wilmington, Del.

The name of John Culbertson along with that of his brother, William Culbertson, has been inscribed on the bronze plate placed on the monument erected in Rocky Spring Church Cemetery near Chambersburg, Pa. to Culbertsons in the Revolutionary War.

CHAPTER XLIII
(IV) MARY CULBERTSON

Mary Culbertson. Records of Orphans Court of New Castle Co., Delaware, Wilmington, Del. Book D, Vol. 1, page 175, 1767, Mary, daughter of John Culbertson, deceased, choseth a guardian. She is mentioned in other records of the settlement of the estate of John Culbertson.

CHAPTER XLIV
(V) BENJAMIN CULBERTSON

Benjamin Culbertson mentioned in record of Orphans Court, New Castle County, Delaware, Jan. 21 and 22, 1772, Book D, Vol. 1, page 332, 1772 by Elizabeth Culbertson, wife of John Culbertson as one of her children in settlement of estate. He is mentioned in other records of the settlement of the estate of John Culbertson of New Castle County, Del.

In Delaware Archives, Vol. 1, page 701, one finds the following service record.

Waggon Brigades under direction of Colonel Francis Wade, pay roll for a brigade of Waggons employed in the Continental Service conducted by David Boggs, W. C. Under the direction of Francis Wade, Esq., D. Q. M. Gen'l 1780.

Owner's Name	No. of Teams	Date of Entry	Time of Discharge
Benjamin Culbertson	1	Feb. 8	March 5

Census 1800 New Castle Co., Del., page 252, Benjamin Culbertson—8 in family.

Will records Wilmington New Castle Co., Del., Book S-1-314, letters of administration on the estate of Benjamin Culbertson to Outten Jester.

Note: Del. Arch. also show "Benjamin Culbertson in Q. M. Dept., Capt. Isaac Alexander's Co., Aug. 17, 1778; also Feb. and Mar., 1779."—Editor.

Letters of Administration were granted in 1829 in New Castle Co., Del. to Outten Jester in the estate of Benjamin Culbertson. Record does not show whether this was the above Benjamin. Will Book S-1-283 gives will of Thos. Culbertson probated 1829. Devisees: Son Thos., if he be dead, then brother Isaac Culbertsons two children, Margaret and James. The Isaac here mentioned made a deed with his wife Catherine in 1817,. both residing in Apoquinimink Tp., New Castle Co., Del. to A. S. Naudain, being ¼ part of land belonging to G. Schee.

The Thomas Culbertson who died 1829 was evidently Thomas Culbertson who is buried in Md., east of New Neck, Elkneck Hundred, Cecil Co., Md. This is evidently the Thos. who was granted land called "Culbertson's Discovery" in Md. about 1820. He had two daughters and one died single. I cannot trace his relationship.

Cecil Co., Md. Court Marriage Records show "Thomas Culbertson married to Elizabeth Ashbau, June 6, 1805, by Rev. Mr. Hindman." It is my opinion that this is Thomas who was granted land, i. e. Culbertson's Discovery above mentioned.

CHAPTER XLV

(VI) SAMUEL CULBERTSON

Samuel Culbertson. Orphans Court Record, New Castle County, Delaware, Book D, Vol. 1, page 314, 1771, John Hyatt appointed guardian of Samuel, David and Jane, children of John Culbertson, deceased. On page 322, 1771, Samuel Culbertson choseth a guardian. On page 406, 1773,. Samuel Culbertson, et al, orders to value estate of John Culbertson, deceased. He is also mentioned by his mother in other records of the settlement of the estate of John Culbertson.

Note: Samuel, son of Irish John of Delaware, is, in my opinion the Samuel Culbertson of Maryland Troops. "Samuel Culbertson, Capt. Maryland Battn. of the Flying Camp, July, 1776; captured at Ft. Washington, 1776, Nov. 16th; exchanged Nov. 2nd, 1780." (Heitman).

Samuel of New Castle Co., Del., does not appear on Del. Records after 1775 and not with Delaware troops so it is possible that he lived just over the Del.-Md. line and served with the Md. troops. I do not know what became of him. Rev. John N. Culbertson thinks that Heitman has put this record in the wrong place and that this is Capt. Samuel, Chester Co., Pa.—Editor.

CHAPTER XLVI

(VII) DAVID CULBERTSON

David Culbertson, Orphans Court, Wilmington, New Castle Co., Del., Book D, Vol. 1, page 314, 1771, John Hyatt appointed guardian of Samuel, David and Jane, children of John Culbertson, deceased. Book D, Vol. 1, page 486, 1773, motion of order for annual valuation of lands of Benjamin, Samuel, David and Jane Culbertson, minor orphan children of John Culbertson is hereby continued. He is mentioned in other records of the settlement of the estate of John Culbertson of New Castle Co., Del., Census of Cecil County, Elk Neck Hundred, Maryland 1790, David Culbertson, himself, wife, 1 boy under 16 years and 2 girls. Census 1800 New Castle County, Del., pages 234-237 New Castle County, Del., D. Culbertson, 6 in family.

CHAPTER XLVII

(VIII) SARAH CULBERTSON

Sarah Culbertson mentioned in settlement of estate of John Culbertson in Orphans Court records by Elizabeth Culbertson as one of her children and married to Wililam Flynn.

CHAPTER XLVIII

(IX) JANE CULBERTSON

Jane Culbertson, Orphans Court, Wilmington, New Castle Co., Del. Book D, Vol. 1, page 314, 1771, John Hyatt appointed guardian of Samuel, David and Jane, children of John Culbertson, deceased. Book D, Vol. 1, page 486, 1773, motion of order for annual valuation of lands of Benjamin, Samuel, David and Jane Culbertson, minor orphans of John Culbertson is hereby continued. She is mentioned again with Samuel and David as Jean.

CHAPTER XLIX

(1. a.) ANN CULBERTSON

Ann Culbertson died young according to family rumor.

* * * * *

CHAPTER L

(2. a.) JOHN CULBERTSON

John Culbertson is mentioned in his father's will. It is difficult to ascertain from its records which apply to this John Culbertson and which to his uncle, John Culbertson, Capter XLII. Records of New Castle Co., Del. give a John Culbertson in tax records of Pencader Hundred, 1800 with this remark: "John Culbertson gone to Kaintucky." Records of marriage licenses issued by Clerk of Cecil County Court, Elkton, Maryland, from June 22,, 1777 to 1840, give a John Culbertson to Sarah Foster, May 8, 1799, Rev. McCosden. Rumor through the family of Robert and Thomas Culbertson says that John Culbertson died as a young man without family. This would indicate that the one married to Sarah Foster was perhaps his uncle John.

Note: I do not hold the same view as F. E. Kempton in regard to the John Culbertson who went to Ky. It is my opinion that this John was the son and not the brother of William (II) of Pencader Tp. He first appeared on the tax lists in 1798 in Del. and John Sr. was not on Del. tax lists prior to this. He disappeared in 1799 when he went to Ky. It is my belief that John, son of John Sr. (K.K.) went to Shermans Valley, Pa. This John was given Census 1800, age over 45 in Teboyne Tp., Cumberland Co., Pa.—Editor L. R. C.

(2. a.) John Culbertson mar. Sarah Foster and moved to Ky. Administration Record of Clark Co., Ky., shows that in John Culbertson's estate administrator was appointed in 1807. His widow, Sarah, died 1830, and administrator appointed. A quit claim was made in Clark Co., Ky., in 1827, which shows his children were:
1. David Culbertson.
2. Harmon F. (Was this Foster?)
3. Mrs. James E. Prockman.
4. Mrs. John Elliott.

CHAPTER LI

(3. a.) DAVID CULBERTSON

FOURTH GENERATION

(3. a.) David Culbertson, b. Del. Married Clarissa Brevard, Dec. 21, 1800, Elkton, Md. Both died in Grant Co., Ind. Known to have lived in Clark Co., Ky., and in Wayne Co., Indiana.
1. b. Nancy, b. Mar. 28, 1803, Del. m. to William Ellsbury, Del. d. Greenfield, Ind., Aug. 5, 1845.
2. b. Rebecca Culbertson, b. Del .m. to George Ellwood. No issue living.
3. b Davison Culbertson, b. Nov. 24, 1814—Clark Co., Kentucky.
4. b. Polly, b. Del married Isaac Nordyke, Del. moved to Wayne Co., issue.
6. Celia, married Mr. Helms, Wayne Co., Indiana.
7. Lawrence married his 2nd cousin Jane Estep. They have four children.

8. Other issue but names not known.
5. b. Sarah married Mr. Griffin. Issue:
9. Mrs. Elmore, Indiana.

FIFTH GENERATION

(1. b.) Nancy Culbertson mar. Wm. Ellsbury, Del. See William Ellsbury (2. Chapter LII) as he is her first cousin. details given there.

(2. b.) Rebecca Culbertson mar. to George Ellwood. They were second cousins.
10-11. Son and daughter, both died young, buried at Olive Hill Cemetery, Wayne Co., Indiana.

(3. b.) David Culbertson born Nov. 24, 1814, Clark Co., Ky. His parents moved to Wayne Co., Ind.,. soon after his birth. Died 1911, age 97, Grant Co., near Marion, Ind. Married first wife,. Bashabee Garrigus, b. Aug. 8, 1819. Butler Co., Ohio. Died 1855. 6 children:
12. Martin Brevard Culbertson, born July, 1836.
13. Calvin Garrigus Culbertson, born Dec., 1838.
14. Jesse Estep Culbertson, born Nov. 1844, Wayne Co., Ind.
15. Joseph Tarkington Culbertson, born Mar., 1842.
16. Allen Hoover Culbertson, born 1844, living Marion, Grant Co., Ind., 1923.
17. Marion Albert Culbertson, born 1852, Grant Co., Ind.

(13) Calvin Garrigns Culbertson, wife daughter of Benjamin Woods was a direct descendant of Daniel Boone.

(16) Allen Hoover Culbertson, born 1844, living Marion, Grant Co., Ind., 1923. Granddaughter, Mrs. Edwards, 18, lives at Kokomo, Ind., 1923.
Second wife married Louisa Howard, born 1828, died 1899.
Children second marriage: 19, Luther; 20, Frank; 21, Mark; 22, Ascury; 23, Charley; 24. Louisa; 25, Mattie; 26, Anna; 27, Rose.

(4. b.) Polly Culbertson married Isaac Nordyke.
Issue: 6, Celia; 7, Lawrence.

(5. b.) Sarah Culbertson married Mr. Griffin.
Issue: 8, daughter (Mrs. Elmore).

CHAPTER LII

FOURTH GENERATION

(4. a.) Jean Culbertson married Frederick Ellsbury about 1797 either in Delaware or nearby. Frederick Ellsbury was born September 4, 1761, in Maryland. Private in the York County, Pa., Militia, serving in the company of Captain Ephriam Pennington, and also with a detachment of the York Co. Company detailed to guard prisoners from Yorktown to Reading with Capt. John Ehrman and Col. Henry Miller in command. In 1782 he served two months in a company commanded by Lieut. Chas. Barnitz. He was killed by the explosion of a cannon which was being used to celebrate a victory of the U. S. on May 12, 1813, according to family rumor. (See Continental Lives Pa. 1779 to 88, page 466. Also Pa. Archives 5 and 6, Vol. 4, Page 466).

Issue 7.

1. b.   Ann Ellsbury.
2. b.   William Ellsbury.
3. b.   Elizabeth.
4. b.   Jacob Nide.
5. b.   Thomas.
6. b.   Fanny.
7. b.   Richard.

Jean Culbertson married as a second husband Samuel Chestnut in Delaware.

Issue 4:

8. b.   Anna Chestnut, born November 20, 1818, New Castle County, Del., married her cousin, William Culbertson, from Wayne County, Indiana. No issue. She later married Thomas Cook. No issue.

9. b.   Clarissa Chestnut married Silas Phillips at Cincinnati, O. Issue: 12, Annie Phillips. Annie married John Skillman. She died in Denver, Col. Issue 1 son, Emory Skillman, who lives at Cripple Creek, Colorado. Issue, names not known. 13. Frank Phillips. He was killed in a railroad accident; no issue. 14. Charles Phillips; he was injured in a gold mine in California, afterwards conducted a news stand in Long Beach, California, where he died. 15. Harry Phillips. He was also killed in a railroad ac-

cident in the west. Names not known. Died
young (two)..

10. b. Sammie Chestnut married three times. Issue by
first wife 2. 16, Jane Chestnut. 17, Robert Chestnut. Second wife issue 1. 18, Sammie Chestnut.
Third wife—no issue.

11. b. Asenith. She was never married. Died in Wayne
County, Indiana.

FIFTH GENERATION

(1. b.) Ann Ellsbury, b. April 5, 1798, N. J. d. Feb. 20,.
1858, Wayne Co., Indiana, married July 21, 1814, Delaware,
to John Ellwood, b. Sept. 24, 1768, d. Aug. 11, 1855. John
Ellwood was in the war of 1812. His record is as follows:
Delaware Archives Military Volume 5, Page 596, petition to
Governor Haslet to change 2nd light infantry into a rifle
company.

To His Excellency Joseph Haslet, Esq.,   1813.

Governor of State of Delaware.

The undersigned officers and members of the 2n.: company of light infantry attached to the 2nd battalion, 2nd
regiment first brigade, Delaware militia, respectfully represent that we deeply impressed with the report of a rifle
corps when opposed to the enemies of our country in that
maurauding species which they have of late and are now
waring with such pernicious and destructive effects upon
our citizens and believing from every day's experience that
that species of force which, at present, we all in this state
alone able to oppose to them will not be found to afford an
efficient defence.

Therefore request that your excellency having the power
by law, would change the said company from Light Infantry into a rifle company by an issue of new commissions
by the same officers which are now attached to the company and that your excellency would as we humbly conceive
you have the power furnish us with Public Rifles, either by
law from the Federal Government or in any other way
which your excellency shall deem most proper and expedient

and with as much promptness as is compatible with your convenience.

And as in duty bound we will ever pray.

LEVI BOULDEN, Capt,.
AMOS FARIES, Lieut.
JACOB FARIES, Ensign.

Signed by the 60 members of the company and among them is the name of John Ellwood who was third corporal, 7th class.

John Ellwood and Ann Ellsbury Ellwood, his wife and 4 of these children—George, Andrew Mary and Levi moved from New Castle Co., Delaware to Wayne Co., Indiana, stopping a short time in Kentucky, arriving in Wayne Co., Ind., Dec. 16, 1824. He bought a farm 4 miles north of Centerville, Ind., where he and wife lived and died. They are buried at Olive Hill, Ind. John Ellwood served in War of 1812, Delaware.

Issue 13:

20. George Ellwood, b. June 26, 1815; d. 1839, Indiana, No issue living.
21. Andrew Ellwood, b. Feb. 26, 1817; d. June 26, 1853.
22. Jean Ellwood, b. May 11, 1819, Del.; d. 6 months of age, Del.
23. Mary Ellwood, b. Feb. 11, 1821; d. Jan. 1, 1886.
24. Levi Cooch Ellwood, b. Jan. 11, 1823, Ind.; d. June 25, 1904.
25. Amelia Ellwood, b. Dec. 18, 1824, Ind.; d. 1856, no issue living.
26. Jane Ellwood, b. March 31, 1827; d. 1905.
27. William Jackson Ellwood, b. May 20, 1829; d. Dec., 1917.
28. John T. Ellwood, b. Feb. 11, 1832; d. April 30, 1886.
29. Louisa Ellwood, b. Aug. 8, 1834; d. July 2, 1853.
30. Frances Elizabeth Ellwood, b. March 20, 1837; d. 19—.
31. Jacob Ellwood, b. March 4, 1839; d. Oct., 1922.
32. Lydia Ellwood, b. March 5, 1841; d. July 21, 1848.

SIXTH GENERATION

(24) Levi Cooch Ellwood, born Jan. 11, 1823, Newcastle Co., Del. Member of Methodist church, died June 25, 1904, Centerville, Wayne Co., Ind. He was married March 14, 1849, Centerville, Ind., to Eleanor L. Kirkman, who was born May 2, 1830, Guilford Co., North Carolina, died May 23, 1894, Centerville, Ind.

Issue 4:

47. Savilla Josephine Ellwood, born March 21, 1850, Centerville, Wayne Co., Ind. (Mrs. Wm. J. Kempton.)
48. Ann Elizabeth Ellwood, born Oct. 23, 1853, Centerville,
Wayne Co., Ind., died Jan., 1858.
49. Willard B. Ellwood, born April 22, 1863, near Centerville, Wayne County, Ind., married Nov. 15, 1888,
to Emma Heim, Brownsville, Union Co., Ind.
50. Ella M. Ellwood, born Feb. 5, 1867, Centerville, Wayne
Co., Ind., married Dec. 18, 1888, to Harry J. Gentry, Centerville.

(3. b.) Elizabeth Ellsbury, b. 1800 married Robert Holmes
of English descent. He died 184—.
Issue:
51. Eliza Ann Holmes.

(27) William Jackson Ellwood born May 20, 1829, died
Dec., 1917, Centerville, Wayne Co., Ind. Married to Rebecca
Bailey, Washington, now Greensfork, Ind., 1851.
Issue:
50½. Sarah Louella Ellwood, married William R. Cooke,
June 5, 1878. Issue 4: Earle G. Cooke, b. March
18, 1879. Alta B. Cooke, b. Sept. 6, 1881, married
Harry Castator, 1900, Harry Castator deceased
Dec. 3, 1917; 1, Susan Castator, b. 1902; 2, Harry
Jr., born 1904, d. 1919. Dot Cooke, born Feb. 19,
1884, married Clem G. Lancaster Sept., 1905; issue
1, Richard, born 1906. Ruby Cooke, b. Sept. 26,
1888; married Fred Schneider Feb., 1906; issue, 1
daughter; 1, daughter, Catherine Schneider, born
1908, died 1911.

SEVENTH GENERATION

(47) Savilla Josephine Ellwood, born Centre Township,
Wayne Co., Ind., March 21,. 1850. Married William James
Kempton, Centerville, Ind., March 5, 1872. Rev. Rupe officiating. William born Jan. 2, 1840, New York City, the son
of John Kempton and Jane (Marshall Kempton, both born
near Cookstown, Ireland.)   William was the 4th child of a
family of 3 sons and 6 daughters born to them.

(Refer to Memoirs of Wayne Co., Ind., Vol. 2, Page 293,
by Western Historical Association, Madison, Wis.)

William was a member of Ohio State Militia and private
in Co. D., 146 Ohio Volunteers, Infantry. Discharged September 15, 1864, died Nov. 23, 1918, at Centerville, Ind.
Presbyterian in religious belief. Politically, Republican.

Educated in Cincinnati schools. He owned two farms in Wayne County, Indiana.

Savilla Ellwood was educated at Whitewater College, Centerville, Ind. Became a member of M. E. church, Kennedys Chapel (now Olive Hill), Centre Township, Wayne Co., Ind. Jan., 1866, membership now Centerville, Ind. Charter member of Eastern Star chapter, Centerville, Ind., a member of Burnside Relief Corps, Washington D. C., D. A. R. Catherine Montgomery, Chapter D. C. and member of District of Columbia Society of the National Society, United Daughters of 1812. To this union was born on a farm 4 miles north of Centerville, Ind., 3 children.

52. Infant son, born and died August 5, 1876.
53. Lora B. Kempton, born June 28, 1881, died Ooctober 29, 1885.

54. Forrest Ellwood Kempton, born October 5, 1883, unmarried, now employed office of Cereal Investigation, B. P. I. U. S. Department of Agriculture, Washington, D. C. as Plant Pathologist in charge of the Barberry Eradication Campaign. Attended Centerville Indiana High School, B. S. Earlham College '06; M. S. Wisconsin University '13; Ph. D. University of Illinois, '18. Teacher, public schools, Wayne Co., Ind., '05-'12; prof. biol. Ill. Col. '13-'14; Asst. bot. University of Illinois, '14-'18; plant pathologist, smelter smoke investigations, St. Louis Smelting and Ref. Co. 17; U. S. Dept. Agr. plant pathologist Porto Rico '18. In charge, barberry eradication campaign, 1919. Member of Amer. Assn, for Adv. of Science; Phytopath. Soc.; Bot. Soc.; Ill. Acad.; Wash. Bot. Soc. Sigma Xi. Publications or research: Cytology of Entylomas; Origin and Development of the Pycnidium; Progress of Barberry Eradication.
(See American Men of Science—Third Edition— The Science Press 1921). He was plant pathologist under Civil Service States Relation Service United States Department of Agriculture, June to December, 1918. Registered in Porto Rico in Third Draft.

(49) Willard Bargis Ellwood. Refer to Memoirs of Wayne County, Indiana, Vol. 11, Page 360, by Western Historical Association, Madison, Wisconsin.

Willard Bargis Ellwood, born near Centerville, Wayne County, Indiana, April 22nd, 1863. Married Emma May

Heim in Brownville, Union County, Indiana, on November 15th, 1888. Rev. Frank Moore officiating.

Emma was born May 21st, 1869, the daughter of George M. Heim and Appalonia (Bachmeyer) Heim both of whom came to America on the same vessel in 1853, from Markelsheim, Germany. Emma was the ninth child of a family of eight boys and six girls born to them.

To this union was born, on a farm south of and adjoining the town of Centerville, Indiana, three children, Mabel, George, Leo. (55-56-57.)

(50) Ella M. Ellwood, b. Feb. 5, 1867, residence 5016 Carrolton Ave., Indianapolis, Ind.; married Dec. 18, 1888, Centerville, Ind., to Harry J. Gentry, born Sept. 8, 1864, Centerville, Ind., son of John and Josephine Woods Gentry.

Issue:

58.   Laura Josephine.

(51) Eliza Ann Holmes and David Thomas were married December 14, 1849, Centerville, Indiana. He was born Jan. 28, 1829. She was born March 29, 1831, and died March 12, 1852. Their only child, 59, Martha J., was born July 8, 1850, and died April 22, 1906, Centerville, Ind.

EIGHTH GENERATION

(55) Mabel Ellwood, b. April 9, 1893, who married George Kutche, a native of Greece, at Centerville Indiana, on June 1st, 1911. Rev. Mrs. Fred Teas, a Quaker minister, officiating. Mabel was granted a divorce and her maiden name restored in the Marion County Circuit Court, Indianapolis, Indiana, in September, 1917. Service during the war: She was Comptometer Operator in the Statistical Department of the Fuel Administration from October, 1918, to March, 1919 and was then transferred to the Auditing Department of the Railroad Administration and has an honorable discharge from that branch of our government.

She was married the second time on March 11, 1919, at Rockville, Maryland, by Rev. Duffy of the Methodist church to Percy Hart Smith, a native of Pittsylvania County, Virginia. He was the fifth child of a family of four boys and seven girls, born to George Dudley Smith and Willie Kate (East) Smith, both of whom are natives of Pittsylvania County, Va.

(56) George Dewey Ellwood, born April 2nd, 1898, un-married, Altavista Va.

(57) Leo Bunker Ellwood, born May 17th, 1900. Married Vera Elizabeth Sale in Lynchburg, Virginia, on Feb. 21, 1920, Rev. R. A. McFarland officiating. Vera was born October 6th, 1901, near Pleasant View Amherst County, Virginia. The third child of a family of two boys and three girls, born to John Lewis Sale and Eva Glen (Wiltshire) Sale, who were married at Pleasant View, Amherst County, Virginia.

To Leo and Vera were born, in Lynchburg, .Virginia. 1. Leo Bunker Ellwood, Jr., on November 26th, 1920. 2, Eva Jean Ellwood, in Altavista, Virginia, June 21st, 1922.

Leo B. Ellwood enlisted on July 1, 1918, in the Petersburg Guards, Infantry Virginia State Volunteers to serve for "the emergency" and was discharged April 1, 1919. He enlisted in U. S. Regular Army, June 23, 1919, Signal Corps, unassigned attached to Camp Signal Office, Camp Lee, Virginia. He was appointed Sergeant First Class, June 25, 1919, later assigned to duty with 10th Field Signal Battalion, Camp Meade, Kansas. Battalion moved to Camp Meade, Maryland. He was honorably discharged from the United States Army, Feb. 7th, 1921.

Enlisted in Hdq. Co., Ist. Bn. 116th Inf. Va. N. G. for a period of three years, March 11, 1922. Made Sergeant, April 6th, 1922. The above information for Family of Willard Bargis Ellwood furnished by him.

(58) Laura Josephine Gentry born Aug. 17, 1890, Centerville. Married Richwood, Indiana, March 6, 1912, to Stanley Sheard born May 22, 1892, Oxford, Ohio, living at (1923) Indianapolis, Ind.

Issue:

Jack Sheard, born June 11, 1913, Indianapolis, Ind.
Jean Sheard, born, Dec. 31, 1915.

(59) Martha J. Thomas and William F. Mathews were married Jan. 5, 1869. He was born May 21, 1848, New York City, and served in the Civil War as a Union soldier. Born to them were seven children: 1, Walter T., b. Jan. 3, 1870; 2, Emma J., b. Sept. 15, 1872; 3,. Elizabeth M., b. April 2, 1875; 4, Eliza A., born Aug. 27, 1877,. and died Sept. 16, 1895; 5, Charles W., born Aug. 9, 1881; 6, Howard C, b. Oct. 24, 1888; 7, A. Noel b. May 17, 1892.

Walter T. Mathews and Clara I. Needham were married Jan. 25,. 1893. Born to them were six children. 1, Rosella, b. Aug. 6, 1893; 2, Paul D., b. Oct. 26.

1894, single; 3, Jesse William, b. Oct. 5, 1896; 4,
Walter Ray, b. Jan. 30, 1901; 5, Frances, b. Aug.
19, 1904; 6, Kendal Emerson, b. Jan. 22, 1909.

Paul D. Mathews, single, enlisted in Co. E, 10th Inf. of the
U. S. Army of the World War, Sept. 3, 1917. Was
stationed at Fort Harrison, Indianapolis, Ind., for
several months. Was then sent to Nitro City, West
Va. for several months and then sent to Camp Cus-
ter, Battle Creek, Mich, where he was corporal. He
was honorably discharged in May, 1919.

Jesse W. Mathews and Nova Shadle were married Feb. 20,
1920. Jesse W. Mathews enlisted in Co. C, 14th
Cav. of the U. S. Army of the World War on the
9th of April, 1917, in Detroit, Mich. Was signed up
on the 22nd of April, 1917, and sent to Columbus,
Ohio. From there he was sent to Del Rio, Texas,
and was stationed on the border for about 18
months. Was then sent to Fort Sam Houston,
Texas for a while and then transferred to Officers' Training Camp, at Camp Hancock, Augusta,
Ga. He was honorably discharged Dec. 17, 1918.

Elizabeth M. Mathews and Frank Hatfield, married July
15, 1895.   Issue: 1, Joseph Keith, b. Nov. 7, 1896;
2, Kenneth Mathews, b. June 14, 1907; 3, Martha
Maria, b. Aug. 29, 1911.

Joseph Keith Hatfield and Laurabel Stevens. Married June
2,. 1920. 1, Joseph Keith, Jr., b. Nov. 2, 1922, d.
Nov. 6, 1922. Joseph Keith Hatfield enlisted in
May 30, 1918. Hospital apprentice Sec. class U. S.
Naval Reserve force. Stationed at U. S. Training
Station Great Lakes, Ill. Released from active
duty Oct. 12, 1919. Saw service during the flue epi-
demic.

CHAPTER LIII

(5. a.) **William Culbertson** the son of William Culbertson
(II) is mentioned in his father's will and is probably the
one recorded as being in Delaware Militia, Third Company,
Third Regiment, First Battalion 1799, Middle District St.
Georges Hundred, William Frazier, Captain. Family rumor
through the family of Robert indicates that only 4 of the
sons of William raised families so there is probably no family record for this William.

CHAPTER LIV

FOURTH GENERATION

(6. a.) Robert Culbertson. The quoted data was supplied by Mrs. Effie Thomas, 123 Ridge Street, Richmond, Indiana, a great granddaughter through Louisa, daughter of Daniel Culbertson and from copies of old family records:

"This is Robert Culbertson's family and his father was William Culbertson and his mother Nancy Thorton. Robert Culbertson was born in Del., March 27, 1781, died May 13, 1875. Rebecca Culbertson (his wife) was born in Kentucky, Feb. 1, 1793 and died July 18, 1857. Robert Culbertson and Rebecca King were married 1809 in Kentucky, later moved to Wayne Co., Ind.

Issue:
1. Drucilla Culbertson, b. Sept. 7, 1810; d. 1811 in Kentucky.
2. Nancy Culbertson, b. Oct. 14, 1811, d. 1812, Kentucky.
3. David Culbertson, b. Jan. 29, 1813, Methodist Minister, d. March 25, 1846, Indiana.
4. John Nelson Culbertson, b. Sept. 6, 1814; d. 1824, in Indiana.
5. Sarah Culbertson, b. March 25, 1816, Indiana; d. Aug. 22, 1846, Indiana.
6. Daniel Culbertson, b. May 24, 1817, d. Indiana.
7. Jane Culbertson, b. July 7, 1818; d. 1825, Indiana.
8. Sanford Culbertson, b. Sept. 10, 1820; d. in 1896, in Indiana.
9. Clarissa Culbertson, b. Sept. 19, 1824 ;d in 188— in Indiana.
10. Lafayette Culbertson, b. Aug 13, 1826, d. in Indiana, 1895.
11. Andrew J. Culbertson, b. Jan. 3, 1828; d . in Indiana, 1861.
12. William Culbertson, b. Oct. 23, 1831, Wayne County, Indiana.
13. Ann Culbertson, b. April 24, 1837; d. 1874, in Indiana.

FIFTH GENERATION

(3) David, b. Jan. 29, 1813; d. March 25, 1846, in Wayne Co., Indiana. Married Mary Hoover, Wayne Co., Indiana. He was a Methodist Episcopal Minister. Issue, 1 daughter, 14, Rebecca Ellen, who died in childhood.

(4) John Nelson, b. Sept. 6, 1814; d. 1824, Wayne Co., Indiana.

(5) Sarah Culbertson, Wayne Co., Ind., b. March 25, 1816; d. August 22, 1846, Wayne Co., Ind. Married to Jesse Estep. Issue: 15, Rober.t Estep, married Della Bean, 1861, both deceased. Issue: Alta and Charles, both married and have issue, Charles Estep lives north of Richmond, Ind. 16, Jane Estep, m.arried Lawrence Nordyke, her second cousin. Issue: Mattie Nordyke, no infor.mation; Sadie Nordyke, no information; Millie Nordyke, no information; Joseph Nordyke, lives in Peru, Indiana.

(6) Daniel Culbertson, born May 24, 1817, died in Wayne County, Ind., buried at Olive Hill, Ind. Married Martha Hoover, Wayne Co., Ind., 1838. Was farmer and later real estate agent and notary public. According to Census 1850.

Issue: 5 by first wife.

17. Thomas Jefferson Culbertson, b. 1840, married and moved to Jeffersonville, Ind. Issue, no other word.

18. Louisa Culbertson, b. 1843; married Harrison Bailey, Issue 4.

19. Martha Susan Culbertson, b. 1845, married John Irvin. issue 2, son a, Allan, married, no issue; b. Minnie Irvin, single. All live Webster, Ind., 1823.

20. John Culbertson, b. 1847, soldier in Civil War; died in service.

21. Anna Culbertson, b. 1850, died 1868, single. 2nd wife Martha Smith, issue 2.

22. Lily, born Fairland, Ind., married. No other information.

23. Carrie, born Fairland, Ind. No other information.

(7) Jane, b. July 7, 1818; d. 1825, buried Olive Hill, Indiana.

(8) Sanford Culbertson, b. September 10, 1820, married Anne Thorn, Centerville, Wayne Co., Ind. He moved to Jay County, Ind., died 1896, issue 2 or more. 24, Rebecca, born 1846; 25, Anna, born 1849. Others not known.

(9) Clarissa Culbertson, b. Sept. 19, 1824, died 1886, not married.

(10) Lafayette Culbertson, b. Aug. 13, 1826, died in Wayne Co., Ind., 1895. Married Martha Cranor.

Issue:

26. E. L. Culbertson, married Sarah Duke, deceased; mar-
       rid second wife. No issue. Grocer, Westville, O.
27. Frank Culbertson, accidentally shot at age of 8 years.
28. Hattie Culbertson, married John Duke, 1887; no issue
       both deceased.
29. Robert Culbertson, deceased, unmarried.

(11) Andrew J. Culbertson, b. Jan. 3, 1828, died 1867,
buried Olive Hill, Ind. He died from accident having been
thrown by a horse. Married Elizabeth Study, Williamsburg,
Ind.
   Issue:
30. Melissa Culbertson, b. 1854, married John Fulton; is-
       sue daughter Bell, died in girlhood.
31. Massa Culbertson, died as infant.
32. Joseph Culbertson, b. 185—.
33. Emma Culbertson, deceased.

(12) William Culbertson, b. Oct. 23, 1831, Wayne County,
Indiana. Died Aug. 18, 1914. Married Mary Jane Ebersol,
Dec. 27, 1853. She was born April 25, 1836, in Pennsylvania.
Died March 23, 1913. Issue 10. Refer to Memoirs of
Wayne Co., Indiana, Vol. 2, Page 578, published by Western
Historical Association, Madison, Wis., 1912.
   Issue:
34. Lafayette Culbertson, b. Sept. 5, 1854.
35. Alice, b. Oct. 27, 1856 (Mrs Sharon).
36. George, b. June 23, 1860.
37. Katherine, b. Dec. 17, 1861.
38. Ella, b. Sept. 5. 1863.
39. Letitia, b. Aug. 25, 1865.
40. William T., b. Aug. 5, 1868.

(13) Ann Culbertson, b. April 24, 1837; d. 1874, Wayne
Co., Ind; married Richard Williams, 1867 as his second wife.
He still lives at Fountain City, Ind. Issue 2.
41. Roy Williams, married lives near Richmond, Ind., issue.
42. Jeannetta Williams, married Clark McNutt. He is now
       deceased. She lives at Fountain City, Ind. Issue 6.

(18) Louisa Culbertson, b. 1843, married William Harrison Bailey. He was in Civil War, enlisted April 21st, 1861,
and served until the close of the war. He reenlisted as a
veteran in Jan. 1,. 1864. Issue 4.
43. Effie M. Bailey, married Mr. Thomas, lives 1231
       Ridge St., Richmond, Ind., 1923. Issue 3; son and
       two daughters. The daughters are married.
44. Sadie Bailey.

SIXTH GENERATION

(32) Joseph Culbertson, b. 185—, married Della Bertram, Centerville, Ind.

Issue 5:

45. Mary Culbertson, married Mr. Logan. Issue 2; Jack Logan and a daughter.
46. George Culbertson, in world War.
47. Tip Culbertson, in World War.
48. Robert Culbertson, minister Friends' church.
49. Lelia Culbertson, married.

(33) Emma Culbertson, married Jacob Wolfe. She is deceased. No issue.

(34) Lafayette Culbertson. Married Emma Potter divorced.

50. Cleo Culbertson.
Married Miss Borton.

Issue:

51. Son, Walter Culbertson.
52. Lydia Culbertson and Emma Culbertson, twin sisters.
Cleo Culbertson and family lives at Webster, Wayne Co., Ind.

(35) Alice, married Oliver Sharon.

Issue:

53. Daughter Rachel, who is married but has no issue. All live in Wichita, Kansas. Rachel Sharon married Harvey Grace.

(36) George Culbertson, b. June 23, 1860. Married Minnie Arnett. She is deceased. Issue 3:

54. Leona, who is married and lives in Toledo, Ohio.
55. Oliver and father, also lives in Toledo, O.
56. Carl, married Miss Owens. Issue 1. They live on West Main St., Richmond, Ind.

(37) Katherine Culbertson, married Henry Horney. They had two children. 57, William Horney, married Mary Beck. They have 3 boys, live at Olive Hill, Ind, 1923. 58, Mary married and lives in Richmond, Ind. Issue 59.

(38) Ella Culbertson. Married Abram Potter, issue one daughter, 60, Mabel. Mabel Potter married Floyd Bell. They have two daughters, 61, Elizabeth Bell, a student at DePaw University, Greencastle, Ind. 62, Margaret

Bell, a younger daughter. Mr. Bell and family live at Princeton, Ind., where he is connected with a creamery.

(39) Letitia Culbertson, married May 31, 1883 to Wm. K. Cheeseman, refer to Memoirs of Wayne County, vol. 2, page 574, published by Western Historical Society, Madison, Wis., 1912. Issue: 63, Earl Cheeseman, b. Oct. 28, 1892, married Beatrice Ward. They have three sons, 64, Earl Cheeseman; 64½, ——Cheeseman, son; 65, Robert Cheeseman.

(40) William T. Culbertson. A letter of William T. Culbertson, Richmond, Ind., April 1, 1923, to Lewis R. Culbertson, Zanesville, Ohio, is as follows:

"Lafayette, Alice, George, Katherine, Ella, Lutecia, Wm. T., Sadie, Laura and Mary. I, Wm. T., youngest one living. Born August 5, 1868, married December 24, 1890, to Mary Elizabeth Miller, two children, boys, 66, Lowell L., b. Dec. 13, 1894, served in World War, was drafted 1918, went to Camp Taylor, Ky., Louisville, July 23, 1918. Sailed for France Oct. 27. Went from New York through England down through Paris. Got within three days' travel of front. Arrived at Boston, May 3, 1919. Discharged May 15, 1919. Sailed from France as Bordeaux Casual Co. No. 70 Artilleryman. Married in March, 1920, to Pricilla Arnold, his address Richmond, Ind. R. R. A. 67, Donald A.., born Dec. 25, 1899, drafted. Called but did not get to camp. Married Sept. 1921 to Dorothy Simpson, one baby girl, born August 7, 1922. His address Richmond Ind., No. 814, South E St.

Yours truly,
(Signed) W. T. CULBERTSON,
Richmond, Ind. R. R. A.

CHAPTER LV

(7. a.) Francis Culbertson and Ann ——, daughter of a prominent Kentucky family, were married in Kentucky, according to an old letter of Daniel Culbertson, son of Robert Culbertson. Census records of Bourbon County, Kentucky, 1810, page 93, gives Francis Culbertson. In 1820, he is known to have lived in Wayne County, Ind., owning a farm near Centerville, Ind. Issue 2, two daughters, names not known. One married a Mr. Burke of Cincinnati, Ohio. Francis and family are known to have moved to Cincinnati,

Ohio, where they were living in 1848.   No further information.

CHAPTER LVI

FOURTH GENERATION

(8. a.) Thomas Culbertson, born 1786, married Anna Beall, July, 1809, as his first wife in Bourbon County, Ky. She was born October 25, 1790.   Census 1810 and 1820 Bourbon Co., Ky., page 93, gives Thomas Culbertson.   He later migrated to Wayne County, Indiana, and lived there as shown by Census Records for Wayne County, Indiana, 1830 and 1840, issue 4.

1.   Jane Culbertson, b. September 7, 1810, married February 14, 1828, Ebenezer Cheesman, Wayne County, Indiana, by Rev. Isaac Cotton; issue 6.

2.   William Culbertson, b. January 16, 1812, in Kentucky, died Wayne County, Indiana, March 5, 1864.   He married as his first wife Ruth Commons in 1835. They were separated that same year and later divorced.   He married as his second wife his cousin, Anna Chestnut, daughter of Jean Culbertson by her second husband, Samuel Chestnut.   Anna Chestnut.   Anna Chestnut was born November 20, 1818, in Delaware, died December 21, 1890, Centerville, Ind. No issue.

3.   James Culbertson, September 16, 1814, married Phoeba Bishop, Wayne County, Indiana; they later moved to Kansas where both died.   Issue 6.

4.   Roxann Culbertson, born February 15, 1826, married Eli Albertson in Wayne County, Indiana.   Later moved to other parts of Indiana, issue.   No further information.

Thomas Culbertson married a second wife Mary B. McKee, May 29, 1841, issue 1 son.

5.   Thomas Newton Culbertson, born March 19, 1842.   He is said to have gone to California.

FIFTH GENERATION

(1) Jane Culbertson married Feb. 14, 1828, Ebenezer Cheesman, Wayne Co., Ind., by Rev. Isaac Cotton. Issue 6.

6.   Amanda Cheesman, married Pressly King, Wayne County, Ind., later moved to Kansas and Oregon. One son lives in Oregon.

7. Martha Ann Cheesman, married Oliver Jones of south of Centerville, Ind. He was a soldier in the Civil War and killed in service 1862. She died in Randolph County, Ind., in 1916, and was buried at Centerville, Wayne Co., Ind. Issue 3. 1, John Jones, Randolph Co., Ind.; 2, Mrs. James Beck, Muncie, Ind.; 3, Alice Jones married James Neal, Wayne Co., Ind.

8. Thomzy Ann Cheesman, b. Oct. 22, 1835, married John Bond, Oct. 11, 1855, Wayne Co., Ind., and lived near Greensfork, Ind., on a farm. She died Sept. 15, 1873. He died Feb. 13, 1895. Issue 5.

9. Davison Cheesman, b. Wayne Co., Ind., married Ann Taylor, 1857. She died in 1911. Davison living April 1923, retired, Farmland, Ind. Owns farm in Randolph Co., Ind. Issue 8.

10. Demaris Cheesman, married Levi King, near Centerville, Ind. She died in 1900. He died in 1907. Issue 4.

11. Amelia Cheesman, married Edward Fites, Bourbon, Ind. She died March 8, 1900. Children 3.

FIFTH GENERATION

(3) James A. Culbertson married Phoeba Bishop, Wayne County, Indiana. Later they moved to Kansas where they both died. Issue 6.

12. Anna Culbertson, died as a young woman.

13. Mahlon Culbertson, married Miss Ensley in Illinois. Issue two daughters—18-19.

14. Henrietta Culbertson, married Oliver Brumfield, Centerville, Indiana, in 1865. She died about 1878. Issue 5.
   Issue 5: 20, Clarence Brumfield, b. 1866; 21, Charles Brumfield, d. in childhood; 22, Ansan Brumfield; 23, Millie Brumfield (Mrs. Linnie King) ; 24, William Brumfield, d. 1893.

15. Dayton Culbertson.

16. Christopher Columbus Culbertson.

17. Jennetta Culbertson, born 1856, married Arthur Charman. She lives in Centerville, Indiana. Issue 2 daughters.

25. Mattie Charmman, married Mr. Reichard. Issue 2 daughters. 1, Ruth Reichard, deceased young. 2, Ethel Reichard, lives with her grandmother, Centerville, Indiana. She is a stenographer.

26. Myrtle Charman, married Verte Connor, Dec. 10, 1921. He was in World War overseas service.

SIXTH GENERATION

(15) Dayton Culbertson mar. Anna ——; lived until recently on farm near Stanley, North Dakota. They now live with sons, at Selah, Washington. Issue 5 .

27. May Culbertson, married and lives at Stanley, North Dakota. Issue 5.
28. Forrest Culbertson, lives at Milo, Iowa, married and has isue.
29. Columbus Culbertson, married and lives at Selah, Washington.
30. Leonard Culbertson is married and lives at Selah, Washington.
31. Clayton Culbertson lives at Stanley, North Dakota.

(16) Christopher Columbus Culbertson married Ella Vochard in McLean Co., Ills. Until his death in 1922 he lived as a retired farmer in Danvers, Ills. His wife died in 1921. Issue 4 sons.

32. Vernon Culbertson, married Kate Friday; lives at Danvers, Ills. No issue.
33. Roy Culbertson, married Almeda Bowers. Issue 4, Danvers, Ills. 36, Eleanor Culbertson; 37, Bowers Culbertson; 38, Marie Culbertson; 39, Miss Culbertson.
34. Clyde Culbertson, married Vera Sea. Issue 1.
35. Lawrence Culbertson, single, Danvers, Ills.

SECTION FOURTH

(L) Richard of Cumberland Co., Pa.

(K) SECTION FOURTH

(L) **Richard Culbertson** (Irish). Revolutionary record: "Transferred from an infantry regiment from Northhampton County, Pa. (Enlisted 1778), April 2, 1779, to Capt. Isaac Corens Co. of Art. His name appears as 'belonging to a Regiment of Foot sent us by order of the Board of War.' Enlisted from Northhampton Co. (Isaac Corens Art. rendered important service under Gen. Washington). In Sept., 1781, enlisted in Capt. Asa Hills 4th Co., 2nd Batt'n of Cumb. Co., Pa. Ass'rs. (Pa. Arch.) Jour. Pa. Assembly, p. 359. He was deeded land in Carlisle, Pa., in 1781 by Wm. Denny. Deed states Richard was a butcher Richard and wife, Margaret, deeded this land in 1782 and they then moved to East Neck Tp., Cecil Co, Md. He appears on the Census of 1790, Cecil Co., Md., self and wife, one son under 16 years, and 3 daughters. He died before 1800 and Census of 1800 Cecil Co., Md. gives Margaret Culbertson (widow) her age between 26 and 45; one son between 16 and 26; two sons under 10 years; one daughter between 10 and 16; two daughters under 10. Richard probably died about 1796-8. Born in Northhampton Co., Pa. The Registrar of Wills writes me that he cannot find him or any Culbertson on his Court Records until 1918. Richard evidently had no property.

Richard's eldest son must have been born after 1775. He could hardly have been James Culbertson who married Elizabeth Stillings about 1794 or '95 and whose descendants allege moved from "Row' to Havre-de-Grace, Md., about 1794, and who they allege died there (no court record there of him).

I do not know the names of any of Richard's children or what became of them.

A thorough search of 1790 and 1800 Census of Md. shows only Richard and Margaret Culbertson.

The story of James (above mentioned) by his descendants might or might not be true. It might be that instead of a step-mother-in-law that it was a mother-in-law by a second husband? The Census report on Margaret for 1800 gives only one female (herself) of marriageable age therefore proving her son could not have been married.

A Margaret Culbertson was married to Wm. Hamilton, Sept. 11, 1806, in Cecil Co., Md. (license). This may have been Richards 'widow or his daughter.

A Mary Culbertson was married Aug. 24, 1811 to Joseph Richardson (license) in Cecil Co., Md. This was probably a daughter of Richard.

SECTION FIFTH

Scotch Irish Culbertson, Some of Whose Descendants Came to America Before and After 1800.

His Name Not Known. Lived in Irish Culbertson Row at Ballygan, Near Ballymoney, Co. Antrim, Ireland.

SECTION FIFTH

FIRST GENERATION

—— Culbertson, of "Culbertson Row," Ireland, remained in Ireland.

Issue:

1. John, d. in Ireland.
2. ——, died in Ireland.

SECOND GENERATION

(1) John Culbertson settled at Ballywalter, near Ballymoney, Co. Antrim, Ireland, about 1720, and died there.

Issue:

3. John, d. in Ireland.
4. Hugh.

THIRD GENERATION

(3) John Culbertson d. in Antrim Co., Ireland.

Issue:

5. John, remained in Ireland.
6. Alexander.
7. James. d. in Ireland.

(4) Hugh Culbertson settled at Ballygan, near Ballymoney, Co. Antrim, Ireland; in "Row."

Issue:

8. John. Emigrated to America.
9. Hugh, d. young.
10. James, d. young.
11. Mrs. Adams.
12. Mrs. Lyons.
14. Joseph. Emigrated to America about 1800.
13. Robert. Emigrated to Philadelphia, Pa.

FOURTH GENERATION

(5) John Culbertson remained in Ireland. All his children emigrated to America.

Issue:

15. James, d.
16. John.
17. William, d.
18. George, d.

19. Robert, d. Lived at Philadelphia, Pa.
20. Isabella, d.
21. Nancy.
22. Jane Mary, d.
23. Mary Ann.

(9) Hugh Culbertson mar. ——. Died in Antrim Co., Ireland.
Issue:
24. Robert.
25. James.
26. William.
27. Andrew. Emigrated. Lives in Philadelphia, Pa.

(13) Robert Culbertson mar. Mary Wright, June 1, 1802.
Issue:
28. Mary Ann, b. Apr. 22, 1805. (Mrs. McDaniel).
29. Joseph, b. Aug. 30, 1806.
30. Maria, b. Feb. 26, 1808.
31. Agnes, b. Dec. 29, 1809.
32. Hugh, b. Nov. 17, 1811.
33. Sarah, b. Feb. 15, 1813 (Mrs. Getty).
34. Joseph (2nd), b. March 1, 1816.
35. Jane, b. Oct. 8, 1817. (Mrs. Hays).
36. Matilda Ann, b. Jan. 1, 1820. (Mrs. Getty).
37. Robert, b. Sep. 22, 1824.

FIFTH GENERATION

(19) Robert Culbertson mar. ——.
Issue:
38. George. Philadelphia, Pa.
39. John.
40. Robert, d.
41. Arthur. Chicago.
42. Wm. d.
43. Irwin.
44. Mary Ann.
45. Isabella, d.
46. Margaret, d.

(32) Hugh Culbertson lived and died at "Culbertson Row," Ireland.
Issue:
47. Robert. Lived at L. Derry, Ireland.
48. James.
49. Mary.

50. Wm. John. The only Culbertson living in Co. Antrim,
Ireland (1892).
51. Andrew emigrated to Philadelphia, Pa., in '89.
55. Annie married. Lives in Ireland.

SECTION SIXTH
The Lancaster County, Pa., Family

SECTION SIXTH

FIRST GENERATION.

(L) Four brothers came over before the Revolutionary War—it is not definitely known whether they came from Scotland or Ireland, but most likely the latter—and settled in Lancaster Co., about four miles from Lancaster. Name of their father not known.

Names of brothers:

I. John, d. in Lancaster Co., Pa.
II. ——, bro., d. Went South,. Virginia or Ky.
III. ——' bro., d. Went South, Virginia or Ky.
IV. ——, bro., d. Went South, Virginia or Ky.

SECOND GENERATION

(I) John Culbertson mar. Ann Maria ——.   (Was a miller.)

Issue:

1. Samuel, .d.
2. John, d.
3. David, d.
4. Louis, d., Lewiston, Pa.
5. Elizabeth.
6. Maria.

After death of husband, widow lived at Petersburg, E. Hempfield Twp., Lancaster Co., Pa. (From a Deed.)

THIRD GENERATION

(1) Samuel Culbertson mar. ——.

Issue:

7. Anna.
8. Fannie.
9. Eliabeth, d.
10. Louis.
10½. Susan.

(2) John Culbertson moved in Spring of 1834, to eight miles from Mansfield, O. Mar. Miss Wiley, of Lancaster,. Pa.

Issue:

11. Eliza, d. 1878. (Mrs. A. Kinnell.)

12. Sarah, b. Feb., 1827. (Mrs. John Kornleans.)
13. Henry, b. Oct., 1828; d. Oct., 1890.
14. John, b. Feb., 1831. Lives at Whitehall, Ills.
15. Aaron, b. Feb., 1835.
16. Maria, b. Oct., 1837. (Mrs. Mitschlen.)
17. David,.b. Feb., 1838.
18. Wm., b. 1840. Killed at battle Jonesboro, Sept., 1864.
19. Samuel, b. Apr., 1842.
20. Levi, b. 1844.
21. Anna, b. Sept. 1846. (Mar. first, Mr. Kornleans; second, Mr. Miller.

(3) David Culbertson mar. ——.
Issue:
22. Elizabeth.
23. David.

(4) Louis. Know nothing of descendants. He lived at Lewiston, Pa.

FOURTH GENERATION.

(13) Henry Culbertson mar. Susan Altoffer.
Issue:
24. John. Mar.
25. Wm. Mar.
26. Henry, d.
27. Charles, d. 1890.

(14) John Culbertson mar. Rebecca Clark. Lives at White Hall, Ills.
Issue:
28. Laura.
29. Ella Frost.
30. Ida Davis.
31. Belle Culbertson.

(15) Aaron mar. Rebecca Hubley.
Issue:
32. Sarah Baldwin. Mar.
33. Arabella Duncan. Mar.
34. Albert. Mar.
35. Tecumseh, d.

(17) David Culbertson mar. first Mary Secrist. Wife died.
Issue:
36. Elmira H.

37. Olivia, d.
38. Elnora Mason.

(17) David Culbertson mar. second, Miss Cobb. Wife died.
Issue:
39. Ervin.
40. Amy, d.
Third wife, Miss Whitmer. No issue.

(19) Samuel Culbertson mar. Miss L. Jones.
Issue:
41. Annie.
42. Edgar.
43. Frank.

(20) Levi Culbertson mar. Caroline Musser.
Issue:
44. Lida, d.
45. Wm.
46. John.
47. Frank.

SECTION SEVENTH .

(M) Elias Culbertson of Washington
Co., Pa. and Descendants.

SECTION SEVENTH

(M) Elias Culbertson on Census 1790, Washington Co., Pa. Given one male over 16 (head) 3 under (males) and one female (no doubt wife).

(M) **Elias Culbertson** came from Ireland about 1782. Lived in Washington Co., Pa. Mar. ———. Name of father not known.

Issue:
1. James, d.
2. Thomas, d.
3. Alexander, b. 1792; d. 1880.
4. John, d.
5. Elias, d.
6. Joseph, d.
7. Jane, b. 1803; d. Mar.
8. Sarah, d. Mar.

THIRD GENERATION

(1) James Culbertson mar. ———. Lived on a farm three miles north of Ashland, Ohio.

Issue:
9. Eli Culbertson, d.
10. Morgan.
11. William.
12. James.
13. Rachael. (Mrs. Bishop.)
14. Keziah. (Mrs. Wertman.)

(3) Alexander Culbertson mar. ———. Lived Fairfield, O.

Issue:
15. Wm. Culbertson, b. 1822.
16. Henry.
17. Jacob. N. Fairfield, O.
18. Emily.

(4) John Culbertson; know nothing about him.

(5) Elias Culbertson mar. Sarah Mason.

Issue:
19. William, d.
20. Elizabeth, dead.
21. Rachael, dead.
22. Elias. Ruggles, Ohio, dead.

23. Martha, dead.
24. Mary, dead.
25. Harriett.

(7) Jane Culbertson mar. J. D. Moore, of Cross Creek, Washington Co., Pa.
Issue:
26. Martha Moore (Mrs. Ford). Des Moines, Ia.
27. Sarah (Mrs. Vandemark). Topeka, Kan.
28. Elmina (Mrs. Boetcher). Bloomville, Ohio.
29. James. Washington Co., Pa.
30. Joseph. Cambridge, Ohio.
31. Gladen. Leadville, Col.
32. Alexander. Topeka, Kan.
33. Elizabeth (Mrs. Duncan). Talleyrand, Kan.
34. John. Savannah, Ashland Co., O.
35. Martin Moore. Topeka, Kan.
36. Elias, d. 1842.

(8) Sarah Culbertson mar. Mr. Brandeberry.
Issue:
37. Conrad Brandeberry.
38. Ezra.

FOURTH GENERATION

(9) Eli Culbertson mar. ——.
Issue:
39. Abe Culbertson.
(11) Wm. Culbertson mar. ——. Lives at Hooperstown, Ill.
Issue:
40. William.
40½. B. J., Charlotte, Mich. Insurance Agent.
40¾. John B., Sterling, Kan.

(13) Miss Rachael Culbertson mar. Mr. Bishop.

(14) Miss Keziah Culbertson mar. Mr. Wertman, of Ashland, Ohio.
Issue:
41. Ida Wertman.

(15) Wm. Culbertson mar. Mary L. ——. Lives at Greenwich, Ohio.
Issue:
42. William, d. Dec. 1850.
43. Emily. Lives at Akron, O.

44. John W., Lorain, O.
45. Charles, d. Nov., 1863.
46. Lewis A. Lives at Mt. Vernon, O.
47. Hiram. Lives at Columbus, O.
48. Mary. Greenwich, O.
49. Albert, d. June, 1886.

(16) Henry Culbertson mar. ——. Lives at Penora, Ia.
Issue:
50. Leroy.
51. Sherman.
52. Frank.

(17) Jacob Culbertson mar. .
Issue:
53. Huldah (Mrs. Stauffer). Greenwich, O.
54. Mary (Mrs. Collier.)

(18) Emily Culbertson mar. Ganning. Lives at N. Fairfield, O.
Issue:
55. Howard Ganning. Cleveland, O.

(20) Elizabeth Culbertson mar. Mr. Heath. Lives at York City, Ind.
Issue: Know nothing about.

(21) Rachael Culbertson mar. Mr. Baldwin.
Issue:
56. Adelbert Baldwin.
57. Sarah Jane.

(22) Elias Culbertson mar. Estella Carley.
Issue:
58. Frank E. Ruggles, New London, O., Rt. 4.
59. Alvin Ruggles, Ashland Co., O. Greenwich, O., Rt. 4.
Mar. Clara Quinn. No issue.

(23) Martha Culbertson mar. Mr. Nobles.
Issue: (?)

(24) Mary Culbertson mar. Mr. McGinn.

(25) Harriett Culbertson mar. Harmon Johnston, of Wauseon, O.

FIFTH GENERATION

(43) Emily Culbertson mar. Mr. Brown, Akron, O.
Issue:
60. Zelia Brown.

61. Mabel (Mrs. Harry Walters), Akron, O.
62. Earl. Akron, O.

(44) John W. Culbertson mar. Jessie Tyler, Mar. 13, 1877. Lives at Lorain, O. (Hardware).
Issue:
63. Guy W.
64. Joseph Ray.
65. Wm. Leo.

(46) Lewis A. Culbertson mar. ———. Lives at Mt. Vernon, Ohio.
Issue:
66. Wm. Ray. Mt. Vernon, O.
67. George. Mt. Vernon, O.
67½. Albert.

(48) Mary Culbertson mar. Mr. Collier. Lives at N. Fairfield, Ohio.
Issue:
68. Kenneth Collier.
68½. Lucille.

(48) Married second Mr. Brown.

(58) Frank Culbertson mar. Cora E. Irish, New London, Ohio.
Issue:
69. H. Reid. New London, O. mar. Jeanette Fauldauer.
    Issue: Marjorie Grace.

SIXTH GENERATION

(63) Guy Wilbur Culbertson mar. Ada Ludington. Lives at Los Angeles, Calif.
Issue:
70. Jack   } Twins, b. Dec. 12, 1912.
71. Betty

(64) Joseph Ray Culbertson mar. Gertrude Bruce. Cashier of Central Bank, Lorain, Ohio.
Issue:
72. Son. ———, b. Oct. 22, 1905.

(65) Wm. Leo Culbertson enlisted Naval Reserves, Aviation Corps. In Camp during World War at Newport, R. I. Living at Providence, R. I. Mar. first Gladys Evans who died four months later without issue. Mar. second Anna Parker.

SECTION EIGHTH
N. Carolina Irish or Scotch Families.

SECTION EIGHTH

IRISH WILLIAM AND JOHN CULBERTSON AND DAVID, SR., OF MECHLENBURG, N. CAROLINA.

(N) **William Culbertson.** In his aplication for pension says: "Born in Tyrone Co., Ireland, in 1740 (Mar. 17). Married Rachael ——, January, 1772, in Ireland. Left Ireland May, 1773. One son, Thomas, born in Ireland. Also has a daughter Sally. Others. I was in Pa. when the British man-of-war, Roebuck, came up the Delaware river to Wilmington. I joined a Pa. company for a few days then later in 1775, I removed to Mecklenburg Co., N. Car. Served in Capt. Oliver Wiley's Co. and in Major Joseph Dixon's company of "Minute Men." Also Barrie's Army and Navy of U. S. (p. 248, Chap. XXVI) "Served short time with Pa. troops, then removed to N. Car.; also served short time with Col. Harris Regt.; Pension $39 a year, commenced Mar. 4, 1831. Residence Burke Co., N. Car. Died Apr. 7, 1838." In battles of Cowpens and King's Mt. and many other actions. (From his pension papers.) William Culbertson was deeded land by John McCall in Mecklenburg Co., N. Car., July 14, 1778, on Crocket Creek, 92 acres. He later moved to Burke Co., N. Car., where he died. His son, David, moved to Burke Co. in 1805.

Census Records of 1840 show him 90 years old; wife 80 years and that he had a son William and son David, between 40 and 50 years old and both married and had children. The widow of one son was named Martha. Court records of this county were destroyed during the Civil War. Census Records 1790 give him wife and eight children (4 girls); one child male over 16 years; residence Mecklenburg Co., N. Car.; 3 males under 16.

* * * * *

(O) **John Culbertson** (Irish) on Oct. 6, 1766, purchased land from Adam Alexander on Goose Creek, Mecklenburg Co., N. Car. From time to time made other purchases on Goose Creek. His son, Moses, first bought land in Apr., 1777, from which I would infer he must have been born 1756 in Ireland. N. Car. Archives, Colonial, show that "John Culbertson of Clear Creek, Mecklenburg Co., N. Car. commissioned Corporal in Capt. Adam Alexander's Co. of N. Car. Militia, June 7, 1766."

John Culbertson, Sr., deeded 82 acres to his son, David, in 1793, on Goose Creek. David sold all of his land in Mecklenburg by 1804, at which date he lived in Anson Co., N. Car. John Culbertson conveyed the tract on which he lived to his son John in 1803 and in 1808 sold all of his land and moved to Anson Co., N. Car. John, Jr., remained in Mecklenberg Co., N. Car., and his estate was administered Aug., 1826. Margaret Culbertson was his widow and M. W. Cuthbertson was Guardian. Gdn. pd. David Cuthbertson, John Cuthbertson and Margaret Cuthbertson. Census 1790 gives John, Sr., 3 children (two girls). Mechlenburg Co. (One son under 16). In some of these deeds the name was Cuthbertson and some it was Culbertson (referring to the same parties). Cuthbertson on 1790 Census. David, son of John Sr., is given Census Records 1790, Mecklenburg Co., one son, under 16; two females. Cuthbertson on 1790 Census. Moses W. Culbertson (Cuthbertson) before mentioned purchased land on Goose Creek in 1777 from David Oliphant (271 A.). Up to 1840 I find no will or administration of him in Mecklenburg Co., N. Car. I find he took out a warrant for 4½ acres in Anson Co., in 1820. His estate may have been administered in Anson Co. He does not appear on 1790 Census (evidently overlooked). Burke Co. court records destroyed during war. Census 1830, age 50 years, wife 40 years. I was first inclined to think Moses W. was a brother of John (Irish) but my belief is that he was a son and born about 1756. David being on Census 1790 married and 2 sons under 16 would indicate he was born 1760-65. We do not know whether John, Sr., came to America before 1766.

*   *   *   *   *

(P) David, Sr., of Burke Co., N. Car., appears on Census 1790 with wife and 3 sons under 16 and 3 girls. He no doubt was a brother of Irish John and William. No deeds to or from him in Mecklenburg. Moses W. Culbertson above mentioned lived on Goose Creek adjoining John, Sr. No deeds from John, Sr., to Moses W. Culbertson.

SECTION NINTH
The Bulaughmore, County Tyrone, Ireland,. Family.

SECTION NINTH

SECOND GENERATION

(Irish) —— Culbertson said to be a cousin of the three Irish brothers of the Pennsylvania "Row." Do not know whether this man lived in "Irish Row," Antrim Co., Ireland; but he probably lived at the latter place.

Issue:

I. —— **Culbertson.** (See Part First.)

(Q) II. **James.** Emigrated to Mason Co., Ky. (Part Second.)

(R) III. **Robert.** Emigrated to Harrison Co., O. (Part Third.)

(S) IV. **Wm. Culbertson,** Irish-American came to U. S. before 1800, place of settlement unknown. (Part Fourth.)

(T) V. **Joseph Culbertson** of Huntingdon Co., Pa., and Belmont Co., O. (Part Fifth.)

* * * * *

Note: It is my firm belief that the above men were related to the Kenton Co., Ky. family, who came from Tyrone Co., Ireland. A daughter of James, one of the four brothers from Tyrone Co., Ireland, who settled in Kenton Co., Ky. stated in 1892 that her grandfather, James, who remained in Ireland, had a brother, Robert, who came to America about 1800, but his place of settlement was unknown. I think this was the above Robert of Guernsey Co., Ohio.

PART FIRST

THIRD GENERATION

(I) —— Culbertson died about 1815 at Bulaughmore or Bulliamore (means "more gold"), Ireland. Was a farmer. According to a statement made eighty-five years ago by his son, Dr. John Culbertson of Hanover, Pa., this man was a nephew (?) of the three Irish brothers of the Penna. "Row." He married Miss Clendennis, of Fintona, Ireland.

Issue:

1. William, lived at Bulliamore, Ireland.
2. James (Dr.) Dublin, Ireland.
3. (U) John (Dr.) b. 1791; d. Mar. 18, 1882.
4. —— (Mrs. Wallace). Lived in Tyrone Co., Ireland.
5. Daughter.
6. Daughter.

FOURTH GENERATION

(1) William Culbertson mar. Jane Christie of Ireland. Issue:

7. Sarah, mar. Wm. Beatty of Fintona, Ireland and emigrated to Australia, 1850. Issue: James, Sarah Jane, Margaretta, Emilie; five others names unknown.
8. Margaret (Mrs. John McCausland) Mulliamore, Ireland. Issue: Catherine Jane (Mrs. James Burns), Sydney, Aus., Cuthbertson; Anna Bella, Fred, William.
9. William, mar. Margaret ——, United States. Issue: Maude, Margaret, Elizabeth, Emma, William.
10. Anna Bella, mar. Henry Page, Sydney, Australia.
11. Margaret, deceased.
12. Maria (Mrs. Robert C. Musgrave), Allegheny, Pa. Issue: Eliabeth H., John Knox, Henry P.
13. Lizzie. Baltimore.
14. Fannie.
15. Matilda.
16. John Knox.
17. Sarah (Mrs. Wm. Christie) Mulliamore, Ireland. Issue: Wm., John, Margaretta Rebecca (U. S. A.), David (Liverpool), Alexander (Liverpool), Alexander (Liverpool), Crawford (Canada), Hubert, Isabella Elizabeth mar. Chas. Mitchell, Fintona, Ireland. Issue: James, Wm., Chas.; Jane (Mrs. Chas. Cootes); Maria (Sydney, Australia); Wm. mar. (Bulliamore, Ireland) five children.

(2) Dr. James Culbertson mar. ——. Lived at Dublin, Ireland, where he was a surgeon of prominence. For some reason part of his children changed their name to Cuthbertson. Three of Dr. James daughters (Emily, Eliza and Louisa were triplets and when they were children were presented to Queen Victoria of England, who gave an expensive present to each.

Issue:

18. John Jeremiah.
19. James.
20. Robert, d. in India, in British Army. (Major).
21. Anna. Lives in Dublin, Ireland. Deceased.
22. Rose. Lives in Ireland, Kingston, d. 1919.
23. Emile. Lives in Ireland, Kingston. Living 1922.
24. Elizabeth. Lives in Ireland, Kingston, d. 1921.

25. Louisa (Stevens). Alberta, Canada, d. 1921.

(3-U) Dr. John Culbertson mar. first Elizabeth Himes. Emigrated to Hanover, York Co., Pa., April, 1819. Mar. second Elizabeth Hawthorne.

Issue:

26. John (Grocer at Keokuk, .Ia.) Do not know whether by first or second wife.

(4) —— mar. Mr. Wallace, of near Fintona, Ireland and lived in Ireland.

Issue:

27. Wm. moved to Columbiana Co., O.
28. Son, d. Iowa.
29. Son, d.
30. Joseph, b. 1817. Columbiana, O.

FIFTH GENERATION

(18) John Jeremiah Culbertson mar. Mary Amelia Fonshall.

Issue:

31. John James. Vice Pres. of Paris Oil & Cotton Co., Paris, Texas.

SIXTH GENERATION

(31) John James Culbertson mar. Emily Lee. Lives at Paris, Texas.

Issue:

32. John James, Jr., Oklahoma City.
33. Emily Lee.
34. Florence Fonshill.

SEVENTH GENERATION

(32) John J., Jr. II. mar. 1911 Bonnie Dulaney of Paris, Tex. Issue: 35, John J., b. 1913; 36, Margaret Lee, b. Oct. 30, 1914.

(33) Emily Lee mar. 1915 to A. B. Potter, M. D., of Oklahoma City. Issue: 37, Albert Bryan, Florence C.

(34) Florence Fonshill Culbertson mar. 1920 Eugene Whittington of Oklahoma City. Issue: 38, Richard C., b. 1921.

PROMINENT DESCENDANTS

(18) John James Culbertson of Paris, Texas, is Vice President of the Southland Cotton and Oil Co. and Member of the Board of Directors of Federal Reserve Bank at Dallas, Texas.

His son (32) John James Culbertson, Jr., is also connected with the Southland Cotton Oil Co. and lives at Oklahoma City, Okla., and is part owner of the Culbertson Block, Oklahoma City.

Embarked in the cotton seed oil manufacturing business in 1883 and is a pioneer; organized and erected a large number of plants which are part of the present company of which he is Vice President. He is a large owner of real estate in Oklahoma and built the Culbertson Block in Oklahoma City.

He was elected president of the Interstate Cotton Seed Oil Crushers Association in 1916. Is a member of the National Foreign Trade Council in New York. Aided in Washington when war was declared in the Cotton Seed Products Section of the Food Administration. Was elected as a Class B. Director of the Federal Reserve Bank of Dallas when the system was organized and has served continuously until the present time. Is reported to be a millionaire.

PART SECOND
SECTION NINTH

(Q) James Culbertson (Irish)
of Mason County, Kentucky.

PART SECOND
THIRD GENERATION

(Q) II. **James Culbertson** emigrated from Bulaughmore, Ireland, to Mason Co., Ky., Ky., about 1800.

Issue:
1. Robert, d. Rushville, Ind.
2. James, d. Lived near Maysville, Ky.
3. William. Glenwood, Ind.
4. David, d. Bachelor.
5. Margaret, d. (Mrs. Reed).
6. Sarah, d. Mar.

FOURTH GENERATION

(1) Robert Culbertson mar. ——. Moved to Rushville, Ind.

Issue:
7. Mary Ann, d.
8. Martha P., d.
9. Jane. Rushville, Ind. (Unmar.)
10. Elizabeth, d.
11. John. Rushville, Ind.
12. James, d.
13. Alexander. Rushville, Ind.

(2) James Culbertson mar. Sarah Weaver. Both dead. Saddle and trunk maker.

Issue:
14. Wm. G. (Mays Station, Ills.)
15. John James, d.
16. Edward O., Tolono, Ills.
17. Amanda (Mrs. Grace). Danville, Ills.
18. Sarah (Mrs. Matkin). Indianola, Ills.

FIFTH GENERATION

(14) Wm. G. Culbertson mar. Nancy Ledger.

Issue:
19. Wm. J.
20. Kate, d.
21. Sarah E. (Mrs. Henry McPhillips).
22. Blanche (Mrs. Hugo Lodge). Paris, Ills.
23. Florence (Mrs. Scott Dougherty), Wabash, Ind.

24. Edward. Unmar. Paris, Ills.
25. Thomas, d.

(16) Edward O. Culbertson mar. ――――. Is insurance adjuster to the Aetna Fire Ins. Co., for five states. (Tolono, Ills.)
Issue:
26. Sarah N. (Mrs. Hartman) La Fayette, Ind.
27. Candace A. Unmar. Tolono, Ills.
28. Jennie (Mrs. Handy) Tolono, Ills.
29. G. W. Tolono, Ills.

(17) Amanda Culbertson mar. Mr. Grace. Live at Danville, Ills.

(18) Sarah Culbertson mar. Mr. Matkin.

PART THIRD
SECTION NINTH

(R) Robert Culbertson (Irish) of Harrison and Belmont County, Ohio

PART THIRD

(R. III) **Robert Culbertson** emigrated in 1820, from Bulaughmore, Ireland (Antrim Co.) to Harrison Co., Ohio. He later moved to Claysville, Guernsey Co., Ohio. (Naturalization papers "came over 1802").

Issue:

THIRD GENERATION

1. John.
2. Ezekial.
3. Samuel.
4. James.
5. Robert.
6. William.
7. Benjamin.
8. Thomas.
9. Hugh, b. 1795-6. Marion Co., Ind.
10. Joseph.
11. George. New Concord, Ohio.
12. Gillespie.
13. Mary, d. young.
14. Annie, (Mrs. Dr. Gillogley), Zanesville, Ohio.

FOURTH GENERATION

1. John Culbertson, born in Ireland. Married a Miss Culbertson from Scotland (a grandson stated in 1892). Settled in Richland Co. Ohio, near Mansfield.

Issue:

15. John.
16. William, d. 1848 in California.
17. Calvin. Lived in Tennessee. Rich Creek.
18. Houstin.
19. Chalmers, d.
20. Martha (Mrs. Dean).
21. Jane.
22. Agnes (Mrs. Dr. McCullough of Chicago).

(9) Hugh Culbertson came to America in 1802 with his father. Lived first in Harrison and Belmont Counties, Ohio, then moved to Guernsey Co., Ohio, then to Marion Co., Ind. where he owned a large farm. Married first ——.

Issue:

23. Nan (Mrs. Baird). Issue: Tom.

(9) Hugh Culbertson mar. second Miss Holt.
Issue:
24. Thomas. In Civil War.
25. Mary (Mrs. Granville Bocock). Issue: Edwin, Silas;
     Maude.
26. Dorcas (Mrs. Bethuel Smith). Issue: Vernon; LeRoy;
     Ethel; Mary; Nettie.

(9) Hugh Culbertson mar. third Katharine Ann Cox.
Issue:
27. John.
28. Hugh.
29. Joseph.

FIFTH GENERATION

(18) Houston Culbertson born in Richland Co., Ohio. Mar.
first ——.
Issue:
30. Ida (Mrs. McCollough).
31. James Wallace; Iowa City, Ia. in 1892.
32. William.

(18) Houston Culbertson mar. second ——.   Lived in
1892 at Winfield, Ia. Hotel proprietor.
Issue:
33. Stella.
34. Roy.

(24) Thomas Culbertson.
Issue:
35. Otto, d.
36. Ellery, unmar. Carpenter. (Marion, Ind.)
37. Mary Millicent unmar. (Marion, Ind.)
38. June, unmar. (Marion, Ind.)

(27) John Culbertson mar. ——.
Issue:
39. Harry, mar.
40. Abraham mar.
41. Earle.

(28) Hugh Culbertson mar. Lives Detroit, Mich.
Issue:
42. Ralph d. infancy.
43. Claude, d. infancy.
44. Oscar, in Marine Corps recently.

45. Louise, d. infancy.
46. Joanna; mar. J. Row (Issue: Elizabeth).
47. Izetta, Washington, D. C. Unmar.
48. Katherine, d. infancy.
49. Mary, unmar. Washington, D. C.
50. Ruth mar. Otto J. Palmer (Issue: Iola Louise).

(29) Joseph Culbertson, mar. ——. Marion, Ind. Both dead.

Issue:
51. McClellan, d. aged 28 years.
52. Nelson, d. young.
53. Dessie, d. young.

PART FOURTH

SECTION NINTH

(S) William Culbertson (Irish) of America.

PART FIFTH

SECTION NINTH

(T) Joseph Culbertson of Huntingdon Co., Pa.--Belmont Co., Ohio.

PART FOURTH

(S. IV) William Culbertson of Ireland came to United States. Place of settlement not given.

The following is from a letter of a Culbertson residing in Mansfield, O. (1895):

"According to my memory, it was said at home that brothers named Alexander, Joseph and Samuel left Scotland at the time of the Revolution (1688?), going to the west part of Tyrone county, Ireland. One settled near Strabane, the other two near Fintona. My great grandfather bought a tract of land, and giving grandfather the house and one-half the land and his brother Joseph the other half. (Grandfather's name was William.) There was another brother who stayed in Ireland. Grandfather came to the United States and settled in Pennsylvania* About 1800 an uncle of my father, named Robert came to this country and first settled in Belmont Co., O., then later in Guernsey county and had twelve sons and two daughters. (S) William Culberson (grandfather) had five children (two daughters, Margaret and Mary, and three sons, John, Andrew and James.) Mary (Mrs. McCracken) had two sons and two daughters, died at Warren, O. Margaret (Mrs. Crawford) died at Pittsburg had four sons. John had a family of eight; William, James, John, Margaret, Elizabeth, Mary Ann, Martha and Jane. John died in Ireland. Andrew had eight children: James, Samuel, William, Eliza, Mary Jane, Margaret, Isabella and Rebecca. James you know of. John Culbertson, who lived at Mansfield, was the oldest son of Robert Culbertson of Belmont County, O. His other sons settled in Kentucky, Indiana and Illinois, and some are still living in Guernsey County, O.

*Instead of Pa., could it have been Maryland? and could he have been Wm. of the Md. Line in Revolution at Valley Forge? (Ed.)

SECTION NINTH

PART FIFTH

THE PA-OHIO FAMILY—IN HUNTINGDON CO., PA., AND BELMONT CO., OHIO.

(T.-V.) **Joseph Culbertson** came to America from either Down or Tyrone Co., Ireland, with his brother (name unknown) and settled in Huntingdon Co., Pa. His brother shortly after left him and his place of settlement is unknown. Joseph mar. Margaret McCune of Pennsylvania, and after residing a few years in Huntingdon County or Westmoreland County, Pa., moved to Uniontown, Belmont Co., Ohio. There was a Joseph Culbertson, Huntingdon Tp., Westmoreland Co., Pa. 1800 Census, self and wife, both under 26 years; two daughters under 10 years.

Issue:
1. Robert, b. 1797; d. 1879. Richland Co., O.
2. Thomas. Mar. but no issue.
3. Joseph, d.
4. James, d. when a young man, unmar.
5. Margaret, d. mar. cousin, William Culbertson, of Guernsey Co., O.
6. Polly, d. Mar. cousin, John Culbertson, of Mansfield, Ohio.
7. Elizabeth, d. (Mrs. Thos. Finney, Mansfield, O.)
8. Nancy, d. (Mrs. Elijah Finney, Mansfield, O.)
9. Sarah, d.
10. Abigail, d. (Mrs. Walker, Belmont Co., O.)

THIRD GENERATION

(1) Robert Culbertson mar. ——.
Issue:
11. Joseph, d. infancy.
12. James, d. aet. 27. Unmar.
13. Jane. Living, 1892.
14. Thomas S. Nankin, O.
15. Joseph.
15. Joseph.
16. Mary Ann. Living, 1892.
17. Margaret. Living, 1892.
18. John, d.

19. George, d. 1865.
20. Rachael,. living,. 1892.
21. ——, d. young.

(3) Joseph Culbertson mar. ——.
Issue:
22. James. Alliance O.
23. Joseph.
24. Wilson S., d. Lived at Cincinnati.
25. Eliabeth.
26. Mary Ann.

FOURTH GENERATION

(13) Jane Culbertson mar. Mr. Hamilton.
Issue:
27. Son.
28. Daughter.

(14) Thomas S. Mar. ——.
Issue:
29. Joseph. Ashland, O.
30. George. Ashland, O.
31. Perry. Montana.
32. Calvin. Montana.
33. Frank. Salt Lake City.
34. Ella. Traer, Ia.

(16) Mary Anne Culbertson mar. Mr. Ritchie.
Issue: Do not know.

(17) Margaret Culbertson mar. Mr. Stertz.
Issue:
35. Elihu Stertz (M. D.). Adopted the name of Culbertson. Norwalk, Ohio, b. Feb. 1, 1854.

(20) Rachael Culbertson mar. Mr. Dunlap.
Issue:
36, 37, 38. Daughters.

(22) James mar. ——. Alliance, O.
Issue: Do not know.

(24) Wilson S. Culbertson mar. Sadie ——. Widow lives at Tusculum, near Cincinnati, O.
Issue:
39. Daughter.

(24) Jos., mar. ——. Ashland, Ohio.
(30) Geo., mar. ——. Ashland, Ohio.

FIFTH GENERATION

(35) Elihu Stertz-Culbertson of Norwalk, Ohio, mar. first Ida Gregory. (Wife died).
Issue:
40. Hugh Emmett Culbertson. Atty., Ashland, Ohio.
41. B. W. Culbertson, Coshocton, Ohio.
42. Burr Douglas, d. infancy.

(35) Elihu S. Culbertson mar. second Lillie Jenkins. No issue. He now lives at Ontario, Richland Co., Ohio.

SIXTH GENERATION

(40) Hugh Emmett Culbertson, Ashland, Ohio, mar. Flora Neal Paul, of Milan, O., March 17, 1906.
Issue:
43. Edna Pauline.
44. Mary Margaret.
45. Helen Louise.

PROMINENT DESCENDANTS.

(40) Hugh Emmett Culbertson, attorney, graduated Law Department Ohio State University, 1905; in 1906 editor on staff of Lansing Law Book Co. Author "Medical Man and The Law," 1913. Mayor, Milan, O., 1907-8. Practiced for a time at Loudonville, O. Now ass't Prosecuting Att'y, Ashland Co., Ohio. Lives at Ashland, O. Mentioned 1917 in "Who's Who in America."

PART ONE
SECTION TENTH

The Kenton Co., Ky. Family From
Tyrone County, Ireland.

(This family was compiled and written by an attorney in
Cincinnati, Ohio, Mr. James A. Culbertson, a descendant.
—Editor.)

PART ONE

The Culbertsons of Kenton County, Kentucky, are of two branches. The first traces its ancestry through immigrants who settled about the year 1800 at Edinboro, Erie County, Pa. The second branch, which is the branch under consideration here, traces its ancestry through immigrants who settled on the Licking River, at Culbertson Station (now Spring Lake) Kenton County, Kentucky, about 1813 and later. There were four brothers and four sisters, as follows:

V. 1.   James, who married Elizabeth Youtsey (See Part Two).

V. 2.   William, who married Jane Reese and Nancy White (See Part Three).

V. 3.   Allen, who married Ester Greer (See Part Four).

V. 4.   Robert, who married Maria Gregg (See Part Five).

V. 5.   Sidney, who married James Taylor.

V. 6.   Margaret, who married —— Kyle.

V. 7.   Mary, who married —— McLaughlin.

V. 8.   Sarah, who married George Youtsey.

This family came from Newtown-Stewart, County Tyrone, Ireland. Their parents were James and Jane Culbertson. James did not come to America, but his wife, Jane, came. She was born in 1761 and died in the year 1833. She is buried in William Culbertson's family cemetery at Spring Lake, Ky.

At pages 904 and 905, Volume 2, of Charles A. Babcock's History of Venango County, Pennsylvania, there is the following interesting account of a memorial stone in William Culbertson's family cemetery.

"There is a unique memorial in Kentucky whose story should have its place in the annals of the Culbertson family, as the following article which accompanied a cut of this odd gravestone explains. The gravestone shown in the illustration stands in a lonely pine grove near Spring Lake, Ky., and is supposed to commemorate a tragedy of many years ago in Ireland. The memorial is hewn out of a single stone slab and is about four feet high. On the front there is carved a small harp and at the bottom appears the letters and date 'W. C. —— B. 1787,' while on the side there is the name, 'Cormick O. Devlin.' As the story is told, it was about 130 years ago that a family of the name of Culbertson, residing in Ireland and enjoying something of rank and position were forced to flee suddenly from their home as the result of politics. Owing to the hastiness of their departure very little of their personal belongings could be taken along. They had gone but a short distance when one of the daughters happened to think of a certain bit of jewelry which she treasured highly, and unknown to the other members of the family, started back to recover it. A few minutes later her absence was discovered and her lover, a young man named Cormick O. Devlin, who was with the party, immediately went in search of her. He was drawing near her house when he heard cries of distress and running inside found that a number of rough looking soldiers had attacked her. Bravely he attempted to fight off her assailants and in the course of the struggle the girl managed to make her escape, but Cormick O. Devlin himself was killed. The Culbertson family came over to this country and settling at Spring Lake erected this unique monument."

A daughter of (V. 1.) James Culbertson, Mrs. Jane Pye, stated to the Author in 1892 that her father was James and that her grand-father was James who lived in Newton-Stewart, Co. Tyrone, Ireland. Descendants say that the father of the Culbertson brothers (Irish-Americans) who came to Kenton Co., Ky., in 1813, died aboard ship en route to America. We know positively that his widow came to this country and settled in Kenton Co., Ky., in 1813, as the following will prove:In the old cemetery on the Licking River in Kenton Co., Ky., is this inscription, "This family cemetery was founded in 1840 by William Culbertson, cooper and horticulturist, a native of Tyrone Co., Ireland, who cleared, planted, built and improved this place 1813, up to this time." Another inscription says "In memory of Jane Culbertson, who died of cholera July 22, 1833, aged 72 years." Also same stone:

> "She told me that shame would never betide
> With truth for my creed and God for my Guide.
> She taught me to lisp my earliest prayer
> As I knelt beside her old arm-chair—
> My Mother.
> "W. C."

This was the mother of the four Irish-American brothers.

SECTION TENTH

PART SECOND

(V. 1.) James Culbertson, a native of Tyrone County, Ireland, who settled at Spring Lake (formerly Culbertson station), on the Licking River, Kenton County, Kentucky, in the year 1813. Born June 22, 1781; died, December 18, 1834. Married Elizabeth (Betsey) Youtsey, of Campbell County, Kentucky, about 1813. She was born December 10, 1791, and died January 27, 1869.

SECOND GENERATION

Issue:

I.   Jane, born November 22, 1814; died ——. Married William Pye. Chapter LVII.

11. James, born December 23, 1816; died November 5, 1880. Chapter LVIII.

III. John Youtsey, born December 15, 1817; died ——, 1887. Never married.

IV. William H., born ——9, 1819; died; killed in Civil War. Chapter LVIX.

V.   Michael, born May —, 1822; died March 25, 1860. Chapter LX.

VI. ——, born September —, 1823; died ——, 1823.

VII. Katherine, born November 22, 1824; died —'. Married Alfred Frazer. Chapter LXI.

VIII. George, born January 4, 1826; died ——. Chapter LXII. No data.

IX. Peter born —— 1827; died in infancy.

X.   Jacob, born November 26, 1828; died 1885. Chapter LXIII.

XI. Sarah M., born March 7, 1830 died. Married —— Hunt. Chapter LXIV.

XII. Robert, born November 6, 1831; died June 19, 1889.

CHAPTER LVII

(I) **Jane Culbertson** married William Pye. They lived at Pye's station, south of Latonia in Kenton County, Ky.

THIRD GENERATION

Issue:
1. James.
2. Mollie. A daughter, ——, married Geo. C. Shays of Cincinnati, O.

CHAPTER LVIII

(II) **James Culbertson** married Mary Eliza Coleman on February 9, 1847. They lived at Ryland Station, south of Latonia, Kenton County, Kentucky.

Issue:

THIRD GENERATION

1. James Coleman, born November 16, 1847; died May 28,. 1912.
2. John Wesley, born February 27, 1849; died July —, 1849.
3. Alice Elizabeth, born August 8, 1850; died July —, 1908.
4. Mary Jane, born September 13, 1852; died March 29, 1856.
5. William Henry, born April 11, 1854; died Feb. 26, 1856.
6. Jeannette, born April 13, 1856.
7. Caroline, born May 2, 1858.
8. Ida Irena, born March 24, 1860.
9. George W., born September 17, 1862.
10. Anna Maud, born November 28, 1867.
11. Mary Eliza, born November 15, 1872.

FOURTH GENERATION

(1) James Coleman Culbertson married Laura Arena Richardson (born September 1, 1848; died July 10, 1918) on the 22nd day of December, 1868. They lived in Covington, Ky.

Issue:
12. Cynthia Catherine, born March 6, 1870.
13. James Edward, born October 23, 1871; died Dec. 6, 1921.

14. Clarence Laird, born March 14, 1874; died March —, 1874.
15. Robert Laird, born November 29, 1875; died October 8, 1910.
16. Austin Rusk, born January 4, 1844.
17. Susan Irene, born October 31, 1888.

(3) Alice Elizabeth Culbertson married John Morris Mendenhall (born April 4, 1843) of Kenton County, Ky., January 28, 1867. They lived at Ryland, south of Latonia, Ky.
Issue:
18. John James, born June 17, 1868.
19. Eliza Ellen, born March 17, 1870.
20. Etha Lena, born September 24, 1873.
21. William Lamborn, born November 2, 1879.
22. Nettie Maud, born March 10, 1882.
23. Edgar Ray, born April 20, 1885.
24. Edna May, born April 20, 1885.
25. Bessie, born January 28, 1888.
26. Jessie, born January 28, 1888; died July 11, 1910.

(6) Jeannette Culbertson married James Madison Loving (born ———, died September 22, 1904) November 3, 1880. They lived at Lenore City, Tenn.
27. Ernest Lloyd, born August 20, 1881.
28. Eva Maud, born January 14, 1883; died January 21, 1904.
29. May Jeannette, born August 10, 1884.
30. James Hendricks, born March 26, 1886.

(7) Caroline Culbertson married Augden Milton House (born April 4, 1851) of Kenton County, Ky., December 16, 1876. They live at Florence, Boone County, Ky.
Issue:
31. Iva Irene, born February 26, 1878.
32. George William, born March 11, 1880; died 1916.
33. Annabelle born August 1, 1883.
34. Florence May, born October 10, 1885; died December 25, 1892.
35. Mabel Luella, born December 8, 1887.
36. Russell Eugene, born July 5, 1899.

(8) Ida Irena Culbertson married Dr. Lafayette Stephens of Kenton County, Kentucky. They lived in Kenton County, Ky.
Issue:
37. Anna May.

38. Edith.
38½. Allen.

(9) George W. Culbertson married Sarah Ida Senour (born April 15, 1865) of Kenton County, Ky., September 17, 1884. They live at Ryland Station (Latonia postoffice) in Kenton County.

Issue:
39. James Atwood, born April 22, 1886.
40. Bessie Irene, born January 24, 1888.
41. Edith Geneva, born September 30, 1891.

(10) Anna Maud Culbertson married George Thomas Ellison (born June 19, 1858) of Kenton County, Ky., February 3, 1886. They live at 625 Greenup Street, Covington, Ky.

Issue:
42. Robert Chester, born August 25, 1887.
43. George Walter, born June 1, 1890.

(11) Mary Eliza Culbertson married Longstreet Lamb, of Lamb's Station, Kenton County, Ky. They live at Nashville, Tenn.

Issue:
44. Grace Ethel, b. Mar. 7, 1896.
45. Alma Jennings, born March 24, 1897.
46. Avis Maud, born February 21, 1900.
47. Helen Lauretta, born December 21, 1910.

FIFTH GENERATION

(12) Cynthia Catherine Culbertson married Victor Wilson (born June 11, 1860; died January 10, 1916) of Covington, Ky., April 23, 1891. She lives at 1942 Oakland Avenue, Covington, Ky.

Issue:
48. Warner Culbertson, born November 3, 1892.
49. Stanley Edward, born August 1, 1894.
50. Irene Lucille, born May 31, 1898.

(15) Robert Laird Culbertson married Edith Pearl Palmer (born November 5, 1877), August 20, 1895. They lived in Covington, Ky.

Issue:
51. James Alfred, born August 19, 1896.
52. Robert Aubrey, born January 10, 1899.
53. Edith Mabel, born June 29, 1903.

(16) Austin Rusk Culbertson married Mary Duvenac, of Cincinnati, August 17, 1903. They live in Covington, Ky.
Issue:
54. Clarence, born February 11, 1905.
55. Dorothy, born October 21, 1906.
56. Austin, born November 12, 1908.
57. Blanche, born October 21, 1911.

(40) Bessie Irene Culbertson married William Verner Mills of Kenton County, Ky., April 21, 1906. They live at Ryland station (Latonia Postoffice R. F. D.), Kentucky.
Issue:
58. Verner Milburn, born October 29, 1909.
59. Kathleen, born December 9, 1912.

(41) Edith Geneva Culbertson married Hugh Van Deren Craigmyle of Cynthiana, Ky., March 12, 1910. They live at Ryland station (Latonia R. F. D.), Kentucky.
Issue:
60. Hazel Scnour, born February 15, 1911.
61. Hugh Joseph Beach, born October 23, 1913.

SIXTH GENERATION

(51) James Alfred Culbertson marriel Rosalie Evansburg (born April 7, 1899), June 1917. They live in Covington, Ky.
Issue:
62. James Edward, February 2, 1918.
63. Virginia Edith, born December 20, 1919.
64. Ruth Elizabeth, born September 5, 1921.

(52) Robert Aubrey Culbertson married Vivian Reitman (born August 10, 1898) September, 1919. They live in Covington, Ky.
Issue:
65. Vivian Carrol, born March 11, 1921.

CHAPTER LIX

(IV) **William H. Culbertson** married Isabelle Elliott, of Kenton County, Kentucky. They lived on a farm near Fiskburg, Kenton County, Ky.
Issue:

THIRD GENERATION

66. Mary Katherine, born June 15, 1843.

67. Betsy.
68. James E., born October 7, 1845; died March 9, 1923.
69. Ann Eliza.
70. John D., born August 14, 1850.
71. William Pye, born February 24, 1853.
72. George Youtsey, born March 14, 1855.
73. Charles T.
74. Franklin, born January 20, 1860.
75. Henry, born ——; died in infancy.

FOURTH GENERATION

(66) Mary Katherine Culbertson married Sidney M. Goshorn (born June 15, 1841; died June 10, 1913), of Marion, Ohio, June 3, 1863. She resides with her son, Wm. L. Goshorn, 22 East 18th St., Covington, Ky.

Issue:
76. Seymour Houston, born September 7, 1863.
77. Laura E., born March 27, 1865.
78. John Henry, August 24, 1869.
79. Mary Isabelle, born May 1, 1873.
80. William Lewis, born October 28, 1878.

(67) Betsy Culbertson married —— Winterling, of Grant County, Ky.

Issue:
81. Joseph Winterling residing at Stewartsville, Grant Co., Ky. Others unknown to compiler.

(68) James E. Culbertson married Eliza Kidwell (born October 10 1844; died December 14, 1919) of Kenton County, Ky. They lived on a farm near Fiskburg, Ky. (Demossville Route 1).

Issue:
82. Henry Houston, born November 27, 1867; died Nov. 1, 1897.
83. William Robert, born March 31, 1869.
84. Jacob, born January 28, 1874.
85. Eddy, born October 28, 1872; died August 2, 1910.
86. Virgie Belle, born November 10, 1878.

(69) Ann Eliza Culbertson married —— McWayne, of Fiskburg, Kenton County, Ky.

Issue:
87. Joseph.
88. Lulu.
89. Milton.
90. Louis.

91. Robert.
92. Queenie.

(70) John D. Culbertson married Mollie Wellman. They lived in Kenton County, Ky.
Issue:
93. Arthur.
94. William B.
95. Kirtley. died.
Second wife Carrie Weakley.
Issue:
96. Gertrude.
97. Effie.
98. Iva.
99. John, died.
100. Edward.

(71) William Pye Culbertson married Martha Jacobs of Dry Ridge, Ky., December 22, 1883. They live on a farm at Lebanon, Ohio., Route 6.
Issue:
101. Kate Elliott, born March 24, 1885.
102. Charles Eugene, born March 1, 1892.
103. Emily Prising, born March 11, 1899.

(72) George Youtsey Culbertson married Emma Frances Kidwell (born April 16, 1862) of Fiskburg, Ky. They live at Demossville, Kenton County, Ky., Route 2.
Issue:
104. Etta Flora, born April 3, 1882.
105. Earl F., born April 22, 1888.
106. Monroe, born May 24, 1892; died October 10, 1918, at Camp Taylor, Ky.
107. Elva Temple, born October 18, 1900.

FIFTH GENERATION

(82) Henry Houston Culbertson married Sadie Loomis of Fiskburg, Ky.
Issue:
108. Olive Irene, born August 6, 1895.
109. Cecil (girl), born October 26, 189—.

(83) William Robert Culbertson married Hattie May Daugherty (born March 19, 1877) of Demossville, Ky., October 24, 1894. They live at Demossville, Ky.
Issue:
110. Iva Ethel, born November 26, 1896.

111. Robert Kirtley, November 3, 1898.
112. Foster Floyd, born February 20, 1902.
113. Leonard Roosevelt, born May 5, 1905.
114. William Henry, born February 28, 1914.

(84) Jacob Culbertson married Ora V. Aydelott, of Fiskburg, Ky., February 20, 1895. They live at Demossville, Ky., Route 1.
Issue:
115. Ada V., born January 19, 1896.
116. Nina L., born October 16, 1897; died Jan. 13, 1917.
117. James Henry, born May 2, 1903.
118. Muzette Corine, born May 29, 1907.
119. Lena May, born December 23, 1911.

(93) Arthur Culbertson married Jessie Colker of Covington, Ky. They live at Phoenix, Ariz.
Issue:
120. Clifton.

(94) William B. Culbertson married Maude Davis of Missouri. They reside at Oklahoma City, Okla.
Issue:
121. William.
122. Florence.
123. John D.
124. Doris.

(97) Effie Culbertson married Edward Welter of Cincinnati. They live at 846 Clinton Street, Cincinnati, Ohio.
Issue:
125. Edward.
126. Virginia.

(98) Iva Culbertson married Harvey Fowler of Cincinnati, Ohio.
Issue:
127. Azedel (girl).

(101) Katie Elliott Culbertson married Eldon A. Short, of Dayton, Ohio, February 24, 1909. They live at 101 South Mathison Street, Dayton, Ohio.
Issue:
128. Harold Vernon, born March 26, 1910.

(102) Charles Eugene Culbertson married Bertha Supinger. They live at 132 Ardmore Stret, Dayton, Ohio.
Issue:
129. William Robert, born January 12, 1920.
130. Fredrick Eugene, born September 26, 1922.

(104) Etta Flora Culbertson married Melvin Mullins of Demossville, Ky., October 18, 1899. They live at Demossville, Ky.

Issue:

131. Roy Mullins, born February 13, 1903.

(107) Elva Temple Culbertson married Raymond Kinsey, of Demossville, Ky. They live at Demossville.

Issue:

132. Virginia Luanna, born January 14, 1922.

SIXTH GENERATION

(108) Olive Irene Culbertson married Eddy Elliott, of Fiskburg, Ky. They live at Demossville, Ky., R. F. D.

Issue:

133. Marzella Irene, born October 10, 1918.

134. James Rudolph, born March 25, 1920.

(109) Cecil Culbertson married Homer Works. They live at Gardnersville, Pendleton County, Ky.

Issue:

135. Elmo.

136. Frances.

137. Edwin.

(110) Iva Ethel Culbertson married Parran C. Spegal, June 25, 1916. They live at Demossville, Ky., Route 2.

Issue:

138. Wanetta May, born August 25, 1917.

139. Cecil Ruth, born November 15, 1922.

(111) Robert Kirtley Culbertson married Ernestine Mann, February 21, 1918. They live at Demossville, Ky.

Issue:

140. Robert Monroe, born August 20, 1922.

(115) Ada V. Culbertson married Newell Spegal, of Fiskburg, Ky., February 12, 1913. They live at Demossville, Ky., R. F. D.

Issue:

141. Anna Viola, died.

142. Doris Velma.

143. Lucy Roberta.

144. Bennetta Ethal.

145. Ora Ada.

William H. Culbertson (IV) served with the Federal forces in the Civil War. He received wounds at the battle of Mills Springs from which he died.

CHAPTER LX

THIRD GENERATION

(V) **Michael Culbertson** married Belle Mefford on the 13th day of March, 1845. They live in Kenton County, Ky.

Issue:

146. Jacob Frank Lester, born April 9, 1848; died April 26, 1919.
147. Minnie Belle, b. July 29, 1850; never married, died.
148. Lala Hinda, born April 27, 1852; died July, 1886.
149. Dora, born September 16, 1854. Unmarried.
150. Boonetta (Nell), born October 18, 1856.

FOURTH GENERATION

(146) Jacob Frank Lester Culbertson married Margaret Belle Hempfling of Grant's Bend, Kenton County, Ky., November 3, 1880. They lived on a farm on Taylors Mill Pike, south of Latonia, where his widow now resides.

Issue:

151. Michael Verner, born August 21, 1882.
152. Jacob Hempfling, born October 20, 1884.
153. Charles Allen, born September 21, 1886; died Feb. 21, 1919.
154. Mary Elizabeth, born August 26, 1888; married John James Cain March 17, 1918.
155. William Henry, born June 3, 1891; married Ruth Irene Porter, May 10, 1922.
156. Alfretta (Etta) Belle, born December 6, 1895; unmarried.

(148) Lala Hinda Culbertson married James Wayman of Kenton County, Ky., May 11, 1881. They lived in Kenton County, Ky.

Issue:

157. Logan, born March 13, 1882. Unmarried.

(150) Boonetta (Nell) Culbertson married Frank Savageot, of Ashland, Ky., March 5, 1887. He died. She and Dora Culbertson, her unmarried sister, reside at Tacoma, Wash.

Issue:

158. Dora, born February, 1888.
159. Inda, born May, 1891.

FIFTH GENERATION

(152) Jacob Hempfling Culbertson married Bertha A. Batcham, of Detroit, Mich., September 7, 1907. They live at Romulus, Mich., near Detroit.

Issue:
160. Everett Lyle, born December 26, 1910.

William Henry Culbertson (155) enlisted in the military forces of the United States at Covington, Kentucky, February 26, 1918. He sailed from the United States July 9, 1918. He participated in the battles of Aise Marne, Oise Aise, and Meuse Argonne. Received no wounds. After the armistice he was stationed at Coblenz, Germany, with the Army of Occupation. He arrived in the United States July 7, 1919, and was honorably discharged at Camp Taylor, July 17, 1919.

Charles A. Culbertson (153) enlisted in the military forces of the United States at Covington, Kentucky, May 22, 1918. Served at Camp Clark, Texas, and Camp Boie, Texas, and was honorably discharged at Fort Sill, Oklahoma, February 14, 1919. He returned to his home immediately, was ill when he returned, and died February 21, 1919, one week after his discharge.

CHAPTER LXI

(VII) Katherine Culbertson married Alfred Frazer, of Kenton County, Ky. They lived at Spring Lake (Culbertson Station), Kenton County, Ky.

Issue:

THIRD GENERATION

161. John.
162. Betty. Married —— Rusk.
163. Albert.
164. Charles.
165. Jennie. Married William Stafford. Died.
166. Lucy. Married Timothy W. Spanton.
167. Dolly. Married —— Rust } Twins.
168. Frank
168. Frank.
169. William.

CHAPTER LXII

(VIII) **George Culbertson** married Malissa Rusk, of Kenton County, Ky. They lived in Kenton County.

Issue:

THIRD GENERATION

170. Elizabeth; died in infancy.
171. Lafayette.
172. Isabelle, born February 20, 1851.
173. Joan, died, aged about 66.
174. Winfield; died in infancy.
175. Monroe; died in infancy.
176. John, died; never married.
177. Thomas.
178. Jennie.
179. Katherine; never married.
180. William; died in infancy.
181. Michael.

FOURTH GENERATION

(171) Lafayette Culbertson married Sallie Hoskins of Kenton County, Ky. He lives at Value, Rankin County, Mississippi.

Issue:

182. Howard.
183. William, died.
184. Mamie.
185. Lafayette.
186. Charles, died.
187. Susan, died.
188. Jennie, died.
189. Bessie.
190. George, died.

(172) Isabelle Culbertson married Samuel Taylor, of Kenton County, Ky. He died about 1902, and she now resides with her daughter, Hinda Pearl Taylor, at 4554 Commonwealth Ave., Erlanger, Ky.

Issue:

191. Ira Edwin.
192. Hinda Pearl.
193. Emmaline.
194. Jennie; died in infancy.

(177) Thomas Culbertson married Alice Thompson. They live at Fostoria, Ohio.

Issue:

195. Joan, died.
196. Frank.
197. Forrest.
198. Charles.
199. Kate.
200. Susan.
201. Thomas.

(178) Jennie Culbertson married Elisha Maddox, of Campbell County, Ky. She lives with her son at 1216 East 44th Street, Kansas City, Mo.

Issue:
202. Stella.
203. Byron.
204. Joan.

(181) Michael Culbertson married ——.
Issue:
205. George.

CHAPTER LXIII

(X) **Jacob Culbertson** married Caroline Beggs, of Campbell County, Ky., about 1850. They lived near Jackson, Mississippi.

Issue:

THIRD GENERATION

206. Charles, born April 10, 1851. Unmarried. Lives at Jackson.
207. Frank, born July 31, 1853.
208. William, born July 3, 1855.
209. May; died about 1890.
210. Maud, born January 30, 1866. Unmarried. Lives at Jackson.
211. Ursula, born Nov. 4, 1877; lives at Jackson, Miss.
212. Elizabeth (Bessie) December 25, 1874; died July 3, 1907.

FOURTH GENERATION

(207) Frank Culbertson married November 26, 1875, Mattie Jones. They live at Brandon (P. O. Value) Rankin County, Mississippi. Wife born Aug. 11, 1854.
Issue:
213. Sue, born Jan. 18, 1877.
214. Beulah, b. Nov. 16, 1866. Columbus, Miss.

(208) William Culbertson married Miss Clara Wade of Durant, Mississippi, August 23, 1892. They live at Jackson, Mississippi.
Issue:
215. Bert, born Feb. 2, 1896.
216. Clara May, born May 29, 1904.
217. Elizabeth, born Oct. 26, 1908.
218. ——.
219. ——.

(209) May Culbertson married —— Anderson. They lived at Jackson, Miss.
Issue:
220. O. M. Anderson, pastor New Monmouth Presbyterian Church, Lexington, Va., Route 1.

(211) Ursula Culbertson married Oct. 13, 1897 G. W. Alford of Jackson, Miss. They live at Jackson.
Issue:
221. Gladys, born Aug. 21, 1898. Married July 2, 1921, to Chas. Wilson Montague, Traverse City, Mich.
222. Charles Culbertson, b. Oct. 4, 1900.
223. Thomas Westley, Jr., born Apr. 24, 1907.

(212) Elizabeth (Bessie) Culbertson married Robert Kennon Jayne of Jackson, Mississippi, November 21, 1895.
Issue:
224. William McAfee, born August 21, 1896.
225. Elizabeth, born January 4, 1898.
226. Robert Kennon, born July 4, 1906.

FIFTH GENERATION

(213) Sue Culbertson married James Rufus Payne, June 22, 1904.
Issue:
227. James R., Jr., b. July 22, 1906.
228. Fred Culbertson, b. Oct. 31, 1910.
229. Robert Keets, b. July 16, 1814.

(X) Jacob Culbertson was a graduate of West Point, class of 1851. At the outbreak of the Civil War he joined the Confederate forces at Bowling Green, Kentucky, with the rank of Lieutenant. He served in the defense of Fort Henry, and, in the absence of a superior officer, commanded the batteries which engaged the Federal gunboats at the siege of Fort Donaldson, where he was captured. He was a prisoner at Camp Chase and Johnson's Island, till exchanged in 186—. He had various artillery company, brigade and division staff appointments with Loring's division until the battle of Baker's Creek, which was his last engagement.

A commission as Major was issued to him early in the war, but it did not reach him till near its close.

CHAPTER LXIV

(XI) Sarah M. Culbertson married —— Hunt. They lived in Illinois.

Issue:

THIRD GENERATION

230. Rollin A., born January 28, 1848.
231. Elizabeth Jane, born May 18, 1849.
232. Mary Ella, born October 22, 1852.
233. Ada A., born November 4, 1854.
234. George W., born September 19, 185—; died December 15, 1877.
235. Serena, born April 12, 1856.
236. Evelyn, born June 28, 1858; died August 10, 1907.
237. Belle, born July 17, 1863.
238. Hester M., born July 12, 1865.
239. William, born August 28, 1867.

CHAPTER LXV

(XII) **Robert Culbertson** married Susan Carr Rusk, of Kenton County, Ky., September 18, 1861. They lived at Ryland, Ky.

Issue:

THIRD GENERATION

240. Richard Herndon, died February 7, 1883; never married.
241. John Baldwin, died February 11, 1883; never married.
242. William, born March 4, 1870; died December 19, 1886; never married.
243. Harry, born February 2, 1874.

FOURTH GENERATION

(243) Harry Culbertson married Clara Sale, of Effingham, Ills., September 18, 1904. They reside at 2142 Maple Ave., Evanston, Ills.

Issue:
244. Robert S., born August 4, 1905.
245. Bowner Q., born September 18, 1907.
246. Harry Altin, born December 19, 1909.
247. Clara Elizabeth, born June 15, 1912.
248. Charles Elliott, born July 10, 1913.

PART THIRD
SECTION TENTH

(V. 2.) William Culbertson of Spring Lake, Kentucky.

PART THIRD

SECTION TENTH

(V. 2.) **William Culbertson,** a native of Tyrone County, Ireland, settled at Spring Lake (formerly Culbertson Station), on the Licking River, Kenton County, Kentucky, in the year 1813. Born about 1787 and died about 1872 in the eighty-fifth year of his age. He is buried at Spring Lake in the family cemetery established by him. He married Jane (or Jennie) Reese. Late in life he married Nancy White.

Issue: By Jane Reese.

SECOND GENERATION

I.   Anna. (Chapter LXVI).
II. Matilda, born March 24, 1824; d. July 15, 1856. (Chapter LXVII).
III. James T., born June 26, 1826; died November 5, 1861. (Chapter LXVIII).

* * * * *

CHAPTER LXVI

(I) Anna Culbertson married James Scott, of Scott's Post Office, Kenton County, Ky.

(Compiler has received no data respecting her descendants.)

* * * * *

CHAPTER LXVII

(II) Matilda Culbertson married William Burrows of Kenton County, Kentucky.

Issue:

THIRD GENERATION

1. Mollie; married —— Lilly.
2. James; never married.
3. William C., born August 6, 1845; died Sept. 6, 1862.
4. James Carlisle, born November 26, 1846; died February 24, 1849.
5. George Washington, born July 7, 1854; died June 22, 1859.

CHAPTER LXVIII

(III) James T. Culbertson married Caroline Stephens, daughter of Joseph Stephens of Kenton County, Ky., January 27, 1850. She was born September 13, 1831; died February 8, 1896. They lived at Spring Lake, Ky.
Issue:

THIRD GENERATION

6. Joseph S., born May 17, 1851; died February 9, 1873; never married.
7. William, born March 19, 1853; died July 27, 1877; never married.
8. James Thomas, born July 15, 1855.
9. Mary J., born December 12, 1858; died June 30, 1875; never married.
10. Emma, born March 17, 1860; died aged about 20 years. Married —— Roth.

FOURTH GENERATION

(8) James Thomas Culbertson married Martha Ann Boyle, of Covington, Ky., February 27, 1876. They reside at Spring Lake, Kenton County, Ky.
Issue:
11. James Thomas, born January 8, 1882.
12. Elizabeth Agnes, born October 26, 1884.
13. Lydia Catherine, born November 17, 1886; died December 6, 1921.
14. Hayden Polk, born November 22, 1888.
15. Georgia Emma, born June 5, 1892.
16. Henry Joseph, born April 1, 1894.
17. Roy Stephen, born April 12, 1896.
18. Jennie Luetta, born May 26, 1898.

FIFTH GENERATION

(11) James Thomas Culbertson married Martha Huffmann, November 28, 1906. They reside at Spring Lake, Ky.
Issue:
19. James Thomas, 4th, born March 25, 1908.
20. Robert William, born December 12, 1913.
21. Margaret Elizabeth, born May 9, 1915.
22. Anna May, March 16, 1917.

(12) Elizabeth Agnes Culbertson married John S. Hall, of Covington, Ky., March 17, 1908. They reside in Covington, Ky.
Issue:
23. Martha Elizabeth, born July 19, 1909.
24. John Thomas, July 4, 1913.

(13) Lydia Catherine Culbertson married August Lewis Brown, of Covington, Ky., September 14, 1910.
Issue:
25. August Lewis, Jr., born February 3, 1913.
26. Lydia Catherine, born April 3, 1915.
27. Matilda Emma, born April 11, 1917.
28. Martha Jane, born June 7, 1919.

(14) Hayden Polk Culbertson married Anna Fitzpatrick, of Covington, Ky., June 18, 1918.
Issue : None, April, 1923.

(15) Georgia Emma Culbertson married Milo Zimmerman, of Spring Lake, Ky., November 25, 1921. They reside at Spring Lake.
Issue:
29. Emma Luetta, born November 17, 1922.

(16) Henry Joseph Culbertson married Nellie McClure of Visalia, Kenton County, Ky., June 9, 1920. They reside at Spring Lake, Ky.
Issue:
30. Henrietta Murrill, born March 21, 1921.

MEMO.

William Culbertson, the emigrant from Tyrone County, Ireland, established a family cemetery at Spring Lake, Ky., which is rock enclosed. A center stone bears this inscription:

"This family cemetery was founded A. D. 1840 by Wm. Culbertson, cooper and horticulturist, a native of Tyrone Co., Ireland, who cleared, planted, built and improved this place since A. D. 1813 up to this time."

His individual stone bears the following inscription:
"If there's another world, he lives in bliss;
If there is none, he made the best of this."

From which it is assumed, and tradition so has it, that he was somewhat of a skeptic.

James T..Culbertson (III) had the military rank of Captain. His gravestone is so inscribed, but his military record is unknown to the compiler.

PART FOUR
SECTION TENTH

(V.3.) Allen Culbertson of Spring Lake, Kentucky.

PART FOUR

SECTION TENTH

(V. 3.) **Allen Culbertson**, a native of Tyrone County, Ireland, settled at Spring Lake (formerly Culbertson Station), on the Licking River, Kenton County, Ky., in the year 1813. Born October, 1790; died, February 2, 1856. Married Ester Greer, of Covington, Ky.

Issue:

SECOND GENERATION

I.   James Greer, born September 27, 1819; died March 15, 1912. (Chapter LXIX).

II. Ann Jean, born March 1, 1822; died May 19, 1900. She married William Reese, Cold Springs, Ky. (Chapter LXX).

III. Mary, born February 16, 1825; died July 15, 1849. She married W. H. Fish.

IV. Sarah Catherine, born February 16, 1827; died June 19, 1833.

V.   William Wright Culbertson, born April 16, 1829; died Sept. 22, 1862.

VI. George Allen, born November 30, 1832; died about 1900.

VII. Margaret, born April 29, 1834; died about 1906. She married Adam McCracken and James Moss. Had no children.

VIII. John, born February 22, 1837; died November 9, 1908 (Chapter LXXI).

IX. Greer, born June 30, 1840; died February, 1843.

William Wright Culbertson never married. He served as Captain of Company K, 18th Regiment Kentucky Volunteers, in the Civil War and was killed at the battle of Richmond, Ky. His battle flag, officer's sash and epaulettes are in the possession of Mrs. Fred E. Lillick (granddaughter of James Greer Culbertson) 6151 Grand Vista Avenue, Pleasant Ridge, Hamilton County, Ohio.

George Allen Culbertson was a bachelor.

CHAPTER LXIX

(I) James Greer Culbertson married Catharine Youtsey, daughter of Jacob Youtsey, Campbell County, Ky.
Issue:

THIRD GENERATION

1. Mary Ann, born August 1, 1845.
2. William H., born February 28, 1847; died December 10, 1898. Never married.
3. Sarah E., born October 15, 1849. Never married.
4. Emma V., born October 15, 1851. Married Jackson Curlis, Feb. 22, 1884; no children.
5. Ella, born October 3, 1853.
6. James Allen, born November 27, 1855.
7. George Andrew, born November 18, 1857; died Sept. 29, 1882. Never married.
8. Nancy J., born April 15, 1859.
9. Jacob Bernard, born October 3, 1862.

FOURTH GENERATION

(1) Mary Ann Culbertson married Ethan Allen Martin, January 15, 1867. They live at Drake, Ky.
Issue:
10. Martha Ann, born October 31, 1867; died August 5, 1922. Married —— Reed, of Scottsville, Ky.
11. James Allen, born June 26, 1869; died —— 1870.
12. William Culbertson, born May 27, 1871; died January 16, 1922.
13. Catherine Esther, born October 24, 1873. Married Elvin Warwick, of Scottsville, Ky.
14. George Andrew, born November 7, 1876; died Sept., 1901.
15. Ira Allen, born October 19, 1877.
16. Clarence Alfred, born October 22, 1880.
17. Mary Emma, born March 24, 1889.

(5) Ella Culbertson married Thomas Reiley, March 11, 1883. She and her sisters, Sara E. and Emma V., live at 710 Dayton street, Dayton, Ky.
Issue:
18. James Elmer, born ——; died in infancy.

(6) James Allen Culbertson married Mollie Church, of

Newport, Ky., December 18, 1878. They live at 919 Cleveland Avenue, Hamilton, Ohio.

Issue:

19. Grace Pearl, born October 24, 1879.
20. Ida, born January 22, 1881.
21. Luella, born March 2, 1883.
22. Margaret, born October 28, 1888; died in infancy.
23. Frank Albert, born July 3, 1891; died July 1, 1894.
24. Harold McKinley, born September 26, 1893.
25. Earl Church, born June 27, 1898.

(8) Nancy J. Culbertson married Alfred Lutton, December 22, 1880. He died February 19, 1896. She lives at 6151 Grand Vista Avenue, Pleasant Ridge, Hamilton County, Ohio.

Issue:

26. Robert, born July 13, 1882; died October 21, 1918. Never married.
27. Clara F. Lutton, born December 25, 1883; married Fred E. Lillick, December 23, 1910.
28. James Greer, born March 26, 1885; died November 1, 1887.
29. Alfred Bernard, born January 9, 1890; died April 6, 1892.
30. Ray, born April 6, 1892; died April 6, 1892.

(9) Jacob Bernard Culbertson married Amanda Rawlings, who died ———, and Julia Lamb, of Kenton County, Ky. He lives in Newport, Ky.

Issue by Amanda Rawlings:

31. Bernice F., born November 2, 1892.
32. Rawlings, born August 26, 1896; died August 24, 1898.
33. James T., born May 24, 1904.

MEMO.

Ira Allen Martin (15), son of Mary Ann Culbertson Martin (1) served in Spanish-American War and also in the late World War. In the World War he was in action 18 days.

FIFTH GENERATION

(19) Grace Pearl Culbertson married Michael J. Reynolds, of Boonville Ky., June 3, 1903.

Issue:

34. Llewellyn Charles, born February 28, 1904.
35. Edwin Ellis, born October 5, 1907.

36.   Loretta Lydia, born Auust 14, 1909.

(20) Ida Culbertson married Wesley D. Emrich, of Hamilton, O., Jan. 1, 1901.
Issue:
37.   Grace Verina, born March 11, 1902.

(21) Luella Culbertson married Robert E. Altman, of Felicity, Ohio, February 26, 1905.
Issue:
38.   Mollie Virginia, born March 22, 1906.
39.   Robert Edward, born June 22, 1908.

(24) Harold McKinley Culbertson married Jennie Grace Price, of Covington, Ky., January 21, 1914. They live at 104 West Fifth Street, Covington, Ky.
Issue:
40.   Grace Elizabeth, born November 17, 1921.

(25) Earl Church Culbertson married Ina Oden of Hamilton, Ohio, August 6, 1919. They reside at 2043 Dixie Highway, Hamilton, Ohio.
Issue:
41.   Ruth Oden.
42.   Lois Virginia.

CHAPTER LXX

(II) Ann Jean Culbertson married William Rees, of Cold Springs, Campbell County, Kentucky, September 14, 1848.
Issue:

THIRD GENERATION

43.   Elida Ester, born November 14, 1849. Married Ralph Stout of Gano, Ohio, Oct. 6, 1880.
44.   Lorena Amanda, born December 15, 1853. Married John Bartell, deceased.
45.   Maggie Ann, born July 24, 1860. Married Charles N. Lamb, of Visalia, Ky., March 30, 1884.

CHAPTER LXXI

(VIII) John Culbertson married Cynthia Richardson, of Kenton County, Ky., January 1, 1861. His widow lives at 3708 Park Avenue, Covington, Ky.
Issue:

THIRD GENERATION

46. Carrie Ester, born May 9, 1864.
47. John Allen, born April 18, 1866. Unmarried.
48. Mary, born April 26, 1868. Unmarried.
49. Cynthia Elizabeth, born September 13, 1874. Unmarried.
50. Tilden Richardson, born December 25, 1876.
51. Robert Lee, born March 1, 1878; died October 16, 1898. Did not marry.
52. Greer, born April 18, 1888. Unmarried.

FOURTH GENERATION

(46) Carrie Ester Culbertson married Lafayette H. Bird, of Falmouth, Ky., September 13, 1886. They reside at 512 Fry Street, Covington, Ky.
Issue:
53. Frank Mortimer, born June 1, 1888. Unmarried.
54. Carrie Elizabeth, born August 1, 1891. Married Ralph W. Rausch, of Cincinnati, June 15, 1914.

PART FIVE
SECTION TENTH
(V.4.) Robert Culbertson of Spring
Lake, Kentucky.

PART FIVE

SECTION TENTH

(V. 4.) Robert Culbertson, a native of Tyrone County, Ireland, settled at Spring Lake (formerly Culbertson Station, on the Licking River, Kenton County, Ky., in the year 1813. He was born about 1793; died February 8, 1856. He married Maria Gregg.

Issue:

SECOND GENERATION

I. James, born ——; died ——.
II. Matthew, born January 1, 1818; died, 1857. (Chapter LXXII).
III. Jane, born ——, 1821; died December 25, 1839.
IV. George Allen, born May 12, 1829; died Sept. 2, 1892. (Chapter LXXIII).
V. Robert, died young.
VI. John J., born ——; died July 30, 1910 (Chapter LXXIV).
VII. Sarah, born ——; died ——. (Chapter LXXV).
VIII. Lucy, born ——; died ——. (Chapter LXXVI).
IX. Ann
X. Catherine } Names given by (VI) John J., their
XI. Mary   brother, in 1892.

MEMO.

James (I) went to Nebraska or Iowa in 185— (?). Robert Edwin Culbertson (1) says that he settled near Nebraska City and others say he settled near Council Bluffs. The compiler has learned nothing respecting his descendants.

On the authority of a letter written by John J. Culbertson (VI) in December, 1892 it has been indicated that Robert was the father of eleven children. The compiler has learned the names of only seven. He does not know the order of their birth.

* * * * *

CHAPTER LXXII

(II) Matthew Culbertson married Sarah Sprague of

Campbell County, Ky., January 1, 1846. He died near Sidney, Fremont County, Iowa, in 1857.
   Issue:

THIRD GENERATION

1. Robert Edwin, born November 24, 1846.
2. George A., born April 4, 1848; died in Kansas. Never
    . married.
3. James G., born January 29, 1852; died 1864 } Twins
4. William W., born January 29, 1852.
5. Charles Mathew, born February 2, 1855.
6. John J., born February 2, 1855. Unmarried } Twins
    resides at Twisp, Washington.

   (1) Robert Edwin Culbertson married Fredericka Augusta Browning, of Browingsville, Ky., May 1, 1877. They reside at 909 Scott Street, Covington, Ky.

FOURTH GENERATION

   Issue:
7. Robert Edwin, born September 2, 1878; mar-
    ried Josephine Cook, of Falmouth, Jan.
    26, 1909. } Twins
8. William, born September 2, 1878; died July
    26, 1909.
9. Maude B., born April 27, 1885; married John Franklin
    Firth, of Covington, Ky., November 26, 1913. No
    children.

   (4) William W. Culbertson married Margaret Kabel, of Cincinnati, Ohio. They reside at Evansville, Ind., Route A, Box 97.
   Issue:
10. Stella, born October 29, 1884; died May 10, 1885.
11. Edna, born November 18, 1885.
12. Nellie, born January 23, 1887; died May 10, 1914.
   No grandchildren

   (5) Charles Matthew Culbertson married Mary J. Rich, of Fiskburg, Kenton County, Ky., March 2, 1876. They reside at Evansville, Ind., Route A, Box 340.
13. Dora E., born January 13, 1877.
14. Ira D., born January 5, 1879; died July 24, 1880.
15. Ernest C., born December 5, 1880; died October 27,
    1883.
16. Louis N., born June 27, 1883.

17. Charles M., born August 25, 1886.
18. Leslie M., born November 30, 1888.
19. Clara Maud, born February 2, 1891.
20. Nellie May, born May 6, 1893.
21. Leo N., born August 28, 1895.
22. Dee Ray, born January 21, 1898.
23. Forrest, born December 7, 1900.

FIFTH GENERATION

(8) Wiliam Culbertson married Sophia Baker of South Portsmouth, Ky., at which place they resided.
Issue:
24. Edwin M., born January 5, 1910.

(13) Dora E. Culbertson married Whitney Bailey of Pratt, Kansas, May 9, 1897, where they now reside.
Issue: She has a family but has not advised compiler of their names.

CHAPTER LXXIII

THIRD GENERATION

(IV) **George Allen Culbertson**, born May 12, 1829. Married Miss Mary Hemingway, of Kentucky. He died September 2, 1892. She died July 4, 1872.
Children:
29. Maggie, born ——; married —— Hampton. Lives at Mexico, Missouri.
30. Thomas H., born——.
30½. Junia E., born ——; died September, 1877.
31. Sarah, born October, 1861; married —— Jones; lives at Billings, Missouri.
32. Charles William, born June 1, 1863.
33. James G., born June 8, 1865; lives Kirk, Colorado, R. F. D. 2.
34. John D., born December 24, 1867; lives Kirk, Colorado, R. F. D. 2.
35. Katie A., born ——; died May 1, 1919.
36. Cora, born ——.
37. George, born ——; died August, 1872.

FOURTH GENERATION

(32) Charles William Culbertson married Lizzie Phillips of Union, Okla., July 1, 1903. (She was born November 27,

1876). They reside at Billings, Christian County, Missouri.
Issue:
38.   Mary Harriett, born June 30, 1904.
39.   Clarence, Maurice, born February 13, 1906.
40.   Henry Charles, born April 19, 1909.
41.   Annie Elizabeth, born February 1, 1911.
42.   Luzella Dorothea, born November 10, 1912; died February 24, 1914.
43.   Donald Ernest, born May 19, 1915.
44.   Harold W., born December 29, 1917.
45.   Paul Verron. born February 27, 1920.

(16) Louis N. Culbertson married Annie Krusie, of Evansville, Ind., June 25, 1910. They reside at Evansville.
Issue:
25.   Charles W., born May 13, 1911.

(18) Leslie M. Culbertson married Sadie Norton, of St. Louis, Mo., December 31, 1920.
Issue:
26.   John, born February 3, 1923.

(19) Clara Maud Culbertson married Clyde Hitch, of Evansville, Ind., March 2, 1910. They reside at Evansville, Ind.
Issue:
27.   Eveline, born July 3, 1911.
28.   Harold, born March 23, 1914.

MEMO.

Charles M. (17), Leslie M. (18), and Dee Ray Culbertson (22) served in the Military Forces of the United States in France during the World War.

CHAPTER LXXIV

(VI) **John J. Culbertson** was married three times. His first wife was Mary Plummer, of Falmouth, Ky., whom he married in November, 1858. His second wife was Emily J. Plummer, of Falmouth, and his third wife was Louvisa Smith, of Burnside, Ky. He died at Lexington, Ky., July 30, 1910, and is buried at Paris, Ky.
;Issue by Mary Plummer:

THIRD GENERATION

46. Martha, born ——; died ——, aged about 58. Married Henry Plummer, of Falmouth, Ky.
47. Mary, born ——; died in infancy.
48. Sarah, born ——; died in infancy.

By Emily J. Plummer:

49. Georgia Ann born March 14, 1859; died at Lexington about 1911. Never married.
50. James Robert, born April, 1860; died about 1873.
57. John B., born June ——, 1861; died November 22, 1886.
52. Emmaline, born January, 1863; did about 1878.
53. William Henry, born February 5, 1864; died November 6, 1887.
54. Matthew Nelson, born February 4, 1866.
55. Lilly May, born May 14, 1872. Married Frank Martin of Bourbon County, Ky, March 3, 1893. No children.

FOURTH GENERATION

(51) John B. Culbertson married Fanny Bollinger of Pendleton County, Ky., March 20, 1879.

Issue:

56. Pearl.
57. Jessie Lee.

(54) Matthew Nelson Culbertson married Margaret Elizabeth Williams, of Paris, Ky. They live at Cincinnati, Ohio.

Issue:

58. Earl William, born December 24, 1891.
59. Thomas King, born August 6, 1893.
60. Matthew Stanley, born November 19, 1895; died Feb. 21, 1896.
61. Ray Davis, born May 28, 1897; died July 3, 1897.
62. Anna Lillian, born December 20, 1898; died July 31, 1899.
63. Edith Marguerite, born August 5, 1900.
64. Irene Cameron, born September 11, 1902.
65. Ethel Irma May, born September 6, 1906.

FIFTH GENERATION

(58) Earl William Culbertson married Margaret Merringer, of Paris, Ky., December 22, 1911. They live on Nineteenth Street, Covington, Ky.

Issue:

66. Anna Earl, born December 25, 1912.
67. Dorothy Louis, born February 6, 1917.
68. Margaret May, born May 1, 1920.
69. William Harris, born December 31, 1922.

(59) Thomas King Culbertson married Margaret Farrow, of Paris, Ky., March 29, 1919. They live at Cincinnati, Ohio.
Issue:
70. Mary Elizabeth, born July 5, 1920.
71. Vivian Irene, born October 29, 1922.

(63) Edith Marguerite Culbertson married Emil Menzel, of Cincinnati, Ohio, April 9, 1919. They reside at 1339 Main street, Cincinnati.
Issue:
72. Edith Lillian, born January 2, 1920.

MEMO.

Thomas King Culbertson (49) served in the World War, Company A, Fourth Infantry.
The data for this chapter was furnished by Matthew N. Culbertson (44)), who depended upon his memory for the dates shown in the Third Generation section.

CHAPTER LXXV

(VII) Sarah Culbertson married —— Cooney, of Covington, Ky.
Issue:
73. James.

CHAPTER LXXVI

(VIII) Lucy Culbertson married ——Redden. Nothing is nown of her descendants, if any.

SECTION ELEVENTH

(W) Patrick Culbertson (Irish) of Chester Co., Pa.—Sherman's Valley, Pa.—Part First.

(Y) John Culbertson of Sherman's Valley, Pa. (Probably a Brother of (W) Patrick Culbertson)—Part Second

Part First of Section Eleven was compiled and written by a wealthy and prominent descendant of (W) Patrick Culbertson, namely Mr. Frank Culbertson of Oil City, Pa. [Editor.]

PART FIRST

Genealogy of Patrick Culbertson and descendants. (W) Patrick Culbertson born in Chester Co., Pennsylvania in 1745, name of wife unknown.

FIRST GENERATION

Issue:
1. Frances, born 1767, died 1853.
2. James, born 1769, dead, bachelor.
3. John, born 1777, dead, know nothing.
4. Robert, born 1772, dead, know nothing.
5. Jane, born 1773, dead, know nothing.
6. Mary, born 1776, died 1863.

SECOND GENERATION

(1) Frances Culbertson married Mary Steeples of Venango County, Pennsylvania in 1805, wife born 1786, died 1843.
Issue:
7. James, b. 1806, died 1840, bachelor.
8. Patrick, born 1807, died 1850.
9. Jane, born 1808, died 1899.
10. Robert, born 1812, died 1852.
11. Samuel, born 1815, died 1866, bachelor.
12. John, born 1818, died 1846.
13. Elizabeth Archer, born 1821, died 1907.
14. Alexander, born 1823, died 1906.
15. Hamilton, born 1825, died 1886.

(6) Mary Culbertson married Hamilton McClintock, of Cumberland County, Pennsylvania, in 1794, husband born 1771, died 1857.
Issue:
16. Jane, born 1797, dead, know nothing.
17. Hugh, born 1798, dead, know nothing.
18. James, born 1801, died 1855.
19. Ann, born 1803, died 1868.
20. John, born 1806, dead, know nohing.
21. Isabelle, born 1808, dead, know nothing.
22. Culbertson, born 1810, died 1855.
23. Mary, born 1812, dead, know nothing.
24. Rachel, born 1814, dead, know nothing.

25. Elizabeth, born 1815, dead, know nothing.
26. Hamilton, born 1816, died 1876.

THIRD GENERATION

(9) Patrick Culbertson married Elizabeth Vangiesen in 1843.

Issue:

27. Washington, born 1844, died 1917.
28. John Munroe, born 1847, Union soldier, killed in front of Petersburg, Virginia, 1864.
29. Lewis Cass, born 1849, died 1894.

(10) Robert married Mary Cary 1835.

Issue:

30. Isabelle, born 1836, dead.
31. James, born 1838, dead.
32. Mary, born 1841, dead.
33. Louisa, born 1845.
34. Maria, born 1848, dead.

(12) John Culbertson, married Rebecca Nellas of Venango County, Pennsylvahia.

No issue.

(13) Elizabeth Archer Culbertson married Joseph Anderson in 1844, husband dead.

Issue:

35. Thomas Alexander, born in 1845, died 1898, Union soldier, during the Civil War, and was wounded in the leg from which he never fully recovered.
36. Rebecca J., born 1847, died 1849.
37. James Patrick, born 1850.
38. Joseph Addison.
39. John Slentz, born 1857, died 1906.
40. Florence Bell, born 1861, died 1895.
41. Amanda Cecelia, born 1865.
42. Wilhelmina, born 1867, died 1868.

(14) Alexander Culbertson, married Ellen Smith of Venango County, Pennsylvania in 1855, wife born 1838.

Issue:

43. Ella, born 1856, died 1857.
44. Francis, born 1857.
45. Albert, born 1860, died 1862.
46. Edith, born 1862.

(15) Hamilton Culbertson married Rachel Davidson, 1851, wife born 1832, died 1897.
Issue:
47. Francis, born 1851, died 1852.
48. Orson Oscar, born 1854, died 1815.
49. Lawrence Leslie, born 1856, died 1879.
50. Harry Holland, born 1863.
51. Ernest Eugene, born 1865, died 1913.
52. Florence Thayer, born 1872.

FOURTH GENERATION

(27) Washington Culbertson married Elmina Lowrie, wife born 1846.
Issue:
53. Frederick Lewis, born 1867.
54. Elizabeth, born 1869, died 1869.
55. Francis Orren, born 1870.
56. Cora Amelia, born 1873.
57. Gertrude Bell, born 1879.

(30) Isabelle Culbertson married David Mason, lived in Michigan, know nothing about.

(31) James Culbertson married Elizabeth Whitehill in 1877.
Issue:
57½. Charles C., born 1880, died 1918.

(32) Mary Culbertson married Alonzo Snodgrass.
Issue:
58. James, know nothing about.
59. Robert, know nothing about.

(33) Louisa married William Willings.
Issue:
60. Laura, know nothing about.

(34) Maria Culbertson married Charles Schoeffler, know nothing about.

(35) Thomas Alexander Anderson married Harriet Louisa Hartshorn in 1866, wife born 1845, died 1923.
Issue:
61. Mabel Duiera, born 1867.
62. Anna Hartshorn, born 1869.
63. Jessie Bannon, born 1871, died 1888.
64. Harry Manfull, born 1878, died 1879.
65. Ethel Florine, born 1882.

(37) James Patrick Anderson married Henrietta Knaus in 1877.
Issue:
66.   Edward Lawrence, born 1878, died 1894.
67.   Frederick, born 1880.
68.   Leroy, born 1883.

(38) Joseph Addison Anderson married Mary McCullough in 1871, wife born 1852, died 1912.
Issue:
69.   James Hamilton, born 1873.
70.   Dudley Hannon, born 1875.
71.   Franklin Reed, born 1878.
72.   David McClure, born 1880.
73.   Milcah Irene, born 1882.
74.   Tacie Florence, born 1883.
75.   Parker Donald, born 1885.
76.   Joseph Russell, born 1888.
77.   Myrtle Goldie, born 1893.

(39) John Slentz Anderson married Emma McCullough in 1875.
Issue:
78.   Blanche G., born 1876, died 1876.
79.   Myrtle F., born 1878.
80.   Charles E., born 1880.
81.   Edith G., born 1882, died 1923.
82.   Hazel M., born 1896.

(40) Florence Bell Anderson married J. Parker Naugle.
Issue:
83.   Josephine Izora, born 1882.
84.   Allen Verlee, born 1884.
85.   Georgia, born 1885, died 1891.
86.   Elizabeth Browne, born 1887.
87.   Dana, born 1888, died 1891.
88.   Emma, born 1895   Above two twins.
89.   Thurma, born 1895.

(41) Amanda Cecelia Anderson married Otto Frederick Haltnorthin, 1893.
Issue:
90.   Carl Raymond, born 1895.
91.   Charles Frederick, born 1898.
92.   Emma Elizabeth, born 1900.
93.   Freda Rhinehart, born 1904.

(46) Edith Culbertson married Samuel Justice in 1888, husband born 1836, died 1920.

No issue.

(48) Orson Oscar Culbertson married Mary E. Kinnear in 1880.

No issue.

(50) Harry Holland Culbertson married Louisa Catherine Eichner in 1892.

Issue:
94. Hilda Louisa, born 1893.
95. Edith Arlene, born 1898.
96. Cathryn Eichner, born 1901.
97. Harry Holland Jr., born 1906.

(5) Ernest Eugene Culbertson married Lyda Zelma Harger.

Issue:
 98. Lawrence Harger, born 1897.
 99. Mildred Amelia, born 1906.
100. Edna Ellen, born 1908.

(52) Florine Thayer Culbertson married Archie B. Rodgers in 1893.

Issue:
101. Ruth Ellen, born 1896, died 1912.
102. Helen Mae, born 1900, died 1914.
103. Grace Marie, born 1905.

(53) Frederick Lewis Culbertson married Susan B. Henry in 1890.

Issue:
104. Mildred Grace, born 1891.
105. Francis Ward, born 1894.
106. Agnes Flavilla, born 1897.
107. Bruce Leslie, born 1900.

(55) Francis Orren married Florence N. Wigggans in 1896.

Issue:
108. Glenn Walter, born 1896.
109. Wayne Lowrie, born 1902.
110. Clarence Frederick, born 1906.

(56) Cora Amelia Culbertson married first, Louis Shade in 1903. Louis Shade died in 1912.

(56) Cora Amelia Culbertson married second, John Dean in 1918. John Dean died in 1918.

(56) Cora Amelia Culbertson married third, E. C. Towne in 1922.

(57) Gertrude Bell Culbertson married Sehon Goshua Gee in 1918.
Issue:
111. Howard, born 1899.
112. Mabel, born 1904.
113. Gertrude Agnes, born 1912.

SEVENTH GENERATION

(95) Edith Arlene Culbertson married Russell S. Henry in 1920.
Issue:
114. Elizabeth Ann, born 1921.

(105) Francis Ward Culbertson married Anna Rita Knotts in 1917.
Issue:
115. Eleanor Sue, born 1919.
116. William Frederick, born 1921.

(104) Mildred Grace married John Ardell Thompson in 1916.
No issue.

CULBERTSON SUMMARY AND PROMINENT DE-SCENDANTS OF PATRICK (W)

Francis Culbertson No. 1 was born in Chester County, Pennsylvania, in 1767.

When a mere boy he commenced to deal in furs, buying them from trappers and Indians. He made a number of trips to what was the western frontier of those days. He had many adventures and narrow escapes. In 1794 in company with an Indian fighter and trapper, named Ricketts, he came to what is now Venango County, Pennsylvania. Both liked the country. They returned to their eastern home gathered their effects and came back to Venango County again in 1795. Ricketts settled near Plumer and Francis on Oil Creek where the town of Rousville now stands. With Francis came his sister Mary and her husband Hamilton McClintock. The McClintocks settled at a place now known as McClintockville. Their farm joined the lands of the famous Indian chief Cornplanter. On the McClintock farm was located the famous oil spring of the Seneca Indians. Francis Culbertson left the Oil Creek Valley in 1805 and settled in the Allegheny River Valley near Eagle Rock in Venango County. He lived there until his death in 1853.

Alexander Culbertson No. 14 taught school and lumbered when a very young man (in 1860) he became interested in oil and continued in this business until his death. On his farm near Eagle Creek, Venango County, Pennsylvania, several good wells were found in 1862 and 1863. He was a scientific farmer many years before this kind of farming became general. On one of his farms located in Chatauqua County, New York, he one year grew a field of wheat that yielded 47 bushels per acre, this being the largest yield of that county in many years. During his entire life, he was liberal giver to charitable and philanthropic organizations. In his young days he was a great hunter and spent considerable time in the pursuit of various kinds of game.

Hamilton Culbertson No. 15 was a successful business man for many years.

Samuel Justice, the husband of (46) Edith Culbertson Justice, was a self-made man of the highest type. When a small boy he earned the money with which to educate himself, and when the Civil War began, he was teaching school in Ohio. He enlisted in the Fifth Ohio Cavalry and served during the war. After its close, he came to the oil country, and was a buyer, producer, and refiner of oil until his death. He left an estate of several million dollars. His wife and daughter have the use of the income during their lives. After their death, the estate is to be used to found and maintain a home for the orphan children of Venango County, Pennsylvania.

None of the descendants of Patrick Culbertson have cared for political careers. Patrick No. 3, was Recorder of Venango County at an early day and Alexander No. 14 was Auditor about the same time. Harry Holland Culbertson No. 50, has been controller of Oil City for a number of terms. (49) Lawrence Leslie Culbertson who was only twenty-three at the time he died, had already made a reputation as a journalist.

DAVIDSONS

(19) Ann McClintock, daughter of Hamilton and Mary Culbertson, married Moses Davidson in 1825, husband born 1794, died 1858.

Issue:

1. Mary, born 1826, died 1893.
2. Charlotte D., born 1829, died 1833.
3. Rachel, born 1832, died 1897.
4. Alexander, born 1835, died 1900.
5. Anna Eliza, born 1837, died 1862.
6. Nancy J., born 1841, died 1920.

THIRD GENERATION

(1) Mary Davidson married William G. Wolf, husband dead.

Issue:

7. James.
8. Eddy, born 1869, died 1871.
9. Sara.

(2) Rachel Davidson married (15) Hamilton Culbertson. See under Hamilton Culbertson in Genealogy.

(4) Alexander Davidson married Phoebe Eleanor Morgan in 1862, wife born 1845, died 1921.

Issue:

10. Ida Irona, born 1863, graduate of Bucknell University, class of 1883.
11. Enise Emerson born 1864, educated at Bucknell University, and Lafayette College.
12. James Urban born 1866, died 1868.
13. Frances Lourena born 1869 educated at Bishop Thrope Seminary, Bethlehem, Pennsylvania.
14. Jennie May, born 1870, died 1903, honor graduate of Bucknell University.

(5) Anna Eliza Davidson married J. S. McClintock.

Issue:

15. Blanche.
16. Theodore.
17. Willis.

(6) Nancy Jane Davidson married Joshua E. Ewing, in 1864, husband born 1823, died 1888.

Issue:

18. Lottie, born 1865.

19. Fred, born 1867, died 1912.
20. Jessie, born 1870, died 1895.
21. Frank, born 1873.
22. Arthur, born 1883, died 1900.

FOURTH GENERATION

(10) Ida Irona Davidson married John Heisley Weaver in 1887, husband born 1860.

Issue:
23. Phoebe Mildred Weaver, born 1893, educated Ogontz School Jenkinton, Penna, and Mt. Vernon Seminary, Washington, D. C.
24. Marion Elizabeth Weaver, born 1899, educated Ogontz School Jenkinton, Penna, and Miss Spence School, New York.

(11) Enise Emerson Davidson married Emily Marie Hastings, 1899, wife born 1869, educated University of Pennsylvania.

Issue:
25. Ruth Marie Davidson, born 1910.
26. John Weaver Davidson, born 1904, student Pennsylvania State College.

(13) Frances Lourena Davidson married first, in 1902 John Gibson Coryell, husband born 1861, died 1911.

Issue:
27. John Burrows, born 1905.

(13) Married second, Dietrick Lamade in 1922, husband born 1859.

FIFTH GENERATION

(23) Phoebe Mildred Weaver married John Farrell Macklin in 1915, husband born 1884, graduate of University of Pennsylvania.

Issue:
28. Ida Weaver Macklin born 1917.
29. J. Heisley Weaver Macklin, born 1918.

(24) Marion Elizabeth Weaver married Robert Simpson Kapman in 1917, husband educated at Princeton.

Issue:
30. Robert Simpson Kapman, Jr., born 1918.
31. Elizabeth Simpson Kapman, born 1919.

(19) Fred Ewing Davidson married Jennie Young 1893, wife born 1872.

Issue:

32.   Guy Ewing, born 1895.
33.   Fred Ewing Jr., born 1903.
34.   Elizabeth Ewing born 1910.

DAVIDSON SUMMARY AND PROMINENT DESCENDANTS

Alexander Davidson No. 4 was a man whom it was good to know. He was owner of the well known Davidson oil farm at Petroleum Center, Pa. The most famous two wells of Pennsylvania, the Maple Shade and Coquette, were located on this farm These two wells produced over eight million dollars worth of oil in about two years. This farm made Egbert Bros., of Franklin, Pa., the first millionaires in the oil world. Alexander Davidson sold his farm and moved to Williamsport, Pa. There he bought two of the finest farms in Lycoming county, making his home on one of them. He also built a large saw mill and ran it for some years. Tiring of this business, he sold the farm and then commenced to raise trotting horses. In this he was very successful. Pilot Medium, one of the world's great trotters was raised on the Davidson farm as well as many other famous racers. Alexander and his wife were fond of entertaining their friends and extending hospitality and good cheer to many hundreds. He was a fine amateur musician in his young days. He was also a good shot and a famous hunter. For many years he devoted part of each season to the gun and rod. His wife Phoebe was indeed a helpmate. Generous and charitable to a fault, she had a wide circle of friends and did a world of good during her long, busy life. She took a great interest in orphans and helped many of them. In touch with great wealth during the closing years of her life she was still the same warm-hearted generous woman of her young days.

(29) John Heisley Weaver, the husband of Ida Irona Davidson is one of the great coal mine owners of the world. He counts his mines by the dozen and his coal lands by the thousands of acres He is the largest individual mine operator and owner of coal lands in the world. He is a millionaire many times over. He also controls a number of railroads. He was made Chevalier of Italy by the king of that country for distinguished service during the world war.

(13) Dietrick Lamade, second husband of Lourena Davidson Coryell established the well known weekly paper Grit at Williamsport forty years ago. He has been at its head ever since and has made it a great success. He has lofty ideals and is foremost in every movement for the benefit of the community in which he lives. He is a member of forty-one business, fraternal, religious and civic societies and is an officer or trustee in nineteen of them. He still finds time to take much enjoyment and pleasure in his home life.

SECTION ELEVEN

PART SECOND

(Y) John Culbertson of Sherman's Valley, Cumb. Co., Pa. He appeared on the tax records of Toboyne Tp., Cumb. Co., Pa., in 1778 and until 1795. There is a Patrick Culbertson appears on tax lists of Toboyne Tp., Cumb. Co., in 1779, but I do not now know what relation—if any—to John.

John Culbertson's Revolutionary Record: "Pr. Sixth Class of 5th Batt'n, Cumb. Co., Pa., Militia. Capt. Samuel Lemmons Co., Col. David Mitchell in 1780. In same service 1781-2." (Pa. Arch. Series 5, p. 338, 353, 358.) Samuel Lemmons lived in Toboyne Tp. as shown by 1790 Census, showing that his company was from this Tp. Census 1790, John Culbertson, self and wife, Toboyne Tp., 1 son over 16, 3 sons under, 2 daughters. David Mitchell and Samuel Lemmon on Census 1790, Toboyne Tp., Cumb. Co., Pa.

The Court Records of Cumb. Co., Pa. show that Mary Ann Culbertson of Mifflin Tp. (north of Shippensburg) made a will Feb. 16, 1843, probated March 6, 1843. She devises to her brothers John and Andrew Culbertson and sister Jane McFit, widow of Robert McFit. Niece Mary (Mrs. Jonathan Kozier).

The name McFit is so similar to McFate that it makes me believe that the parties named McFit in her will are the McFates named in the will of John Culbertson of Crawford Co., Pa., who made his will in 1847 and same probated June 8, 1860. In his will he names nephew Robert McFate and niece Elizabeth McFate. John McFate executor. Lived in Fairfield Tp. I think this is John, son of John Culbertson of Shermans Valley, Pa.

Census of 1800, Toboyne Tp., Cumb. Co., Pa., gives John Culbertson Sr., age between 45 and upward; one male 10 under 16; one male 16 and under 26; two males 26 under 45. Females one 26 and under 45; one female under 10.

Francis Culbertson Sr. of Toboyne Tp. does not appear on this Tp. Census 1800 but is found on Census of Venango Co., Pa.

Patrick Culbertson also is not found here or in Venango Co. Census for 1800. I have not been able to find any deed, will, administration, Power-of-Attorney or any record to give any positive evidence that this John Culbertson came from Delaware. The fact that John Culbertson, son of John Sr. St. Georges Hundred (K.K. in Section Third), disappears entirely from court and Revolutionary records in Nov. 1777, and not found thereafter might lead one to suspect that he went to Toboyne Tp., Cumberland Co., Pa. in 1778, as John of Toboyne Tp., is first found on tax records there in 1778.

SECTION TWELFTH

(Unclassified)

CHAPTER LXXVII

MISCELLANEOUS AND UNCLASSIFIED DATA ON
CULBERTSONS

North Carolina Warrants not investigated.

John Culbertson (Rowan) 1799; David Culbertson 250 acres Anson Co., 1804; David Culbertson 150 acres Anson Co., 1813; Andrew Culbertson 50 acres Buncombe Co., 1817; Moses Culbertson 4½ acres Anson Co., 1820; Josiah Culbertson 5 acres Moore Co., 1820.

In Va. (Territory of Ky.) were four or five warrants; 1781-1787 for several thousand acres in Central Ky. to Samuel Culbertson. Could not find out who he was. Also David Culbertson 4½ acres, Todd Co., Kentucky; Joseph and John Culbertson, Whitely Co., Ky.

In Maryland, 8 acres to Thomas Culbertson in Cecil Co., in 1821.

In Penna, James Culbertson in Mifflin Co., 1794; John in Bedford; James in 1751 Cumb. Co.

A history of Roxburgshire Co., Scotland, says there is a small stream in the county called "Culberts (or Cuthberts) Hope."

* * * * *

The following Culbertsons paid pew rent in 1794 in Rocky Spring (Harrisburg Daily Telegraph, July 7, 1894).

Pew No. 1

Capt. Joseph Culbertson..£2;
Col. Samuel Culbertson ....£2.
John Rea (afterwards Maj. Gen.) ....10 s..

Pew No. 29
Capt. Alexander Culbertson

Pew No. 31
Samuel Culbertson (Creek)
Capt. Robert Culbertson

Pew No. 50
Oliver Culbertson

CHAPTER LXXVIII

(X) John Culbertson Sr. (fuller) died 1811. His widow Mary appointed administratrix. Settlement records show he owned land in Bedford Co., Pa. This is the John who was taxed on land only in Hopewell township, Bedford Co., from 1779 until 1811. This was sold at sheriff's sale in 1812. He first paid tax in what is now Wayne township, Mifflin county, in 1782, which he bought of J. Burg, and at this date he lived in Fermanaugh township, Cumberland County, Pa. in what is now Juniata Co. Census 1790, self and wife, 1 son over 16, one daughter.

Issue:
The following is from Orphans' Court records of Mifflin County, Pa.: "Jan., 1822. Petition of Jeremiah Cunningham, alienee of Eleanor Daniel, which said Eleanor is an heir of John Culbertson, dec'd, son of John Culbertson, Sr. (fuller), said John, Jr. dying intestate and without heirs, estate goes to his brothers and sisters, i. e., Agnes Wilken, widow, Margaret, intermarried with —— McFarland; Mary, intermarried with Patrick Leator; Sarah Cole, widow; Eleanor Daniels; Nancy, formerly married to Alex. Wilken (since dead), said Nancy now resides in County Donegal, Ireland; Margaret (Mrs. Geo. Foster), resides in Tyrone county, Ireland. Petition for sale of 200 acres and Fulling Mill, in Wayne township."

CHAPTER LXXIX

(Z) Rev. John Cuthbertson, Lancaster Co., Pa. (from Hannah's Scotch-Irish of America. Vol. 2, page 70.) John Cuthbertson the first missionary of the Reformed Presbyterian church to reach America labored in Pennsylvania and the adjoining colonies for nearly forty years visiting families and communities of his faith, ordaining elders, establishing churches, organizing presbyteries. During the period of his missionary travels (1751-1790) he rode on horseback more than 60,000 miles, preached more than 2400 days, baptized 1600 to 1800 children, and married nearly 250 couples.

Among the places mentioned where he preached were Carlisle, Big Spring, Rocky Spring, Green Castle.

Then follows several pages of his diary.

Page 100, The Reformed Presbyterian church in America was first organized from congregations by the Rev. John Cuthbertson who came from Ulster in 1751 and labored as a missionary through the frontier settlements of Pennsylvania for nearly forty years; in 1773 he was joined by the Rev. Mess'r Alexander Lind and Matthew Dobbin, both also from the north of Ireland; these three ministers met at Paxtang, near Harrisburg, Penna. on March 10, 1774, and constituted themselves as The Reformed Presbytery of North America. Mr. Culbertson retained the charge of Middle Octorora and Muddy Creek congregations, Lancaster county and Lower Chanceford in York county.

John Cuthbertson (Rev.) rec'd patent for his farm in Bart Tp., Lancaster Co., Pa. in 1760. His son John app. admn'r in 1794 in this township, leaving a wife, Sarah, and daughter Sarah and son John. The diary he left was in Heirogliphic and portions of it have been deciphered. He says "Preached at Rocky Spring, Sept. 14, 1755, also Aug. 22, 1757, Apr. 1, 1756, met many Indians on Conococheague Creek. Preached at Middle Spring, lost pistol on way to Carlisle. Apr. 9, 1759 preached at Rocky Spring. Oct. 13, 1762, preached at Shippensburg, bugs so bad could not sleep; Mar. 27, '65, Nov. 11, '65 preached at Rocky Spring."

As the massacre of McCords Fort occurred April 1, 1756, and Battle of Sideling Hill, Apr. 2, 1756, it is very probable that he held funeral services (or assisted) of victims at McCords Fort and of those of Sideling Hill. Rev. John had a son, Dr. John.

Rev. John Cuthbertson came to America in 1751 from Lanark Co., Scotland. His sister was the wife of Archibald Bourns who accompanied him to Lancaster Co., Pa. (see McCauley's Hist., Franklin Co., Pa., page 299.) Census 1790 Bart Tp., Lancaster Co., Dr. John, males one, females two (mother and sister Sarah).

I do not believe McCauley is correct in stating Rev. Cuthbertson was from Scotland. I take Hannah as authority here.

CHAPTER LXXX

Pension Records show "Robert Culbertson 3rd Mo. Mil. war of 1846, Capt. Benj. W. Smithers, Co., enlisted Sept. 1846, died in service. Father William Culbertson, filed claim Sept. 1852, aged 61, lived in St. Clair Co., Mo. Wife's name Elizabeth. (soldier was unmarried). Children: Robert, the soldier. Mary, Andrew, Elizabeth, Wm., Jas., Ezra B., John A., Green B. H. Who is he?

Land Office Records of Tenn, down to 1830 show no warrants to Culbertsons.

Census 1790 for S. Car. in Beaufort County gives Mrs. Penella Culbertson, 2 sons under 16 years; 2 daughters. The County Clerk of Court of that county has no record of them or any Culbertsons and that their court records were destroyed during the Civil War. ˉ

Census 1790, York County, Pa. (Hamilton Tp.) gives Samuel Culbertson and wife, no children. No will in York County. This township was thrown into Adams County in 1880. Letters of administration were granted John A. McKesson June 2nd, 1814 on the estate of this Samuel Culbertson but nothing further was done in court and there are no deeds to or from him.

* * * * *

William Culbertson born in Cork, Ireland. Revolutionary Record: Jan. 28, 1776, enlisted in Capt. Nathaniel Smith's Co. Md. Art'y. Nov. 17, 1777 transferred to Capt. Richard Dorsey's Co. Md. Art'y. Dorsey's Co. was at Valley Forge with Md. troops. (Md. Arch.).

Note:—In the Delaware Archives is also found (Vol. II) "William Culbertson in Capt. Isaac Alexander's Co. Del. Militia Nov. 1, 1778 to March 31, 1779." "Also same Capt. and Co., Aug. 17, 1779." I can find no other William Culbertson at this date in New Castle Co., Del., to whom this record could be ascribed.

* * * * *

Census 1790 gives a James Culbertson, Luzerne Co., Pa., males one, female one.

* * * * *

John Culbertson served in Capt. James Bryson's Co., of Westmoreland Co., Pa. Rangers, 1781-2. (Pa. Arch. Vol. 23, p. 223-325). I cannot place this party.

CHAPTER LXXXI

Dr. Norman E. Culbertson of Whitehorse, Yukon, Alaska, was born near Meaford, Ontario, Can., Dec. 9, 1882. Graduated in Medicine, Toronto, in 1909. Spent two years in Toronto General Hospital—then went to Dawson City, Yukon, and since 1920 has practiced at Whitehorse, Yukon, Alaska. His father moved from Renfrewshire, Scotland, in early life to Meaford, Ontario, and died in 1896, Jan. 30, aged 60 years. He had a brother Alexander and sister Agnes. His wife's father came from Scotland and was born in Ayrshire. She was born Jan. 11, 1842; name Agnes Hunter. Living. Dr. Norman's father was Edward Culbertson, born near Barrie, Ont.

Dr. Norman E. Culbertson also took Post Graduate work in New York.

CHAPTER LXXXII

Stephen Culbertson, a prominent druggist of Kansas City, Mo., gives this information regarding his family:

My father Stephen Culbertson (d. Sept. 21, 1889), married Melissa Anna Day of Greenville, Ind., April 13th, 1864, at Topeka, Kansas. Had 5 children: Sara Jane, born Sept. 28th, 1865, died Nov., 1865; John Wesley, born March 10th, 1867, died July 13th, 1884; Francis Ausbury, born May 16th, 1869; living in Miami, Ariz., unmarried; Anna Marie, born Aug. 10th, 1875, married F. A. Goss of Leavenworth, Kans., Sept. 9th, 1894, had two children, Alfred F. and Stephen C., now in Fresno, Cal., was divorced and remarried, now lives in Los Angeles, Cal. Stephen born March 25th, 1880, married Elizabeth Robertson of Sibley, Mo., Aug. 3, 1902, has two children, Elizabeth Mary, born Feb. 19th, 1906; Helen J. born Jan. 7th, 1908.

CHAPTER LXXXIII

Wm. Culbertson, member of Col. Brooks' Regt. Continental Line, Mass. Lived in N. Y. close to Mass. line. Born 1761 in Tyrone Co., Ireland. Enrolled Oct. 1, 1781. Oct. 1778." (Quoting Rev. John N. Culbertson, Wash., D. C.)

In Census 1790, Schenectady, N. Y. Not in Mass. Census 1790.

CHAPTER LXXXIV

DAVID CULBERTSON OF LINCOLN CO., KENTUCKY.
ANCESTRY UNKNOWN.

David Culbertson of Lincoln Co., Ky. was given in the first edition of Culbertson Genealogy, page 103, (12) as a son of Col. Samuel Culbertson of Pa. "Row." This is an error. The statement on p. 134 of first edition "David had not received his inheritance from Col. Samuel's estate" is not true as Settlement Records of Franklin Co., Pa. show that the executors of Col. Samuel Culbertson in their final account paid David in full (1823).

The County Clerk of Court of Lincoln Co., Ky. (and several other counties in Ky. as well as at Bedford, Indiana) informs me that there is no will or administration of David Culbertson and no deeds from him. The only record was a marriage license of Sarah Bright to David Culbertson in 1805.

The Census of Lincoln Co., Ky., for 1820, gives David Culbertson, age 45 years, Sarah Culbertson, age 45; children eight. Census 1830 does not give David but gives Sarah, age between 40 and 50 with eleven children. David, son of Col. Samuel Culbertson of "Culbertson Row," Pa., was born 1789 so this eliminates him as the ancestor of this family. David, Sr., son of John, Sr., of Del. was born before 1762, so this eliminates him. David, Jr., son of Wm. of Pencader, Del., married Clarissa Brevard of New Castle Co., Del. in 1800 and went to Clark Co., Ky, so this eliminates him. We cannot tell where David Culbertson of Lincoln Co., Ky., came from.

David's descendants say he was eighteen when he ran away from home in Pennsylvania (?).

David of Lincoln Co., Ky.—his widow told her son that David ran away from home when 18 years old and never received his share, $1100, in his father's estate, and that he came from Pennsylvania and his whereabouts was unknown. He was one of Kentucky's greatest pugilists and was a giant six feet, nine inches tall.

Sarah (Bright) Culbertson died in Bedford Co., Ind. in 1869. Her husband died about 1830 in Lincoln Co., Ky. He owned no property. His wife inherited her property from her father, John Bright of Ky. Family tradition had it that David came from Culbertson Row, Pa.

SECOND GENERATION

David Culbertson mar. Sarah Bright, 1805. Widow died 1869 in Lawrence Co., Ind.

Issue:
1. John B., drowned in Ohio River, April 2, 1852.
2. George, d. in fifties. Lived in Ky.
3. David.
4. Lucy.
5. Christena.
6. Margaret.
7. Emily.
8. Clementine.
9. Elizabeth.
10. Mary.
11. Sarah.
12. Drusey.
13. Henry, b. 1817.

THIRD GENERATION

(1) John B. Culbertson, mar. 1842. Moved from Lincoln Co., Ky. to Lawrence Co., Ind. about 1838, widow moved to Clay Co., Ill. in 1860.

Issue:
14. George, d. July 27, 1864 at Vining Sta., Ga. (Priv. Co. B. 38th Ills. Vol.)
15. Henry, d. 1849.
16. Tucker W., b. Nov. 12, 1846. Served in Civil War with Sherman, Pr. Co. B, 48th Ills. Vols.
17. Christena, d. in youth.
18. Sarah, d.
19. Mary Jane, d.

(2) George Culbertson mar. ———. Lived in Lawrence Co., Ind.

Issue:
20. Son. Lived Georgia, Lawrence Co., Ind.

(3) David Culbertson mar. Miss Robinson of Ky. Both died same year.

Issue:
21. James Henry. 24th Ky. Inf. Killed at Battle Cedar Mt. Raised by his uncle Henry.

(4) Lucy Culbertson mar. W. H. Bryant of Bryantsville, Ind. Had issue.

(5) Christena Culbertson mar. first Mr. Kerns; married second Col. Henry D. Bedford of Indiana. No issue.

(6) Margaret married Thos. Hickman of Council Bluffs, Cal. Issue not known.

(10) Mary Culbertson married Mr. Embree of Bryantsville, Ind. Issue not known.

(7) Emily Culbertson mar. Franklin Russell of Mitchellville, Ia.
Issue:
22. David Russell.

(8) Clementine Culbertson married Joseph Russell of Perry, Ia. Issue not known.

(9) Elizabeth Culbertson mar. Mr. Embree of Bryantsville, Ind.

(11) Sarah Culbertson married Thos. Robinson of Bryantsville, Ind. Issue not known.

(12) Drusey Culbertson mar. first Geo. Bright, second Mr. Woolrey of Bedford, Ind. Issue?

(13) Henry Culbertson mar. Mary E. Williamson of Green Castle, Ind. Lived at Bedford, Ind. until 1855. In Washington, D. C., 1892. 23 to 30. Daughters. Youngest Sarah was in the Pension Dept. at Washington in 1892.

THIRD GENERATION

(16) Tucker W. Culbertson mar. Margaret J. McKnelly, June 16, 1866. Hotel propr. Tuscola, Ills. Also Capt. Co. I, 9th Ills Vols. Spanish-American War. Fought in Cuba, 1898.
Issue:
31. Luella (Mrs. Sherman Moss).
32. Fannie.
33. Mary J. (Mrs. Allen Lindsay).
34. Rebecca E.
35. Anna E.
36. Alonzo A.
37. John B.
38. Theodore.
39. Thomas.
40. Adaline, d. infancy.

(18) Sarah Culbertson married A. C. Kellurns.
Issue:
41. Laura Kellurns.
42. Nannie.
43. Eva.
44. William.
45. George.

(19) Mary June Culbertson mar. Lorenzo D. McKnelly.
Issue:
46. Henry.
47. Isabelle.
48. Sallie.
49. Thomas.

CHAPTER LXXXV

I received a letter from Mr. Samuel Culbertson Feland of Washington, D. C. about ten years ago in which he stated: "My great grandmother's name was Sarah Culbertson. She was born in Old Fort Culbertson in or near Culbertson Row, Pa. and was the first child born in that fort. She was married to my great grandfather, Thomas Feland, and they lived in Kentucky and raised a large family of children. I do not know when they were married but would like to know the name of her father and mother."

It seems to me that this man's ancestress can be only one of two different parties. One party who might have been his ancestress was Ann Culbertson, daughter of Irish Robert of Peters Tp., Cumb. Co., Pa. She was living in 1788 (born about 1760) at Shermans Valley, Cumb. Co. (present Perry Co.), Pa. Some of the Culbertsons of Delaware state moved to Kentucky (Clarke Co.) but I could find no evidence that Mr. Feland married any of these.

I find on examining the Census Records of 1790 for Pennsylvania that no Thomas Feland or Felan appears thereon, showing that Thomas Feland did not live in Pennsylvania in 1790.

I find on the Tax Records of Northumberland Co., Va. for 1782 that a Wm. Fallin is given with family of eight and seven slaves.

Samuel Felland of Washington states that his great grandmother, Sarah Culbertson Feland was born in old Fort Culbertson. There were two Fort Culbertsons, one in Culbertson Row, Pa., and one at Culbertson Bottom, Va., on the New River, the latter built in 1753 by Andrew Culbertson. It is possible that his ancestress may have been a daughter of Andrew Culbertson of Shippensburg, who built Fort Culbertson in Virginia.

Have never been able to ascertain the name of this Andrew Culbertson's daughters, if any.

Wm. Fellin of Northumberland Co., Va. having a family of eight in 1782 would indicate that he must have been born by 1750-55 and his wife about the same period. The Census of 1790 for South Carolina does not show any Felands.

Census of 1790 for South Carolina shows this family not in North Carolina.

Thomas Feland (so his grandson says) moved from Campbel Co., Va., to Danville, Ky., and then to Glasgow, Barren Co., Ky. Campbel Co., Va. is close to Rockbridge Co. Campbel Co., Va. was organized in 1782, therefore Thos. Feland must have left this county after 1782.

* * * * *

Sarah Fallin is given on tax lists 1782, Northumberland Co., Va., three in family.

CHAPTER LXXXVI

(3) James Culbertson married Elizabeth Stillings of Franklin Co., Pa. (according to his great grandson, R. L. Culbertson). Said Elizabeth Stillings born about 1770 and died 1860 at Pittsburg. R. L. Culbertson in 1892 stated that James Culbertson, his ancestor, came from Culbertson Row, Pa. and that about 1794 he moved to Havre de Grace, Md., and died there in 1815 (Court Records at Bel Air, Md. give no record of him). He stated that after James' death his widow moved to Chambersburg and then to Pittsburgh, where she died. That after 1815 she went to Chambersburg where her step-mother-in-law lived; then to Pittsburg.

SECOND GENERATION

Issue:
1. Anne, b. 1796; d. 1854.
2. Jane, b. 1800; d. 1868. Unmarried.
3. Hannah, b. 1802; d. 1866.
4. Martha, b. 1804.
5. Levi, b. 1806.
6. James, b. 1808.

THIRD GENERATION

(1) Annie Culbertson mar. John Bennett.
Issue:
8. Wm. Muscatine, Ia.

(3) Hannah Culbertson mar. Standford Jester of Allegheny, Pa. in 1821.
Issue:
9. Melissa.
10. Eliza.
11. Francis.
12. James.
13. Sarah (Mrs. Forne).
14. Maria.
15. Amanda (Mrs. J. Ricorder). Lorain Co., O.

(4) Martha Culbertson mar. David Curry. Went west.
Issue:
16. Margaret (Mrs. Coates). Duquesne, Pa.

(5) Levi Culbertson married Miss Nancy Smith, a cousin of Gen. U. S. Grant, and moved to Wis.

Issue:
17. James.
18-21. Daughters.

(6) James Culbertson married Miss Jane Guthrie of Mercer Co., Pa.
Issue:
22. Montilian, b. 1830; d. 1842.
23. Clorinda, b. 1834.
24. Elizabeth, b. 1838; d. 1868.
25. Robert L., b. 1842.
26. Sarah J., b. 1846; d. 1880.

FOURTH GENERATION

(23) Clorinda Culbertson mar. Hugh Roberts of Shire Oas, Wash. Co., Pa.
Issue:
27. —— (Mrs. L. L. Cavenaugh), Hope Church, Allegheny Co., Pa.
28. —— (Mrs. John Dalle), Charleroi, Pa.
29. Nettie (Mrs. Bently), Washington Co., Pa.
30. Elizabeth (Mrs. Beodell), W. Elizabeth, Pa.
31. George B. W. Elizabeth, Pa.
32. Phillip B. Shire Oaks, Pa.

(24) Elizabeth Culbertson married A. F. Ferrell.
Issue:

33. W. J. Ferrell, W. Elizabeth, Pa. (Carpenter).

(25) R. L. Culbertson married Kate E. Borky in 1866. Served four years under Gen. Sherman in Army of the Cumberland. Pr. 79 Pa. Inf. Lived W. Elizabeth, Pa. Dry gcods merchant.
34. Maud A., d. 1880.
35. Elizabeth, d. 1870.
36. Effie, d. 1878.
37. Jenny (unmarried).
38. Charles.
39. Thelma.

(26) Sarah J. Culbertson married L. H. Dolly of W. Elizabeth, Pa.
Issue:
40. Edwin L., of W. Elizabeth, Pa. (Painter).
41. Harry, W. Elizabeth, Pa. (Coppersmith).
42. H. (Telegrapher).
43. C. H. Duuesne, Pa. (Coppersmith).

CHAPTER LXXXVII

TAX LISTS CUMBERLAND CO., PENNSYLVANIA.

Carlisle, Pa., Dec., 1921.

Dr. L. R. Culbertson,
Zanesville, Ohio.

Dear Sir:—Preparatory to giving you the result of my canvassing the tax lists of early Cumberland County, I trust I may be permitted to say that the task involved more labor than I anticipated as I am sure I canvassed not less than 3000 to 4000 names to cull out what I herewith give. But in order that you may have a more definite understanding of the early Townships of the County, I mean those which were formed before the respective counties were strickn from Cumberland.

Bedford County was stricken off Cumberland in 1771; the townships formed prior to that date were Colerain, Cumberland and Bedford, all 1767.

Franklin was taken off in 1784; townships prior to that date, Antrim in 1741 (whilst yet a parcel of Lancaster Co.), Peters 1750, Hamilton 1752, Guilford 1760, Lurgan 1750, Fannett 1761, Letterkenny 1762, Washington 1779, Montgomery 1781 and Southhampton in 1783.

Huntingdon Co. taken 1787; Barre township formed 1767. Taken from Bedford.

Fulton Co. taken from Bedford 1850; townships in its present confines formed when yet in Bedford, Dublin in 1767, and Ayer 1769.

Mifflin taken from Cumberland and Northumberland in 1739; Townships Derry and Armaugh 1770; Wayne from Derry 1782-3.

Perry Co. was taken from Cumberland 1820. Townships prior to that, Tyrone 1754, Toboyne 1763, Greenwood 1767, Juniatta 1793, Buffalo 1798, and Saville in 1817.

Juniatta Co. taken from Mifflin 1831; townships prior when part of Cumberland, Fermanah 1763, Lack 1778 and Milford, don't have date.

The name of Robert Culbertson as it appears in different places is somewhat confusing and I give it as I find it here, together with other assessments, etc., which may be of value to you. As to Thomas Culbertson I cannot find his name anywhere in our records. The townships I give you above embrace all the territory known as Shermans, prior to the separation of the respective counties from Cumberland.

The first evidence I can find of a Robert Culbertson is he is assessed in Peters Township in 1751.

In that same year I find James, Joseph and Oliver assessed in Hopewell, at present in Cumberland but which then covered a large part of Franklin County.

In 1753 Samuel, Oliver and Joseph were assessed in Lurgan Township.

ASSESSMENTS.

1771—Robert, James and Alexander are assessed in Cumberland Township and a Thomas Clark and Robert assessed this year also in Colerain.

Samuel (Irish) Robert, Samuel, James son of Samuel, Joseph, Samuel and John assessed in Letterkenny.

1772—Robert assessed 300 acres in Letterkenny or Antrim (Irish Samuel's son).

1773—Alexander assessed in Guilford; Samuel, Robert, Joseph and John in Letterkenny.

1774—John assessed in Armaugh, Robert in Hopewell, Oliver in Lurgan, and Samuel, John and Alex. in Letterkenny.

1775—John assessed in Armaugh, Alex. in Guilford, Oliver, John and Samuel in Lurgan, John in Letterkenny, as well as Samuel 1st, Samuel 4th, and Joseph in Letterkenny. Samuel (3rd), John (Mountain), Robert, John, Alex., freeman Joseph, Jr.

1776—John assessed Armaugh; Robert, Hopewell; John in Lurgan; John 1st and John 2nd, Oliver and Alexander in Letterenny; ditto Samuel (1st), Samuel (4th); Joseph, Samuel (3rd); freeman Joseph.

1778—John assessed Armaugh, Alexander in Guilford, Robert in Hopewell and John in Teboyne.

1779—Alex. and Elizabeth assessed in Guilford; Samuel Sr.; Samuel (Creek); Alex., John 1st, John (Mt.), Joseph, Sr., and Joseph, Jr., in Letterkenny; John and Patrick in Teboyne; Samuel (Col.) in Letterkenny; Elizabeth (widow of Robert).

1780—John and Robert assessed in Lurgan Co., Samuel, Robert, Joseph Sr., Samuel Sr., Samuel (Creek) in Letterkenny; Patrick and John in Teboyne.

1781—Robert's heirs, John, Oliver, Samuel (Creek), Col. Samuel, Robert, Joseph, Alex. (Tanner), Samuel Sr., in Letterkenny, Patrick and John in Teboyne.

1782—Rober⁺ in Hopewell, John in Lurgan, Capt. Joseph, Col. Samuel, Robert, Jno., Samuel (Creek), Oliver, Alex., Samuel Sr. and Samuel Jr., in Letterkenny, also Robert's heirs and Robert.

1785—John in Armaugh, John in Wayne, Robert, Hopewell; John and Robert a renter in Teboyne; Guilford, Elizabeth, widow; Letterkenny, Robert, John, Samuel (Creek), Oliver, Alex., Samuel Sr., Samuel (2nd) ; Lurgan, John.

1786—John in Armaugh, Col. Robert Hopewell; John and Patrick in Teboyne and John in Wayne.

1787—Col. Robert in Hopewell, John and Patrick in Teboyne.

1783—John in Armaugh, Col. Robt. and Andrew in Hopewell, John and Patrick in Teboyne, and two Johns in Wayne.

1789—John in Armaugh, Robert and Andrew in Hopewel, John and Patrick in Teboyne and John in Wayne.

1793—John and Patrick in Teboyne and the same in 1795.

1763—John, Joseph, Samuel and Robert in Letterkenny.

1766—Robert in Hopewell and Oliver in Lurgan.

1768-1769—Robert Culbertson in Hopewell.

1770—Robt., John, Samuel (widower), Saml. (Jos. son) ; Joseph, Saml Sr., Saml (wagoner), in Letterkenny.

The foregoing is all the Culbertson names I can find in the old assessment lists preserved here. I trust the list may be of value to you.

Respectfully yours,

JOHN R. MILLER, Atty.
Carlisle, Penna.

1772—Alex. son of Irish Sam'l, real and personal in Guilford.

1762—Hopewell, Wm. Robert, real and pers.; Fannett, Alex. (land on:y) ; Letterkenny, Sam'l, John, Joseph, Sam'l, Robt.; Lurgan Oliver.

NOTE:—The above letter gives tax lists. I have also inserted into these lists names I found on tax lists when I examined same 25 years ago. The following I found on lists of Chester Co., Pa.

1713—Robert Culbertson, Kennett Tp.; John Culbertson, Londongrove Tp.

1726—Andrew Culbertson, Kennett.

1740—Robert Culbertson, Kennett Tp.; Samuel Culbertson, Londongrove.

1735—Oliver Culbertson, Londongrove Tp.

1762—Widow Jane (Roberts) Culbertson. Kennett.

1757—John Culbertson, Londongrove.

1769—John, Londongrove.

1767—Abigail Culberson (widow John) East Coln.

1767—John Culberson (Major), East Coln.

1769—John Culberson (Major), East Coln.

1769—James Culberson, East Coln.

1757—John Culberson, East Coln.

1767—Andrew Culberson, East Coln.

1767—John Culberson, Londongrove.

1767—Jane Culberson, Kennett.

1776—East Coln Tp., John and Samuel, Benjamin freeman.

1776—Pikeland Tp., Samuel. 1774, same.

1787—Samuel Culbertson; Samuel Culbertson Jr. East Coln Tp.

1762—Vincent Tp., Samuel.

1732—Londongrove, Samuel; Kennett, Robert.

1730—Samuel Culberson, Londongrove Tp. (not on book 1729).

1766—John Culbertson, East Nottingham Tp., freeman.

CHAPTER LXXXVIII

THE "THE FLYING CAMP"—WHAT WAS IT?

On June 3rd, 1776, Congress resolved that a Flying Camp be organized in the Middle Colonies, of 10,000 men, for service anywhere, until Dec., 1776. 6,000 from Pa., 3400 from Md., 600 from Del. July 3, 1776, Congress urged Pa. to forward all the troops she could spare to Gen. Washington in N. J. (See Minutes of Council of Safety, Vol. X, p. 60-61. Also Md. Arch. Vol. —, p. 29.)

"Minute Men": On July 18, 1775, Congress recommended that all able-bodied men between 16 and 60 years be enrolled and that one-fourth be selected for "minute men to march anywhere." (See Minutes of Council of Safety, Vol. X, p. 292-293.)

[THE END]

ADDENDA

In Chapter XXIV, one of the sons of (31) George W. Culbertson on page 195 is given William (78). There was no William but there was given on page 195, George William Culbertson, of near Sonora, Muskingum Co., Ohio. He was usually called William. He married Fanny Cullens of Sonora, O., in 1893. His children are given in the latter part of Chapter XXIV.

(76) Howard M. Culbertson, brother of the above, is unmarried and lives near Sonora, Ohio.

* * * * *

On page 152, Mrs. Emily (Culbertson) Walker (245), daughter of (143) Sidney M. Culbertson of Denver, Col., was married Dec. 11, 1922 to Bruce Kistler of Denver, Col. Miss Kathrine Culbertson (246), her sister, was married March 3, 1923, to J. Franks of Denver, Col., a chemist.

(245) Emily Culbertson mar. first Gerald Walker of Denver, Colo.

* * * * *

Joseph Culbertson, Chapter XV, page 75, son of (III) Andrew Culbertson of Rockbridge Co., Va. The question of whether this man had a Revolutionary record is discussed on page 75. This evidence does not give him a military record and we find no more data. Who the Joseph Culbertson in Capt. Gilder's Co. in 1776 was we cannot say. A granddaughter in 1892—as well as others—claimed he was in the Revolutionary War and was wounded. This was tradition. It is possible they got him mixed with Chas. Kilgore, who was the father-in-law of Joseph Culbertson's son James of Scott Co., Va.

* * * * *

Chapter XXVII, page 230.

EIGHTH GENERATION

(57) Alexander Culbertson, b. June 13, 1848, mar. ——
(wife b. Aug. 31, 1843).

Issue:

$104\frac{3}{8}$. Harry, b. Jan. 4, 1873.
$104\frac{1}{2}$. Aubrey, b. Sept. 1, 1876.
$104\frac{5}{8}$. Pearl, b. Aug. 7, 1878.
$104\frac{3}{4}$. Nell, b. Apr. 18, 1882.
$104\frac{7}{8}$. Fred, b. June 30, 1885.
104 8-8. Margaret, b. March 1, 1895.

Note:—There are also given Armenia, b. July 22, 1910; Jeanette, b. Nov. 23, 1913. It is not clear from data sent whether these are children or grand-children of (57) Alexander and wife.

(59½) William Culbertson married Miss Mary Anderson, Jan. 1, 1866. (wife b. 1846; d. Dec. 16, 1922). Their issue on page 232 was incorrect. Issue here given is corrected.

Issue:

105.   James, b. Nov. 27, 1866.
105 1-5.   George, b. May 7, 1869.
105 2-5.   Hugh, b. Aug. 18, 1872.
105 3-5.   Belle, b. Apr. 20, 1884. Married to Wilmer McArthur, Oct. 1, 1902. Issue: Florence McArthur (Mrs. Andrew Bair), b. Dec. 31, 1903; Leona, b. June 19, 1906; Leroy. b. Sept. 12, 1918; Lester, b. June 14, 1922).
105 4-5.   Archie Culbertson, b. Jan. 31, 1887. Florence McArthur married Andrew Bair, Dec. 22, 1922. Issue: Wm. Edward Bair, b. Nov. 19, 1922.

*   *   *   *   *

On pages 28 and 31 will be found (195) John Thomas Culbertson, married Orlena M. Kidner. Lives at Duluth, Minn.

Issue:

261.   Lucius Linn, b. ——, 1876, in Iowa. Lives So. Minneapolis, Minn.
262.   Byron John Culbertson, born in Iowa 1879. Lives Duluth, Minn.
263.   Vern Randolph, b. ——, 1884, in Ia. Lives So. Minneapolis.

(261) Lucius Linn Culbertson married to Louisa Grady, (wife b. 1877, Wis.)

Issue:

274.   John Randolph, b. Duluth, Minn., 1907.
275.   Wm. Harrison, b. Duluth, Minn., 1910.

(262) Byron John Culbertson, married Nina Nelson (wife b.——).

Issue:

276.   John Byron, b.——. Duluth, Minn.

(263) Vernon Randolph Culbertson married Cora Chandler. Issue: None.

On page 111 of this (Revised) Edition was omitted the name of (40) Priscilla Culbertson. Her name is found on page 119.

Delayed data which was written by Joel W. Shackelford, Aug. 11, 1895, is as follows:

"Priscilla Culbertson, p. 84 (40), married James Madison Shackelford of Ky. in 1836 (He was born in Richmond, Ky., Jan. 4, 1812, son of George Lyne Shackelford and wife, Martha Hockaday. George Lyne Sr. was born in King and Queen Co., Va. in 1780, the son of Lyne Shackelford and wife Elizabeth Taliaferro).

Priscilla Culbertson Shackelford's children were:

(116) 1. (Col.) George Taliaferro, born Springfield, Ills., 1837 (now Denver, Colo.).

2. John Taliaferro, born Springfield, Ills, 1839; died young.

(117) 3. Edmund James, born in Illinois on way to Kentucky, 1840; now Mt. Sterling, Ky.

4. Mary, born in Richmond, Ky., 1842; died young.

Priscilla C., wife of James M. S., died in Richmond, Ky., in 1845.

James M. Shackelford remarried in 1847, Melissa Walker of Richmond, Ky. There were 4 children by this marriage, Patty, Jenny, Joel Walker and William. All died in infancy, excepting Joel W., born 1851, who is married and has 7 children. He lives at Denver, Colorado.

James M. Shackleford, husband of Priscilla C., died 1867 in Richmond, Ky. He and his young wife, Priscilla, moved ot Springfield, Ills., when first married. He called on the school teacher, Abe Lincoln, to survey him a piece of land and they were warm friends ever afterwards. Studied law together. Pres. Lincoln offered him Brig. Generalship, which was declined. His son, George T., was Col. 6th Ky. Vols. He has family and living at Denver, Colo.

* * * * *

On page 149, Alice Estella Daily married Alex K. Goudy. Husband dead. Was Nebraska State Supt. of Schools.

Issue:

Daughter, died aged four.

(64) Emily Edith Woods, page 142 (No. 64).

Issue:

Carrie, mar. Philip Cyester.

Charles, d.

Anna, mar. —— Briggs; daughter Frances.
Arthur, d.
Nellie, mar. E. W. Gillette. Issue: Lola, Arthur, d., Edith.

* * * * *

On page 154 (271) Ralph Benj. Bedell is Supt. of Schools, Ashland, Kans. His sister (270) Bess C. Bedell, is principal of Rose Hill School, Omaha, Neb.

On page 153 (263) Alice Culbertson (married James Peterson) is Principal of Dundee School, Omaha, Neb.

On page 154 (170) Leafie Emma Culbertson married George Rogers. Issue: 272. Floyd Culbertson Rogers, b. 1891; 272¼. George Melbourne, b. Apr. 4, 1898; 272½. Donald Alan Rogers, b. June 19, 1909.

(272) Floyd C. Rogers is First Assistant Engineer in Merchant Marine Service. Married Anna ——, in Sweden. Issue:

310.   Leafie Charlotte, b. Jan. 1921.

311.   Alice Estella, b. Mar. 1923.

272¼. George M. Culbertson is a young attorney in Omaha, Neb.

* * * * *

On page 197, William C. Van Horne (109) is given as having been a Capt. in the World War. This is an error. It was his brother-in-law, Capt. Smith, husband of Mary Van Horne (113).

On page 153 Charles W. Culbertson (164) there was omitted his daughter 264¼, Elizabeth.

(153) mar. third Elizabeth ——.
Issue:
264½.   William, b. Jan. 1, —— (This Wm. married twice).

(167) Nettie Culbertson mar. C. M. Wherry. One child omitted, i. e. 269½, Lydia Culbertson Wherry, b. Sept. 6, 1894.

(168) Harry Wilbur Culbertson mar. first Otto Butler.
Issue:
Samuel Culbertson.

(168) Harry W. C. mar. second Idress Lawrence. No issue. He then mar. third Mrs. Ruby Collins. No issue.

(170) Leafie Culbertson mar. George Rogers.
Issue:
272.   Floyd B., b. Dec. 5, 1889.

272¼. George Melbourne, b. April 5, 1899.
272½. Donald Alan, b. June 19, 1909.

(171) Grace Dailey Culbertson mar. Elbridge W. White, Baptist evangelist. No issue.

NINTH GENERATION

(261) Charles D. Culbertson mar. Mame Mahan.
Issue:
A boy.

(262) Laura Culbertson mar. Lotta Davis.
Issue: Six.

(263) Alice Culbertson, mar. James C. Peterson, June 10, 1908. No issue.

(264) Edith Culbertson mar. George Batty, Dec.——.
Issue: George Edward; Robert.

(264¼) William Culbertson mar. first ——.
William Culbertson mar. second ——.

(265) Grace Fort mar. John Wiles, Sept. 1898.
Issue:
Charles, b. June 24, 1899.

(267) Nettie Fort mar. Carl Ferguson.
Issue:
Alice, July, 1906.

(268) Nellie Fort mar Dr. Albert Gardner.
Issue:
Albert, b. ——.

(269) Lee B. Wherry, mar. Claire O'Brien, Nov. 16, 1920.
Issue:
Marjorie, b. Oct. 1, 1921.

(269½) Lida Wherry mar. George Yoeman, April 30, 1914.
Issue:
George Wallace, b. Feb. 1, 1915.
Janice, b. Aug. 10, 1920.
Sam Culbertson mar. Rose ——. (Son of 168).
Issue: Two.

(271) R. B. Bedell mar. Mabel Adair Bowen, Aug. 20,

1911 at Osborne, Kans. Wife b. Nov. 13, 1884, at Smith
Center, Kans.
    Issue:
Margaret Bess, b. June 26, 1915.
Alice Ann, b. Oct. 28, 1918.

    (272) Floyd Rogers, mar. Anna ——.
    Issue:
Charlotte Leafie, b. Jan. ——, 1920.
Alice, b. ——, 1923.

    (261) Charles Culbertson, now living at Shelbyville, Ind.,
is president of the First National Bank there.
    Alice Peterson, Benbow Apts., Omaha, is principal of the
Dundee School. One of the largest in the city.
    Bess Bedell, Peru, Nebr., Principal of Rose Hill School,
Omaha.
    R. B. Bedell, Ashland, Nebr., Supt. of Public Schools. A.
B., Peru Normal; M. A. University of Nebr.
    George Rogers, Omaha, Nebr., Attorney.
    Lida Yoeman, lives at Hastings, Nebr.

               *   *   *   *   *
Charles Draper, d. Aug. ——, 1907.

TABLET PLACED ON ROCKY SPRING MONUMENT
IN 1922

John Culbertson, Pa. Line*†
John Culbertson, Pa. Mil.
Andrew Culbertson, Pa. Mil.
James Culbertson, Pa. Line*†
John Culbertson, Pa. Mil.*
Samuel Culbertson, Pa. Mil*
Benjamin Culbertson, Pa. Mil*
Samuel Culbertson, Sr., Pa. Line†
Samuel Culbertson, Pa. Mil.
John Culbertson, Pa. Mil.
John Culbertson, Pa. Mil.
Robert Culbertson, Pa. Mil.
Alexander Culbertson, Pa. Mil.
James Culbertson, Pa. L. H.
Joseph Culbertson, Pa. Mil.
Robert Culbertson, Pa. Mil.
Richard Culbertson, U. S. Art.
William Culbertson, Md. Art.
    (Valley Forge)
William Culbertson, Del. Mil.
John Culbertson, Del. Mil.

Alexander Culbertson, Pa. Line *†
Samuel Culbertson, Pa. Mil.
Robert Culbertson, Pa. Mil.
Alexander Culbertson, Pa. Mil.
John Culbertson, Pa. Mil.
James Culbertson, Pa. Mil.
Joseph Culbertson, Pa. Line*
Robert Culbertson, Pa. Mil.
Josiah Culbertson, S. Car. Mil.
William Culbertson, N. Car. Mil
Robert Culbertson, N. Car. Mil.
Samuel Culbertson (Dr.) Va. Line
Joseph Culbertson, Va. Line.
James Culbertson, Va. Line.
James Culbertson, Va. Line.
John Culbertson, Va. Line.
Robert Culbertson, Pa. Mil.
William H. Culbertson, Pa. Mil.
John Culbertson, Pa. Mil.
William Culbertson, Pa. Mil.
William Culbertson, 4 Mass Line.

*Due to service.
†In Indian War. Trenton. Princeton. Monmouth. Saratoga.

"By the rude bridge that arched the flood
Their flag to April's breeze unfurled—
Here once the embattled farmers stood
And fired the shot heard 'round the world."
—Emerson.

DATA TAKEN FROM TABLETS ON MEMORIAL STONE TO CULBERTSON SOLDIERS IN PROVINCIAL WARS AND THE REVOLUTIONARY WAR (AMERICAN).

ANDREW CULBERTSON,	1729
JOHN CULBERTSON,	1730
ALEXANDER CULBERTSON,	1733
SAMUEL CULBERTSON,	1733
ROBERT CULBERTSON,	1733
JOSEPH CULBERTSON,	1734

SIDELING HILL,	APRIL 2, 1756
ISLE AUX NOIX,	JUNE 21, 1776
LONG ISLAND,	AUGUST 27, 1776
FORT WASHINGTON,	NOVEMBER 16, 1776
BRANDYWINE	SEPTEMBER 11, 1777
GERMANTOWN,	OCTOBER 4, 1777
VALLEY FORGE,	DECEMBER 19, 1777
MONMOUTH,	JUNE 28, 1778
RAMSOURS MILLS	JUNE 20, 1780
CAMDEN,	AUGUST 16, 1780
KINGS MOUNTAIN,	OCTOBER 7, 1780
COWPENS,	JANUARY 17, 1781

"On Fame's eternal camping ground
Their silent tents are spread,
And glory guards with solemn round,
The bivouac of the dead."

—O'HARA.

DATA TAKEN FROM TABLETS ON MEMORIAL STONE TO CULBERTSON SOLDIERS IN PROVINCIAL WARS AND THE REVOLUTIONARY WAR (AMERICAN).

Sons of
The Gael

Shoulders
Together

HONOR ROLL OF THE CULBERTSON CLAN

WAR OF 1748

John Culbertson, Pa. Prov.   John Culbertson, Pa. Prov.

1755   INDIAN WARS   1758

*John Culbertson, Pa. Prov.   *Alexander Culbertson, Pa. Prov.
*James Culbertson, Pa. Prov.   Samuel Culbertson, Pa. Prov.

1775   THE ANSWER TO FREEDOM'S CALL 1783

John Culbertson, Pa. Mil.   Samuel Culbertson, Pa. Mil.
Andrew Culbertson, Pa. Mil.   Robert Culbertson, Pa. Mil.
Samuel Culbertson, Pa. Mil.   Alexander Culbertson, Pa. Mil.
*Benjamin Culbertson, Pa. Mil. John Alexander, Pa. Mil.
William Culbertson, Mass Line   James Culbertson, Pa. Mil.
Samuel Culbertson, Pa. Mil.   *Joseph Culbertson, Pa. Line
John Culbertson, Pa. Mil.   William Culbertson, N. C. Mil.
John Culbertson, Pa. Mil.   Robert Culbertson, Pa. Mil.
*Robert Culbertson, Pa. Mil.   Josiah Culbertson, So. C. Mil.
Alexander Culbertson, Pa. Mil. Robert Culbertson, N. C. Mil.
James Culbertson, Pa. Cav.   Samuel Culbertson, Va. Line
Joseph Culbertson, Pa. Mil.   Joseph Culbertson, Va. Line
Robert Culbertson, Pa. Mil.   James Culbertson, Va. Line
Richard Culbertson, U. S. Art. John Culbertson, Va. Line
William Culbertson, Md. Art.   James Culbertson, Va. Line
William Culbertson, Del. Mil.   Robert Culbertson, Pa. Mil.
John Culbertson, Del. Mil.   William Culbertson, Pa. Mil.
William Culbertson, Pa. Mil.   John Culbertson, Pa. Mil.

* "They Gave the Last Full Measure of Devotion."—Lincoln *

Trenton, December 26, 1776   Saratoga, October 17, 1777
Princeton, January 3, 1777   Yorktown, October 19, 1781

This Stone Was Erected by

The Culbertson Memorial Ass'n of Culbertson's Row, Pa.
September 15, 1907

Lightning Source UK Ltd.
Milton Keynes UK
UKHW020301081222
413533UK00006B/278